RELIGION AND SOCIETY
COTSWOLD VALE

RELIGION AND SOCIETY IN A COTSWOLD VALE

Nailsworth, Gloucestershire, 1780–1865

ALBION M. URDANK

UNIVERSITY OF CALIFORNIA PRESS
BERKELEY   LOS ANGELES   OXFORD

University of California Press
Berkeley and Los Angeles, California

University of California Press, Ltd.
Oxford, England

Copyright © 1990 by The Regents of the University of
California

Library of Congress Cataloging-in-Publication Data

Urdank, Albion M.
    Religion and society in a Cotswold vale: Nailsworth,
Gloucestershire, 1780–1865 / Albion M. Urdank.
        p.   cm.
    Bibliography: p.
    Includes index.
    ISBN 0-05-200667-0 (alk. paper)
        1. Nailsworth (England)—Church history—18th century.
    2. Nailsworth (England)—Church history—19th century.
    3. Nailsworth (England)—Social conditions.   4. Nailsworth
(England)—Economic conditions.   I. Title.
BR765.N35U73   1990
306.6'09424'1909033—dc20   89-32044
                                                       CIP

Printed in the United States of America

1 2 3 4 5 6 7 8 9

In memory of Stephen Koss,
mentor and friend

"These Days

whatever you have to say, leave
the roots on, let them
dangle
And the dirt

    just to make clear
    where they came from"

        —Charles Olson
         Archaeologist of Morning
         (courtesy of Joseph Salerno)

Contents

Tables   IX

Maps   XII

Figures   XIII

Acknowledgments   XV

Introduction: Background and Perspectives   I

Contexts and Approaches   I
Sources and Methods   5
Organization   8

Part I: Structures of Communal Life

1. Community of the Vale: Landscape and Settlement   15
   Boundaries and Settlement Pattern   16
   A Transitional Social Structure   27
   The Landscape   35
   Regionalization   42
   Summary and Conclusion   51

2. Hinterland of the Vale: Landownership and Tenure   54
   Structures of Landownership   55
   Land Tenure   64
   Agrarian Transformation   74
   Summary and Conclusion   82

3. Churches and Chapels: The Pattern of Religion   84
   The Origins of Dissent and the Evangelical Revival   85
   The Revival and the Church of England   96
   Epilogue   101

4. Manors, Parishes, and Dissent: The Structure of Politics   102
   Manorial Jurisdiction   103
   Parochial Administration   113
   Dissent and the Composition of Lordship   118
   Summary and Conclusion   125

Part II: From Community to Society

5. Birth, Death, Migration, and Dissent   131
   Population Change: An Overview   132
   Natural Population Change: Horsley-Nailsworth,
       1775–1851   138
   Mortality by Age-Sex Cohort, 1808–1838   154
   The Age-Sex Structure in 1841 and 1851   163
   Summary and Conclusion   168

6. Capital and Labor in the Industrial Revolution   170
   The Course of the Business Cycle   171
   Capital Formation   179
   Capital and Labor   190
   Summary and Conclusion   205

7. Class Formation and the Growth of Social Stability   208
   The Weaver Strike of 1825   208
       First Stage   220
       Second Stage   222
       Third Stage   227
       Aftermath and Discussion   228
   Strikes and Protests, 1827–1848   231
   Summary and Conclusion   243

Part III: Contrasting Communities: Two Case Studies in Dissent

8. An "Introversionist Sect": Nailsworth's Society of Friends   249
   Organizational Change and Decline   249

Church Order and Discipline 256
  Discipline I: Courtship, Marriage, and Kinship 260
  Discipline II: "Moral Economy" and Religious
    Orthodoxy 267
Spirituality 272
Conclusion 274

9. Secularization and the Shortwood Baptist Church 275
Membership Growth and Decline, 1775–1864 276
The Impact of Geographic Mobility 280
Attendance at Shortwood, ca. 1850 284
Church Order and Discipline 293
Summary and Conclusion 303

Part IV: Conclusion: The Impact of the Industrial Revolution

10. Synchronicity? Local Changes in the Industrial Revolution 307

Appendixes A–N 313

Abbreviations 335

Notes 337

Bibliography 409

Index 433

Tables

1 Nailsworth Village and Hamlets: Occupational Structure,
  1841 22
2 Inner Periphery: Occupational Structure, Dispersed
  Settlements Bordering the Vale 23
3 Outer Periphery: Occupational Structure, a Sample of
  Surrounding Villages 24
4 Proportion of Selected Occupations in Three Zones in 1841:
  Core, Inner Periphery, and Outer Periphery 26
5 Values of Personal Estates by Occupation and Status 33
6 *t*-Tests of Wealth Differences by Occupation and Status 33

7 Willmakers as a Percentage of the Population: The Lower Classes, 1841 — 34

8 Acreage under Tillage: Horsley, Avening, and Minchinhampton, 1800–1841 — 40

9 Arable Acreage by Types of Crops: Horsley and Avening, ca. 1801 — 40

10 Crop Yields for Avening Parish in 1838 — 41

11 Parochial Typologies: The Standard Model — 56

12 Concentration of Landholding: Avening Parish, 1784–1838 — 58

13 Concentration of Landholding: Horsley Parish, 1784–1841 — 60

14 Concentration of Landholding: Minchinhampton Parish, 1777–1839 — 62

15 Long-Term Leaseholders at Horsley — 71

16 Cattle Grazed on Minchinhampton Common, 1843–1851: Unadjusted Values — 81

17 Turnover among Forest Green Congregationalist Ministers, 1688–1866 — 91

18 Attendance by Social Class of Suitors at the Court Baron, Horsley Manor, ca. 1811 — 108

19 Religion by Social Class of Suitors at the Court Baron, Horsley Manor, ca. 1811 — 108

20 Religion by Attendance of Suitors at the Court Baron, Horsley Manor, ca. 1811 — 109

21 Occupations of Encroachers Prosecuted at the Court Baron, Horsley Manor, ca. 1802 — 111

22 Items Granted through Outdoor Relief, Horsley Parish, 1802–1822 — 114

23 Election Returns for the Borough of Stroud, 1832 — 124

24 Population Growth in Overview: Stroud, Avening, and Horsely Parishes, 1801–1851 — 133

25 Population Estimates for Nailsworth, 1801–1851 — 134

26 Geographic Mobility at Horsley-Nailsworth, 1801–1851 — 134

27 Compound-Interest Growth Rates in Births, 1775–1838 — 145

28 Regression Coefficients: Wheat Prices (Residuals) and Cloth Production on All Baptisms and Births, 1804–1838 — 147

29 Regression Coefficients: Wheat Prices (Residuals) and Cloth Production on Nonconformist Births, 1804–1838 148

30 Regression Coefficients: Cloth Production, Conversions, and Members Lost on Baptist Births, 1804–1838 150

31 Regression Coefficients: Cloth Production, Members Lost, and Total Membership on Baptist Births, 1804–1838 151

32 Compound-Interest Growth Rates in Burials and Total Births, Horsley-Nailsworth, 1775–1838 153

33 Crude Vital Rates at Horsley-Nailsworth, 1781–1841 153

34 Crude Vital Rates: England and Wales, 1781–1841 154

35 Regression Coefficients: Wheat Prices (Residuals) and Cloth Production on Infant, Child, and Adolescent Burials, 1808–1838 158

36 Regression Coefficients: Wheat Prices (Residuals) and Cloth Production on Adult Burials by Age Cohort, 1808–1838 159

37 Age-Pyramid Data Values, 1841 (for fig. 15) 165

38 Age-Pyramid Data Values, 1851 (for fig. 16) 166

39 Summary of Age-Pyramid Data, 1841–1851, with Differences-of-Proportions Tests 167

40 Qualitative Shift in Age Composition, 1841–1851 167

41 Bankruptcy and Mill Sales by Type of Sale, 1803–1839 172

42 Mill Property in Gloucestershire, 1831–1841 175

43 Sales of Mills, Machinery, and Stock, 1804–1839 179

44 Steam and Water Power in Gloucestershire and West Riding, Yorkshire Woolen Mills, ca. 1838 185

45 Per Capita Power in Gloucestershire and West Riding, Yorkshire Woolen Mills, ca. 1838 186

46 Steam- and Water-Powered Cloth Mills 188

47 Craftsmen, Weavers, and Laborers, Horsley Parish, ca. 1811 191

48 Occupations of Household Heads in Horsley Parish, ca. 1811 and 1841 192

49 Occupations of Factory Weavers' Wives, ca. 1838 193

50 Mean Earnings of Weavers' Wives by Occupation, ca. 1838 194

51 Weavers' Attitudes toward the Factory: A Parliamentary Survey, ca. 1838 199

52 Earnings and Productivity of Factory Weavers by Former
Status, ca. 1838   200

53 Wages and Wheat Prices by Occupation, 1808–1838   202

54 Wheat Prices as a Percentage of Wages, 1808–1838   205

55 Weaving Rates Negotiated in 1825   210

56 The Master Weaver's Stated Expenses, ca. 1824   212

57 Three-Month Moving Averages of Wheat Prices (in Shillings,
per Bushel), 1804–1826   213

58 Quaker Marriages with Known Occupations of Grooms,
1660–1839   251

59 Quaker Membership, 1812–1834: Occupations and
Residence   253

60 Quaker Membership Turnover by Type of Acquisition and
Dissolution   254

61 Years of Membership by Type of Dissolution   255

62 Time Series of Baptist Membership Growth Rates, 1775–
1864   279

63 Average Membership Losses among Shortwood Baptists,
1775–1864   279

64 Average Membership Losses as Percentage of Average Total
Membership Losses   279

65 Attendance Patterns of Shortwood Baptist Church Members,
1852/53   286

66 Significance Tests of Variable Interactions   287

67 Attenders at Founding of the Avening Baptist Church   296

68 Members and Hearers Buried at Shortwood, 1808–1873   299

Maps

1 Boundary Map of Nailsworth, with Inset: Nailsworth in
Longtree Hundred   18

2 Elevations of Hills at Nailsworth   36

3 The Frome River Valley and Streams   38

4 Stonehouse-Nailsworth Branch Railroad Line, ca. 1863   50

5 Field Map: Southeast Section of Minchinhampton, ca. 1804:
Pasture, Arable, and Common Lands   78

Figures

 1 Champion and Wood-pasture Settlements   20

 2 Selected Occupations in Nailsworth and Surrounding
    Villages, ca. 1841   25

 3 Section of the Hills near Nailsworth, Gloucestershire   39

 4 Stroud Canal Dividend Series, 1785–1824   47

 5 Series of Suitors and Nonattenders at the Court Baron,
    Horsley Manor, 1794–1814   107

 6 Series of Items Granted through Outdoor Relief, Horsley
    Parish, 1802–1822   115

 7 Time Series of All Births, 1775–1838   143

 8 Time Series of Nonconformist Births, 1775–1838   144

 9 Time Series of Births, Marriages, and Burials, 1775–1838   145

10 Time Series of Infant Mortality as Percent of Births and Youth
    Burials, 1808–1838   155

11 Child and Adolescent Mortality as Percent of Youth Burials,
    1808–1838   156

12 Young Adult (Ages 18–49) Mortality, by Gender, as Percent
    of Youth Burials, 1808–1838   160

13 Middle-Aged (Ages 50–64) Mortality, by Gender, as Percent
    of Adult Burials, 1808–1838   161

14 Elderly (Ages 65+) Mortality, by Gender, as Percent of Adult
    Burials, 1808–1838   162

15 Age Pyramid of Four Horsley-Nailsworth Hamlets, ca. 1841   163

16 Age Pyramid of Four Horsley-Nailsworth Hamlets, ca. 1851   164

17 Three-Year Moving Averages of Business Turnover, 1804–
    1839   176

18 Gloucester Market Wheat Prices, 1808–1849   201

19 Social Pyramid: Status of Quaker Grooms, 1660–1719   252

20 Time Series of Shortwood Baptist Church Conversions and
    Membership Losses, 1775–1864   277

21 Time Series of Total Shortwood Baptist Church Membership,
    1775–1864   278

22 Familial Bonds between the Clothier-Deacons of Shortwood   297

Acknowledgments

I have many to thank for the support and guidance given me over the last few years. Basic research was made possible by two years of support under Columbia University's President's University Fellowship. A Faculty Senate Grant from the University of California, Los Angeles made possible additional research assistance at the final stage of revising the manuscript.

Staff members of libraries and archives provided especially invaluable assistance: Eileen McIlvain and Anita Lowry of Columbia University's Butler Library; Brian S. Smith, former keeper of the Gloucester Record Office; David J. H. Smith, the present keeper, and his staff officers, Kate Hazlum and Margaret Richards; Jill Voyce and Rosalind Lane of the Gloucester City Library; and the more numerous staffs of the Public Record Office and the British Museum.

Many local residents of Stroud, Nailsworth, Avening, Horsley, and Minchinhampton were exceedingly helpful in making available church and family records not otherwise obtainable through local archives. I wish to thank especially Betty Mills of Newmarket House; David and Beatrice Playne of Minchinhampton and Avening; Frank Smith, keeper of the Avening Baptist Church; Canon Welander of the Gloucester Cathedral; the ministers of the Stroud and Minchinhampton Baptist churches; and the vicar of Nailsworth's parish church. Roger Schofield very generously provided access to data, collected by the Cambridge Group for the History of Population and Social Structure.

Portions of chapters 6 and 7 have already appeared as articles in the *Journal of Economic History* (June 1985) and the *Journal of British Studies* (April 1986), and I am grateful to the editors for granting me permission to incorporate these materials in this study.

I also thank Andrew Foster, James P. P. Horn, David Rollison, Brian Frith, Nick Herbert, John Jurica, John Walsh, Dennis Mills, Pat Thane and James Obelkevich for their encouragement and stimulating conversation during the initial period of my research in England, as well as Eric Monkkonen, Jon Butler, Isser Woloch, Robert Edelman, Ed Berenson, Eugen Weber, Peter Loewenberg, Ben Elman, Joyce Appleby, Joseph Salerno, Reba Soffer, Henry Addis, Robert Burr, Peter Stansky, Richard Rouse, Hans Rogger, Anthony Brundage, Dick Weiss, Dan Howe, Robert Brenner, Geoffrey Symcox, Lauro Martines, Claus-Peter Clasen, Steve Zipperstein, Philip Nord and Scott Waugh for their supportive advice during the final stage of this project. I wish to thank especially Eric Monkkonen, Jon Butler, Nancy Fitch and Steve Ross, participants in our local quantitative history group convened at UCLA, and two anonymous readers for their helpful comments on either all or parts of this work. This does not imply, of course, their complete agreement with the study's theses nor complicity in its errors or deficiencies; these remain my responsibility alone.

I owe a special debt of gratitude to Isser Woloch and the late Stephen E. Koss, both of whom gave me invaluable support and direction during the early stages of this project, and to Malcolm Bean and Sheila Biddle, who introduced me to the advanced study of English local history. Richard Jensen's wonderfully illuminating statistics lectures at the Newberry Library likewise influenced the approach of this study. At the outset, E. P. Thompson very generously gave important advice regarding research strategy, even though we had never met; although this study's findings depart from some of his well-known theses, his work remains an inspiration for me. I also thank my good friends David Metz, Stewart Lange, Susan Scales, David Barlow, Veronica Tatten-Brown, Susan Burrell, and Andrew and Liz Foster, who made my visit to England in the years just prior to Mrs. Thatcher's accession very much more than an academic enterprise. Kathleen Biddick gave both spiritual nourishment and intellectual stimulation during the years of writing and revision for which I will always remain grateful.

Los Angeles, California   A. M. U.
December 1988

Introduction: Background and Perspectives

Contexts and Approaches

At the turn of this century, Elie Halèvy advanced the thesis that evangelical religion, through the influence of Methodism, served as midwife at the birth of modern English society. Halèvy believed that despite its early association with enthusiasm, evangelicalism imbued an emerging proletariat with a rational approach to life and thereby facilitated the modernization of society in the long term.[1] The Halèvy thesis further incorporated the concept of modernization in its assumption that the Industrial Revolution and the process of class formation associated with it marked a crucial phase of transition to the contemporary world. Historians have since affirmed the broad outlines of his thesis, however much they have qualified some of its details.[2]

Three areas touching this literature remain comparatively neglected, however. The link between changes in popular religious feeling and socioeconomic transformation has been described more than demonstrated because historians of religion have adopted the style of cultural anthropology in a manner that eschews economics.[3] Moreover, by devoting their efforts primarily to the study of Methodism, historians have neglected the local study of New Dissent, to whose influence Halèvy also attached much importance.[4] Local studies of English industrial villages, furthermore, are rare for the eighteenth to early nineteenth century[5] and are especially scarce for Nonconformist villages with protoindustrial economies that passed over the watershed of the Industrial Revolution, although failing thereafter.

Religion and Society in a Cotswold Vale adds to these several literatures—on popular religion, local history, and European industrialization—by offering a socioeconomic history of the Vale of Nailsworth, a rural-industrial Gloucestershire settlement and center of evangelical Nonconformity. By devotion to the landscape as a framer of community life and collective mentalité, this study follows the English and French traditions of local history and "histoire totale" developed respectively by the Leicester and *Annales* schools.[6] This book reveals how the ecology of the landscape and forms of landownership characteristic of the region influenced the shape of the economy, the social structure and a religious culture centered on the Nonconformist Chapel, combining in this way a materialist outlook and structuralist analysis with a belief in the efficacy of both individual and collective human experience.

Most importantly, *Religion and Society in a Cotswold Vale* is concerned with the processes of change that occurred in different spheres yet combined finally to transform a protoindustrial, transitional community into a modern society, albeit one that failed to sustain itself in the long term. Changes in agricultural organization, manufacturing industry, and demography developed autonomously yet interacted in a manner that fundamentally altered the ways in which men and women lived. These changes underlay the regionalization of village and parish life, the final eclipse of manorial government, the formation of social classes, and the transformation of Baptist and Congregationalist churches from small sects into broadly based albeit less stable denominations. A more mobile society had emerged, in other words, which stressed the values of individualism while basing itself fully on an integrated national market, a factory system, and a pluralistic, denominational religious culture. The findings of this study thus affirm the essential features of a familiar but controversial paradigm, "the transition from traditional to modern," however much they qualify its teleological vision of progress.

Dean C. Tipps, in a synthesis of this controversy, has identified several attributes of the concept of modernization that have provoked criticism but are germane to the concerns of this study and therefore merit consideration.[7] Tipps calls attention to the view that "traditional" and "modern" are dichotomous, mutually exclusive categories, the definitions of which are both vague and reductive; "modern" conforms ostensibly to what is contemporary, and "tradition" is merely its negation. The transition from one to the other, furthermore, is regarded as "inclusive" insofar as it embraces a multifaceted process that moves in a unilinear and progressive direction. The process also describes a pattern in which modern characteristics gradually supplant traditional ones, while stability is conceived as a natural state and departures from it as pathologies; a "normal" society, in this view, is one capable of maintaining or returning to equilibrium.

Unfortunately, this general description appears as "a simpleminded vision of modernization," an unfair distortion of "positions no serious scholar has ever held"; revisionists who have criticized this formulation by offering a more nuanced interpretation appear to have set up a straw man.[8] In this study, "traditional" refers to those attributes of corporatist life that existed historically and assumed diverse and dynamic forms, while "modern" is defined by distinctive qualities that can hold an indirect or anticipatory relation to the contemporary.[9] Traditional and modern characteristics, moreover, can be seen to have interacted dialectically in the course of a community's development to form a synthesis. In this way, remnants of a traditional world can be seen to have survived into a modern one but are given new meaning by the different constellation of social and property relations. Desire for security at the expense of profit maximization, embodying an aversion to risk, can, for instance, be viewed as a traditional attitude to the ownership of property or to work and consumption;[10] entrepreneurial behavior, conceived broadly as a willingness to undertake risk in pursuing higher earnings, or a more advanced standard of living, can be viewed as the quintessentially modern approach.[11] Yet modern investments, in combining both mentalities, sometimes choose long-term security—yielding moderate returns—over riskier short-term, high-yield ventures.[12]

This study, furthermore, rather than representing a multifaceted single process moving in a unilinear and progressive direction, reveals the existence of *multiple* processes, linked by mutual interaction and fluctuating around a trend, the end of which issues in socioeconomic decline rather than long-term growth and development.[13] The overall direction of this trend may appear linear, but the fluctuations around it constitute deviations, or elements of contingency, affecting both the pace and the configuration of modernization.[14] Stability, or social equilibrium, is considered, additionally, as neither natural nor normative but as a socio-cultural construct that gives way to instability or discontinuity, first gradually and then abruptly, as the forces of change gain momentum. Archaic structures of authority survived at Nailsworth in muted form into the early nineteenth century and were further eroded and then decisively broken up by the course of socioeconomic change and the rise of class conflict, only to be replaced by new structures of authority and stability and a new configuration of social relations, however much these may have incorporated some elements of the old. Although a new equilibrium may have reconstituted itself by 1850, this did not preclude the reassertion of conditions of conflict in the future.

On one hand, therefore, equilibrium and discontinuity are treated in this study as oscillating *alternatives*, insofar as each may broadly characterize a given historical period; on the other hand, consensus and conflict are treated in the short term not as dichotomous categories but as modalities that could interpenetrate and shape one another, as can be seen especially in the weavers' strike of 1825, discussed in chapter 7.

The local study of religion offers opportunities for tracing links between the institutions of popular culture and this changing socioeconomic environment; through these links, Nonconformity, in particular, is shown to have mediated a historic transformation. Puritanism has long been associated with modernity: with the promotion of individual autonomy, expressed by control of affect and sobriety of habits, which made possible the spread of such materialist values as the rational pursuit of self-interest and concomitantly the growth of the private sphere at the expense of the public or communal. David Underdown has shown the extent to which seventeenth-century Puritanism could be associated with rural villages and parishes dominated socially by the "middling sort" and by members of an individualist-minded religion bent on assaulting a communal popular culture.[15] Keith Wrightson and David Levine have demonstrated that the pattern of fertility control within marriage, widespread in post-1870 Britain but generally uncharacteristic of early modern English society, could be found at the sixteenth-century Puritan village of Terling, which, like Underdown's settlements, was also dominated by the "middling sort."[16] For the nineteenth century, James Obelkevich has shown that changes in agricultural organization in South Lindsey, associated with the progress of enclosures and the emergence of capitalist farmers as a class, precipitated the breakup of traditional communal solidarity based on the parish and coincided with the emergence of Methodism in its diverse denominational forms.[17]

This association of puritanism with modern materialist values, however, is largely the outcome of an indirect and unintended consequence of Protestant "worldly asceticism."[18] Anxiety concerning salvation induced adherents of a predestinarian theology to adopt Puritanical social values as a means of self-assurance regarding their salvation. Puritanism thus equipped its "pilgrims" to engage successfully the fallen world in which they lived but of which spiritually they were not a part. In actuality, Puritan asceticism condemned, as a matter of principle, preoccupation with the acquisitiveness of a materialist world, regarding such preoccupation as a diversion from one's proper calling, devotion to God.[19] Out of this asceticism arose the need to build a godly community as a bulwark against the depravity and sin of the world. Hence a customary, communitarian tradition, however voluntarist in foundation, came to serve as a counterpoint to Puritan individualism, coexisting with it in an uneasy tension, and can be traced from the earliest Puritans down through the advent of Methodism and beyond.[20]

Sources and Methods

By thus offering a study of religion within the dimensions of social and economic change, *Religion and Society in a Cotswold Vale* seeks principally to evoke the texture of human experience. A great deal of highly localized information has been worked into a layered mosaic, which grows increasingly complex with the passage of each chapter. This level of detail calls upon readers to assimilate the particulars of "local knowledge" slowly;[21] patient readers will gain a distinctive aesthetic reward by doing so, but this study also promises them a fully integrated picture of local life emerging surely and steadily.

An emphasis on human experience suggests a traditional narrative approach to the sources, a kind of qualitative portraiture drawn from a wide array of archival documents. For the study of social structure, these documents have included probate records, manorial listings of suitors, and local census enumerations. Proceedings of two Courts Baron, manorial records of leaseholds, tithe surveys, and land tax returns have permitted the recreation of structures of landownership and tenure, as well as patterns of agrarian transformation that destroyed the remnants of the traditional open-field system. A wide array of records belonging to Nonconformist Chapels made possible the careful study of religious Dissent and its relationship to the Anglican Establishment. These records included Chapel minute books, membership lists, and marriage, birth, and burial registers, as well as letters written by the most ordinary of members. In combination with Anglican parish registers, Nonconformist vital registration made possible an analysis of population change that included a significant cultural component, while other Chapel records facilitated the reconstruction of the inner spiritual and social lives of two important Nonconformist communities. The *Gloucester Journal*, a regional newspaper founded in 1720 and published weekly ever since, yielded diverse materials, ranging from news accounts to bankruptcy notices and sales advertisements, which permitted the close study of industrialization and economic decline in Gloucester's woolen industry, as well as the pattern of class formation through changing configurations of strikes and protests. Bankruptcy examination and Home Office papers, housed in the Public Record Office, crucially supplemented the evidence the *Journal* provided.

These sources have also facilitated critical analyses of theoretical models, appearing in various historical literatures, and employed here as ideal types against which the available empirical evidence can be studied. This approach has great utility. For descriptive purposes, it matters little whether the evidence actually conforms to the model in question, since its patterns of conformity or deviation cast into sharper relief than otherwise possible the contours of reality. If the evidence should either confirm or challenge the validity of a particular model, however, the findings can also be assumed to have contributed to our knowledge of a given historical problem.

These models have been tested, where possible, with the aid of quantitative methods. The "open" and "closed" parish paradigm in chapter 2, used to explain the settlement patterns of Dissenters, has been studied for the three parishes of Nailsworth's hinterland between 1777 and 1841 through the distribution of mean acreage across several categories of landownership defined according to size.[22] This analysis helped established the existence of a more complex relationship than previously appreciated between the Establishment, Dissent, and popular individualism, on which the qualitative material subsequently expanded. In chapter 5, the use of multiple-regression analysis in time series established the significance of a religious-cultural variable to the causes of population growth, a phenomenon usually conceived only in economic terms. Aggregative analysis of demographic data is certainly a blunter instrument than family reconstitution, a technique beyond the scope of the present study; the use of multivariate statistics on such data, however, has precedent and significantly expands the utility of the aggregative method.[23] In chapter 6, the model of the factory system as a symbol of progress was tested and challenged by drawing on the findings of path analysis, a form of multiple regression that deconstructs direct and indirect causal flows. Finally, in chapter 9, the transition from "sect" to "denomination," undertaken by the Shortwood Baptist Church, and the problem of the "chiliasm of despair," a metaphor regarding religious experience first enunciated by E. P. Thompson, were studied with the aid of multiple classification analysis, a form of analysis of variance.

Quantitative methods utilized by this study—ranging from descriptive statistics to multivariate analysis—have enhanced the dimensions of the qualitative material and have been deployed sensitively to render analyzable data from sometimes recalcitrant sources. Quantifiable variables have made it possible to draw meaningful inferences about popular *mentalité* and behavior, particularly in the absence of written records. By doing so, they have articulated the mission of social science history, while affirming their compatibility with narrative modes of historical discourse; in part, this book has sought to make an original contribution by effecting such a reconciliation.[24]

Organization

The dialectical manner in which socioeconomic changes evolved has dictated the general organization of this book. Part I emphasizes in a descriptive fashion the structural features of community as they existed in the eighteenth century, while part II focuses on the dynamic elements of socioeconomic change as these transpired over the period from 1780 to 1865. The dichotomy between structure and process, however, should not be overdrawn, since part I also illustrates how far the erosion of traditional forms of communal life had transpired by the early decades of the nineteenth century. Part III closely examines two contrasting religious responses to a changing social environment and, reciprocally, how this environment altered the texture of religious life.

The forms of traditional communal life set forth in part I include the boundary settlement, the industrial village, the Nonconformist Chapel, the manor, and the parish. Chapter 1 shows how landscape and ecology shaped Nailsworth as an isolated boundary settlement, industrial village, and Chapel community, while chapter 2 illustrates how the structures of landownership and tenure in the Vale's hinterland created a material basis for the proliferation of Dissent. Chapter 3 outlines the patterns of settlement and growth of Nonconformist Chapels, and chapter 4 explains why the structure of politics, framed by the institutions of Nailsworth's manorial and parochial hinterland, permitted the Vale to become a Nonconformist stronghold.

The chronology of settlement of Dissenters' churches revealed the early sectarianism of these communities that established them as a kind of religious *gemeinschaft*.[25] Indeed, each form of community described in part I began historically as a kind of corporate community, if not always a full-fledged gemeinschaft, and by the end of the eighteenth century, the passage of time had seriously eroded their structures. Ferdinand Toennis based his concept of gemeinschaft on an idealized vision of the medieval past, in which village or parish life appeared closed and static, without conflict or access to markets and without social differentiation or geographic mobility. Medieval English historians have since revealed, quite to the contrary, the economic and social dynamism of such communities and the extent to which conflict pervaded them.[26] The concept of gemeinschaft has retained, however, at least a metaphorical relevance to evoke the image of relatively stable or homogeneous communities, and several historians of the modern period have profited from its use in this way.[27]

Nailsworth's sects might be conceived as gemeinschaften because at the outset they were relatively homogeneous, relying primarily on an artisan membership, and reinforced in this occupational uniformity by kinship ties. Although founded initially as voluntary associations, they assumed in the late seventeenth to early eighteenth century this organic, corporatist quality. By the late eighteenth century, however, the Congregationalists and Baptists had begun to acquire the more open characteristics of a "denomination," while the Quakers persisted in their sectarianism throughout the period under study.

What was true for its sects was true for Nailsworth as a boundary settlement. Nailsworth's initial isolation and relatively homogeneous social structure, consisting mainly of weavers, clothworkers, and day laborers, created the kind of informal, face-to-face contact associated with a corporate community, however unregulated Nailsworth remained as a settlement at the edge of a thick woodland zone. Nailsworth's weavers and clothworkers, moreover, found their homes concentrated in the Vale's dispersed, surrounding hamlets and developed attachments even to these circumscribed neighborhoods. Still, Nailsworth had suffered only a relative isolation in the eighteenth century, and by 1830 the growth of a regional communications network had fully integrated the Vale with the rest of the Stroud valley. Nailsworth's social structure, furthermore, had commenced the transition from a hierarchical to a class system, highlighted by a pattern of social mobility promoted by Nonconformist individualism.

By contrast to the sect or boundary settlement, the manor and parish functioned as *formally* corporatist institutions. As instruments of local government, they enforced the rules that bound the village communities together. In this sense, they provided the framework for interaction between the landed governing class and the rest of local society. Face-to-face contact, in other words, existed between diverse social strata rather than merely within a single group and in the eighteenth to early nineteenth century was still founded on relations of paternalism and deference, however much punctuated by episodes of social conflict.

For the manors of Nailsworth's hinterland, the passage of time had become manifest in structural changes in landholding and the decline of their customary courts, which were feudal in origin, as these transferred their civic duties to the parish and to the Justices of the Peace; in the early nineteenth century, the parish, too, lost considerable authority, as it became incorporated into the regional framework of Poor Law Unions. The power of traditional lordship had not waned completely by the end of the eighteenth century, as some have supposed,[28] although medieval customary practices had certainly deteriorated significantly. This deterioration was reflected in leaseholding arrangements, the shifting nature of manorial court business, and the piecemeal enclosure of common arable fields and rapidly accelerated in the period thereafter. The structure of leaseholding, although archaic in origin, had evolved by 1800 into a system that validated individual property rights among the laboring as well as the upper classes, thereby providing a setting for the spread of Nonconformity.

Historians have sought to explain the strength of Nonconformity in rural communities as an inverse relation to the power of landlordship. They have assumed correctly that individualism correlated with religious dissent and a differentiated social structure but have wrongly assumed that these qualities necessarily rendered Nonconformists adversaries of the Establishment. Lordship throughout Stroud was Whig, liberal, and paternalistic; in Nailsworth's hinterland, despite the relatively high concentration of landownership there, it established cooperative relations with Dissenters in a manner facilitating the growth of their communities.

Part II is devoted to a more detailed explication of the mechanisms by which the most fundamental changes affecting these traditional communities had developed: population growth and industrial transformation. Debate regarding the causes of population growth during the late eighteenth to early nineteenth century has centered on the comparative importance of a rising birth rate or a falling burial rate. Using compound-interest growth rates and multiple-regression analysis, chapter 5 introduces Nonconformity as a distinctive element in this discussion and identifies its independent contribution to population growth. Historical demographers have usually treated Nonconformity solely as a factor of underregistration in the Anglican record; this chapter makes an original contribution by suggesting that cultural differences, as manifest in the relative cohesiveness of religious communities, help explain patterns of population change. Migration is shown, furthermore, to have influenced demographic change more strikingly than did natural increase and was itself shaped by the vagaries of the tradecycle in woolen manufacturing. Trade-cycle and wheat price fluctuations each affected levels of mortality, when examined by age-sex cohort and in a manner that contributes to the debate over working-class living standards during the Industrial Revolution. In general, the demographic status of the locale by 1851 mirrored its economic condition and, once established, provided the basis for a detailed consideration of the emergence of the factory system.

The economies of Gloucester's woolen manufacturing districts collapsed, while their market towns failed to urbanize appreciably despite passage through the classic stages of the Industrial Revolution. Chapter 6 reconstructs the pattern of the business cycle in order to document the decline of small clothiers and the parallel rise of large capital-intensive firms and further examines capital formation processes to explain the causes of Gloucester's longterm economic decline. Economic historians have generally thought of "deindustrialization" before 1850 as a failure of those regions dominated by cottage industries to effect the transition to the factory system.[29] This chapter shows, to the contrary, that economic decline coincided with the actual transition to the factory system and was caused largely by the peculiar features of this very process. Analysis of the impact on labor of all these changes follows, and the standard of living debate once again frames the discussion of local experience.

The transition from a protoindustrial to a factory-based system deeply altered the social structure of the Vale community. "Instead of the pyramidal balance of rank and degree, or the vertical range of interest groups," characteristic of earlier eras, "there emerged the horizontal outlines of a class society."[30] Chapter 7 examines how changing patterns of strikes and protests between 1825 and 1848 reveal the process of class formation. The strikes indicate how master weavers, as small employers, rapidly became factory workers, while the protest movements that followed them illustrate the dynamic by which middle-class values gained universal legitimacy.[31] Evangelical religion occupied, moreover, a crucial place in this dynamic: striking weavers, protesting operatives, as well as their working-class opponents, articulated grievances in enthusiastic religious language. Evangelicalism thereby revealed both a radical and a conservative potential and indicated the extent to which early industrial society remained unsecularized.

Still, extreme fluctuations in the business cycle, increased geographic mobility, and the emergence of the factory system induced deeply secularizing experiences;[32] these altered patterns of human behavior but changed individual attitudes more slowly. Part III contrasts two Nonconformist responses to the impact of changing social conditions. The Nailsworth Society of Friends resisted all adaptation to external influence by reaffirming its sectarianism and eschewing evangelicalism but paid the price of a rapid demise. The Shortwood Baptists discarded their early sectarianism under the impact of the Revival to become a denominational and latitudinarian community. This shift made them the premier Nonconformist church in the region and the largest Baptist community outside London yet only forestalled their decline until after midcentury.

Secularization among Shortwood Baptists followed a fluctuating course. The early Industrial Revolution created "an initial phase of anomie"[33] that induced in turn a heightened popular religious enthusiasm; by tapping this sentiment, early Baptist evangelicalism created a radical communitarian environment that softened the impact of anomie. However, this same evangelicalism also contained the seeds of a denominational religious culture because of a theological emphasis on individual experience and the high turnover in membership that eventually issued from it. Denominationalism thereby became associated gradually with a conservative rather than a radical spirituality; in the long term, this change institutionalized the very alienation the Chapel had ameliorated at the outset of the Revival. Chapel life, in other words, although itself deeply transformed by socioeconomic change, helped pave the way for a more thoroughly secular society.

Part 1

Structures of Communal Life

Community of the Vale:
Landscape and Settlement

Definitions of the term "community" can vary according to whether one conceives of a regional landscape or a regional society, "a topographical area on a map...or a human organism with a conscious life of its own, a conscious identity or a sense of belonging together."[1] In the case of the Vale of Nailsworth, both definitions applied coterminously; its topography promoted a pattern of settlement and a type of economy that gave this once remote district a distinctive communal identity. A boundary settlement and protoindustrial village,[2] located in a wood-pasture region, the Vale provided fertile ground for the growth of Dissent, becoming in the eighteenth to early nineteenth century a prototype of a Dissenting community.[3]

The Vale, consisting of Nailsworth village and its dispersed hamlets, was situated four miles south of the town of Stroud in the Cotswold region of Gloucestershire. Stroud served as the hub of a region of fifteen rural-industrial parishes well known for the manufacturing of woolen cloth and an association with Nonconformity. By 1830 Nailsworth had become the Stroud region's most important locus of manufacturing and contained some of the largest Nonconformist congregations in the county. With the growth of industry and communications, however, Nailsworth lost its isolated character, as its Congregationalist and Baptist sects transformed themselves into broad-based denominations:[4] in this combined fashion, the community of the Vale completed its transition to modernity.

The present chapter establishes some of the sociological and topographical features of this transition. It begins with a description of the boundaries and settlement pattern of the Vale community in the eighteenth to early nineteenth century and includes a geographic distribution of occupations. This distribution, although drawn from a census taken in 1841, sets forth a social structure that already possessed a deep history; a more developmental treatment of social structure follows, which focuses closely on its transitional quality. This more dynamic analysis establishes the extent of erosion of a hierarchical social system from the late eighteenth century and the beginning of the formation of modern social classes, whose antecedents lay nevertheless in earlier eras.

The chapter returns next to a discussion of topography, by demonstrating how the configuration and ecology of the landscape helped shape Nailsworth's settlement pattern. The landscape initially promoted a degree of isolation and a protoindustrial economy; its hills, rock formations, streams, and forests gave form to the Vale's topography and underlay its character as an industrial village and Dissenting community. This discussion is carried forward by showing how Nailsworth became integrated geographically into the life of its hinterland; road, turnpike, canal, and railway construction proved critical to the growth of a regional society, yet the slowness of their development also illustrates the incompleteness of their modernizing effects.

Boundaries and Settlement Pattern

A discussion of communal boundaries in rural England begins inevitably with the parish, the primary unit of ecclesiastical administration, which set the parameters of social organization at least from the early modern period. Following the Webbs, the parish can be defined in simplest terms as "a 'shrift-shire', the sphere of reciprocal duties between a duly commissioned priest and the inhabitants in his charge."[5] Parishes, consequently, centered on their churches, although the territory they encompassed often varied considerably, as did the size of their respective populations.

Smaller parishes usually possessed nucleated settlements and for this reason were better served by their incumbents. Their churches were located accessibly at the center of the parish, which made gaining a foothold difficult for Dissenters.[6] In larger parishes, settlement patterns tended to be irregular; chapelries might, therefore, be created in their more remote districts in order to give the inhabitants some contact with established religion.[7] Chapelries did not, however, enjoy the same status as churches; they were not supported from their own tithes, nor always consecrated,[8] a condition that made them less appealing alternatives to Dissenters' chapels. Still, Anglican authorities did not always create chapelries in outlying parochial districts, leaving them wide open to competition from Dissenters. These same districts, moreover, sometimes spawned boundary settlements.

A boundary settlement developed at the borders of two or more parishes, with its various neighborhoods emerging under competing parochial jurisdictions. The Vale occupied just such a position prior to its creation as a civil parish in 1892. The boundaries of Horsley, Avening, and Minchinhampton crossed Nailsworth village, its surrounding hamlets likewise distributing themselves among these three parishes. Shortwood and Newmarket were in Horsley; Forest Green, Inchbrook, and Winsoredge were in Avening; and Watledge, including Scar Hill, was in Minchinhampton.[9] Village and hamlets together constituted the community of the Vale, although it was possible to distinguish even smaller valleys lying between them[10] (see map 1).

Nailsworth's peculiar treatment in land tax returns and extant manor records, as well as its contradictory classification in the early censuses,[11] reflected the confusion regarding its proper boundaries. The land tax returns describe Nailsworth as a tithing of Avening; as an outlying district on that parish's western border, the assessor allocated it a separate listing of owners and occupiers, indicating a semiautonomous status.[12] Nailsworth's connection with Avening arose from the annexation of the manor of Nailsworth to the manors of Avening and Minchinhampton in the sixteenth century. The manor of Nailsworth had existed as early as the reign of Henry II and extended from Aston Farm to Winsoredge.[13] The records of Horsley manor also refer to a tithing of Nailsworth, which ought to have included only that portion of the village already under the jurisdiction of Horsley parish.[14] Nevertheless, the boundary of this tithing extended into Avening proper, as far as Winsoredge, in what was clearly disputed terri-

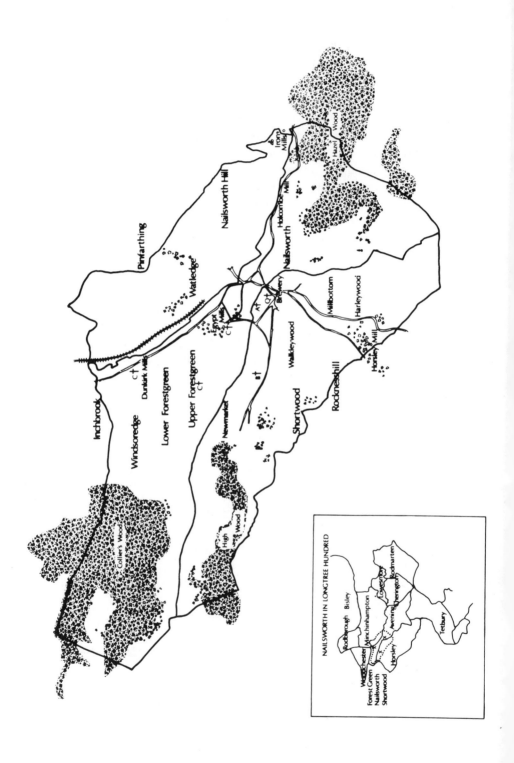

Nailsworth Hill

Pinfarthing

Watledge

Iron
Mills

Hazel Wood

Holcombe Mill

Brewery Nailsworth

Millbottom

Harleywood

Egypt
Mills

Walkleywood

Hunsley Mill

Inchbrook

Dunkirk Mills

Lower Forestgreen

Upper Forestgreen

Newmarket

Shortwood

Rockneshill

Windsoredge

High Wood

Colliers Wood

NAILSWORTH IN LONGTREE HUNDRED

Rodborough

Bisley

Minchinhampton

Woodchester

Lowesmoor

Rodmarten

Forest Green

Nailsworth

Shortwood

Horsley

Avening

Cherington

Tetbury

tory: Nathaniel Wilkins, a broadweaver of Horsley, had been granted a ninety-nine year lease in 1692 on "all that one close of pasture ground lying . . . near to a place called Winsorhedge [*sic*] within the parish of Horsley [!] aforesaid."[15]

Such peculiarities were in part the result of the gradual expansion of the Vale's original settlement, which depended on the development of its economy. The growth of the cloth trade and population increase tended to form its dispersed hamlets into a more unified entity, although they never entirely lost their individual autonomy. Naturally, the original settlement antedated the arrival of Dissenters and was considerably influenced by the landscape.

The most fundamental distinction regarding the English rural landscape is that between the Champion regions, or predominantly arable societies, and the forest or wood-pasture regions that emphasized stock rearing.[16] These economic activities were not mutually exclusive, the distinction between them depending on degrees of specialization. The Cotswold region of Gloucestershire was a wood-pasture society in which sheep rearing was important, although the proportion of land under tillage was higher there than in the Vales of Berkeley and Gloucester, which concentrated on dairying, fruit growing, and market gardening.[17] Champion regions were associated with nucleated settlements, small parishes, and a low incidence of Dissent. The poorer soils of wood-pasture areas, in contrast, encouraged the growth of industrial by-employments, while hilly terrain created irregular settlements in which Dissent more easily proliferated. How well Nailsworth conformed to the criteria of a wood-pasture society can be seen from its economic geography (see fig. 1).[18]

The etymology of Nailsworth evokes a very early association with the wool trade. The Anglo-Saxon "Nael" is a derivative of the teutonic "nagel," which is a measure of seven pounds in

---

Map 1. Boundary map of Nailsworth, with inset: Nailsworth in Longtree Hundred. *Scale*: six inches = one mile. *Source*: Boundary Survey Map, 1892. Inset: *The Victoria County History of Gloucestershire*, Vol. XI.

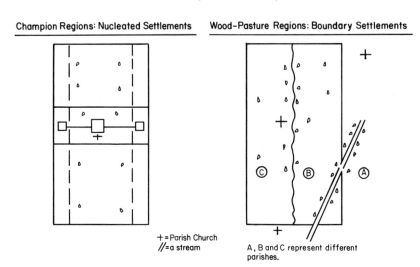

Champion Regions: Nucleated Settlements   Wood-Pasture Regions: Boundary Settlements

+ = Parish Church
// = a stream

A, B and C represent different parishes.

Fig. 1. Champion and wood-pasture settlements.

weight for wool; the stem, "worth," is derived from the Anglo-Saxon "weorth," meaning market or enclosure.[19] "Nailsworth," therefore, means "wool market," although this very likely reflected a later characterization. The earliest reference to Nailsworth appears as early as 716 in a charter of King Ethelbald in which "Negelsleag Minor" is mentioned.[20] The stem "leag" refers to a pasture or wood and seems to indicate that part of a forest was cleared and the land used as sheep pasturage. Thus the region was initially associated with the wool trade chiefly as a supplier of raw material. With the settlement of the village as a market center, "leag" must have been altered to "weorth." This change undoubtedly coincided with the establishment of fulling mills in the area, as the transition was made to a more active engagement in production. Fulling mills were present at Nailsworth during the reign of Henry II,[21] and by the end of the thirteenth century the Vale and the rest of the Stroud region had emerged as important centers for the manufacture of woolen cloth.[22]

Early rural manufacturing, from the medieval period, was based on cottage industry. Clothiers from Nailsworth village distributed raw wool to the spinners and the spun threads to the weavers; they collected the woven pieces, had them finished, and then marketed the final product. Marketing took place initially at Nailsworth village; later at county fairs held at Stroud, the nearest market town; and, as time progressed further, with agents of the London cloth factors.[23]

Unburdened by urban guild restrictions, clothiers had at first engaged cottagers on the basis of secondary, industrial by-employment,[24] a development associated with settlements on wastes, commons, and woodlands. Weavers, clothworkers, laborers, and artisans established settlements by building cottages on wasteland, or in a forest clearing, and fencing off a patch of ground to be tilled as a garden or a small farm. John Chambers of Nailsworth, cordwainer, was formally accused in Horsley's manor court of erecting "a cottage and encroaching eight lug of the waste on Rockness Hill." Samuel Manning, weaver, encroached ten yards of waste and built a cottage at Wash Pond; and Abraham Kitteral, with twenty others, was charged with "tak[ing] away the turf on the waste lands."[25] More prosperous artisans and laborers occupied lands either in the common arable fields, where these survived from medieval times, or in enclosed patches that they either leased or purchased outright. John Pavey, a clothworker from Avening, bequeathed to his wife Mary "a tyning of arable"; to five grandchildren he bequeathed in trust "all messuages, lands and woods which I bought and purchased of my son-in-law, John Penley"; and to his eldest grandson he bequeathed two acres of wood and woodland ground "which I lately bought and purchased to myself. . . situate at Winsoredge."[26]

This practice of dual occupations persisted into the 1850s: "The existence of manufactures in the midst of an agricultural district," one observer commented in 1854, "made the inhabitants not as entirely dependent on either calling."[27] He undoubtedly exaggerated. In the medieval period, spinning and weaving may have been undertaken as activities ancillary to agriculture. By 1841 the reverse was true; a division of labor, created first by protoindustrialization and later intensified by the factory system, made woolworkers dependent on manufacturing, however much they engaged in argicultural by-employment.

The industrial character of the region, as it had matured from the seventeenth century, can be illustrated from the 1841 census. Tables 1 to 3 give the occupational distributions for Nailsworth

TABLE 1. Nailsworth Village and Hamlets: Occupational Structure, 1841

	Nailsworth Village[a]			Shortwood			Newmarket			Forest Green			Winsoredge			Watledge		
	N	% Pop.	% Emp.	N	% Pop.	% Emp.	N	% Pop.	% Emp.	N	% Pop.	% Emp.	N	% Pop.	% Emp.	N	% Pop.	% Emp.
Retailers[b]	20	1.5	4.2	8	2.4	8.2	5	1.5	3.1	2	0.6	2.0	7	2.1	6.1	8	1.7	7.6
Artisans	87	6.8	18.1	11	3.3	11.2	23	6.8	14.5	16	5.0	15.7	12	3.6	10.4	23	4.8	21.9
Weavers	43	3.4	9.0	21	6.3	21.4	34	10.1	21.4	30	9.3	29.4	24	7.2	20.9	10	2.1	9.5
Spinners	1	0.07	0.2	—	—	—	—	—	—	—	—	—	—	—	—	—	—	—
Cloth-workers	57	4.5	11.9	17	5.1	17.4	34	10.1	21.4	36	11.2	35.3	36	10.8	31.3	84	17.4	80.0
Subtotal	101	7.9	21.1	38	11.3	38.8	68	20.2	42.8	66	20.6	64.7	60	18.0	52.2	95	19.6	90.5
Agricultural-laborers	45	3.5	9.4	13	3.9	13.3	3	0.9	1.9	21	6.5	20.6	17	5.1	14.8	11	2.3	10.5
Laborers	18	1.4	3.8	4	1.2	4.1	22	6.5	13.8	—	—	—	—	—	—	—	—	—
Farmers	9	0.7	1.9	2	0.6	2.0	1	0.3	0.6	2	0.6	0.3	2	0.6	1.7	1	0.2	0.95
Total pop.	1,273			335			337			321			334			484		
Total emp.[c]	480			98			159			102			115			105		

[a]Nailsworth Village here includes parts of Box and West End districts.

[b]The occupations here represent all of those in the district, not merely the ones of household heads as in the comparison with the 1811 enumerator's listing.

[c]"Emp." refers to the number employed, that is, with stated occupations.

Source: Census Enumerator's Lists, 1841: Home Office 107/362.

TABLE 2. *Inner Periphery: Occupational Structure, Dispersed Settlements Bordering the Vale*

	Theescombe			Barton End			Rockness		
	N	% Pop.	% Emp.	N	% Pop.	% Emp.	N	% Pop.	% Emp.
Retailers	5	1.2	4.0	1	0.4	0.9	3	1.1	2.9
Artisans	13	3.0	10.4	7	2.6	6.4	16	5.8	14.7
Weavers	—	—	—	11	4.1	10.0	10	3.7	9.8
Spinners	1	0.2	0.8	4	1.5	3.6	1	0.4	0.98
Clothworkers	47	10.8	37.9	23	8.6	20.9	38	14.0	37.3
Subtotal	48	11.0	38.7	38	14.8	34.6	49	18.0	48.0
Agricultural-laborers	1	0.2	0.8	38	14.8	34.6	18	6.6	17.7
Laborers	5	1.2	4.0	1	0.4	0.9	1	0.4	0.98
Farmers	4	0.9	3.2	4	1.5	3.6	1	0.4	0.98
Total pop.	436			268			272		
Total emp.	124			110			102		

Source: Census Enumerator's Lists, 1841: Home Office 107/362.

and its neighboring villages; table 4 and figure 2 interpret them by comparing three zones. Zone I (in fig. 2) represents Nailsworth village and its dispersed hamlets. Zone II is an inner periphery consisting of those districts that border the Vale: Theescombe, in Minchinhampton and Barton End and Rockness in Horsley. Zone III, an outer periphery of sample villages at a distance from the Vale, included Horsley and Avening villages as well as Box, Burleigh, and Littleworth villages in Minchinhampton.

Examining the Vale first, it can be seen that the number of woolworkers, as a proportion of the total workforce, was much higher in Nailsworth's surrounding hamlets than in the village itself. At Nailsworth they accounted for only 9.5 percent of the workforce, while in the surrounding hamlets they accounted for 56.0 percent. Nevertheless, woolworkers constituted the largest occupational group resident at the village. This anomaly may be explained by the fact that Nailsworth had acquired a quasi-urban, cosmopoli-

TABLE 3. Outer Periphery: Occupational Structure, a Sample of Surrounding Villages

	Box			Burleigh			Horsley			Avening			Littleworth		
	N	% Pop.	% Emp.	N	% Pop.	% Emp.	N	% Pop.	% Emp.	N	% Pop.	% Emp.	N	% Pop.	% Emp.
Retailers	14	3.2	5.6	20	4.0	10.5	9	2.0	5.1	6	1.2	3.8	12	1.9	7.1
Artisans	28	6.4	11.2	31	6.3	16.2	24	5.5	13.6	40	7.8	25.0	24	3.8	14.1
Weavers	63	14.5	25.1	14	2.8	7.3	18	4.1	10.2	3	0.6	1.9	38	6.0	22.4
Spinners	4	0.9	1.6	1	0.2	0.5	12	2.7	6.8	3	0.6	1.9	—	—	—
Clothworkers	121	27.8	48.2	66	13.4	34.6	22	5.0	12.4	25	4.8	15.6	41	6.5	24.1
Subtotal	188	43.1	74.9	81	16.4	42.4	52	11.8	29.4	31	6.0	19.4	79	12.5	46.5
Agricultural-laborers	—	—	—	1	0.2	0.5	59	13.4	33.3	48	9.3	30.0	—	—	—
Laborers	31	7.1	12.4	29	5.9	15.2	2	0.5	1.2	6	1.2	3.8	27	4.3	15.9
Farmers	3	0.6	1.2	—	—	—	—	—	—	1	0.2	0.6	3	0.5	1.8
Total pop.	436			494			440			516			634		
Total emp.[a]	251			191			177			160			170		

[a] "Emp." refers to the number employed, that is, with stated occupations.

Source: Census Enumerator's Lists, 1841: Home Office 107/362.

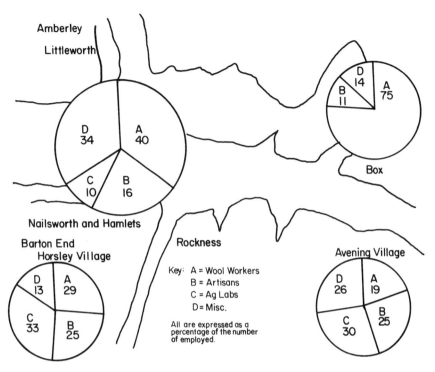

Fig. 2. Selected occupations in Nailsworth and surrounding villages, ca. 1841.

tan status, containing a very high proportion of artisans and retailers and even miscellaneous occupations such as "police officers." As early as 1806 an advertisement for the sale of merchant property described Nailsworth as "a very populous and flourishing village." Another advertisement, for the sale of a millinery shop, had described Nailsworth proper as "genteel and populous," and a third, for the letting of a baker's shop, referred to the property's location as "the preferable part of Nailsworth."[28] Clearly, the village had acquired the social distinctions characteristic of a small town.

Toward the outer periphery in the directions of Horsley and Avening villages, the proportion of resident woolworkers fell significantly, while that of agricultural laborers rose. The reverse was true of the Minchinhampton villages; their clothworking popula-

TABLE 4. *Proportion of Selected Occupations in Three Zones in 1841:*
Core, Inner Periphery, and Outer Periphery

Occupations[a]	Vale hamlets	Inner periphery	Avening-Horsley	Box-Bur-Littleworth
Woolworkers	0.56	0.40	0.25	0.57
Agricultural-laborers	0.112	0.169	0.317	0.001

[a]In difference-of-proportions tests between the Vale hamlets and the inner periphery, for woolworkers, $Z = 4.675$, significant at the 0.0 level; and for agricultural laborers, $Z = 2.448$, significant at 0.007.
Source: See text.

tions proportionately equaled those of the Vale's hamlets, and they contained even fewer agricultural laborers.

The inner periphery consisted of dispersed hamlets situated between more heavily concentrated areas. Theescombe division, in Minchinhampton, lay between Amberley and Nailsworth village just north of the Vale. Rockness district, in Horsley, bordered Avening parish to the east and was virtually part of the Vale's settlement. Barton End district, located to the south of Nailsworth, extended to the outskirts of Horsley village. Table 4 presents the differences between the three zones in their respective proportions of woolworkers and agricultural workers. Figure 2 offers a more schematic summary of the occupational differences between the Vale, Horsley and Avening villages and Box village, which lay at the outskirts of the town of Minchinhampton. Horsley and Avening parishes, exclusive of the Vale community, were clearly more agricultural, and Minchinhampton emerges as almost completely industrialized.[29]

Apart from the clothworking population, the industrial villages included a variety of artisans, such as carpenters, blacksmiths, and masons, as well as retailers ranging from bakers to publicans and vintners. Middle-class occupations included farmers, clothiers, pinmakers, maltsters, and brewers. The landed gentry, naturally, were situated at the top of the social hierarchy.

"Gentlemen" were not included as an occupational category in the 1841 census but were listed as such in an 1811 manuscript census for Horsley parish.[30] Horsley's resident gentlemen numbered twelve in 1811, representing 2.5 percent of all householders with occupations. They included one "gentlewoman," a Sarah Harvey, the recent widow of John Harvey of Drawley Estate,[31] and the head of a household of five females. The eclipse of the title "gentleman" reflected the dilution of its meaning under the pressure of upward social mobility. At the other end of the social spectrum, woolworkers came to represent a more homogeneous class as a result of the emergence of the factory system.[32]

A Transitional Social Structure

Extant wills permit the study of social mobility within the context of class formation. Laborers, clothworkers, artisans, and weavers wrote proportionately fewer wills than did members of the gentry or middle classes. However, the testators among them probably belonged to the elite of their occupations, although the personal estates of several valued less than £20. Still, a sufficient number of wills survive for us to appreciate how definitions of status, changes in the distribution of wealth, and opportunities for upward social mobility were interrelated. Individual cases, combined with statistical analysis, illustrate the fluidity of a transitional social structure.

The presence of a number of large-scale manufacturers among the gentry suggests upward social mobility among the middle class. William Playne, "Esquire," one of the most prominent clothiers of the Stroud region, bequeathed to his heirs in 1850 "all that my Manor of Avening and all freehold messuages and tenements, mills [and] lands. . . ."[33] Edmund Clutterbuck of Avening, likewise styling himself "Esquire," had also descended from a line of gentlemen-clothiers, and for this reason the estate duty officer added the designation "clothier" to the abstract of his probate.[34]

Lords of manors were called "Esquire" regardless of their social origins or occupations. However, it was also possible for ordinary members of the middle class to become substantial landowners without acquiring this title. In 1814, Edward Barnfield's personal estate was valued under £10,000; his principal bequest referred to "all messuages, dwelling houses, lands and premises at Watledge . . . lately purchased. . . ." that did not include his 100-acre estate at Nailsworth.[35] Peter Playne, although perhaps wealthier than his brother William, designated himself a clothier in his will. He may not have owned manors, but he bequeathed a farm at Frampton Mansell in Sapperton, Gloucester, and the tithe survey of lands, undertaken in 1839, recorded him owning and occupying an estate of over 100 acres in Minchinhampton alone.[36]

Indeed, seven of ten clothiers' wills proved at the Prerogative Court of Canterbury made direct references to lands owned or in the testator's possession. The ratio was not as high for those clothiers' wills proved locally in the Consistory Court of the Diocese of Gloucester, as one might have expected:[37] five out of eighteen, or 27.8 percent, made direct references to land owned or in possession, excluding those wills that referred only to cottages or other buildings. In general, the purchase of land and even manors by manufacturers had become commonplace throughout Gloucester since the beginning of the eighteenth century.[38] In an earlier period, a family that had created its fortune in trade might abandon this occupation once a landed estate had been acquired. By the early nineteenth century, however, the prejudice against remaining in trade had waned.[39]

Perhaps the most vivid evidence documenting this change of attitude comes from advertisements placed in the *Gloucester Journal* by some of the exclusive boarding schools in the area. The St. Chloe School instructed "a limited number of gentlemen" in the classics and French and English Grammer, but also in "merchant's accounts . . . surveying and mapping of land timber," as well as in "geography, navigation and astronomy." The Minchinhampton Park School was equally candid in evaluating the uses of its curriculum when it described itself as a "classical and commercial academy for young gentlemen."[40] Younger sons of the aristocracy and gentry customarily sought fortunes by marrying heiresses from wealthy merchant families or by acquiring a profession in the law, armed forces, or overseas trade and banking.[41] Commercial subjects, however, were not always thought appropriate to a gentleman's education; their inclusion in school curricula in the early nineteenth century symbolized the extent to which previous social distinctions had eroded.[42]

Wills of the lesser "gentry" and of the lower middle classes provide further evidence of mobility. Samuel Jenkins was "formerly of

Leonard Stanley, baker, late of Stroud, yeoman, but now of Nailsworth in Horsley, gentleman."[43] His personal estate was valued under £2,000 and was probably the decisive reason for his acquisition of a "title." The principal witness to his will, nonetheless, was a wheelwright, and his executors were two Baptist deacons of humble station: his brother, Charles, a baker, and Isaac Hillier, who at this early date was a pig butcher.

The career of Isaac Hillier perfectly illustrates a pattern of substantial upward social mobility. Having started as a pig butcher, he later became a bacon-curing manufacturer of considerable wealth, with a personal estate valued for probate at £15,000.[44] His marriage to Maria Playne, the daughter of Elizabeth and Thomas Playne, undoubtedly facilitated his advancement; her father was the illegitimate brother of William Playne, the gentleman-clothier and leading Anglican of the locality.[45] Nevertheless, Hillier had worked diligently to develop a large-scale enterprise for the many years he remained in business. The sober habits of a Baptist deacon, who served his church in this capacity for more than two decades,[46] undoubtedly contributed to his worldly success.

Others were more willing to join the Church of England, upon achieving a measure of respectability. In 1788 Nathaniel Dyer had been a carpenter with Nonconformist connections.[47] In 1794, as an "architect" and prominent Anglican, he designed and built the Anglican chapel at Nailsworth. By his death in 1833, he had acquired "manors, messuages, farmlands, and tithes" and was titled "Esquire"; the court at Canterbury valued his personal estate just under £12,000.[48] Although his social advancement appears more meteoric than Hillier's, Dyer never discarded his previous attachments. He named John Clark, a Horsley carpenter and nephew, a beneficiary and made bequests to others with even humbler occupations. He awarded £20 annuities for life to Deborah Bamford, wife of ——— Wigmore of Minchinhampton, shoemaker; Ann Parslow, wife of Isaac Parslow of Horsley, laborer; and Eunice Evans, his niece and the wife of Thomas Evans of Tresham, Gloucester, wheelwright. Most very likely were close relatives or objects of Dyer's newly acquired paternalism.

Richard Bartlett of Minchinhampton, "gentleman," provides yet another although more curious example. The executor proved

Bartlett's will at Canterbury, with the court valuing his personal estate under £600.[49] This estate included a London inn called the "Fortune of War," an odd piece of property from which a gentleman might draw an income, although Bartlett seems to have occupied it until his retirement to Minchinhampton. His brother Edward, also from Minchinhampton, acted as his trustee and was a baker by occupation.

These are the more obvious examples of upward social mobility that can be cited. However, other wills often contained anomalies that qualify the actual status of the testator.[50] A general point that can be made is that wealth rather than mere occupation or title became increasingly important as a mark of status over the eighteenth to early nineteenth century. Men called themselves "gentlemen" if they succeeded in acquiring even a modest fortune, despite the humbleness of their origins; if they acquired landed estates, they called themselves "Esquires" as well. Some of the more spectacular examples of mobility, moreover, came from among Nonconformists whose sobriety and individualism, fostered by the Calvinist churches of the Vale, brought them worldly success and respectability.

Similar tendencies prevailed among those at the lowest rung of the social scale. Daniel Cook of Shortwood, haymaker, an occupation equivalent to a laborer, held at his death a personal estate worth £1,500; like Isaac Hillier, he served as a deacon of the Shortwood Baptist Church.[51] The source of Cook's bequests, moreover, epitomized a capitalist spirit, paid as they were from the interest and dividends accruing from capital placed in trust and invested in public funds. Cornelius Bowne of Nailsworth, a Congregationalist laborer, offered a similarly striking example of entrepreneurship; his activities were especially significant because of the network of associates they revealed. Bowne directed his trustees, both deacons of the Forest Green church, to divide his £100 estate:

Amongst such persons as shall . . . hold and be entitled to a share in certain monies now in the public funds which is to fall to these at my death (and for the consideration whereof each and every one of them (sixty in all) [!] now pay me a penny a week under certain articles of agreement duly executed) share and share alike.[52]

Bowne evidently served as broker to other laborers, sixty in all, whose sense of mutuality had a decidedly capitalistic bent.

Nor was this an isolated case of popular individualism. Clothworkers, laborers, weavers, and artisans made bequests routinely from the profits of investments in cottages and other buildings. Robert Mason, clothworker, owned seven cottages and a shop with a broadloom, all leased to tenants, and that the Consistory Court valued at £200. Thomas Baker, clothworker, bought two houses on mortgage, besides his own residence, leased them to tenants, and bequeathed their rents and profits to his beneficiaries.[53]

Bankruptcy records reveal similar examples of entrepreneurship. Both elder and younger, Thomas Neales were bankrupt clothiers indebted to two shearmen, each of whom had lent them sizable sums at interest. George Oldland held two promissory notes; the first, dated August 9, 1819, amounted to £50 with interest, and the second, dated September 28, 1825, amounted to £30 with interest. Joseph Vines held a promissory note, dated December 18, 1823, for £150 at 5 percent interest, which he had signed in 1822, four years prior to the debtors' default. The bankruptcy examiner emphasized that these notes were given "for money lent and advanced," which leaves no doubt regarding the creditors' intentions.[54] Indeed, the two shearmen must have accumulated considerable capital to invest; they had not only made sizable loans but also left them outstanding for several years.

The entrepreneurial spirit of the lower classes did not generally produce the upward social mobility experienced by Nathaniel Dyer or even Isaac Hillier. Usually, it encouraged horizontal social mobility through which artisans, retailers, weavers, and laborers associated with each other on a more equal footing. In a typical example, Thomas Bird, shopkeeper and small clothier, appointed John Webb, clothworker (whom he described as a "friend"), one of the executors of his estate.[55] Bird clearly found his social milieu among his employees or among those whom he served as customers in his shop, and with whom he very likely collaborated in small ventures. They may even have attended chapel together.[56]

These patterns of social mobility, however, must be set against a framework of continuity. Although the traditional hierarchy had severely eroded in substance, its form appeared to remain intact. In customary society, differences in wealth reflected rather than created rank ascription, although in the long term they reinforced social distinctions. "[S]tatus honor...normally stands in sharp opposition to the pretensions of mere property," Max Weber once wrote. "[Yet if] property as such is not always recognized as a status qualification... in the long run it is, and with extraordinary regularity."[57] Although wealth may have served as the hidden foundation of honor, the governing class of the eighteenth century still treated "gentleness" as a virtue bred by birth and upbringing and ranked the lower classes according to the criterion of occupation or function.[58] In such a society, one might have expected differences in wealth to have followed the gradations of rank. The growth of capitalism from the sixteenth century helped erode this hierarchical system, however, and as industrialism advanced from the late eighteenth century, new standards of defining status developed alongside the old as the personal wealth of individuals increased.[59]

The inability of the old order fully to assimilate the change revealed itself statistically. The social pyramid can be examined through analysis of wealth distribution across occupations, or status designations such as "gentleman," using valuations of personal wealth recorded in probate records.[60] Differences in mean personal wealth, when analyzed alongside their respective coefficients of variation, expressed degrees of continuity and social mobility, either horizontal or vertical (see tables 5 and 6).

Table 5 contains a breakdown of mean personal wealth by social groups appearing in rank order.[61] The solid lines indicate the points at which the differences proved to be significant according to statistical *t*-tests presented in table 6. As in customary society, the mean wealth of each group generally reflected rank ascription. However, the fact that the differences proved not to be significant in every case suggests that important changes had occurred.

Gentlemen and the middle classes clearly constituted a homogeneous category, as did the yeomanry, retailers, and artisans immediately below them. Weavers, laborers, and clothworkers did the same. This structure clearly affirms the upward social mobility of the middle classes (already revealed by the qualitative

TABLE 5. *Values of Personal Estates by Occupation and Status*

Status and occupation	N	Sum (£)	Mean (£)	Standard deviation (σ)	Coefficient of variation (%)
Gentlemen	53	155,260	2,929.4	6,056.5	206.7
Middle class	59	159,895	2,710.1	5,237.6	193.8
Yeomanry	76	53,795	707.8	1,297.4	183.8
Retailers	86	44,525	517.7	1,325.5	256.0
Artisans	92	21,800	236.9	433.2	182.8
Weavers	74	8,177	110.5	105.7	95.7
Laborers	25	2,685	107.4	115.0	107.1
Clothworkers	30	2,838	94.6	81.5	86.1

TABLE 6. *t-Tests of Wealth Differences by Occupation and Status*

Occupation and status	t-Value	Degrees of Freedom	p^a	Pass/Fail
Gentlemen, middle class	0.202	107	<0.2	F
Middle class, yeomanry	2.844	65	0.01	P
Yeomanry, retailers	0.910	280	<0.2	F
Retailers, artisans	1.862	103	0.1	F
Artisans, weavers	2.686	106	0.01	P
Weavers, clothworkers	0.813	73	<0.2	F
Clothworkers, laborers	0.38	45	<0.2	F

[a]The minimum acceptable probability level for significance is 0.05.

evidence from wills) and of small retailers and artisans, who approached the yeomanry on a more equal footing. The weavers were an exception; their position had noticeably deteriorated since the eighteenth century, when they ranked fully as artisans. Nevertheless, many more weavers wrote wills than did either clothworkers or laborers, as table 7 illustrates. As a group they probably suffered less poverty, although their mean personal wealth hardly differed in value; or they may have held a greater apprecia-

TABLE 7. *Willmakers as a Percentage of the Population:*
The Lower Classes, 1841

Occupation and status	N_1 (wills)	N_2 (sample population)	N_1 as % of N_2
Retailers	86	120	71.6
Artisans	92	355	25.9
Weavers	74	319	23.2
Laborers	25	688	3.6
Clothworkers	30	647	4.6

Source: See text.

tion for property rights, a residual consequence of their waning artisan status.

Thus, if the shape of a customary hierarchy remained formally intact, according to the distribution of mean personal wealth, it eroded nonetheless as more distinct social classes began to appear. The middle classes and gentry became the high bourgeoisie of later Victorian society; the yeomanry, retailers, and artisans constituted a petit bourgeoisie; and weavers, clothworkers, and laborers formed a proletariat. At the same time, none of these classes remained monolithically encased. Had that been so, the standard deviations would have fallen well below their respective means. In every case, except for weavers and clothworkers, they fell significantly above their means, indicating extreme variability. For weavers and clothworkers, the standard deviations fell just below their means but were high nonetheless. The coefficients of variation express the standard deviations as percentages of their respective means and invite comparisons across occupational and status boundaries. The high percentages, particularly for the first five groups, provide a useful corrective to the mere distribution of means; they show that many individuals from different strata possessed overlapping estate values. This pattern ran counter to the tendencies of their respective means, which accentuated the differences between them, and accounted for the failure of several *t*-tests, designed to measure such differences. Even where no such failure existed, the high coefficients of variation rendered the difference between means largely a formal one.

Thus, the erosion of the hierarchical system had a dual aspect, pointing toward the formation of modern social classes, in a manner affirming Marx's original perception of this process, as well as to a pattern of individual mobility which fundamentally denies it.[62] The lower middle and working classes, furthermore, shared a petit-bourgeois attitude toward upward social mobility that Nonconformity appears to have reinforced. The Chapel community, as Halèvy had suggested, served as the mediator between a transitional and a modern England by encouraging an ethos of individualism tinctured by the spirit of deference.[63]

However transitional, the social structure of the Vale community had assumed a distinctive settlement pattern considerably influenced by the landscape. Woodlands invited clearing, and the streams flowing down the hills marked the distribution of weavers', clothworkers', and laborers' cottages. The elevation of the hills, the quality of the soil, and the direction of the streams in turn affected the landscape's configuration.

The Landscape

The Stroud district is located at the midpoint of the Cotswold hills, which occupy the eastern part of Gloucestershire. At their highest point, they reach an elevation of 1,093 feet at Cleeve Hill, and the average height of twelve of the highest peaks is 834 feet above sea level. Elevations near Stroud are lower, ranging from 200 to 600 feet.[64] Nonetheless, such extremes in elevation occurring within short distances transmitted an aura of remoteness to localities such as Nailsworth, as well as a sensation of social complexity (see map 2).

Approaching the Vale from the southwest, and moving northeasterly, the traveler, while on walking tour, encounters Horsley village on its immediate periphery at an elevation of 500 feet. Continuing in a northeasterly direction, the hamlets of Newmarket, Forest Green, Winsoredge, and Inchbrook emerge, varying in elevation from 300 feet at Newmarket to 400 feet at Forest Green and dropping to 200 feet at Winsoredge and Inchbrook.[65] Turning

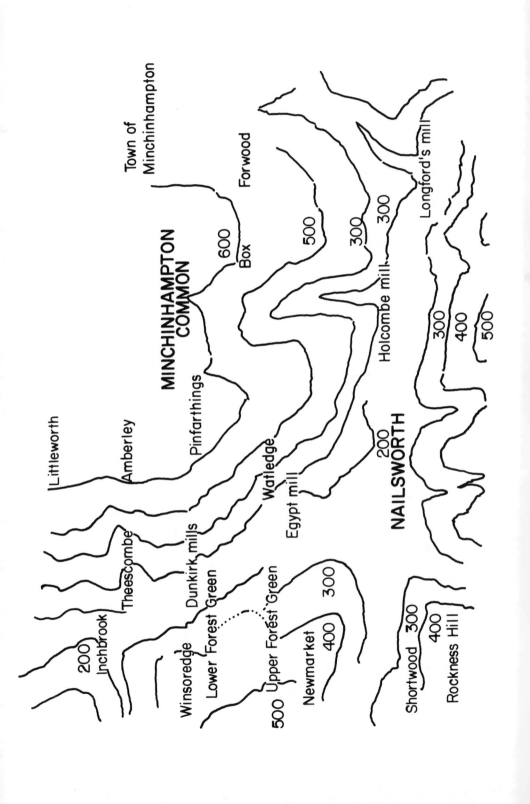

Littleworth

Town of
Minchinhampton

Amberley

Forwood

**MINCHINHAMPTON
COMMON**

Pinfarthings

600

Box

500

Theescombe

Watledge

300

300

Inchbrook

Dunkirk mills

Egypt mill

Holcombe mill

Longford's mill

200

Winsoredge

Lower Forest Green

NAILSWORTH

200

300

400

500

500 Upper Forest Green

Newmarket

400

300

Shortwood 300

400

Rockness Hill

southeasterly, while moving along the bottom of the valley, the traveler passes Dunkirk and Egypt mills until reaching Nailsworth village. The Nailsworth valley continues in a southeasterly direction as the traveler passes Holcombe and Iron mills, finally reaching Longfords mill. Thereafter, the ascent begins once more, rising to 500 feet at Avening village on the southeasterly periphery of the Vale.

Beginning the ascent from Nailsworth village, however, and moving in a northeasterly direction, the traveler encounters the hamlets of Watledge and Nailsworth Hill, which rise, respectively, to levels of 400 and 500 feet. They constitute the Vale's outer limits as one moves toward the southernmost edge of Minchinhampton Common. Continuing northeasterly along the edge of the Common, the traveler passes Box and Forwood villages before finally arriving at the old wool town of Minchinhampton. The town and the villages that ring the Common (suggesting its importance to their original pattern of settlement) stand at 600 feet above sea level, the highest point in the neighborhood, overlooking the broad valley of the river Severn to the north. From these heights originate the streams and rivulets that fertilize the valleys below.

Each valley of the Stroud district is associated with a comb or "bottom"; and each comb, with a spring or rivulet that emerges from the strata of Lias Clay and Supra-Liassic or Cotswold Sand. The drainage of the area follows the slopes of the hills, and the valleys give a westerly direction to the flow. The Stroud district is drained by the river Frome, which empties into the Severn. At the town of Stroud, the springs flowing down from the north are joined by the Slad and Painswick brooks, and at Dudbridge by those of Ruscombe and Nailsworth, which flow in from the south.[66] The Nailsworth stream is formed by the junction of two rivulets that rise, respectively, near Avening and at Horsley and contains the drainage of the Vales of Nailsworth and Woodchester[67] (see map 3).

Map 2. Elevations of hills at Nailsworth. *Source*: Ordinance Survey Map, with elevations (1885).

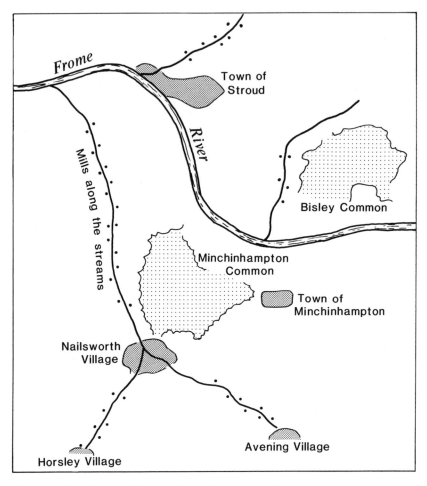

Map 3. The Frome River valley and streams. *Source*: 1-inch Ordinance Survey Map, ca. 1885, Gloucester Records Office Q/RUM 304.

These streams, together with the water-bearing soils that allowed them to flourish, crucially determined the settlement of the Vale. "These villages," William Cobbet remarked in 1830, "lie on the sides of a narrow and deep valley, with a narrow stream of water running down the middle of it." Nor could he fail to observe how "this stream turns the wheels of a great many mills and sets of machinery for the making of woolen cloth."[68]

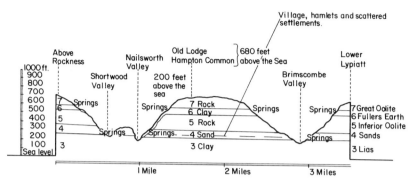

Fig. 3. Section of the hills near Nailsworth, Gloucestershire. *Source:* In the possession of David Playne, Bannut Tree, Avening, Stroud, Gloucestershire, Playne Family Papers.

The regularity of the supply of water and the actual power the streams generated were mutually dependent on the quality of the soil and the distances the flow of water needed to travel from hill to vale. The formation of Upper Lias Clay and Supra-Liassic or Cotswold Sand, because of their porous and friable natures, acted "as . . . spung[es], into which all the water that percolated through the beds [from above] is received and stored."[69] Notwithstanding variations in the rate of drainage, a reasonably good supply of water was usually obtainable year-round.[70] The positions of the clays and sands, furthermore, were always marked by the lines of cottages that dotted the slopes of the hills: "Everywhere [the villages and hamlets] are all built near the base of the sands and just above the line where the water is thrown out by the Upper Lias."[71]

Apart from the clays and sands, which were crucial to the establishment of cloth mills, numerous quarries of both the Inferior and Great Oolites were developed at Scar Hill, near Nailsworth, and around Minchinhampton Common. They provided much of the building material that has added another distinctive feature to the landscape (see fig. 3).

The Fuller's Earth, which normally lies between these two formations, is largely responsible for the fertility of the slopes. In the Vale of Nailsworth, especially, the hills tend to be capped by the Great Oolite; the slopes of Inferior Oolite are thereby covered with slipped Fuller's earth, which "has upon its surface a rich

TABLE 8. *Acreage under Tillage: Horsley, Avening, and
Minchinhampton, 1800–1841*

Parish	Total acreage	Percent arable 1800–1804	Percent arable 1838–1841	Percentage change
Horsley	4,145.0	33.3	47.6	42.7
Avening	4,512.5	34.0	63.8	87.4
Minchinhampton	4,942	48.8	43.6	−10.5

Source: See text.

TABLE 9. *Arable Acreage by Types of Crops: Horsley and Avening,
ca. 1801*

Parish	Total arable land	Wheat	Barley	Oats	Peas	Beans	Turnips
Horsley	1,382.5	734	190	300	43	9.5	106
Avening	1,536	481	278	638	32	31	66

Source: See text.

soil well adapted for cultivation."[72] In Horsley, Avening, and
Minchinhampton—the parochial hinterland of the Vale—wheat,
barley, and oats were the principal crops grown, while peas,
beans, and turnips were secondary. Tables 8 and 9 indicate,
respectively, the percentages of parish lands under tillage in 1800
and 1840 and the amount of acreage devoted to each type of crop
around 1800. The increase in arable land under cultivation at
Avening was caused by the shrinkage of the wasteland and at
Horsley, very likely, by more intensive husbandry resulting from
greater concentration of ownership; the fall in cultivated arable
land at Minchinhampton was due to that parish's more complete
industrialization.[73]

Actual crop yields, however, are difficult to ascertain. Of the
three parishes, only the tithe survey for Avening gives any indica-

TABLE 10. *Crop Yields for Avening Parish in 1838*

Crop	Estimated arable acres sown	Bushels	Bushels as % total yield	Bushels per acre estimated arable land
Wheat	904.9	7,416	18.8	8.2
Barley	522.9	13,153.4	33.3	25.2
Oats	1,200.3	18,933.3	47.9	15.8

Source: See text.

tion. However, since each parish contained the same type of soil, one can assume that Avening's crop yield was typical of that of its region. If the tithe charge were one-tenth of the yield (as the name of this tax suggests), the total yield could be estimated;[74] this estimate is depicted in table 10. Wheat was marketed for human consumption and oats for animals, while the very high barley yield reflected the strong demand from the malting and brewing industry.[75] The low wheat yield and the significantly higher yields for oats and barley affirm that the region, as a wood-pasture society, was better adapted to stock rearing and industrial activities, some of which remained ancillary to agriculture.[76]

A wood-pasture society, Nailsworth once was covered by dense forests, which were only partially cleared as settlements became established. Local place names such as Shortwood, Harleywood, and Collier's Wood testify to their importance, as occasionally do the field names. A parcel of arable land, occupied by a tenant of Robert Kingscote and consisting of 17 acres, was called "Horsley Wood field" in Horsley's 1841 tithe survey. Clearly, it had once been part of a common arable field, which served as woodland ground in an earlier period. The same could be said of three acres of arable land near Nailsworth called "Woodleaze," which was put up for sale in 1823. At Newmarket in this same year a half acre, sold by auction and "covered with a plantation of thriving timber trees of different kinds," revealed the extent to which the region remained forested even at this late date.[77]

Field names, moreover, evoked the image of a once quite isolated district. "Hither Robbers Green," "Middle Robbers Green," and "Far Robbers Green" suggest the uses to which a forest region, combined with an uncertain parochial jurisdiction, might have once been put by shrewd evaders of the law,[78] at least until the advent of a better communications system. "Until then," commented one local historian, "we can see what rough and steep perilous routes [the roads] must have been for the traveller, and not lightly to be followed."[79]

By 1825 the Vale had become fully integrated into its surrounding region; increased geographic mobility, facilitated by improved communications, rendered Nailsworth a far less isolated locale. The growth of communications, while promoting the regionalization of local society, also contributed to the process of industrialization. Turnpikes, canals, and railway lines constituted a new infrastructure, on the basis of which the woolen industry expanded. Despite the advent of the factory system the woolen industry failed, however, reflecting the slow development and incompleteness of this very infrastructure. As a result, the network of improved communications, although promoting regionalization, altered the landscape only to a limited degree.

Regionalization

Little had been accomplished before 1780 to bring economic unity to the Stroud region, and especially to Nailsworth and its hinterland. The roads connecting the villages and towns of the region were generally old tracks that had hardly experienced improvement. One exception was the Minchinhampton-Tetbury road, which was found in 1667 in a state of disrepair; in 1758, it was one of the first roads to be turnpiked.[80] Nevertheless, the road, while running north-south through Avening parish, bypassed Nailsworth, leaving this outlying settlement in comparative isolation.

Before 1780, Nailsworth depended on a series of tracks to bring it into contact with places as far as Tetbury, six miles to the southeast, and Dursley, five miles to the southwest. Tetbury was the second most important market town in the Stroud region and like Horsley, Avening, and Minchinhampton, was located in Longtree Hundred. Dursley was located at the center of the lower cloth-manufacturing district of the county, near the Vale of Berkeley.

Regular intercourse with such places was made difficult by the

fact that the tracks were narrow and not especially durable to support the weight of carriages.[81] Prior to general road improvement,
the transport of cloth in both its raw and finished states was
undertaken by packhorses. The boundary map of Nailsworth
(map 1, above) provides an overview of the local transport network. It shows the extent to which proximity to newly built roads,
and later to the railway, provided convenient service to the neighboring mills. One of the more important roads linking Nailsworth
to its surrounding hinterland passed from Woodchester in the
northwest through Inchbrook and Forest Green, continuing east
through Nailsworth and then southeast to Avening village and
eventually to Tetbury. This last stretch came to be known as the
Nailsworth-Tetbury road. Nailsworth was also connected to
Avening village by an old route that ran along the hillside through
Hazelwood, while another track through Balls Green connected
it to the town of Minchinhampton. A road from Nailsworth
to Dursley passed through Horsley village to the south and thereafter turned southwest toward the lower cloth-manufacturing
district.

The first significant improvement occurred in 1780 with the
construction of the Bath-Gloucester road, a major thoroughfare
that passed through Nailsworth at closer proximity to the mills
than the old road from Woodchester; the new road bisected Horsley parish from north to south. At the same time, an additional
road was constructed at Nailsworth, connecting the new Bath
road to Box village on the outskirts of Minchinhampton, while the
old Nailsworth-Tetbury road was turnpiked. The Nailsworth-
Dursley road through Horsley was turnpiked in 1800, and in 1822
a new road was constructed along the valley toward Avening,
complementing the old hillside track.

Numerous efforts were made in the early nineteenth century to
widen existing tracks and to make new additions. In February
1820 the trustees of the Nailsworth, Woodchester, and Dudbridge
turnpike roads met for the purpose of "making and maintaining a
road from Tiltups Inn, in . . . Horsley, to join the turnpike road
from Cirencester to Dudbridge . . . in the parish of Rodborough,
and from the bridge at Nailsworth . . . to Minchinhampton Common."[82] In the same year, an application to widen some of the
smaller, ancillary roads in the area was noted:

from the field called Boulden Sleight to the end of a lane adjoining the road from Horsley to Tetbury, near Tiltups Inn; and from the Market House in Tetbury to the turnpike road on Minchinhampton Common; and from the said road in Hampton field unto the turnpike road from Cirencester to Stroud, near Burnt Ash; and from the said turnpike road to Tayloe's mill pond in Chalford Bottom; and through Hyde to the bottom of Bourn Mill.[83]

Such undertakings, together with the construction of turnpike roads, facilitated the transport of commodities and the geographic mobility of the population. From 1780, accelerated membership growth of the Shortwood Baptist Church, as we shall see, coincided with the building of the Bath-Gloucester road. The scattered population of the surrounding area found itself better able to travel to Nailsworth, although local residents responded more slowly to the stimulus. In 1794 Nailsworth was still widely viewed as a somewhat isolated district. Not until after 1812 did the local populace become more mobile,[84] and by 1825 it was found moving routinely between Nailsworth and other villages.[85]

The regionalization of local society was evident, furthermore, by the manner in which turnpikes and improved local roads were managed. The trustees of the Nailsworth, Woodchester, and Dudbridge roads made joint decisions that clearly applied to places at some distance from Nailsworth.[86] The toll gates, over which they also exercised joint control, were likewise scattered throughout the neighborhood;[87] their jurisdiction, in other words, was extra-parochial.

In order to maintain the roads, the trustees were empowered by the General Turnpike Act of 1780 to call meetings of parish surveyors and to require them to mobilize the resources of their respective communities. Although turnpike trusteeships were not regulated by a manor court (and, in fact, were ad hoc bodies of landowners and clothiers), the form in which their orders appeared had a medieval aspect. In 1809 the trustees of the Nailsworth, Woodchester, and Dudbridge roads required the surveyors to produce

a true and perfect list... of the names of all inhabitants and occupiers of lands, tenements and herediments... that are liable to do statute work or duty; and in such lists to distinguish . . . [those who] keep a team or teams and . . . to what annual reputed value they respectively occupy [land, etc.] and which of them are labourers, and liable to do statute duty as labourers only.[88]

The order was akin to what a steward of a manor might direct to a Court of Survey; the specific reliance on statute labor, rather than wage labor,[89] evoked the tradition of the corvée.

The collection of tolls, furthermore, was undertaken by the traditional method of tax farming. Farmers would compete for the privilege at auction; the winners were required to pay a monthly rental from receipts and were permitted to keep the surplus as compensation for their efforts. In 1824 it was reported that five gates in the Nailsworth-Woodchester-Dudbridge area rented for an average sum of £254; and in 1835 it was reported further that the toll revenue of the previous year was £1,320 above the expenses of collecting them,[90] a sum sufficiently high to attract eager bidders.

In general, the turnpikes were not constructed with a view to turning a profit for a group of shareholders. The initial capital may have been raised through subscriptions, but this sum was usually treated as a loan to be repaid at low interest rates, although repayment was rarely accomplished.[91] Funds for maintaining the roads were dispensed from monthly toll gate rentals and, evidently, from a property tax levied on small owners, who were permitted to commute their statute duty into a monetary payment. Such was the peculiar dialectic by which the quasi-feudal conscription of labor and resources, toll farming, and the reliance on a kind of "rent perpetuelle" for the raising of initial capital aided the modernization of the local and regional road systems.[92]

The local elite employed more current financing methods to build canals; these ventures were viewed as profit-making enterprises and required investment of larger amounts of capital.[93] A joint-stock company was formed in the 1770s to build two canals that would link the Severn and Thames rivers at Wallbridge, Stroud, and both to a small inland port at Brimscombe; the linkages were designed to facilitate the transfer of cargoes.[94] The Stroudwater canal connected Framilode on the Severn to Wallbridge, and the Thames-Severn canal connected Wallbridge to Lechlade on the Thames.[95] The project, begun in 1775, was completed by 1785.[96]

Contrary to expectation, the canals did not significantly improve the flow of traffic to London.[97] They did, however, facilitate commercial contact between the city of Gloucester and inland settlements such as Nailsworth. Improved contact was especially important for the grain trade, as Nailsworth relied on both the Tetbury and Gloucester markets. Messrs. Lewis and Company, owners of the Stroud barge, announced that their vessel "regularly loads every Saturday at Lewis's, warehouse, on the quay, Gloucester, sails from Gloucester to Stroud, Brimscombe, and all intermediate places every Monday and returns on the Friday following, delivering grain and other goods."[98] One such "intermediate place" was Dudbridge wharf in Rodborough, which served as a delivery terminal for the Rodborough-Woodchester-Nailsworth area. An advertisement for letting a corn mill at Woodchester Park had noted the mill's strategic location just three miles from Dudbridge wharf and twelve miles from Gloucester.[99]

The canals, however, were intended primarily to benefit the clothiers of the district, most of whom were initial backers of the various schemes to build them.[100] Nevertheless, those who owned or occupied mills along the river resisted their construction since water drawn from the streams into the canals deprived these mills of their only source of power prior to the advent of the steam engine.[101] Much later, after the arrival of steam power, clothiers could be found protesting against high transport rates for coal,[102] charging that the canal company engaged in excess profiteering.[103] The canal company sought to rebut the charge, and in doing so revealed much about the extent of regional economic growth.

The prevailing popular view was that the company's dividend payments had grown to £30 percent per annum, based on an initial subscription of £100 per share. The company published its annual dividend payments for the 1785–1824 period and pointed out that the initial capital of £100 per share was an underestimation of the true cost to each shareholder. Because of delays in construction, an additional £50 contribution was needed from the shareholders, and because of a ten-year interval between the initial proposal to build the canals and commencement of their opera-

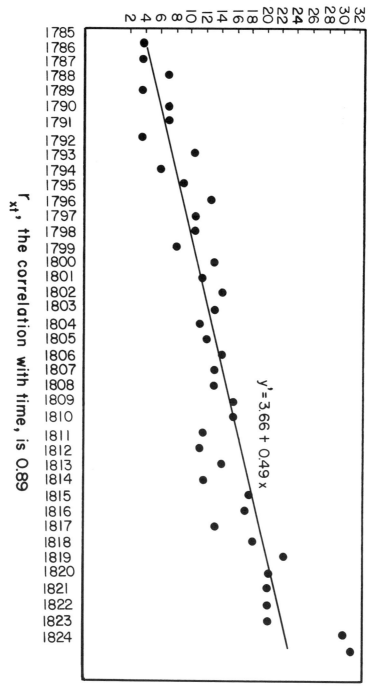

Pounds Sterling

$y' = 3.66 + 0.49x$

Fig. 4. Stroud canal dividend series, 1785–1824.

r_{xt}, the correlation with time, is 0.89

tions, the company sustained a further loss of interest arrears amounting to £75. Altogether, then, subscribers invested an initial capital amounting to £225 per share or £45,000 when all 200 shares of the issue are counted. The total dividend payment over the forty-year period totaled £528.10s. per share, which represented a 235 percent increase in capital. The company protested, however, that the average annual dividend amounted to less than £6 percent per annum; indeed, the time series of dividend payments shown in figure 4, indicates a growth rate or 4.7 percent per annum.

Despite the company's lamentations, such a rate of profit was not unreasonable under then prevailing conditions. In the first fifteen years of the canals' operations (1785–1799), the growth rate in dividends was 8.2 percent per annum, well above the 5 percent interest rate for private lending set by the usury laws.[104] From 1811 to 1824, the trend in the Stroud canal company's dividend payments kept pace with the national movement of canal share prices. The partial correlation coefficient $r_{xy(t)}$ between the two was a strong 0.65.[105] This fact, however, could provide little solace since the rates of profit of most canal companies fell well below the expected 10 to 12 percent per annum.[106] Indeed, the Stroud canals failed to become the major thoroughfare their backers had hoped for. Transport to London proved too slow, sometimes taking up to four months for goods to arrive.[107] Coal and grain seem to have been the only important items carried to the inland settlements and at irritatingly high costs. Although the canals helped to effect the regionalization of local society, slower regional economic growth, revealed by their rates of profit, meant that the landscape remained untrammeled. Implementation of the railway eventually eclipsed the Stroud canals, but its effect on the regional economy and lanscape was hardly more revolutionary.

Both the slowness and high cost of water transport led many clothiers to advocate construction of the Great Western Railway. The line would run between Gloucester and Swindon via Stroud and would link up to the main Bristol-London trunk. Threats to promote such a scheme were made in 1824 and 1831,[108] but no serious action was taken until 1834. In that year an important meeting was held at Stroud to consider public endorsement for building the railway; those attending "represented the most con-

siderable part of the wealth and influence of the neighborhood."[109] Because of sharpening competition with the North of
England in textiles and the promise of further development of
the region's resources, especially coal,[110] the project was given a
unanimous vote of confidence. Moreover, the railway provided
a significant investment opportunity for individuals. "Looking
at it as a matter of investment," one speaker had commented,
"if it paid only £6 percent, it might be considered a pretty good
speculation. . . . The £100 shares [issued] were now producing
£200." Nor was it expected that the burden of raising capital
would fall entirely on the shareholders, who were not held bound
to their subscriptions until all shares were sold, and the government promised assistance to the extent of half the needed capital at
only 4 percent interest.

Despite these liberal terms, and apparent enthusiasm for the
project, the railway was not completed until 1845.[111] Delays were
probably caused by the resistance of landowners whose properties
lay along the proposed route,[112] and by competition between
promoters of the Bristol-London and Southampton-London lines;
the latter would have bypassed the Stroud region entirely.[113] In
addition, there may have been greater skepticism toward the
scheme than was apparent at the Stroud meeting. Although several
speakers emphasized the importance of the railway for industrial
development, one of the principal promoters clearly regarded
passenger service as its primary advantage. His attitude, while
generally optimistic, may have caused potential investors to doubt
the long-term viability of the enterprise.

One indication of such resistance was the failure to consider
construction of branch lines from the proposed Gloucester-
Swindon trunk to the inland areas. W. H. Hyett, MP (Member of
Parliament) for Stroud, confidently maintained that there would
be little difficulty establishing such lines in the future. Yet the only
branch in the region, from Stonehouse to Nailsworth, was not
constructed until 1867,[114] ostensibly because of the scattered
settlement pattern of the district.

This difficulty had been cited as the main obstacle a decade earlier in a debate at the Nailsworth Literary and Mechanics Institute.
"Nothing short of an indefinite number of stations," one speaker
contended, "would be much if any service to the inhabitants" and

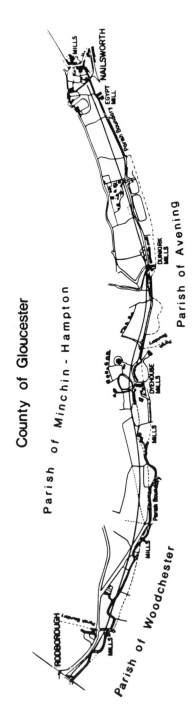

Map 4. Stonehouse-Nailsworth Branch Railroad Line, ca. 1863. *Source:* Gloucester Records Office Q/RUM 304.

therefore of limited profitability.[115] Certainly he had exaggerated the problem. When finally built, the section of the line from Stonehouse to Rodborough, depicted in map 4, provided full service to mill owners on the south side of Stroudwater canal; and the section from Rodborough, running south to Nailsworth, passed close to the mills along the Nailsworth stream. Yet implementation of the railway did little to arrest Stroud's economic decline. Unlike Birmingham, with which contemporaries often drew contrasts,[116] the Stroud region never urbanized significantly and therefore retained its rural character.

Summary and Conclusion

This chapter has depicted the interaction between landscape, ecology, settlement pattern, and social structure in and around the Vale of Nailsworth and has offered structural analyses of two aspects of the experience of modernization: class formation and regional integration. Local topography determined that Nailsworth was initially isolated and characterized by a dispersed settlement pattern. Located in a wood-pasture region, Nailsworth was a boundary settlement, not falling squarely within the jurisdiction of any one parish or manor. Nailsworth's ecology determined its industrial and social characteristics as the Vale emerged from the medieval period with an economy based on a system of cottage industry in woolen manufactures. Nailsworth's initial remoteness, dispersed settlement pattern, and socioeconomic configuration combined to make it a center of Nonconformity in the eighteenth to early nineteenth century, while its progressive integration into a wider regional community was reflected in and facilitated by improvements in transport and communications, however ineffective these remained from an economic standpoint.

A district with a hierarchical social structure in the eighteenth century, Nailsworth's transition to the factory system helped bring into being a more horizontally structured, class-based society in the nineteenth century. Analysis of class formation documents a pattern of accelerated upward social mobility among the "middling sort," the corresponding erosion of the traditional status of "gentleman," and a pattern of downward social mobility, or derogation in status, among artisan weavers. This process had antecedents in earlier periods, but between 1780 and 1850, wealth had become a more obvious criterion for defining status than in the past, so much so that men with the humblest occupations might call themselves "gentlemen" if the size of their personal estates seemed to warrant the title. This change reflected itself further among the traditional gentry and the wealthier bourgeoisie in the closer intermingling of landed and industrial wealth, as well as by the depreciated role of the classics in commonly accepted standards for educating gentlemen. The experience of downward social mobility among weavers became manifest in the analysis of wealth distribution by the failure of their estates to rise appreciably in value above the mean wealth of clothworkers and laborers, however much they outnumbered the latter as testators.

Evidence from wills also suggested a pattern of horizontal social mobility, by which small retailers, artisans, and ordinary laborers could find common ground in feelings of neighborliness, forged by an entrepreneurial spirit. Clothworkers, laborers, and shearmen could be found purchasing real estate in either land or buildings, pooling resources for investment in the public funds, or acting as creditors even to their employers, and all with the expectation of turning a profit. The most spectacular examples of such initiative came from among Nonconformists and thereby lent credibility to the Weberian relationship of a "Protestant ethic" and a spirit of capitalism, at least as applied to Calvinists. These findings take issue with E. P. Thompson's view of working-class culture in the early industrial period, insofar as working people appear more receptive to capitalist values and less committed to communitarian ones than he has suggested. Yet they support, with some irony, his and Elie Halèvy's contention that evangelicalism mediated the transfer of middle-class values to a working class in formation; the Calvinist ideal of the "calling" seems to have promoted individualism and personal autonomy, more than a collective form of work discipline.

Finally, the growth of a regional transport and communications network brought an end to Nailsworth's historic isolation. Although the locality remained a boundary settlement until 1892, Nailsworth village urbanized moderately and integrated itself into the economy and society of its parochial hinterland. Geographically and socially, as a boundary settlement and industrial village embedded in a wood-pasture region, Nailsworth captured the spirit of individuality conducive to the spread of religious dissent. The hinterland of the Vale, in its structures of landownership and authority, likewise provided an appropriate setting for communities of Dissenters and for this reason also warrants close study.

Chapter Two

Hinterland of the Vale:
Landownership and Tenure

The community of the Vale may have been an outlying district throughout most of the eighteenth century, but its remoteness never fully insulated Dissenters from the purview of the Establishment. The boundary settlement typology, however useful a framework for analysis, exaggerates the degree of antagonism implicit in the mutual relations of Dissenting and Anglican churches.[1] The two communities coexisted and interacted: Dissenters maintained their autonomy, their sense of separateness from the world, while engaging the Establishment and Anglican laity in normal intercourse. Leading Nonconformists desired collaboration, and by obtaining it their churches complemented rather than undermined the preeminence of the Church of England. The present chapter studies the underlying structure of this relationship by focusing on landownership and tenure. Since land was the material basis of the Establishment's power, the concentration of ownership and forms of land tenure characteristic of the region ought to have affected the spread of Nonconformity.

The chapter first analyzes the changing structures of landownership in the three parishes of Nailsworth's hinterland between 1777 and 1841, with reference to a standard model used widely to explain the settlement patterns of rural Nonconformity.[2] If relations between Dissenters and the Establishment had been characterized by a fundamental antagonism, as the model holds, a high concentration of landownership would have coincided with a low

incidence of Dissent. However, a high concentration of ownership coinciding with a high incidence of Nonconformity implies
compatibility.

The chapter carries this analysis forward by focusing on the
prevailing forms of land tenure. Tenurial conditions, which reinforced the authority of large landowners, theoretically should have
deterred Dissenters from settling in their parishes, and the reverse
should have been true in areas where tenurial arrangements
favored a dispersion of holdings. In Nailsworth's hinterland, leaseholds were structured in such a way that they succeeded in promoting the latter, while not fully challenging the rights of the
landlord, especially if he were lord of the manor. The prevailing
form of leaseholding combined for the tenant the customary element of security of tenure with an emphasis on greater freedom to
alienate the lease, thereby revealing how far property relations had
become individualized and making possible the growth of an
entrepreneurial spirit, even among the lower classes.

Shifting patterns of landholding, brought about by changes in
the agrarian economy, must also have affected the settlement pattern of Nonconformity. For this reason, the third section of this
chapter, on agrarian transformation, studies the progress of enclosures of common arable land and wasteland and the pattern of
restricted access to common grazing lands; these changes abetted
the formation of an industrial working class and stimulated the
evangelical revival among its members. Thus changes in landholding patterns, reflected in the shifting concentrations of landownership, the evolution of forms of land tenure, and land utilization,
contributed indirectly to the growth of Nonconformity and offered
a broad measure of its compatiblity with the Establishment.

Structures of Landownership

Several historians have used a model of parochial typologies,
based on the criterion of landownership, to describe the Establishment's relationship to Dissent. Like the boundary settlement and
industrial village typologies, this model associates individualism
with Dissent and counterposes each, respectively, to deference
and established authority. As we shall see, however, relations
between Dissenters and the Establishment usually were more

TABLE 11. *Parochial Typologies: The Standard Model*

Types of parish	Number of large owners	Percent land owned
Squires'	One	>50.0
Oligarchic	Few	>50.0
Divided	Several	<50.0
Freehold	None	None

Source: See text.

ambiguous. Still, like the two village typologies, the parochial model provides a convenient framework for analysis; after adjusting for its theoretical deficiencies, a more dynamic, more complex, and less reductionist treatment of the pattern of rural Dissent can be obtained (see table 11).

The model distinguishes four typologies, two of which were associated with a high incidence of Dissent and two with a low incidence. "Open" and "closed" parishes stood at opposite ends of the spectrum. The latter (also called "squires' parishes") were characterized by a high concentration of ownership in which one landlord owned more than half the acreage. In open or "freehold" parishes, ownership was widely distributed among small holders whose properties averaged less than forty acres. Two other categories, located between these extremes, offered slight variations. "Oligarchic" parishes resembled squires' parishes, although their high concentrations of ownership were less centralized. A few principal landowners held more than half the acreage, but none of them predominated individually. "Divided" parishes constituted a greater mixture that more closely approximated freehold parishes; a few large landowners, in this case, found themselves surrounded by a majority of small holders. Dissent ostensibly flourished in divided and freehold parishes where individualism thrived, because of more dispersed landholding, and where social control seemed weaker.

This model is deficient in two important respects. First, it lacks an appropriate time dimension. Typologies established on the basis of a single year's analysis cannot always account for possible changes in the concentration of ownership,[3] and such changes ought to have affected the pattern of Dissent. Second, the model defines "landownership" in too broad a sense, failing to distinguish freehold land from leasehold real estates. Failure to consider the significance of land tenure, especially, neglects a crucial assumption of the model, namely, the correlation between Dissent and individualist attitudes toward property.[4] Such failure also ignores an important mechanism, in the structure of leaseholding, through which the landlord could exercise his authority. A region characterized by a dispersion of landholding was, indeed, likely to have had a higher incidence of Dissent. Contrary to the model's central assumption, however, such a correlation was not necessarily incompatible with strong landlordship. This ambiguity becomes more apparent when the model, adjusted to account for these deficiencies, is applied to the local setting.

Analyses of the concentration of landownership are based on data derived from several tithe surveys and from a land tax return, which cover the years 1777 to 1841 for Avening, Horsley, and Minchinhampton parishes.[5] This period witnessed the considerable growth of Nonconformity. If the concentration of landownership had been crucial to explaining its proliferation, one would expect a significant fragmentation of holdings to have occurred at the expense of larger owners. Our findings, however, reveal a different general pattern, although the change each parish experienced assumed a distinctive form (see table 12).

Avening was an oligarchic parish in 1784, since seven owners possessed 69 percent of its occupied acreage.[6] By 1838 a paradoxical development had occurred; a further increase in the concentration of ownership accompanied a greater fragmentation of holdings among marginal owners. The parish's occupied acreage rose 24 percent over the period, shrinking the wasteland, and large owners increased their share 37.5 percent. At the same time, intermediary and small owners lost a significant amount of acreage,[7] as each fell in number, while the number of marginal owners rose dramatically, almost halving their mean acreage.[8] The aggrandizement by large owners clearly took place at the expense of intermediary and small owners, while growth in the numbers of marginal owners and occupiers occurred partly in response to the shrinkage of the waste, however more marginalized they became. Avening did not, therefore, conform to the standard model. Be-

TABLE 12. Concentration[a] of Landholding: Avening Parish, 1784–1838

Size of holding	Year	N	Owner-occupied acres	Tenant-occupied acres	Total owned acres	Leased by owner	Total occupied by owners	Common field land
Large (200+)	1784	7	330.5 (13.9)	2,039.0 (86.0)	2,369.5 (100.0)	455.5 (19.2)	786.0 (33.2)	0.0 (0.0)
	1838	7	1,066.5 (32.7)	2,192.6 (67.3)	3,259.1 (100.0)	246.9 (7.6)	1,313.4 (40.3)	0.0 (0.0)
Inter-mediate (90–199)	1784	5	63.8 (13.5)	407.3 (86.5)	471.0 (100.0)	147.0 (31.2)	210.8 (44.7)	0.0 (0.0)
	1838	4	0.1 (0.02)	308.5 (99.98)	308.6 (100.0)	100.7 (32.6)	100.8 (32.6)	0.0 (0.0)
Medium (30–89)	1784	7	127.2 (43.3)	166.7 (56.7)	294.0 (100.0)	26.5 (9.0)	153.8 (52.3)	0.0 (0.0)
	1838	5	160.2 (43.3)	115.6 (56.7)	275.8 (100.0)	47.3 (9.0)	207.4 (76.2)	0.0 (0.0)
Medium–small (10–29)	1784	12	55.5 (31.0)	123.3 (69.0)	178.8 (100.0)	11.5 (6.4)	67.0 (37.5)	0.0 (0.0)
	1838	20	129.9 (51.6)	122.0 (48.4)	252.0 (100.0)	122.0 (48.4)	252.0 (100.0)	0.0 (0.0)
Small (4–9)	1784	13	48.0 (56.5)	37.0 (43.5)	85.0 (100.0)	6.5 (7.6)	54.5 (64.2)	0.0 (0.0)
	1838	12	34.5 (53.6)	29.9 (46.4)	64.4 (100.0)	20.2 (31.4)	54.8 (85.0)	0.0 (0.0)
Marginal (<4)	1784	24	14.4 (69.4)	6.4 (30.6)	20.8 (100.0)	1.0 (4.8)	15.4 (74.2)	0.0 (0.0)
	1838	162	24.5 (30.9)	54.7 (69.1)	79.2 (100.0)	20.6 (26.0)	45.0 (56.8)	0.0 (0.0)

[a] Acreage percentages appear in parentheses.
Total occupied acreage, 1784: 3,419
Total occupied acreage, 1838: 4,239
Total parish acreage: 4,512
Source: Tithe survey; see text.

tween 1784 and 1838, the parish grew more oligarchic in character while simultaneously experiencing the opposite trend. This anomaly suggests that while the diffusion of landownership among marginal holders may have been related to the growth of Nonconformity, the proliferation of Dissent could also have coincided with the strengthening of the Establishment. The two trends, in fact, were not mutually exclusive.

Horsley's structure of landownership changed more dramatically, although in a similar direction (see table 13).[9] Horsley could be classified as a divided parish in 1784, with seven owners possessing 50 percent of the occupied acreage, but by 1841 it had become a "squire's" parish. The lord of the manor emerged in 1841 as by far the largest landowner, with an estate comprising 2,050 acres or 57 percent of all occupied acreage. Lands belonging to his sole competitor, Edward Wilbraham, the only proprietor in the "large" category listed in table 13, comprised 281 acres or 7.8 percent of all occupied lands. Medium-small, small, and marginal owners all suffered serious losses in both numbers and acreage.[10] Medium-size owners were the only ones to increase their holdings significantly, although their numbers declined slightly. Thus, the increase in the concentration of ownership was far greater at Horsley than at Avening, while the dispersion of ownership among medium holders remained more limited than the expansion of Avening's marginal sector. The diminished authority of the resident lord of the manor, despite the large holdings of his estate, may have contributed to the spread of Nonconformity, although the lord's active use of the manor court in 1784 had not sought to deter it.[11] As in Avening's case, a high concentration of ownership, even when accompanied by a resident manor lord, proved to be compatible with a strong tradition of Dissent.

Nor did Minchinhampton conform to the parochial typologies found in the literature (see table 14). Unlike Avening and Horsley, no significant change occurred in the concentration of ownership between 1777 and 1839. Although the number of large owners decreased by two, collectively they retained control of 57 percent of all occupied acreage. The total amount of occupied acreage actually fell as the parish became more heavily industrialized.[12] Clothworkers undoubtedly abandoned parcels of arable land as they grew more dependent on industrial work;[13] and population

TABLE 13. Concentration[a] of Landholding: Horsley Parish, 1784–1841

Size of holding	Year	N	Owner-occupied acres	Tenant-occupied acres	Total owned acres	Leased by owner	Total occupied by owners	Common field land
Extra large	1784		—	—	—	—	—	—
	1841	1	184.5 (9.0)	1,866 (91)	2,050.5 (100.0)	0.0 (0.0)	1,866 (91)	0.0 (0.0)
Large (200+)	1784	7	230.4 (12.4)	1,623.7 (87.5)	1,885.1 (100.0)	767.0 (41.3)	997.4 (53.7)	0.0 (0.0)
	1841	1	0.4 (0.2)	280.9 (99.8)	281.4 (100.0)	0.0 (0.0)	0.4 (0.2)	0.0 (0.0)
Inter-mediate (90–199)	1784	9	305.5 (33.9)	595.6 (66.0)	902.0 (100.0)	285.4 (31.6)	590.9 (65.5)	0.0 (0.0)
	1841	6	113.1 (22.7)	385.0 (77.3)	498.1 (100.0)	315.0 (63.2)	428.2 (85.9)	0.0 (0.0)
Medium (30–89)	1784	11	43.0 (17.8)	198.2 (82.0)	241.6 (100.0)	257.2 (106.5)	300.2 (124.2)	0.0 (0.0)
	1841	10	142.9 (34.1)	275.8 (65.9)	418.5 (100.0)	120.4 (28.8)	263.3 (62.9)	0.0 (0.0)
Medium–small (10–29)	1784	21	117.2 (35.0)	217.2 (65.0)	335.6 (100.0)	87.7 (21.1)	204.9 (61.1)	0.0 (0.0)
	1841	14	80.4 (36.4)	140.5 (63.6)	220.9 (100.0)	32.0 (14.5)	112.4 (50.9)	0.0 (0.0)
Small (4–9)	1784	20	66.1 (57.3)	49.2 (42.7)	115.3 (100.0)	13.3 (11.5)	79.4 (68.8)	0.0 (0.0)
	1841	13	19.5 (28.0)	49.9 (72.0)	69.4 (100.0)	13.4 (19.4)	32.9 (47.4)	0.0 (0.0)

Marginal (<4)		86.0 (70.5)	36.1 (29.5)	122.1 (100.0)	12.7 (10.4)	98.8 (80.9)	0.0 (0.0)
1784	69						
1841	40	25.7 (46.6)	29.5 (53.4)	55.2 (100.0)	4.4 (7.9)	30.0 (54.5)	0.0 (0.0)

[a] Acreage percentages appear in parentheses.
Total occupied acreage, 1784: 3,573
Total occupied acreage, 1841: 3,594
Total parish acreage: 4,145
Source: Tithe survey and land tax returns; see text.

TABLE 14. *Concentration of Landholding: Minchinhampton Parish, 1777–1839*

Size of holding	Year	N	Owner-occupied acres	Tenant-occupied acres	Total owned acres	Leased by owner	Total occupied by owners	Common field land
Large (200+)	1777	6	639.1 (33.7)	1,260 (66.3)	1,899 (100)	369.6 (19.5)	1,008.7 (53.1)	492.6 (25.9)
	1840	4	49.7 (3.2)	1,467.9 (96.8)	1,516.5 (52.1)	790.1 (100.0)	838.8 (55.3)	0.0 (0.0)
Intermediate (90–199)	1777	3	311.3 (100.0)	0.0 (0.0)	311.3 (100.0)	0.0 (0.0)	311.3 (100.0)	83.4 (26.8)
	1840	3	226.5 (64.4)	124.9 (35.6)	351.4 (100.0)	41.0 (11.7)	267.4 (76.1)	0.0 (0.0)
Medium (30–89)	1777	10	284.1 (59.7)	192.1 (40.3)	476.2 (100.0)	0.0 (0.0)	284.1 (59.7)	10.0 (2.1)
	1840	9	115.4 (33.2)	232.6 (66.8)	348.0 (100.0)	1.6 (0.5)	164.7 (47.3)	0.0 (0.0)
Medium–small (10–29)	1777	25	158.0 (34.7)	297.1 (65.3)	455.1 (100.0)	12.0 (2.6)	170.0 (37.4)	3.0 (0.6)
	1840	14	88.3 (40.9)	127.7 (59.1)	216.0 (100.0)	44.1 (20.4)	132.5 (61.3)	0.0 (0.0)
Small (4–9)	1777	14	42.1 (51.9)	39.0 (48.1)	81.1 (100.0)	0.0 (0.0)	42.1 (51.9)	0.0 (0.0)
	1840	12	72.5 (46.2)	84.5 (53.8)	157.0 (100.0)	0.0 (0.0)	72.5 (46.2)	0.0 (0.0)

Marginal (<4)	1777	40	48.5 (60.7)	31.4 (39.3)	79.8 (100.0)	0.0 (0.0)	48.5 (60.7)	0.0 (0.0)
	1840	40	28.8 (41.2)	41.1 (58.8)	69.9 (100.0)	6.4 (9.1)	35.2 (50.3)	0.0 (0.0)

[a] Acreage percentages appear in parentheses.
Total acreage including Hampton Common = 4,942
Total acreage excluding Hampton Common = 3,595
Total occupied acreage, 1777 = 3,302.4
Total occupied acreage, 1839 = 2,657.5
Source: Tithe survey; see text.

loss, combined with greater use of Minchinhampton Common by large landowners, also contributed to the growth of the wasteland.[14] Under these conditions most classes of landowners suffered some loss. Intermediary owners experienced a very modest advance, while only small owners registered a significant improvement in total acreage owned. Minchinhampton thus remained oligarchic while experiencing a very limited dispersion of ownership among small proprietors. As at Horsley and Avening, a high concentration of landownership at Minchinhampton remained compatible with the advance of Dissent.

The fact that Dissent progressed precisely in those areas where the Establishment remained strong suggests a more ambivalent relationship between the two religious forces than historians have normally conceded. We can explore this ambivalence further by considering the nature of tenurial arrangements. The forms of land tenure found in the region embodied a contradiction; they contained mechanisms of social control, but they also fostered a countervailing tendency necessary for the growth of individualist attitudes.

Land Tenure

The effect of landownership on the incidence of Dissent manifests itself directly in relations between landlords and tenants. The most important landlord in all three parishes was the lord of the manor. The tenures by which tenants held of the lord were the most ancient, although the rigor with which feudal obligations were exacted had softened over the course of time. Many such obligations had disappeared entirely. Some of the more important ones survived and not merely nominally, however, serving as instruments through which the lord could exercise his authority.[15] At the same time, such tenures as freehold, leasehold, copyhold, and tenancies-at-will underwent a complicated evolution from the medieval period, which led in the direction of greater property rights for the tenantry. Individualism based itself on a refined sense of property right and in turn became associated with Dissent.

In general, small and intermediary landholders, who were not copyholders or tenants-at-will, held leases for lives determinable on 99 years, while large landholders held simple term leases often for periods of 500 years or more. The lease for lives determinable on years was a hybrid form of leaseholding, combining elements of lifehold and term leasing.[16] Lifehold leases were "real interests" in land or freeholds; they provided security of tenure because the indenture recorded the names of heirs.[17] The household head, in other words, could not alienate the property against their will. Similarly, if he died intestate, his heirs were assured of succession to the estate.[18] Nevertheless, if held of a lord of the manor, such leases invariably contained customary obligations that modified their freehold status. Although originally superior to copyholds, they descended directly from them; with their accent on security, they represented the most traditional form of leaseholding.[19] The term lease, in contrast, was a "real chattel" and hence part of the household head's personal estate. He could alienate the property at will, either through sale of the lease or through probate, and was given security of tenure only if the length of the term were considerable.[20] Term leases held on long tenures were most closely associated with individual property rights and entrepreneurship and can therefore be regarded as the most modern form of lease-holding. The lease for lives-determinable-on-years occupied an intermediary position. The law regarded it as a real chattel, as it would any term lease, while giving "the tenant . . . all the other advantages of a lifehold estate."[21] This hybrid form of leasehold-ing synthesized the principles of security and independence associ-ated, respectively, with traditional and modern attitudes toward property and, in this sense, emobodied the most mature concep-tion of the right to own property. However, such leases sometimes contained customary obligations that, as in simple lifehold estates, could restrict a landholder's sense of ownership.

Since manorial lordship persisted quite late in the region, the degree to which individualism spread depended not only on the form of leaseholding but also on the degree of survival of custom-ary obligations as well as on how vigorously they were enforced. By inference, we can use the same standard to determine whether the region proved conducive to the spread of Dissent. It is neces-sary to consider first the structures of leases held of the lord of the manor and then the extent of nonmanorial leaseholding.

The evidence from Horsley manor indicates that customary obligations survived to a limited extent in leaseholds held of the lord of the manor. In ten of the forty-four leases dated from 1666 that are listed among the manor court's records, heriot payments were required on the decease of each tenant. The heriot was perhaps one of the keenest reminders of a tenant's inferior status because it permitted his lord to share in the inheritance of his heirs; in the medieval period, the lord was entitled to the best part of his tenant's estate as well. Of the heriots present in the leases held from Horsley manor, seven were commuted to money payments, while in only one case (that of Cornelius Chambers, woolcomber) was the cash levy especially severe. In a lease contracted in 1707, he and the two living individuals listed in the indenture were required to pay a heriot of £3 at the decease of each individual; the remaining heriots were paid in kind. Joseph Hiller of Horsley, broadweaver, agreed to pay heriots consisting of "one couple of good fat capons," while John Smith of Horsley, yeoman, agreed in 1693 that the "best goods...on the death of each tenant" would be paid.[22]

The practice at Horsley manor of including such provisions in leases seems to have waned from 1666, although the document that describes their particulars may not have been comprehensive. Nowhere, for example, does it mention entry fines, required of the heir to a tenancy, that were surely a standard part of such leases.[23] Nor does it refer to the obligation to pay suit at the manor court, although other manor records make clear that suit of court was still enforced by the levying of fines through 1814.[24] Nor does it indicate the extent to which copyholds and tenancies-at-will survived within the manor, despite the announcement of the lord's perambulation of 1816 having mentioned them.[25] The heriot was the only customary obligation that can positively be said to have survived in leases. The absence of any mention of entry fines and suits of court may have been purposeful; these may have applied only to surviving copyholds. Most heriots had been commuted to money payments, a change that must have lessened their impact on the tenants' propensity to defer. At the same time, three-fourths of the leases listed in the document did not contain heriots and were held for ninety-nine years determinable on the lives of three individuals. In this form, manorial leaseholds had come to embrace individualized property relations.

A similar development transpired at the manor of Minchinhampton-Avening. Unfortunately, no document strictly comparable to Horsley's record of leases survives for this manor. A recent roll for the period 1744–1746 is extant, however, and gives an indication of the extent of the evolution of tenures.[26] It is more precise than the listing of Horsley's manorial leases since it provides a clear indication of the number of copyholders. However, it is less precise in not always clearly differentiating leaseholds from tenancies-at-will, which must be inferred; nor are the contents of leases described in full detail when specifically referred to. The rental lists 271 tenants, together with the values of their rents. Twelve, or 4.4 percent, held copyhold tenures. Only three are specifically mentioned as holding a lease, although all were clearly doing so as subtenants. Samuel Smith paid a rent of 1s. 3d. on Sarah Hill's lease; John Pinfold paid a rent of 10s "for Nathaniel's lease"; and Mr. Ridler of Edgeworth held a lease, the rent of 1s. 3d. on which was "to be paid by Mrs. Bliss."

More than three leaseholds undoubtedly existed on the manor. The document probably made specific reference to them because of the recent transfer of each tenancy. Ten others can be identified as subtenants, as well as eighty-three who seem to have acquired their holdings by conveyance from the previous tenant. Since tenants-at-will were not likely to have conveyed their holdings, these eighty-three were presumably leaseholders. For the 163 remaining tenants, the document makes no reference to the condition of their holdings other than to specify the values of their rents. They held directly from the lord of the manor, but there is no way to distinguish leaseholders from tenants-at-will among them. The ninety-six leaseholders cited above must therefore be understood as a conservative estimate, although constituting 35 percent of all listed tenants.

Subtenancies and conveyances were forms of commercial activity that reveal an individualist attitude toward property. Leaseholders turned a profit either by subletting or through conveyance, and subtenants or purchasers of a lease may have sought to build up an estate or merely to establish a claim to property. Such estates may therefore have varied considerably in size.

Among the manor's subtenants, William Ratter was charged a rent of 1s. 3d. "for Bath's land"; William Vick, 5s. "for Driver's"; and Joseph Mayo, 2s. 6d. "for Fowler's land." The

smallest subtenant, judging from the size of his rental, was
William Minching "for Avery's" at 6d., while the largest was
Samuel Peach "for Driver's land" at £2. 3s. 6d. Samuel Peach
must have been a substantial gentleman-clothier; besides his
landholdings, he also occupied Brimscomb and Symbry mills at
rentals of 1s. 11d. and 8s. 9d., respectively.

The rent roll does not give the occupations of tenants. It is still
possible, however, to obtain an idea of their relative status. The
mean rental value of subtenants' holdings may be compared to the
mean rental value of the holdings of Horsley's lessees, whose
occupations appear in appendix A. If Samuel Peach (an obvious
exception) were excluded from the analysis, the mean rental values
of the two categories would not prove to be significantly different;[27]
these lessees, like those at Horsley manor, were plebeian.

A similar comparison can be made between Horsley's lessees
and the eighty-three tenants who seem to have acquired their holdings by conveyance. The latter are distinguished in the rent roll by
the phrase "that was" following the name of the original tenant.
For example, Jeremiah Aldridge held lands once occupied by the
widow Dean and by Joseph Wood. The entry reads as follows:
"Jeremiah Aldridge. The widow Dean's that was. 6d."; "Jeremiah
Aldridge. Jos. Wood's that was. 1s." Nor does it appear that either
the widow Dean or Joseph Wood were deceased tenants whose
parcels had been relet by the lord. If reletting had occurred, this
fact would have been recorded as follows: "Mr. Blackwell of
Chalford for Decd. Webb's that was." Another example, which
affirms this conclusion, is that of the case of Mary Avery. In 1744,
as the tenant of record, she was charged a rent of 9d. "for a house
on Hocker Hill," but a marginal notation, "now Wm. Mundy,"
indicates that the property must have just been transferred. In
1745 William Mundy appears as the tenant of record, at the same
rent, "for a house on Hocker Hill, Mary Avery that was." The
document clearly captured the act of transference of the property
that, had it involved reletting by the lord, should have resulted in a
higher rent. Since it did not, the transfer was probably a conveyance of the lease. These lessees hardly differed in status from
the subtenants of the same manor; the holdings of each had virtually the same mean rental value and standard deviation as the
other. The status of lessees by conveyance at Minchinhampton-

Avening likewise differed little from that of the lessees of Horsley manor.[28]

Considering the general practice of the region, these leaseholds were probably term leases determinable on lives. Only one of the leases referred to seems to have contained customary obligations. Samuel Smith, cited above, was required to pay 5s. in addition to his rent "for a heriot on the death of Mary and Sarah Hill" from whom he had sublet the holding. A term of years, however, is not specified, so that at minimum the tenure must have been a lifehold lease. It is likely that the leaseholds referred to were all real chattels, however, for there is one case, involving a transfer of property, that specifically mentions a freehold. In 1746 a Mr. Essex was charged a rent of 2s. "for the freehold, Mrs. Crooms that was." Mrs. Crooms had evidently held a lifehold lease of the manor that she conveyed to Mr. Essex. Since none of the other conveyances refer to a freehold, it is reasonable to conclude that they were term leases; and given the practice in the region, among the lower classes, at least, they were probably determinable on lives as well.

If customary obligations do not appear to have survived well among lessees, they may nevertheless have been understated in the rent roll. This seems to have been the case among copyholders, who, by the very definition of their tenures, were required to pay heriots. Yet of the twelve copyholders cited, only one, John Vick, was mentioned as being liable for "capons etc." in addition to his rent of 9d. This citation suggests, moreover, that he was liable for other customary obligations besides. Other tenants, who held directly of the lord but whose tenures were not distinguished in the rent roll, were sometimes cited for such obligations. Edward Dee was required to pay "2s. for a relief" (entry fine) in addition to his rent of 6d., and William Clark occupied a house in Forest Green that required "2s. 6d. for a heriot at the death of the tenant in possession."

References to heriots and entry fines may have been random. In the absence of firmer evidence, however, it seems more reasonable to conclude that their appearance had been waning. It is, nevertheless, of interest that one of the few examples of a customary obligation surviving should have been on a house at Forest Green in the heart of the Dissenting community of the Vale. This shows

that a locality noted for its autonomy and independence nevertheless remained unemancipated from manorial jurisdiction.

The transactions appearing in the records of both manors seem,
in the main, to have involved the lower classes. Yet the example of
Samuel Peach at Minchinhampton-Avening shows that the middle
and upper classes were not unaffected by leasehold practices.
Leasehold practices among them, however, differed considerably
and usually involved simple term leases. The terms of such leases,
moreover, were often extremely long, in some cases approaching
perpetuity. As term leases they were personal, not real estates;
however, their duration could render this distinction irrelevant as
a practical matter. Eric Kerridge has written that very long term
leases were anomalous and that during the reign of Henry VIII, at
least, they "were granted only with ulterior motives and were dis-
allowed by the common law on the ground that such leases were
never without the suspicion of fraud."[29] Frederick Pollock has
accorded them a more legitimate place under the law but suggests
that in some sense they were nonetheless fictitious: "Longer terms,
as of 200, 500 or even 1,000 years, are conferred upon trustees as
part of the machinery of family settlements, and were for some-
time commonly used in mortgages. . . . In these cases there is no
rent and no real tenancy."[30]

This was not the case at Horsley and Minchinhampton-
Avening. At Horsley, leases for very long terms can be traced back
to the reign of Elizabeth. Table 15 indicates the number, the dates,
the term of years, and the median rental of those long-term leases
listed in the manor's records.[31]

A wide spectrum of tenants held 1,000-year leaseholds, and a
genuine rental was charged on each property. In three cases the
rent varied between £1 and £2 for the largest estates; in four cases
it varied between 12s. and 13s. for the intermediary estates; and
for smaller estates the mean rental was 2s. 4d.[32] The manor records
list occupations only for the 800-year term lessees. John Wood
of Horsley, clothier, held a lease dated from 1729 at a rental of
6d. The property was modest, containing a messuage or tenement,
a garden, one acre of arable, three acres of pasture, and two acres of
wood. Thomas Barnard of Horsley, yeoman, held another lease at
a rental of 1s; it was equally modest, consisting of only one messuage in Horsley village. The holding of such leases persisted well

TABLE 15. *Long-Term Leaseholders at Horsley*

Number of Leases	Dates of leases	Terms of years	Median rent
16	June 20–21, 1562	1,000	
3	October 19–31, 1564	1,000	
1	February 19, 1563	1,000	
1	November 1, 1729	800	
1	November 1, 1768	800	9s.4d

Source: Horsley Manor Records; see text.

into the nineteenth century. An advertisement appearing in 1823 for the sale of the lease of three messuages at Horsley noted that "the premises are held for the remainder of a term of 780 years, whereof 683 are unexpired."[33] Such long-term leases were very common in the region during the nineteenth century, and because they were personal estates, they enhanced the lessee's sense of private ownership. Edward Bliss of Nailsworth, a Baptist deacon and clothier with a personal estate in 1832 of £9,000, directed in his will that a certain bequest of landed property be sold and the proceeds invested in securities. "This bequest," commented the estate duty officer, "proves to be a leasehold estate for the term of 500 years and the value is included in the residuary account."[34] Bliss had undoubtedly referred to the lease of the property and not to the property itself. However, his will's imprecise language, and the resulting need for clarification by the estate duty office, betrayed a confusion that must have arisen from the very duration of the lease. The testator had obviously come to feel that the property, held for such a long period, was tantamount to a freehold estate. Perhaps for this reason, Henry Stephens, lord of the manor at Horsley, prohibited his heirs (who were not his own issue) from granting leases, while requiring them to reside at the manor house.[35] Long-term leases could result in the virtual alienation of the property by the lessor and, if practiced on a sufficiently wide scale, could lead to the dissolution of a manor.

Even in the case of long-term lessees, it was, nevertheless, possible for a lord of the manor to require an act of homage. Edmund

Clutterbuck, the gentleman-clothier of Minchinhampton-Avening, held landed property from the lord of the manor for two terms of 300 and 500 years, respectively. Yet in 1814 he was required to "surrender" the assignments to David Ricardo, the new lord, "to attend the inheritance of the Manor of Minchinhampton."[36] The formality may have served to remind Clutterbuck of the true ownership of his holdings. In actuality, considering the length of the term of his tenure, it could have done little to discourage his sense of property right.

Not all long-term lessees held of the lord of the manor. Further analyses of the tithe surveys (shown in tables 12 to 14) reveal that considerable leasing occurred both by and from other owners. The amount of tenant-occupied acreage remained high among all classes of landowner for all three parishes, despite any variations over time. Direct information concerning the contents of such leases is not available, but the leases undoubtedly followed the pattern established by much of local manorial leasing, already widespread throughout the region. The lower classes would have held leases for lives-determinable-on-years, but shorn of heriots and other customary obligations; and following manorial practice, the term of years would have run for a considerable period.[37] The middle and upper classes would have tended to hold simple long-term leases even if the property involved were modest. Both forms of leasehold promoted a sense of property right, and their proliferation thus serves as a partial index of individualism.

Evidence for such individualism abounds in probate records. Some of this material has been cited in the first chapter, to illustrate either patterns of dual occupation or social mobility in and around Nailsworth. Further examples can also be invoked to show that individualized property relations, embodied in local forms of land tenure, provided a backdrop against which testators of very humble status often sought profitable investments in either buildings or land.[38]

William Kemish, a Horsley laborer with a personal estate in 1812 valued under £100, bequeathed to his heirs *four* tenements or messuages in the occupation of his own tenants, together with two "laggards of land" adjoining his dwelling, which he had evidently purchased from two different sellers. Thomas Lewis, a Horsley clothworker, with a personal estate in 1825 worth nearly

£200, bequeathed *two* dwellings to his heirs, besides the one he occupied at Nailsworth, and a small shop. Joseph Heskins, another Horsley clothworker, with a personal estate in 1818 worth nearly £200, left his heirs *four* leasehold messuages, three of which were occupied by his own subtenants. In 1764 Phillip Howell, a Horsley shoemaker, bequeathed *two* cottages besides his own dwelling and a shop occupied by tenants, as well as pasture ground called "Selwin's field" and a close of pasture called "the Hill," with a "haystall of wood thereto." Similarly, in 1757 Thomas Locker, broadweaver, bequeathed *two* dwelling houses occupied by tenants, a plot known appropriately as "Locker's Leaze," with accompanying pasture ground, as well as a grove of beechwood, likewise called "Locker's grove."

Similar cases can be found among working-class testators from Minchinhampton and Avening. In 1778 Robert Mason, a Minchinhampton clothworker, with a personal estate valued at nearly £250, bequeathed *six* freehold cottages occupied by his own tenants, one of which possessed three-quarters of an acre of meadow, and a leasehold cottage for the term of the lease, occupied by a subtenant. In 1803 James Bingell, a Minchinhampton wool scribbler, bequeathed his own dwelling with an adjoining enclosure of land "which I lately bought of Mr. Humphry Collins." In 1827 Thomas Baker, a Minchinhampton clothworker with a personal estate valued at £200, bequeathed to his daughter the right to collect rents from "the house now occupied by George Ockford." In 1823 James Sansum, a Watledge clothworker, with a personal estate worth nearly £200, bequeathed *three* tenements besides his own, each occupied by a tenant. At Avening, Harris Dee, laborer, with a personal estate valued at £100 in 1797, left his heirs a house occupied by Richard Clifford that he "now rents of me adjoining to mine [*sic*]." In 1826 Daniel Sansum, a clothworker from Forest Green, with a personal estate of nearly £200, bequeathed *three* messuages, two of which were occupied by his own tenants.

As at Horsley, Minchinhampton and Avening artisans usually possessed more property than did laborers or clothworkers, often in land as well as buildings. In 1763 William Dowdy, a Minchinhampton tailor, bequeathed in trust freehold and leasehold tenements, with lands, both arable and pasture, and including barns, stables, and outhouses, at Bestbury and Box villages. In 1772 Jacob Harrison, a Minchinhampton mason, bequeathed to his heirs "all real and personal estate whatsoever," including *two* tenant occupied houses and an orchard. In 1779 John Cull, an Avening carpenter and yeoman, left an estate that included *two* small parcels of land and *two* tenant occupied messuages; although the value of his personal estate remained unrecorded in his will, its monetary bequests alone amounted to more than £230. In 1774 Thomas Holliday, a Minchinhampton pargeter, bequeathed his heirs "freehold lands to hold forever," *two* tenant-occupied freehold messuages and *two* sublet leasehold cottages for the term of the lease.[39]

Changes in the agrarian economy, operating through the mechanism of enclosures, further articulated the spread of popular individualism and eventually spelled the demise of manorial authority. In the period antecedent to industrial takeoff, enclosures of common arable were spearheaded by small owners and occupiers operating within the framework of customary institutions. Such activities helped to erode these institutions and thereby laid the groundwork for their disappearance in the period of accelerated industrialization. Agrarian enclosure and industrialization were reciprocal processes affecting the social equilibrium of the region and in particular the formation of a proletariat. They provided the backdrop for the growth of evangelicalism and the spread of Dissent and for this reason require closer scrutiny.

Agrarian Transformation

The enclosure movement in English agriculture has occupied a controversial place with respect to the process of class formation in the Industrial Revolution. Marx, followed by a generation of historians, had articulated a catastrophic view: the spate of 3,000 parliamentary enclosures between 1760 and 1815 displaced a mass of small farmers, who were subsequently transformed into industrial proletarians.[40] Contemporary historiography has largely rejected this connection between agrarian and industrial transformation. Thirsk and Yelling have depicted enclosures as a protracted process extending over centuries and characterized by wide typological and regional variations.[41] G. E. Mingay has questioned whether the position of the small farmer seriously eroded during the late eighteenth century, and J. D. Chambers has argued that the growth of agricultural productivity, resulting from enclosures, was sufficient to absorb the surplus rural population that Marx believed had found its way into industry.[42] The first, more traditional, view holds greater validity in the region under study, although for different reasons than Marx would have entertained. The persistence of the small landholder was, indeed, compatible with the formation of a proletariat, especially in areas where piecemeal enclosure had engineered changes in the agrarian structure. Piecemeal enclosure, the process of consolidation occurring by attrition over a long period,[43] was brought about largely by common folk, although not with the intention of subverting customary institutions. Their parcels were modest and initially functioned compatibly within the existing customary framework. Nonetheless, the cumulative effect of piecemeal enclosure subverted customary practice. The erosion of common arable land laid the foundation for shrinkage of the wasteland at Avening and for the aggrandizement of lands by the lord of the manor at Horsley, both of which had catastrophic consequences for small holders and landless, encroaching cottagers.

Shrinkage of the waste at Avening, however, had also resulted from the activities of encroachers themselves and accompanied a great increase in their numbers. Superficially, this increase suggests the persistence of small holders, but the great fragmentation of the size of their holdings, coinciding with the industrial revolution pointed to their proletarianization. At Minchinhampton, as we have seen, a fall in arable land under cultivation and an increase in waste coincided with a decline in occupied acreage among small holders, the result of industrialization. At the same time, the manor preserved the grazing lands of Minchinhampton Common, so long as access could be restricted to the wealthier members of the community. In the hinterland of Nailsworth, demise of the common arable land and wastelands was completed by the 1820s and restricted access to Minchinhampton Common inaugurated during the 1830s. Correspondingly, the manor courts, the traditional custodians of customary practice, either ceased to function or became the agencies of private aggrandizement.

Piecemeal enclosure of common arable land accelerated from

the late seventeenth century and culminated, in all three parishes, during the early decades of the nineteenth century. References in manorial records, tithe surveys, deeds, and wills, together with an early survey map for Minchinhampton, make it possible to document the process. Manorial records at Horsley make ample reference to common arable fields and the scattered holdings of their occupants during the sixteenth century. In 1570 Edward Rowbottom held of the lord of the manor "three acres of arable land in Telly field, five acres in Wimbley Barrow field and five acres of arable in Binders field and pasture in the Common Fields for 50 sheep."[44] John Wilkins held "34 acres...in Conigre [field] and Common pasture for 150 sheep," to cite two typical examples from the seventeen long-term leases recorded in this period. Reference to a "close" can be found in only three of the lease abstracts; with the exception of one lease, such holdings were in a considerable minority. Walter Keynes possessed a two-acre tenement and a five-acre tenement called, respectively, Barley close and Short-wood close; he occupied "three acres of pasture in the midst of Lethredge, Kellcombes" and "one close in West field containing four acres." The paucity of closes or "tynings," as they were also called, suggests that piecemeal enclosures were first being initiated at this time. It also illustrates the form of the pattern of attrition: small, virtually inconspicuous enclosures in the midst of common fields and clearly not deemed a threat to customary rules.

In the seventeeth century, references to "closes" and "tynings" increased; occasionally such references offer evocative descriptions of the very act of enclosure. In 1707 Cornelius Chambers, wool-comber, held, among several small closes, "two acres of arable land lying in a field called Nupend field lately taken & inclosed with some other lands into a tyning." In 1732 Chambers occupied "Lutsome Tyning lately taken and inclosed out of a field called Wimbley barrow field." A tyning, evidently, could be a larger unit of enclosure than a mere close; its more frequent appearance in the eighteenth century suggests an acceleration of the process of attrition. Nonetheless, most references to acreage in this period would seem to indicate that traditional scattered holdings remained the norm at Horsley, at least until 1770, when the manorial accounts stop. However, the Courts Baron and Leet of the manor continued to operate as late as 1816. As the fourth chapter will demonstrate, the steward of the manor maintained annual lists of householders; the jury fined nonattendants who owed suit-of-court, prosecuted encroachers on common wastelands, and regularly inspected leaseholds of the manor to prevent fraud against the lord's interests. And all of these activities were undertaken with the solemn air of feudality that suggests the persistence of strong, traditional lordship. Under these conditions, one can reasonably expect that the rate of piecemeal enclosure did not accelerate appreciably until the collapse of manorial authority following the transfer of lordship to the management of a trustee after 1816.

A similar process of attrition can be documented at Avening and Minchinhampton. Daniel Harvey of Avening, yeoman, had bequeathed in his will a parcel of arable land of about three acres "formerly taken out of a piece of arable."[45] Thomas Hill of Avening, butcher, and his wife Bridget, in anticipation of the marriage of their son, transferred to two trustees "all those four acres more or less of arable land lying in a newly enclosed tyning formerly taken and inclosed out of one of the common fields of Avening called Northfield."[46] At Minchinhampton the common fields were also called "North," "South," "East," and "West" fields, although they possessed other more descriptive titles as well. In 1777, Revd. Peach released in fee for £283. 10s. "all those 63 acres of arable lying dispersedly in the common fields of Minchinhampton aforesaid called Longfield and Longstone or Southfield now in the possession of Edward Sheppherd, Esq."[47] Longfield was also known as Northfield,[48] although it was referred to as "Upper Field" when Richard Harris of Woodhouse, Minchinhampton, a substantial clothier, conveyed to David Ricardo, the lord of the manor, "all that inclosed piece of arable lying in a common field. . . called Longfield, containing by estimation 35 acres"[49] (see map 5).

The 1777 tithe survey for Minchinhampton records more than 600 acres under occupation in common fields. These fields persisted as late as 1804, when a valuation survey was undertaken for the parish, although by this date much arable land had been left open to the waste and only 200 acres of common lands remained. Map 5 depicts the southeast section of Minchinhampton in 1804 and shows the location of the surviving scattered strips, as well as the proportion of enclosed pasture to arable land characteristic of

S. E. Section of Minchinhampton, c. 1804

Pasture

Arable

Common Field Lands

Quarry

- - - Common Field Strips

the parish as a whole.[50] The arable plots, containing these open field strips, were technically part of the common fields but were beginning to resemble enclosures; the strips were either owner-occupied or held as leaseholds. Table 14 shows the distributions of owner-occupied, tenant leaseholds and common field holdings for Minchinhampton in 1777 and 1839.[51]

By 1777 small and marginal landholders ceased to hold lands in the common fields, while medium and medium-small holders let the great majority of their lands as enclosed holdings. They continued to do so in 1839 with only marginal changes, despite the fall in the parish's total occupied acreage. The greatest change occurred among large and intermediary landholders. In 1777 they held as much as 26 percent of their lands in common fields, and these constituted nearly 18 percent of the parish's total occupied acreage. By 1839, however, common lands ceased to exist. This shift had clearly marked the final progress of piecemeal enclosure of common arable, although surprisingly large holders had lagged behind their smaller brethren.

Common people, such as broadweavers, glaziers, carpenters, small clothiers, and even woolcombers, had initiated the erosion of customary practices in all three parishes. The persistence of manorial control through the eighteenth century had had a restraining effect on the scope of their activities. The cumulative result of piecemeal enclosure was to weaken that same authority, however, particularly as small closes expanded into larger "tynings." As a result, large and intermediary occupiers, in the post-1815 period, were able to effect more systematic assaults on the remainder of common arable and on the wasteland. The erosion of common arable land and wasteland, moreover, legitimated efforts to restrict access to common grazing areas to the more prosperous elements of the community.

Until the 1840s, members of the lower classes, who occupied some land, exercised the right to graze stock on Minchinhampton

---

Map 5. Field map: southeast section of Minchinhampton, ca. 1804. Pasture, arable, and common lands. *Source*: Gloucester Records Office P217a/VE1/1, Survey and Valuation of Minchinhampton Parish Lands, ca. 1804.

Common. A notice of 1813, which warned against overstocking the Common, had reiterated the customary rule: only residents of the parish occupying land, regardless of the amount of acreage, qualified as Commoners, although none could pasture more beasts than their lands could winter.[52] These minimal requirements were still being enforced in 1830 when as little as 1.25 to 2.5 acres of land could carry with it "the right to extensive pasturage to Minchinhampton and Rodborough Commons."[53]

The rules of 1843 regarding the stinting of beasts on the Common had not changed in forty years. According to a new resolution adopted by the Court Leet, however, access to the Common would be restricted to those whose lands were capable of wintering "one cow or two yearlings, or one horse or two asses to every five acres [and] one sheep for every two acres of land occupied in the parish."[54] The resolution also introduced a small charge of 2d per beast. In 1847 the Court Leet made the qualification even more restrictive: Commoners were now allowed "one beast for every £5 . . . and one sheep for every £2 to which they may be rated for land to the poor."[55] The Court emphasized that this higher qualification would be based on the ratable value of lands and not the value of their crop yields. It increased the levy per beast to 6d, a rise of 200 percent. The qualifications of 1843 were indeed restrictive, but those of 1847 were considerably harsher. As a result, a noticeable shift in the Common's usage became apparent even within this short interval. The manorial accounts of cattle marked for grazing in 1843 and 1851 permit such a reconstruction. The findings appear in table 16.

A 31 percent fall occurred in the numbers using the Common, although the number of beasts per Commoner rose only slightly from 3.1 to 3.8. Still, a high turnover in personnel had clearly transpired. Only fifteen of the Commoners recorded in 1843 reappeared in the 1851 list, and two of them were among the largest animal owners of that earlier period. Table 16 describes the joint distribution of the different types of animals grazed by each year. Comparison of observed and expected values suggests that large landholders came to dominate the Common.

Despite the fall in the number of Commoners, only the number of bullocks and affers changed significantly, both absolutely and relative to their expected values.[56] Bullocks increased far beyond

TABLE 16. *Cattle Grazed on Minchinhampton Common, 1843–1851: Unadjusted Values*[a]

	Y	ev	w	B	ev	w	C	ev	w	Ho	ev	w	A	ev	w	Total
1843	164	152	0.9	171	200	4	17	16.4	0	96	87.4	0.8	42	33.3	2.3	490
1851	115	126	1.1	196	166	5	13	13.6	0	64	72.6	6.1	19	27.6	2.7	407
	279			367			30			160			61			897

[a]Chi-square (χ^2) = 18.3916, degrees of freedom (df) = 4, significance (P) < 0.001.
Note: Y, B, C, Ho, and A stand for yearling, bullock, cow, horse, and affer, respectively; *ev*, and *w* refer, respectively, to "expected values" under the null hypothesis and the "weight of the difference" between these and observed values in determining the size of χ^2.
Source: Minchinhampton Manor Records; see text.

their 1843 level in both number and expected value, while affers declined. The number of horses and yearlings declined moderately, while the number of cows remained generally low. Small occupiers were more likely to have grazed cows, affers, and horses; affers were draught animals, and horses were used mainly for carting. The small number of cows in both years reaffirms that by 1843 many of the marginal small holders had already been excluded from the Common. The significant fall in the number of affers and the moderate fall in horses suggests that by 1851 the more prosperous small holders had followed them. The moderate decline in yearlings and the startling rise in the number of bullocks indicate a shift in concentration on the latter type of animal; this increase suggests greater production for butchery, a commercial activity in which larger landholders took a special interest. By 1851 large landholders clearly had come to monopolize Minchinhampton Common.

Summary and Conclusion

Three great changes in the agrarian sector of the economy of Nailsworth's hinterland had coalesced during the critical interval from 1780 to 1840. Enclosures of common arable land and wasteland, together with restricted access to Minchinhampton Common, contributed in a combined yet auxiliary fashion to the formation of an industrial proletariat. At the same time, the forms of leaseholding characteristic of the region showed how far property relations had become individualized.

Leases-for-lives, determinable on ninety-nine years, were generally held by members of the lower classes including woolcombers, clothworkers, laborers, and weavers. When completely shorn of manorial restrictions, such as entry fines and heriots, such leases effectively combined the customary element of security of tenure with greater freedom for the tenant to alienate the lease. The element of lifehold leasing, which survived from medieval times, assured the family security of tenure, while the element of term leasing permitted the head of household to treat the tenement as part of his personal estate. Since manorial restrictions contained in such leases had declined considerably by 1800 and were completely absent in nonmanorial leases, the property relations articulated by these forms of leasehold permitted the growth of individualism among members of the lower classes; the evidence of subletting and conveyancing on the manors of Horsley and Minchinhampton, no less than the progress of piecemeal enclosures, affirms the existence of such a pattern of behavior, already alluded to in chapter 1. Further analysis of probate records in this chapter has also revealed the widespread nature of popular individualism. The forms of very long term leasing, prevailing among the gentry and high bourgeoisie, reinforced the conclusion that long-term leases, although part of the personal estate of a testator, amounted virtually to a freehold and thereby facilitated the growth of individualism.

The particular form tenurial relations took in this neighborhood thus served to encourage relatively independent attitudes even among the dependent, and this circumstance proved to be crucial for the growth of Nonconformity. Although large landowners dominated the region, in this respect not conforming to the standard model of a district likely to foster Dissent, local Whig landowners showed sympathy toward Nonconformity, partly on the grounds that it offset the weakness of the established church in the region. Evidence from local manorial courts provides additional evidence that Dissenters in this neighborhood were not alienated from established authority in all its forms.[57] Still, Nailsworth's Dissenters were not completely subordinated to established authority. On the contrary, individualist attitudes toward property, combined with the scattered nature of parochial settlements, established an underlying structure of independence, fostering the autonomy of religious sentiment, and thereby linking Nonconformity to a spirit of individualism.

Evangelical Nonconformity, however, appealed equally to the poor and outcast, for whom the communal atmosphere of Chapel life softened the destructive psychological effects of social change during the eighteenth to early nineteenth century. The next chapter considers the formation at Nailsworth of the two largest Dissenting communities, the Forest Green Congregationalists and the Shortwood Baptists, their developing relations with the Establishment, and the beginnings of their evolution to a more denominational status.

Chapter Three

Churches and Chapels: The Pattern of Religion

In northern England and parts of the southwest and midlands, the Evangelical Revival contributed to the growth of Methodism,[1] but in Gloucestershire it stimulated the reawakening of some of the older Protestant sects.[2] At Nailsworth, these sects included the Particular Baptists of Shortwood, the Congregationalists of Forest Green and the Nailsworth Meeting of the Society of Friends.

The Society of Friends were the first Dissenters to appear in the locality and were soon followed by the arrival of the Congregationalists. The Shortwood Baptists emerged as a community following a schism among the Congregationalists and after 1800 flourished as Nailsworth's principal Nonconformist church and the largest Baptist community outside London. The Friends eschewed enthusiasm and remained an "introversionist sect" throughout their history, while their Dissenting brethren embraced the Revival and acquired "denominational" characteristics.[3] The Church of England responded competitively to the challenge of Nonconformist expansion and in the process transformed itself into a denomination as well.[4]

Since the Quakers represented a unique example of unrepentent sectarianism, their religious order deserves special consideration elsewhere.[5] Also, since the Shortwood Baptists successfully mediated the pressures of secularization, at least through 1851, their collective experiences since 1800 likewise require separate treatment.[6] This chapter is concerned with the pattern of early Nonconformist sectarianism and how its metamorphosis, under the influence of the Revival, affected relations with the Church of England. As a boundary settlement, and hence with an ostensibly remote Anglican Establishment, Nailsworth conformed, as we have seen, to a community typology widely used to explain the spread of rural Dissent. Yet contrary to this model, Dissenters established from the outset a rapprochement with the local Establishment that far surpassed mere toleration and eventually led to widespread social and political cooperation.[7]

The Origins of Dissent and the Evangelical Revival

A nonconformist tradition within the parish churches of Horsley and Minchinhampton can be traced back to Henry Stubbs, the Puritan preacher who held the benefice of Horsley from 1665 to 1678. Stubbs had not actually taken Holy Orders, and the poor quality of the parish records during his tenure probably reflected a wish to remain inconspicuous by minimizing the performance of baptisms, marriages, and burials.[8] Stubbs's survival at Horsley, during a period of anti-Puritan reaction in the Church, can be attributed to the leniency of the local authorities and ultimately to the puritan sympathies of the substantial clothiers of the region.[9] In 1669 the Privy Council complained to Gloucester's Lord Lieutenant about the conventicles that "of late assemble in greater numbers and more dareing than formerly . . . from they're not being suppressed by the Justices of the Peace."[10] Among these assemblies they cited the example of an open air meeting at Minchinhampton at which forty auditors listened to an unidentified butcher and another speaker called "Mr. Stubbs."[11] The Privy Councillors enjoined the local authorities to consult one another "about the speedy suppression of th[is] dangerous tumult" and to use "military power to suppress [it] . . . along with the civil power."[12] In addition, they required the churchwardens of several parishes to "present the names of all kinds of persons [who] come not to your church as well as lewd and profane persons . . . [whom] you may grant your warrants to."[13]

Although the local magistrates and churchwardens clearly disobeyed these instructions, Stubbs still felt considerable pressure to flee. "He evidently found his position untenable," remarked one local historian, "for... he ejected himself and retired to London" in 1678, joining his friend Richard Baxter, the great Presbyterian Divine and proponent of a moderate Calvinist theology.[14] Stubbs's tenure at Horsley revealed an ambivalence toward dissent on the part of the Anglican gentry that later facilitated the proliferation of Nonconformist churches. As the severity of persecutions under the Clarendon Code waned, and limited toleration was legalized, practical collaboration between Anglicans and Dissenters became more widely accepted, although not all Dissenters adapted to this development with equal speed. The Society of Friends, because of its distinctive discipline, suffered disabilities the longest, while the Congregationalist church at Forest Green effected a reconciliation quite early, with important consequences for its later history.

The Congregationalists occupied an intermediary position between the Quakers and the Baptists in the history of Dissent at Nailsworth. In church organization they moved away from Presbyterianism, which resembled the Quaker order, toward Independency, which the Baptists adopted in imitation of them. Doctrinally, they adhered to a moderate Calvinist theology that the Baptists also eventually imitated. Yet they differed from the Baptists in the practice of infant baptism and in their ambivalence toward the Evangelical Revival, once that great movement gained momentum.

The Forest Green Congregationalists were the first Nailsworth Dissenters to attract a significant following. They erected their meetinghouse in 1668, but prior to this date had held their "conventicle" in Colliers's Wood, near Forest Green, in order to evade persecution. Their founding of a chapel coincided with their abandonment of Presbyterianism in favor of a Congregationalist church order.[15] In 1687 "persons of repute in Nailsworth and its neighborhood availed themselves of King James's Indulgence and purchased the plot of ground on which the [meeting] house stands."[16] These "persons of repute," although very likely associated with the Church of England, clearly had Puritan sympathies; perhaps they had been the same ones who saved Henry Stubbs from the central authorities.[17]

In 1677 Phillip Sheppard, lord of the manor at Minchinhampton, leased the plot of ground that became the site of the chapel (situated on a "common or waste called Forest Green") to Richard Barnard, clothworker. Barnard, in turn, sold the lease for £4 to Aaron Osborn, cordwainer and Richard Bird, broadweaver.[18] The £4, however, was paid by several individuals in whose names the property was then assigned and who, a year later, were mentioned in a conveyance as trustees of the meetinghouse that had been built in the interval. Three clothiers, two dyers, and one maltster were among the seven mentioned,[19] but it cannot be assumed that all were leading members of the chapel at this time.[20] By covering the purchase price of the ground and serving as trustees, they appear to have acted as patrons of more humble Dissenters. Why else would they have needed a cordwainer and a broadweaver to act as surrogates for them? Puritan sympathies had probably compelled them to give support, despite their continuing loyalty to the Church of England. Indeed, until the erection of the Anglican chapel at Nailsworth in 1794, the Forest Green Church "[had been] attended by many of the Established Church laity."[21]

The practice of open communion adopted at Forest Green made possible Anglican attendance at services and the paternalist exercise of trusteeship. In the early eighteenth century, especially, this meant that Anglicans could exercise a social predominance enforced by a novel species uniformity. The waning of Puritan "enthusiasm" permitted Anglicans and Congregationalists to converge in the mutual adoption of a more rational theology, grounded in the moderation or abandonment of Calvinism.[22] Anglican patronage therefore undercut the dissenting edge of Nonconformity. The social and political consensus this created persisted until the 1740s, when the beginning of the Evangelical Revival disrupted it.

"Enthusiasm" experienced a powerful rebirth with the appearance at Minchinhampton Common in 1743 of George Whitefield, the founder of Calvinistic Methodism. An anti-Methodist riot accompanied his appearance and polarized relations between Anglicans and Dissenters.[23] In 1747 the middle- and upper-class trustees of the Forest Green Church suddenly curtailed their relations with it, thereby registering the impact of Whitefield's preaching.[24] Early evangelicalism had made Congregationalism momentarily more plebeian and sectarian. Still, enthusiasm laid the groundwork for whatever future prosperity the Forest Green

Church would enjoy and offered a basis for the new Anglican-Nonconformist consensus, which emerged in the late eighteenth century.

The extent of the Forest Green Church's prosperity after 1750 is difficult to measure because of the paucity of its records.[25] We must rely mainly on the narrative of a Chapel history composed in 1849 by one of the church's ministers. From this history, and from the demographic records analyzed later,[26] the Congregationalists appear to have occupied an intermediary position, in the chronology of their settlement and in their relative strength after 1780, between the Society of Friends and the Shortwood Baptists. The history of the Forest Green Church is of interest primarily because it represented an Independent tradition that proved a comparative failure. Although the Revival affected its members earlier than it did the Baptists, they do not seem to have sustained their enthusiasm with equal ardor. Certainly there were great enthusiasts among them, such as William Biggs, whose conversion experience epitomized the meaning of millenarianism. Biggs had had terrible dreams about sin, and one in particular proved instrumental in his conversion:

He says that he saw in the middle of the night a strange representation in the heavens which appeared directed to him, it awoke him in a awful state of terror and alarm—he felt as though instant destruction awaited him, his sins appeared in their naked deformity—he felt himself as if he were sinking beneath their load; so great was the mental distress on this occassion that the perspiration issued from the pores of his body—he struggled to his knees, and there begged for mercy—he prayed, cried, wrestled—at length he saw . . . a representation of the great Redeemer, shining in the glory of the Godhead, looking toward him with pardon and love bespoken in his very countenance—this his heart instantly seized, and all terminated in gratitude inexpressible—he now dreaded the thought of ever committing another sin.[27]

Still, the membership's rigid insistence on infant baptism, which led to the resignation of at least one minister,[28] in the long term detracted from the evangelical emphasis on conversion. What an historian of early Methodism said of John Wesley applies with singular aptness to the entire evangelical movement: "The birthday of a Christian was . . . shifted from his baptism to his conversion, and in that change the partition line of two great systems is crossed."[29] The church's success, however, depended to a considerable degree on the qualities of its ministers, many of whom after 1750 did not always follow an evangelical course. Reverend Jarvis, the pastor from 1753 to 1769, was considered "a man of considerable attainment [who] kept a school of very respectable character,"[30] which in this period was not likely to predispose him to the "coarseness" then associated with enthusiasm. His appointment seems to have reflected a retreat from enthusiasm by the church and a restabilization of its membership, following the social schism of 1747.

From the 1770s leadership of the church rested in the hands of middle-class individuals such as William Biggs and members of the Thomas family, who were clothiers.[31] Another pastor, Revd. Frames, who held office from 1788 to 1799, was "a Homerton [Cambridge] student, and rather formal in his mode of preaching";[32] although the neighborhood regarded him highly, his formidable intellectual style did not attract a large congregation. It was during the ministry of his successor, Revd. Paine (1800–1817), that the church began to tap the resources created by the Revival. Paine was "a preacher with a warm heart and by his ministry large numbers were converted."[33] Thomas Edkins, who followed him in the ministry, held this position longer than did any other and maintained Paine's evangelical approach.[34] The schism of 1821, however, which led to the establishment of a second Congregationalist church, severely marred his efforts.

The schism had no explicit doctrinal cause and in two respects reflected the impact of secularizing changes. The desire of the wealthier members to shift the church's location to Lower Forest Green was the heart of the dispute. They hoped to attract a wider audience by proximity to Nailsworth, which had grown into a small town, while those who opposed them clung to older traditions. Both class division and urbanization, therefore, engendered difficulties soon to be compounded by trade depression: high rates of outmigration dealt a near death blow to any immediate chances for the recovery of the Congregationalist influence.

Under these conditions, Edkins was unable to hold together the unraveling thread of church membership. Outmigration was a much greater problem at Lower Forest Green (which retained the great majority of Congregationalists) than at Shortwood, and in

1844 Edkins had to face the virtual collapse of his church. Following his resignation in that year "such was the state of the church that it could scarcely be ascertained who were the acknowledged members."[35] In 1845 John Burder, minister of the Stroud Congregationalists,[36] and for many years a leading figure in the political life of the region, helped to reorganize it. By 1851 Congregationalism had recovered sufficiently, but not for very long. "[T]he church seems to have suffered considerably," from the sudden departure of its minister, Revd. Clapham in October 1851;[37] and Revd. Leifchild, his replacement, was more content to follow his interest in geology than his vocation as minister, reflecting indirectly the negative effect on the church of secularizing trends.

It was not only the quality of the church's ministers that mattered but also continuity in the ministry (see table 17). Although the Forest Green Church had a few ministers with reasonably long tenures, the general pattern, depicted in table 17, was one of frequent change punctuated by several periods in which the pastorate laid vacant. The Congregationalists began auspiciously, but their membership later fluctuated erratically in proportion to the turnover among their ministers. By contrast, the Shortwood Baptists were small and considerably more doctrinaire at the outset but were led from 1758 by four able ministers, three of whom served for especially long terms, and this continuity contributed greatly to their growth. To appreciate better their later success, it is necessary to set forth the events and conditions surrounding their origins and early history.

The Shortwood Baptist Church was founded in the aftermath of the schism of 1707 that occurred among the Forest Green Congregationalists. The issues were doctrinal and underscored the more conservative character of the schismatics at a time when the Congregationalists were effecting a rapprochement with the Establishment. It was Revd. Giles's "preaching up the Presbyterian Scheme," which touched on the issues of Election and infant baptism, that precipitated the crisis.[38] William Harding and John Horwood, two broadweavers from Horsley, were troubled by Giles's "Baxterianism," and to obtain doctrinal clarification, they visited the Baptist church at Kings Stanley. There they reaffirmed their high Calvinist principles and their commitment to believers' baptism.[39] Horwood later succumbed to Giles's persuasiveness,

TABLE 17. *Turnover among Forest Green Congregationalist Ministers,*
1688–1866

Name of minister	Year arrived	Year departed	Total	How departed
Wooden	1688	1707	19	Died
Dr. Giles	1707	1714	7	Dismissed
Rawlins	1714	1715	1	Died
J. Allein	1716	1718	2	Died
J. Jones	1719	1724	5	Died
Jos. Jones	1724	1725	1	Dismissed
J. Allen	1726	1730–31	5	Dismissed
W. Bushell	1731	1744	13	Dismissed
Jackson	1745	1749	4	Died
T. Langher	1750	1752	2	Dismissed
Jarvis	1753	1769	16	Dismissed
Vacant; occasional itinerants	1769	1772	3	
W. Moffat	1772	1787	15	Dismissed
Frames	1788	1799	11	Dismissed
Paine	1800	1817	17	Died
Edkins	1817	1844	27	Dismissed
Vacant; itinerants Church reconstitution	1844	1845	1	
Charles Russell	1845	1849	4	Dismissed
W. G. Clapham	1849	1851	2	Dismissed
Vacant	1851	1852	1	
S. R. Leifchild	1853	1855	2	Dismissed
Vacant	1855	1856	1	
J. Burrell	1856	1866	10	Dismissed

but Harding did not, and in an effort to sway him Giles agreed to "preach up" the issues in dispute. Giles did so for fourteen consecutive Sundays, but succeeded only in creating more dissatisfaction; fifty members, after another pilgrimage to the Baptist church at Kings Stanley, decided to withdraw from membership at Forest Green.

This schism fit a national pattern. Richard Baxter, the great Presbyterian divine, had introduced Dissenters to a moderate form of Calvinism in the late seventeenth century. "Moderate Calvinism" involved the retreat from a strict adherence to predestinarian doctrine and, correspondingly, a willingness to embrace the idea of universal redemption. Because it appeared dangerously liberal in its implications, the change produced a number of schisms. As "Baxterianism" spread among Presbyterians in the late seventeenth century, dissatisfied members formed Congregationalist churches, and as the Calvinism of these churches gradually moderated, further schisms occurred that led to the formation of Particular Baptist churches.[40] In the atmosphere of the early eighteenth century, the Shortwood Baptists were to remain a small and isolated sect. Yet, paradoxically, their survival depended from the outset on sympathizers from the Church of England.

After having withdrawn from the Forest Green Church, the band of schismatics decided to meet at William Harding's home, since the distance of three miles to Kings Stanley seemed prohibitive.[41] They continued to do so until 1716, when they succeeded in founding a meetinghouse. From a copy of the original trust deed, one can judge just how plebeian were these founders. Six others besides William Harding were broadweavers; one was a clothworker and another a mason.[42] Their patrons, however, came from middle- and upper-class backgrounds and were often resident at some distance. Henry Allen of Froom, Somerset, a dyer, together with a Mr. Ball, "seeing the people's poverty," gave £10 toward establishing a meetinghouse and raised additional contributions from among their relations.[43] Among the other trustees were Samuel, Henry's brother and a Bristol druggist; Robert Houlton of Trowbridge, Wiltshire, a clothier; John Grant of Trowbridge, a gentleman; and Samuel Sevil of Bisley and Painswick, another gentleman.[44]

The early Baptist church received the kind of support from Sevil that probably saved it from extinction. By the time of the founding of the meeting house, the original band of schismatics had dwindled to thirteen,[45] and for the next three years, two others besides Sevil carried on the ministry of the church. One contemporary history described Sevil as being "a young gentleman of Painswick who came of from [sic] the Church of England and was a very zealous preacher."[46] He died in 1719 and bequeathed £10 to the church to add an extra room to the meetinghouse,[47] an act that testfied to his success; and following his death no preaching took place for about four or five months.[48]

Because of its exclusiveness, the Shortwood church did not

attract a large following for a considerable period. From Sevil's death in 1719 until 1732 only twelve persons joined in fellowship.[49] Between 1737 and 1752 the church met with greater success, as fifty-four were added to the membership. Yet during the last three years of this period a "perplexed and divided condition" prevailed among the members.[50] Nor did this atmosphere abate from 1752 to 1757, the period of Samuel Bowen's ministry. Bowen had made the first tentative move toward adopting an evangelical approach, although he lacked the force of personality to make it effective. On his accession, he had insisted that the members "endeavor to make the ordinance of singing more general."[51] Although the congregation formally agreed to his demand, they "were at one with the Quakers" on this issue and tacitly resisted its implementation. Like the Friends, they valued an austere atmosphere, in keeping with their adherence to high Calvinism. The "unanimity" at Bowen's accession, therefore, "was not lasting, the hopes not realized, the conditions of its acceptance not fulfilled."[52]

Benjamin Francis's accession to the ministry in 1758, by contrast, marked a great watershed in Shortwood's history. Under his tutelage, the church moderated the High Calvinism of its founders, while informing it with a Methodist-like evangelicalism. Francis imported into the locality from Wales a revivalist approach,[53] partially inspired by George Whitefield and based doctrinally on moderate Calvinism.[54] Once Revd. Joshua Thomas of the Leominster Baptist Church had asked him, "When may one conclude that he enjoys God in the performance of Duty?" Francis replied in a manner that testified both to his evangelical ardor and his belief in Calvinist Free Grace:

When his heart is so filled with sacred joy and overpowered with heavenly light: and when the Holy Spirit witnesseth to his spirit, his Election and Vocation so clearly and irresistibly that he can't forbear breaking out in such language as this, "O, my GOD! My GOD indeed! Now I can't question thy Love: O, I feel it! I feel it!"[55]

Despite its origins in "Baxterianism," moderate Calvinism was an eclectic doctrine that first Whitefield and then Francis transformed into a radical evangelizing instrument. By reconciling the doctrines of Particular Election and Universal Redemption, moderate Calvinism made possible the conversion of "sinners." The schismatics of 1707, although artisans,[56] became Baptists because of their adherence to High Calvinism. In the seventeenth century such people often embraced High Calvinist doctrine since it confirmed their belief that God had chosen the "poor" among His elect. Such a doctrine conferred a sense of nobility that uplifted converts psychologically: "Men fought for God's cause and expected it to prevail because it was God's," Christopher Hill has observed. "The humbler the agents of divine Providence, the more manifest God's favor in their success."[57] In the late eighteenth century, however, when the Industrial Revolution began to fashion a proletariat, the democratic doctrine of universal redemption started to supplant the doctrine of Election in popular favor. These considerably poorer and more dependent people regarded themselves as sinners in need of healing; their spiritual condition became one of "affliction," mirroring their temporal state.

Francis's enthusiasm thus attracted large congregations, and his preaching to neighboring villages led to the growth of the Baptist interest far beyond Shortwood. His itinerant travels covered a range of ninety miles into Worcester and Wiltshire, and he preached for a week at a time over a period of seventeen years.[58] In 1774 the congregation drew itself from more than fifteen adjacent parishes, a fact offering testimony to the depth of its commitment, since distances of more than two miles in this period were not easily traversed. "Any friend of evangelical religion," one contemporary recalled,

must have enjoyed the sight of the several companies descending the surrounding hills on the Lord's day, to assemble at Shortwood, where on the rising ground above the meeting house one group after another would appear emerging from the woods; some of them coming from ten miles distant and upwards; nor was it uncommon for persons to unite in worship under that roof whose dwellings were thirty miles apart.[59]

Between 1758 and 1774, when the second major renovation of the Shortwood church fabric took place, the conversion rate averaged 2.1 percent per annum and annual membership levels rose at a rate of 6.5 percent per annum because of the relative immobility of the local population at this time. By February 1775, Francis had added 193 members to the church roll, and the general congregation in that year stood between 500 and 600 communicants, according to one contemporary estimate.[60] In 1760, 1774, and again in 1787, the meetinghouse required enlargement in order to accommodate the growing number of members and hearers.[61]

The composition of Francis's audience also began to change. Under his ministry the church drew its leaders primarily from among the middle class, while "the general congregation consist[ed] of clothworking people."[62] Francis often spoke of "my poor affectionate people at Horsley," a phrase he meant literally. Referring once to their ability to give him a higher salary, he observed; "I have discountenanced them from doing this hitherto; they can make but a dull sound in the harping upon this string while their own circumstances are so extremely indigent."[63]

Thomas Flint, who succeeded Francis as minister, gave an equally apt description of the congregation, linking its social status to its spiritual condition. In a diary entry, circa 1800, he commented: "Many residing at a considerable distance—poor and afflicted—and requiring a degree of watchful superintendance of which none can judge who are not acquainted with the nature of manufacturing districts."[64] The accent Flint placed on the words "afflicted" and "watchful superintendance" illustrates the significant shift toward moderate Calvinism that had occurred at Shortwood since 1758. If the doctrine of universal redemption made the salvation of the "afflicted" possible, it also established the groundwork of their spiritual enthusiasm.[65]

Thomas Flint's tenure, however, had lasted only four years (1799–1803). Having developed a scruple against believers' baptism, he moved to Uley, in the neighboring district, where he presided for eleven years over "a mixed society of Independents and Baptists, the former . . . considerably preponderating both in numbers and influence."[66] His shift to Congregationalism seems to have accompanied a reversion to High Calvinism. If moderate Calvinism had grown evangelical and found many of its adherents among the poor of the manufacturing districts, High Calvinism in the early nineteenth century, because of its exclusive nature, became associated with wealthier Dissenting congregations. Following his tenure at Uley, Flint settled at Weymouth, where he "preached to a select class of people,"[67] and his son, Benjamin F. Flint, whom he had strongly influenced, became a prominent deacon at a Baptist church in Margate that was "tinctured with High Calvinism."[68] Flint's failure as an enthusiast clearly accounted for his limited tenure at Shortwood. William Winterbotham (1804–1829) and Thomas Fox Newman (1830–1864), by contrast, maintained the evangelical traditions of Benjamin Francis. Like him, they provided stable, long-term ministries and figured prominently in local society. Winterbotham served a prison term in the 1790s for preaching a politically radical sermon and was widely praised as a "great man."[69] "Both in politics and religion," Shortwood's chronicler concluded, T. F. Newman "was a man of mark in this neighborhood, and was well known throughout the country as a powerful and attractive preacher."[70] Consequently, Shortwood drew ever larger numbers of adherents. In 1758 its membership stood at sixty-six, but by the time of the erection of a new chapel in 1839, had risen to over 500 with a congregation of 1,000.[71] The year 1758 had, indeed, marked the beginning of Shortwood's transition from sect to denomination.

The Revival and the Church of England

The Church of England could not remain indifferent to such developments. On practical grounds it became necessary to meet the challenge of Dissent; on spiritual grounds, too, enthusiasm was finding a place among its communicants and within its ministry. At the Restoration the Establishment met the challenge of Dissent by repression, although at Nailsworth, as we have seen, they did not apply it with great rigor. By the late seventeenth century, this challenge was being met by tolerance and collaboration, but on terms set by the Establishment. By the late eighteenth century tolerance and collaboration had been restored, following the disruption created by the early Revival, but now on terms set by Dissenters.

Sensing the need to partake of the Revival, the Anglican laity raised a subscription in 1794 for the building of a chapel at Nailsworth, which would offer the Dissenting congregations friendly but real competition. The inhabitants of Nailsworth were "chiefly ...people employed in different branches of cloth manufacture": most of them had large families and were "consequently rendered so poor that it is entirely out of their power (of themselves) to raise a sum sufficient for the erecting of a small chapel."[72] Population increase and accompanying industrialization, combined with an intensification of religious enthusiasm, caused reflective Anglicans to consider the best means of directing popular sentiment into socially acceptable forms.

In a quiescent period, such as the early eighteenth century, a Dissenting chapel that eschewed enthusiasm could be trusted to serve the religious needs of an isolated community, thereby complementing the work of the parish churches. In the period of the Revival, the chapels could not be fully trusted, despite the pretensions to respectability of their leaders. The latent tendency toward tumult always seemed present, and it was therefore preferable that an Anglican "enthusiast" relate directly to popular sentiment in order to provide better guidance.

David Ricardo, the younger, and lord of the manor of Minchinhampton, writing to Revd. P. Bliss in support of a candidacy for a curacy, summed up this attitude:

> You are but too well aware what progress Dissent has made in this neighbourhood, and it is of great importance that we who do love our Church should make great efforts at this moment when so many attempts are being made to overwhelm it.[73]

For this reason, Ricardo supported the candidacy of Revd. F. Rupel, whom he described as "a most excellent clergyman, a most powerful preacher and a true religious man."[74] The minister's credentials as an enthusiast were especially important. Ricardo described how, when Rupel first took up the duties of a living elsewhere: "all the Dissenting houses were thronged and the parish church, a very large one, was generally attended by about twenty or thirty persons. I was there a year afterwards, the church was then quite full and I understood the Dissenting ministers were obliged to give it up as they could not provide themselves a maintenance."[75] These remarks demonstrated a concern for the Church that issued locally and nationally in a concerted church-building program as the Establishment sought to engage Dissenters.[76] Bishop Bethell, in his charge to the clergy of the Diocese of Gloucester in 1825, voiced the widely held concern of the Establishment that "in many parts of the diocese the attendance on the public worship of the Church is by no means proportionate to the population, even where there appears to be no want of sufficient accommodation."[77] Bishop Monk repeated this same concern in 1832. He pointed to the failure of pastoral care resulting from the inadequacy of clerical incomes that had made nonresidency and the plural holdings of benefices an unfortunate necessity.[78] He proposed to increase clerical income in order to discourage pluralism and nonresidency, as well as to expand existing accommodations.

In 1831 and 1835 the Avening minister, as registrar of Oxford University, was nonresident.[79] In 1838 he was recorded as resident, but in 1839 and the years thereafter he had obtained a license for nonresidency.[80] In 1847 he was again recorded as resident, but in 1850 and for several years following had once again obtained a nonresidency permit. The incumbent of Horsely was technically nonresident, although he actually lived at Nailsworth.[81] Minchinhampton was more fortunate in having secured the services of a resident incumbent throughout the entire hundred-year period covered by the diocesan surveys.[82]

Nevertheless, Minchinhampton found it necessary to undertake the expansion of the church fabric in order to accommodate a larger number of poor. This meant providing a greater number of free sittings as opposed to rented pews. Minchinhampton had undergone a considerable reconstruction in 1841 partly for this purpose, yet the reform had the apparent effect of consolidating ownership of the pews in the hands of the gentry as the number of free sittings expanded. Indeed, individual seats held by many who signed their names with a mark were "engrossed" by such families as the Playnes, Sheppards, and Ricardos,[83] and the reform of 1841 represented the culmination of this process.

Yet Minchinhampton was a large parish, and some of its outlying districts could be well served by the building of new churches. The Nailsworth Episcopal Chapel had been established for this reason in 1794, although by the 1830s it had failed to achieve this objective. In 1836 Amberly Church was built just north of Nailsworth. Erected and endowed by David Ricardo, the younger, the lord of the manor, the church was "a very elegant structure in the gothic style."[84] Its consecration was a major event in the neighborhood and testified to the vigor of the Establishment despite the progress of Dissent. The *Gloucester Journal* reported that the "impressive ceremonial [had] excited great interest," for "there was a very numerous assemblage of the manufacturing and labouring population" present. David Ricardo received the Lord Bishop and upward of fifty clergy of the diocese for the consecration services, during which time the church was filled to its capacity of 1,200 persons, and nearly 2,000 were reported to have been outside. The church seated 700 exclusive of the galleries,[85] which meant that, in addition to providing a considerable number of sittings for the poor, there was ample standing room.

The parish church of Horsley was similarly in need of reconstruction, and in 1837 an "appeal for the rebuilding and enlarging" of its fabric was issued.[86] The parish contained nearly 4,000 inhabitants, yet "the church seats only about 500 adults, and affords no free sittings." The children of the Sunday school, who numbered upward of 200, "are necessarily placed where they see and hear very imperfectly, and those of another school are unable to attend for want of room."[87] Indeed, there was "constant demand for sittings, and many who wished to frequent their own parish church cannot possibly be accommodated." The problem, however, was that the church fabric was extremely old and had to be replaced in its entirety, except for the tower. The cost of rebuilding on a scale to accommodate 1,000 persons, with 500 of them as free sittings, was estimated at £2,500. This was ostensibly beyond the capacity of the inhabitants since the population consisted "chiefly of day-laborers and persons employed in the woollen trade and is proverbially poor."[88] The appeal succeeded, and the foundation stone was laid in May 1838. The new church could accommodate upward of 2,000 persons with more than 500 free sittings.[89]

The movement to refurbish parish churches spread throughout the Stroud region. The parish of Stroud, only four miles from Nailsworth, had experienced the same crisis of accommodation as had Horsley and Minchinhampton. In 1833 the incumbent, Revd. Powell, anxiously expressed the desire to "carry into effect the wish of many of the inhabitants, respecting building of a new parish church for the accommodation of many who live at a distance of two or three miles from the present parish church."[90] The *Gloucester Journal* supported this initiative editorially, "notwithstanding the very respectable dissenting places of worship in the neighborhood."[91] As a result of the movement to refurbish parish churches, the Establishment achieved parity with Dissenters. In the Stroud region, this meant that, on the more fundamental level of popular religious practice, the two reaffirmed a tradition of social and political collaboration between them. The initiatives of men such as David Ricardo, the younger, underscored an important phenomenon: the eclecticism of popular religious feeling that in no way detracted from its intensity. The efforts of the Establishment enabled ordinary men and women to maintain the custom of attending both Church and Chapel. Indeed, ecumenicism, rather than sectarian rivalry, was the fruit of enthusiasm.[92]

Nor was this eclecticism merely a local or regional aberration. The controversy surrounding the Dissenters's Marriage Bill of 1835, which Sir Robert Peel conceived of as a liberal measure, provides ample evidence for this assertion. The bill compromised the demands of Dissenters, who wished to marry in their own places of worship, with the interests of a conservative Anglican hierarchy, which sought to maintain the Church's legal monopoly in such matters. One friendly critic observed that the requirement of formally declaring one's own nonmembership in the Church of England, as a condition for taking advantage of the bill's provisions, strengthened the propensity to Dissent when the natural tendency was often more ambiguous. The individual "fluctuates in his attendance at religious worship between the meeting house and the parish church."[93] By requiring such a declaration, the authorities were forcing on him a choice that he normally would not have considered making, "especially where the Dissenting place of worship . . . differs more in discipline than doctrine."[94]

From this standpoint, the bill was defective in one other respect. It provided only for the contingency where "both parties are to be Dissenters. . . . The rights of conscience," the critic held, "are as sacred in one person as in a thousand; those of a woman as sacred as those of a man."[95] These remarks suggest that a significant degree of pluralism of religious affiliation existed at the time of marriage and that the phenomenon sprang from the consciences of men and women. As such, the bill proved incompatible with a profound religious sensibility; more importantly, however, criticism of it showed how much ecumenicism had contributed to the secularity of Victorian society.

Epilogue

If the Church of England had succeeded in establishing parity with Dissent throughout the Stroud region, it still failed to make significant progress at Nailsworth itself. Indeed, the desire to refurbish the parish churches of Minchinhampton and Horsley and to build new churches in the surrounding region was motivated partly by the realization that the Nailsworth Episcopal Chapel had not attracted a following comparable to that of the more important Dissenters. The chapel had been left unconsecrated and therefore with a diminished status.[96] In 1851 the Nailsworth Episcopal Chapel attracted 369 worshipers on census Sunday, or 11 percent of the local population.[97] The Forest Green Congregationalists had divided into two separate congregations, but their combined attendance stood at a respectable 939, or 27 percent of the local population. The Society of Friends was virtually extinct, following a protracted period of membership decline. Only the Shortwood Baptist Church experienced a continuous, linear growth until 1851. In that year its recorded attendance stood at 1,235 on census Sunday, or 36.5 percent of Nailsworth's population.[98] This capacity made it "one of the most flourishing churches of [the Baptist] denomination in the Kingdom."[99] Yet Shortwood's prosperity at midcentury masked an underlying change, represented by a trend toward denominationalism, that in the long term spelled disaster for it, as much as for the other evangelical churches of the Vale.[100]

The growth of Nonconformity before 1851, while stimulated principally by the Evangelical Revival, had owed much to the latitudinarianism of the Establishment. Not only had the Church of England demonstrated willingness to compete peacefully with Dissenters for a religious following; the structure of local politics itself revealed a lay Anglican commitment to the widest tolerance. Liberal paternalism affected the operations of manorial and parochial governments by promoting individualism and thereby laid the foundation of political consensus, which survived the turbulence of the 1830s.

Chapter Four

Manors, Parishes, and Dissent: The Structure of Politics

The survival of customary practices partially constrained the popular individualism fostered by the landholding patterns of Nailsworth's hinterland. Although customary obligations to pay heriots, entry fines, and suits-of-court had waned, they had not disappeared entirely, while Courts Baron and Leet, however much attenuated, continued to enforce them. Between 1780 and 1840 these courts either ceased to function or came to share their authority with the parish, the agency of local government that emerged from the sixteenth century. Although their competence had diminished, by operating as late as they did, Courts Baron and Leet perpetuated the legitimacy of traditional lordship. This legitimacy easily transferred itself to leading nonmanorial land-holders, as they, too, came to exercise civic authority through the parish and the institution of Justice of the Peace.

How did the persistence of manor courts and the transference of their governing powers affect popular attitudes toward established authority? Chapter 2 has shown that changing patterns of land-holding, despite the class polarization they reveal, suggest an underlying structural compatibility between Nonconformity and the Establishment. Patterns of Nonconformist settlement and growth, depicted in chapter 3, have reinforced this contention by illustrating a cultural compatibility as well. The present chapter carries forward consideration of this same theme by examining how the manor and parish mediated social relations throughout Nailsworth's hinterland.

The chapter considers the scope of manorial jurisdiction, as this descended from the medieval period, and discusses how far the operations of the manor court continued to foster deference among its suitors, as well as the extent to which Dissenters came within its purview. Attention is focused next on the parish as a unit of local government, with special consideration of how it supplanted the manor as a center of communal life while perpetuating the elite's exercise of a customary paternalism. A discussion of governmental structure would be incomplete, however, without some consideration of politics; the chapter thus documents the Whiggish political sympathies of the elite and sets forth the structure of electoral politics. Analysis of elections reveals once again the persistence of a deference community yet also illustrates how far the regionalization of Stroudwater society gave scope to more individualized, interest-group politics.

Manorial Jurisdiction

The jurisdiction of the manor court extended over the lands and tenements of which the manor itself was constituted. These consisted of demesne lands that the lord of the manor occupied, as well as "freeholds, farmes and customarie or coppihold tenements."[1] As previously demonstrated, customary tenements possessed "divers services besides their rents properly belonging thereunto,"[2] and the manor court existed in large measure in order to enforce their performance.

The manor had been the center of medieval village life, but its boundaries ranged widely, sometimes including only one village or embracing several of them; several manors could have existed even within one vill (township).[3] The medieval manor of Minchinhampton-Avening included the townships of what later became the parishes of Minchinhampton and Avening. The bankruptcy of Edward Shepphard, the lord of the manor, had precipitated the estate's division in the early nineteenth century;[4] in his place, David Ricardo, the elder, assumed the rights of lordship at Minchinhampton, while William Playne did the same at Avening.[5]

This division meant that the newly constituted manors would be congruent with their respective parishes. Horsley manor seems always to have been congruent with its parish, however, although minor boundary shifts clearly occurred over the course of time.[6]

During the Middle Ages especially the lord of the manor assumed, through his Courts Baron and Leet, the constitutional authority of the King's agent. His status depended, more precisely, on the type of court over which he presided. Sometimes manors possessed only customary courts, the business of which remained confined to the enforcement of obligations due the lord. These courts included Courts of Recognition and Survey; the first took place on the accession of a new lord to a manor, while the second protected the lord's interests against fraud by his tenants. Simple customary courts were held more routinely for the purpose of collecting rents and fines. Since these courts were preoccupied solely with the private business of the lord, the law recognized the "manor" only as a Seignory. The Seignory became a manor when in addition the lord obtained the right to preside over a Court Baron.[7]

The Court Baron exercised jurisdiction over minor civil infractions and established rules for communal agricultural practice. It also possessed the privilege of View of Frankpledge, which required the freeholders of the manor to attend its proceedings; customary tenants were required to pay suit by virtue of their tenures. View of Frankpledge often accompanied the right of the manor to hold a Court Leet, which exercised jurisdiction over criminal offenses such as assault or poaching. Not all manors held the privilege of a Court Leet, however, and criminal cases falling within their jursidictions were referred instead to the Hundred Court, which embraced a larger territorial unit.[8] The manors of Minchinhampton-Avening and Horsley were located in Longtree Hundred, and each retained the privilege of a Court Leet, while Horsley served additionally as the Hundred Court.[9] In practice, the proceedings of the customary courts followed those of the Courts Baron and Leet, but in the period under study, the lord conducted the proceedings of all three simultaneously.

Administratively, the manor divided into tithings, and the court elected their "tithingmen" or constables. Minchinhampton-Avening consisted of Minchinhampton, Rodborough, Avening,

Aston, and Pimbury tithings,[10] and Horsley of Barton End, Dowend, Nupend, Tichmorend, and Nailsworth tithings.[11] Avening tithing embraced lower Nailsworth and its hamlets such as Forest Green and Winsoredge, while Nailsworth tithing in Horsley included upper Nailsworth with the hamlets of Shortwood and Newmarket.[12]

Tithingmen acted as mediators between villagers and the lord, enforcing court orders in their respective jurisdictions and reporting any infractions of customary rules. They drew up lists of offenders and presented them at court and on the day of a Court Baron could be seen leading the residents of their tithings in procession to the courtroom.[13] The Court Baron, in other words, through the agency of the tithingmen, mobilized villagers in periodic demonstrations of obedience to authority, from which more remote settlements such as Nailsworth were not exempted. Nailsworth may have been somewhat isolated in the medieval and early modern periods[14] but, as a tithing, was integrated into the administrative structures of both manors and must therefore have maintained contact with their communal activities. Dissenting communites would eventually form at Nailsworth because of its relative isolation, but even in the earliest period of their histories, they enjoyed amicable contact with established authority.[15]

The mobilization of the inhabitants, on the occasion of a Court Baron, contained a democratic aspect. The court consisted not only of the lord presiding as judge but also of suitors themselves serving as elected jurors. Jurors were selected from among freeholders, regardless of rank, and "the better class of customary tenants."[16] Juries may have originated in the will of the lord, but they were charged nonetheless with delivering verdicts on the most important issues touching the interests of the entire community, while the lord, too, remained legally subject to their jurisdiction.[17]

Courts Baron and Leet continued to operate at Horsley and Minchinhampton well into the nineteenth century. At Horsley, lists of "persons giving suits and service [to] the manor" survive for the period 1794–1814. These surveys, compiled annually by the steward of the manor, group suitors by tithing and record next to each name any fines paid for nonattendance. By linking the manorial survey for 1811 to the Horsley parish census listing of that year, we can determine the occupations of suitors. By establishing a further linkage with the names contained in the church roll of the Shortwood Baptist Church, we can also measure the extent to which committed Dissenters participated in the communal affairs of the manor.[18]

Several questions require consideration. Did class differences between suitors have a significant bearing on their attendance at court? Did class differences and attendance at court vary significantly between Baptists and non-Baptists? The answers to these questions reveal the structure of deference with respect to both class and religion. If Dissenters owed suit-of-court, did they attend its proceedings? If they did not attend, did they pay a fine, or did they refuse to make any payment? Answers to these questions shed light on Dissenters' attitudes toward the Establishment at the moment when the Evangelical Revival began to intensify.

It is worth noting first that overall attendance at court remained low, yet significant enough, as figure 5 reveals. In most cases the court levied a fine of 1d. on tenants whom it failed to excuse, although sometimes it fined them 4d. to 6d. A mean of 85 percent of all suitors for the period failed to attend, but either were excused or complied by paying the fine. Virtually all unexcused absentees chose to pay the fine, however, while only a few, who appear sporadically in the records, refused all payment. In 1803 the court listed twenty-one names, or 4.6 percent of the suitors in that year who specifically refused to comply, while 412, or 91.8 percent, chose to do so. The only other protest against payment of the fine came in 1808: John Hyde of Tichmorend "wont pay [*sic*]."[19]

An absentee rate of 85 percent meant that the authority of the manor court had eroded, partly because it had gradually come to share its governing powers with the parish vestry and the Crown's Justices of the Peace, and partly because of a developing spirit of independence among its tenantry. Although the manor continued to exercise a certain amount of public authority, it must have been viewed increasingly as an agent of private aggrandizement. Still, the overwhelming majority of unexcused nonattendants tacitly acknowledged the lord's authority by consistently electing to pay fines. For laborers, clothworkers, and journeyman weavers, 1d was not necessarily a nominal sum, and their willingness to accede must be understood as an act of obeisance.

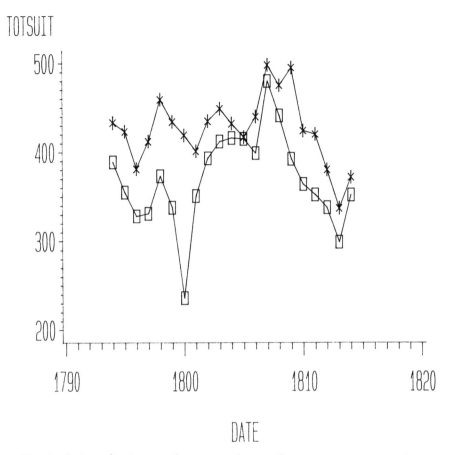

Fig. 5. Series of suitors and nonattenders at the Court Baron, Horsley Manor, 1794–1814.

Key: Star = All Suitors
     Square = Absentees

The following reconstruction of attendance patterns at court is based on a sample of suitors in 1811 whose names could be linked to those appearing in the parochial census for that same year. For the purposes of analysis, their occupations have been grouped into the following categories: (1) gentlemen, yeomen, and clothiers representing the middle and upper classes; (2) retailers and artisans, constituting the lower middle class; and (3) weavers (many undoubtedly journeymen), spinners, shearmen, clothworkers, and laborers, making up the working class. Patterns of attendance by

TABLE 18. *Attendance by Social Class of Suitors at the Court Baron, Horsley Manor, ca. 1811*

Social class	Number present	(ev)	(w)	Number absent	(ev)	(w)	Total
Upper middle	4	(1.7)	(2.9)	13	(15.3)	(0.33)	17
Lower middle	7	(4.9)	(0.8)	42	(44.0)	(0.09)	49
Working class	9	(13.3)	(1.4)	122	(117.7)	(0.15)	131
Total	20			177			197

Note: *ev* is expected value, and *w* is the weight or strength of the cell frequency's contribution to chi square ($x^2 = 5.799$, $df = 2$, $x^2 \geq 5.991$ at the 0.05 significance level).
Source: See text.

TABLE 19. *Religion by Social Class of Suitors at the Court Baron, Horsley Manor, ca. 1811*

Social class	Non-Baptists	(ev)	(W)[1]	Bap-tists	(ev)	(w)	Total
Upper middle	13	(13.7)	(0.04)	4	(3.2)	(0.2)	17
Lower middle	43	(40.5)	(0.15)	7	(9.5)	(0.7)	50
Working class	118	(119.7)	(0.02)	30	(28.2)	(0.1)	148
Total	174			41			215

Note: *ev* is the expected value, and *w* is the weight or strength of the cell frequency's contribution to chi-square ($x^2 = 1.189$, $df = 2$, $x^2 \geq 5.991$ at the 0.05 significance level).
Source: See text.

class appear in table 18, and those by religious affiliation appear in tables 19 and 20.

After excluding the "excused" from analysis in table 18, the chi-square (x^2) statistic just barely fails the test of significance.[20] The social class of suitors did not determine attendance patterns, since each class registered a high absentee rate proportional to its

TABLE 20. *Religion by Attendance of Suitors at the Court Baron,*
Horsley Manor, ca. 1811

Atten-dance	Non-Baptists	(ev)	(w)	Baptists	(ev)	(w)	Total
Present	16	(16.2)	(0.0)	4	(3.8)	(0.0)	20
Absent	145	(143.2)	(0.0)	32	(33.7)	(0.1)	177
Excused	13	(14.5)	(0.2)	5	(3.4)	(0.7)	18
Total	174			41			215

Note: *ev* is the expected value, and *w* is the weight or strength of the cell frequency's contribution to chi-square ($\chi^2 = 5.799$, $df = 2$, $\chi^2 \geq 5.991$ at the 0.05 significance level). Source: See text.

size in the population. Since refusal to attend at court represented alienation from authority, these results suggest that all classes were alienated to the same degree. Yet most unexcused suitors, as we have seen, paid the fine in lieu of attendance, a display of deference that also became manifest despite religious differences (see table 19).

Baptists may be distinguished from others owing suit-of-court by linking the sample of suitors, derived from the 1811 parish census, to the membership roll of the Shortwood Baptist Church. Of the 215 suitors drawn from the original linkage, forty-one, or 19.1 percent, were members at Shortwood. This was an especially high percentage, since formal church membership among Baptists involved greater commitment than that of mere "hearers." Class differences between Baptists and non-Baptists, however, failed to materialize[21] (see table 20).

Class differences did not, therefore, alter the near universal willingness to submit to the lord of the manor that the high rate of fine payment suggests. However, the high absentee rate, which resulted in the levying of fines, suggests a degree of alienation from the authority of the manor. This ambivalence resulted from a contradiction, already apparent in the structure of land tenure, between the growth of individualism and the persistence of ties of dependence. The growth of individualism was reflected especially in the progress of piecemeal enclosures and the decline of customary manorial practices, while the persistence of dependence became manifest in the slow waning of lordship and the transfer of its authority to parishes and Justices of the Peace. A significant percentage of Baptists, moreover, could be counted among the suitors of the manor court; they displayed the same combination of individualism and deference toward authority as did other suitors, whether Anglican or Dissenter. Their appearance in the court roll indicates, too, that their communities were not as isolated from manorial jurisdiction as commonly supposed; the growth of Dissent, as demonstrated equally in earlier chapters, may be seen to have coexisted with customary structures of authority.

The routine business of the manor court further substantiates this conclusion. Of the thirty-one persons presented before the court in 1802, ten, or 32.3 percent, were members at Shortwood.[22] The presentments made before the court survive for a limited period (1802, 1807) but are indicative of the nature of its business. Land transactions were no longer recorded, but a great deal of activity, associated with the maintenance of communal agricultural practice, is clearly evident. Such maintenance mainly involved protection of the wasteland from encroachments by squatters, who erected cottages and created small enclosures.[23] Encroachers, whose occupations are listed in table 21, were artisans, woolworkers, laborers, and lower-middle-class retailers or small clothiers. Their encroachments, however, were prosecuted with doubtful seriousness. Only small fines were levied, and the same offenders often reappeared in subsequent proceedings. In a sense, the lord accepted fines as de facto rent charges for what really amounted to trespassing. One can detect in this practice the tolerance associated with paternalism.

Still, in order to maintain his rights as a landowner, the lord could establish conformity to the letter of the law more insistently. At the Court Baron and Court of Survey for 1802 several tenants with possibly defective tenures were required to make appearances. Stephen Churches, for example, was required to appear, bearing "the original lease. . . granted. . . to Josiah Hutchings of the Parish of Horsley, broadweaver, of the messuage, garden and orchard now occupied by you."[24] The lease ran for ninety-nine years determinable on the lives of the original tenant, his wife, and

TABLE 21. *Occupations of Encroachers Prosecuted at the Court Baron,*
at Horsley Manor, ca. 1802

Occupation	Number
Artisans	
Cordwainers	3
Masons	1
Pargiters	1
Carpenters	1
Saddletreemakers	2
Woolworkers	
Broadweavers	6
Spinners	3
Clothworkers	1
Retailers	
Pigkillers	1
Innholders	3
Manufacturers	
Clothiers	2

Source: Horsley Manor Records; see text.

his son. Stephen Churches was "to prove whether either and which of these lives are now living and if these lives be dead to shew by what title you now hold and occupy the said premises." The notices sent by the steward in 1802 to eight others in the same situation assumed this standard format. Evidently, the original tenants had sublet the properties without obtaining permission from the lord, who necessarily profited from such transactions.

If the Court Baron of 1802 concerned itself principally with prosecuting encroachers, the Court of Survey accompanying it sought to preserve the rights of lordship, of which the proper maintenance of tenancies was one aspect. In his charge to the jury, reproduced as appendix C, the steward of the manor outlined its responsibilities with respect to the lord's rights. Besides inquiring into the state of leaseholds, or making lists of tenants who owed suit-of-court, the jury was "to enquire if advantages have happened to the lord by Escheats or Forfeitures."[25] Escheat was distinctively feudal in origin; it involved "the possibility of the land falling back into the hands of the lord, as representing the original donor, on a failure of the tenant's heirs."[26] As Frederick Pollock remarked, however, this remained a considerable anachronism in an age when "alienation by will is allowed without limit."[27] Escheat applied at Horsley in 1802 in cases where a freeholder committed a felony and where "any Bastard having purchased Land within this Manor be dead without lawful Issue of his Body."[28] Otherwise, the rights of inheritance remained sacrosanct. The survival of Escheat, even in an attenuated form, illustrates what the structure of land tenure and the attendance patterns at court have affirmed: the growth of individualism in the form of tenant property rights coexisted for a time with customary structures of authority.

Formally, Horsley's manor court retained the right to inquire into "any Thing unjustly done or omitted between lord and tenant or between Tenant and Tenant."[29] Yet the absence of presentments concerned with such matters, other than those that touched the lord's interests directly, hints at the waning of the manor court's competence with the passage of time. It was to diminish further. The records of its proceedings had, indeed, survived into the late nineteenth century, but after 1815 presentments for offenses no longer appear in them. Only tithingmen were presented for election to their offices but in a very perfunctory and formal style.

The manor of Minchinhampton remained active longer because of the survival of Minchinhampton Common as a common grazing area and the need to regulate it. Preservation of the Common was a community concern, at least until the 1830s,[30] to which the Court Baron gave institutional expression. A Court Baron, for example, was held at the Crown Inn on August 1, 1820 "for the purpose of adopting speedy and effectual measures to prevent the stealing of dung from off Hampton Common."[31] At the same time, the jury deputed a number of freeholders from each tithing "to inspect the water courses, pools and wells, belonging to the aforesaid Common."[32] As late as the 1820s, the Manor of Minchinhampton exercised its traditional function by mobilizing the inhabitants in communal action, which reinscribed deferential attitudes. Nevertheless, the manor continued to function only on this restricted basis, since it had come to share its communal responsibilities with parochial government. The parish provided an alternative sphere of community, which nevertheless complemented the manor.

Parochial Administration

Parochial institutions evolved over a considerable period. The parish vestry had been established as early as the fourteenth century for the management of ecclesiastical affairs but was a later creation than many parochial offices.[33] Sidney and Beatrice Webb argued that the parish, as a unit of local obligation imposed by the central authorities, symbolized the triumph of national government over regional diversity.[34] As they also pointed out, however, this triumph remained incomplete, since local society itself acted as its instrument. Parochial officials, elected at vestry meetings, were rate-paying freeholders required by law to assume the burdens of office. They were strictly subordinate, however, to the Crown's Justices of the Peace, who met at Quarter Sessions to dispense justice Countywide. The Justices belonged to the locally resident gentry and exercised their legal authority on an individual basis as well as within their respective communities.[35]

The gradual accretion of secular power in the parish vestry and the emergence of Justices of the Peace restricted the traditional prerogatives of manor courts while acting as complementary structures of authority. Minchinhampton's vestry minutes for 1805, for instance, noted that the manor court had appointed a perambulator to inspect Minchinhampton Common. The vestry expressed its approval and then proceeded to assign the new appointee his first task. Similarly, although the tithingman was appointed by the manor, he was supervised by the churchwarden in the latter's capacity as a parochial official.[36] The vestry meeting brought together the rate-paying inhabitants of the parish to consent to the levying of poor rates and taxes for the repair of roads or the maintenance of the church fabric. It also elected the churchwardens, tithingmen (when not appointed by a Court Baron), the surveyor of highways, and the overseers of the poor, who were responsible for daily administration. Vestry minutes and accounts also recorded a wide variety of expenditures, which show clearly how parochial government supplanted the manor in structuring the reciprocal attitudes of paternalism and deference.

TABLE 22. *Items Granted through Outdoor Relief, Horsley Parish,*
1802–1822

	Clothes	Rent	Cash grants	Shoes	Yarn	Appren- ticeship
November 1802– January 1813	295	132	87	35	27	7
February 1813– April 1822	42	66	15	14	27	6

Source: Horsley Parish Vestry Minutes; see text.

Such attitudes were revealed especially in the treatment of the poor.[37] Before the Whig reform of 1834 created new "poor law unions," each parish maintained its own workhouse and dispensed a considerable proportion of monies appropriated for the poor on outdoor relief. At Minchinhampton, circa 1800, 250 persons received relief, of whom seventy, or 28.0 percent, resided in the workhouse.[38] The inmates included the infirm, children of large families, or the illegitimate whose parents were unable or unwilling to provide for them, the aged and dependent women.[39] The variety of outdoor relief offered at Minchinhampton can be only conjectured since its vestry minutes failed to offer a detailed accounting. Monies were certainly spent for the apprenticeship of poor children, on which a £3 limit was placed in June 1818, "excepting under peculiar circumstances."[40] Horsley's vestry minutes give a clearer picture for the period in which they are available, 1802 to 1822. Table 22 gives the frequency distribution by type of expenditure, and figure 6 illustrates the annual fluctuations for the three most important items.[41]

The periodic division in table 22 follows the division of the minute books themselves. There is no difference in the amount of yarn distributed and hardly any in the number of apprenticeships paid for. A great disparity appears between the two periods, however, with respect to the other four items, which can be explained by the French wars.[42] Expenditure on clothing was high from 1803 and declined sharply from 1813; rents and cash grants

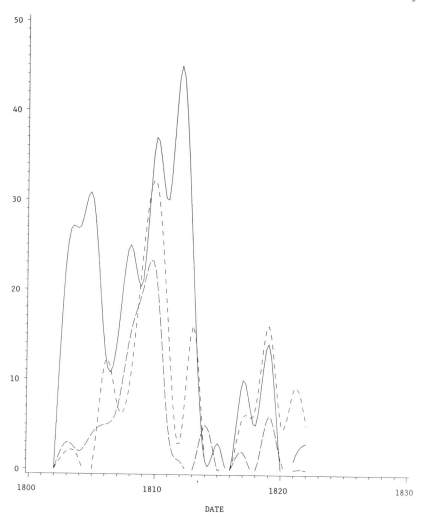

Fig. 6. Series of Items Granted through Outdoor Relief, Horsley Parish, 1802–1822.

Key: Solid Line = Clothes
Small Broken Line = Rent
Large Broken Line = Cash

peaked between 1805 and 1810, although both declined sharply thereafter. Expenditures on all three items were virtually nonexistent between 1814 and 1816 but made a gradual recovery thereafter, probably because of the postwar stagnation in the cloth trade. Sometimes cash grants were made to enable a family or an individual to migrate, often in compliance with the settlement laws. Generally, however, such grants were not specified for any item and must be assumed to have been supplements to wages.

Such expenditures were clearly paternalistic. From 1800, however, gentry paternalism was directed increasingly toward promoting the "independence" of the laboring classes, ostensibly for their social betterment. This interest in working-class independence combined with a self-serving but by no means hypocritical concern regarding the great weight of taxation and the need to maintain social order. A plan for the better regulation of the poor, adopted by the Minchinhampton vestry in 1800, aimed "to lighten the heavy burden of the parochial taxes but also [to] contribute to the health and comfort of those [for] whose benefit the tax is imposed."[43] Implementation of such a goal required the creation of a special board of directors, consisting of twenty-five gentlemen, who would make regular visits to the workhouse as well as to recipients of outdoor relief and in this manner supervise the work of the overseers of the poor.

The board also considered the feasibility of reducing the number of families receiving outdoor relief by taking some of their children into the workhouse and granting a weekly stipend to the friends or relations of workhouse inmates "for maintaining them in preference to keeping them in the House."[44] It would cost less to maintain a child in the workhouse than to support an entire family out of doors and to lodge an adult pauper with a household than to keep him at public expense, where the administrative costs of maintenance would have to be included.

Such economies, it was believed, would effect the moral and material betterment of the poor. The head of a household who sent his child to the workhouse could become self-reliant, an issue of great moment to contemporaries;[45] and the child, removed from a condition of squalor, would benefit from his new environment, particularly if the regime of the workhouse were reformed.[46] Thus, economy in local government, normally associated with

Whig reformism, was compatible in the minds of contemporaries with the humaneness of traditional paternalism. Indeed, the proposal to create a gentleman-board of directors aimed at institutionalizing this tradition, however much it foreshadowed a later and much stricter version in the boards of guardians created by the New Poor Law.

Many were convinced, furthermore, that paternalism, by promoting independence of character, would ensure a deferential working class and thereby the stability of the social order; the example of George Hodges, a Horsley laborer, is an especially apt case.[47] In 1811 Hodges lost all of his possessions in a fire. They were valued at the considerable sum of £100 and included "his cottage, outhouse, pig-stye, furniture, husbandry utensils, clothes and the clothes of his wife and children." He and his family had been industrious, which made their loss especially tragic. As a reward for thriftiness, the local gentry raised a subscription to assist them.

Such voluntarist display was not unusual; the meeting of the parish vestry served often as a community forum for organizing special relief efforts on behalf of the "deserving poor." At Minchinhampton in December 1816, the vestry minutes mention a meeting organized by the parish's "principal inhabitants," the purpose of which was "to take into consideration and adopt measures as may be deemed necessary for the temporary relief of the worthy poor...now out of employ by reason of the stagnation of trade."[48] Those in authority clearly understood that economic conditions and not "immorality" could easily create unemployment. The resolution adopted by the meeting called for "a subscription [to] be immediately entered into for the purpose of employing the manufacturing and laboring poor...who through want of employment stand in need of some temporary and immediate relief."

It is especially noteworthy that the initiators of the scheme should have funded this activity through voluntary subscription rather than from the rates. The employment of labor, on a scale required to offset the effect of a trade depression, was, in principle, too great for any government to undertake. Besides, the local gentry were eager to avoid tax increases, which would have fallen on small holders as well. In true paternalist style, they willingly assumed the entire burden themselves and succeeded in raising over £60. They were concerned, moreover, to avoid the demoralizing impact of parochial relief. The men to be employed under their scheme were accustomed to receiving regular wages, even if sometimes supplemented by outdoor relief. To have thrown them entirely on the mercy of the parish could only have encouraged habits of dependence.

Thus, the rules governing employment under the scheme were drafted with a particular rigor. The rules were designed not only to ensure the performance of the work undertaken but also to sustain habits of work discipline. "Men who absent themselves from their [road repairing] work in part of any day in the ensuing week in case of wet weather," the subscribers resolved, "[then] in such case it is ordered that their pay be reduced $\frac{1}{4}$ and if the foremen . . . do not attend the whole of each day they are to be paid nothing."[49] The scheme was conceived partly by the pragmatic need to prevent outbreaks of violence, which mass unemployment might induce. It remained, nonetheless, an act of paternalism, since no contradiction existed, in the subscribers' view, between pragmatic and moral goals. Paternalism aimed at preventing disorder, restraining taxation, and creating a self-reliant working class. Realization of the first two goals could lead to fulfillment of the third.

This synthesis of paternalism, deference, and individualism embodied a liberal outlook. It embraced an ideal of autonomy and mobility within a hierarchical setting, which served as an alternative to the conservative vision of an "organic society."[50] Whigs, Peelite Tories, and the laboring classes of the region embraced it overwhelmingly. Such broad acceptance, moreover, resulted from cooperative relations between Dissenters and the Establishment and from the social character of lordship. Leading middle-class Dissenters mediated relations between their followers and the authorities, while leaders of the Establishment belonged either to older Whig families, which had maintained a cosmopolitan outlook, or to the more socially mobile elements of the middle class.

Dissent and the Composition of Lordship

Those who amassed fortunes in trade, especially the clothiers of the region, often established landed estates and even acquired the lordship of manors.[51] The Sheppherd family acquired the manor of Minchinhampton-Avening in the seventeenth century after amassing a fortune in the cloth trade. When bankruptcy forced the sale and division of the manor in 1814, David Ricardo, political economist and banker, as we have seen, acquired the lordship of Minchinhampton, while William Playne, gentleman-clothier, acquired the lordship of Avening. The lordship of Horsley manor possessed greater continuity of occupation by one family, although its pedigree possessed no more of an authentically aristocratic origin. The manor of Horsley had descended to the Stephens family of Eastington in the reign of Elizabeth; in 1676 Richard Stephens built the mansion house at Chavenage that remained in the possession of his direct line until 1795. Richard Stephens had settled Chavenage Farm on his wife, Anne, one of the daughters of John Stone, a London haberdasher,[52] and like the Sheppherds and Ricardos, the Stephens family maintained connections with substantial clothier familes. The tithes of Horsley parish, for instance, had been held in trust from 1686 as a result of the negotiated marriage settlement of Ralph Willet, the younger, and Elizabeth Phillips, the daughter of John Phillips of Minchinhampton, both of whom came from substantial clothier families. One trustee was Thomas Davies of Stroud parish, gentleman, whose only daughter had married John Stephens of Chavenage, and on the basis of this connection Henry Stephens, the lord of the manor in the late eighteenth century, claimed possession of Horsley's tithes.[53]

The Ducies of Tortworth Court, furthermore, were the largest nonresident landlords at Nailsworth, with a 272-acre estate in Horsley.[54] The Ducies were the most prominent Whig family in Gloucestershire and were peers of the realm since the Conquest. Tortworth was seven miles from Nailsworth, and at this distance it was unlikely that Lord Ducie would have sustained any regular relations with the community. His influence in the Stroud region, however, was considerable. In 1820 he led the Countywide protest on behalf of Queen Caroline, whose cause had been taken up by the parliamentary Whigs.[55] The Ducies were prominent during the agitation for parliamentary reform, and in 1832 Henry Moreton, the future Lord Ducie, stood as the Whig candidate for the East Gloucestershire seat in the reformed House of Commons.[56] In 1846, as Lord Ducie, he led the agitation for repeal of the Corn Laws, [57] which drew the support of Stroudwater clothiers. The

Ducies's political activities epitomized the Whig social and political alliance, which enabled the landed aristocracy to retain its traditional leadership during an epoch of rapid change.[58] By acting as spokesmen for the "popular classes," the Whigs appealed successfully to Anglicans and Dissenters alike.

In what manner did this alliance manifest itself locally? Although Dissenters could not legally hold parochial office, they participated routinely in parochial affairs and often established amicable relations with Anglican landlords. Joseph Browning, a Nailsworth maltster, revealed his Congregationalist credentials by bequeathing £6 to the Forest Green Church, yet was able to bequeath 20s. to Horsley's churchwardens and overseers of the poor.[59] John Blackwell, a Baptist deacon and clothier, resided at Winsoredge near Nailsworth[60] and leased 73 percent of his 182-acre Avening estate from Edward Sheppherd, the lord of the manor.[61] Nor did religious differences prevent him from participating in parochial affairs. The vestry had overvalued his cloth mill at £52 but corrected the error willingly. All agreed that "Mr. Blackwell shall be charged only £45 as Mr. Tombs being present have declared that it is a mistake in the charge."[62] Dissenters may have objected in principle to the payment of church rates and tithes, but members of the largest Nonconformist churches failed to articulate their grievances sufficiently until the 1830s, when agitation for reform became commonplace.[63]

The Quakers remained the great exception. They had protested against church rates and tithes throughout the eighteenth century and, by the early nineteenth century, had been exempted informally from paying these taxes. Anthony Fewster, a leading Quaker, was exempted in 1838 from paying tithe charges of £3. 3s. 10d. on lands owned and occupied in Avening. Fewster also leased twenty-seven acres (including the parsonage) from Revd. Samuel Lloyd, the Anglican vicar of Horsley and as an additional mark of tolerance governing the neighborhood was elected in 1836 to represent Horsley on the Board of Guardians of Stroud's Poor Law Union.[64]

The examples of Blackwell and Fewster were hardly isolated instances. In 1800 James Thomas, deacon of the Forest Green Congregationalist Church, had been one of those gentlemen to propose the new plan for regulating the Minchinhampton poor.

He appeared again in 1816 as a subscriber to the scheme for setting Minchinhampton's unemployed to work; so did John Blackwell and John Heskins, who, like Blackwell, served as a Shortwood Baptist deacon.[65] David Ricardo, political economist and lord of the manor, moreover, headed the list of subscribers. The joint appearance of these four men epitomized the Whig social and political alliance. Not only did Anglican and Dissenter share the same assumptions about paternalism, deference, and individualism; Dissenters, by appearing under the auspices of the vestry, demonstrated loyalty to a sphere of local community led by the Establishment.

The Whig social and political alliance became manifest most explicitly during the postwar years when agitation for reform became widespread. The Queen Caroline Affair (ca. 1820), although formally concerned with the King's efforts to dissolve his marriage, gave rise to popular protests that enabled the Whigs to emerge as a genuine political opposition.[66] The affair reverberated as much in the provinces as in London. At a Countywide meeting held at Gloucester's shire hall, B. W. Guise, Baronet and M.P., excoriated the Government for proceeding against the Queen, denouncing them for the "ill-advised and impolitic measures . . . which had reduced the country to its present situation of difficulty and distress." David Ricardo congratulated Lords Ducie and Sherbourne for their "manly and independent conduct" in defending Caroline and called for a reform of Parliament to effect "a perfect harmony between the people and their representatives."[67]

Ricardo's ideal of social harmony, as we have seen, already operated informally at the local level, but the Whig-dominated protest gave it further symbolic expression. At the close of the affair, a "demonstration of gladness" held at Stroud sealed the social and political solidarity, forged during the crisis, through the ritualized exploitation of popular emotion.[68] "A fine Ox intended to regale the poor," the *Gloucester Journal* reported, "was led through the town, decorated with laurels and ribbands [*sic*], bearing appropriate inscriptions; and a large green bag, the symbols of ministerial abasement, was suspended at [its] tail." As a result of pelting by the populace, "its outside soon became a striking emblem of the labours of the disgraceful Milan Commission." This public display clearly discharged much pent-up psychic energy. In addition to circuses, however, the demonstration's sponsors also offered "bread" to the poor: "Wednesday was occupied in preparing for the feast intended for the poor on the following day; and on Thursday the Ox and four sheep were distributed, with four hogsheads of strong beer, to the great satisfaction of the poor inhabitants, by whom the day will be long remembered." At a complementary feast held two days later in the George Inn, the gentry celebrated the triumph of their liberal union with such toasts as: "Prosperity to the town & vicinity of Stroud. . . . [To] Religion, Law and Loyalty, which have alike been violated in the persecution of our great Queen."

Liberal opinion soon took up Ricardo's linkage of the Queen Caroline Affair and parliamentary reform,[69] although reform agitation nationwide did not begin in earnest until 1830. When it did, Stroud emerged as one of its principal centers.[70] Following passage of the Great Reform Act, and subsequently the creation of the parliamentary borough of Stroud, elections were held to the new House of Commons. Analysis of this election reveals the formal structure of politics at Stroud; its character underscores more definitively the borough's Whiggish complexion and the persistence of a "deference community"[71] in Nailsworth's hinterland.

The three candidates for Stroud's two parliamentary seats belonged to the same political party.[72] W. H. Hyett stood above all factions and was unanimously selected M.P. He was a country gentleman without personal or family ties to commercial interests but had been an active parliamentary reformer.[73] Poulet Scrope was an outsider from Castle Combe, Wiltshire, who came from a commercial family.[74] His support was concentrated in the town of Stroud and its immediate neighborhood, and he enjoyed the backing of "the greater part of the clothing interests."[75] David Ricardo, son of the now deceased political economist, was lord of the manor of Minchinhampton. He drew support mainly from his own neighborhood but enjoyed the backing of only "a few manufacturers."[76] Scrope was the more cosmopolitan figure and clearly received wide support because of his connections with government and the City.[77] Ricardo, despite the association of his father's great name with banking and the City, cultivated the life of a local squire and made this attribute the cutting edge of his campaign.[78]

Scrope and Ricardo fought bitterly and with the kind of theatrics reminiscent of the Queen Caroline Affair. Theater on the hustings, however, sometimes assumed an unsavory quality:

A stupid attempt to ridicule one of the candidates [Ricardo] by dressing up a fellow in the garb and with the beard of a Jew Peddler was treated with the contempt it deserved. But a country-gentleman who personated [*sic*] a Wiltshire moon-raker [Scrope] met with very rough reception—his rake was broken in pieces and the moon was eclipsed in a cloud of missiles.[79]

Evidently, the crowd was far more exercised by the innocuous attempt to ridicule Scrope than by the anti-Semitism of his supporters.

Ricardo emerged victorious in any case, but by a narrow margin due entirely to his local strength. His support at Minchinhampton, Avening, Horsley, and Woodchester outweighed overwhelmingly his failure to carry the town and environs of Stroud, as well as the several industrial parishes of Stroud's hinterland. The election returns,[80] depicted in table 23, illustrate the persistence of parochialism and deference, traditionally accorded a lord of the manor, despite the growth of regionalism.

Given the extent of regional economic integration, the clothiers' candidate, although a "foreigner," should have stood the best chance of winning. Ricardo's victory was in this sense anachronistic, and perhaps for this reason his tenure as M.P. proved embarrassingly short; he resigned in 1833, allegedly for personal reasons, and was promptly replaced by his former rival, Poulet Scrope.[81]

Nevertheless, the political differences between the two men were more matters of style than substance. Each combined a vigorous commitment to free-market principles with a utilitarian paternalist sensibility. Ricardo engaged himself in a wide range of local efforts to help the "deserving poor," from parochial sponsorship of emigration during trade depressions to the formation of the Nailsworth Loan Society, which helped the poor acquire property.[82] Scrope also believed in "property doing its duty" but, unlike Ricardo, focused much of his attention on the development of a "paternal [national] Government."[83]

As M.P. for Stroud, Scrope sponsored legislation on savings

TABLE 23. Election Returns for the Borough of Stroud, 1832

Region[a]	Hyett	(ev)	(w)	Ricardo	(ev)	(w)	Scrope	(ev)	(w)	Total
1	344	(356)	(1.2)	359	(217)	(93)	88	(208)	(69)	791[a]
2	370	(365)	(0.1)	137	(217)	(29)	284	(208)	(27)	791
3	271	(254)	(1.1)	89	(150)	(25)	190	(145)	(14)	550
Total	985			585			562			2,132

Note: ev is the expected value, and w is the weight or strength of the cell frequency's contribution to chi-square ($\chi^2 = 261.165$, $df = 4$, $\chi^2 \geq 18.465$ at the 0.001 significance level).

[a] Region 1 = Minchinhampton, Horsley, Avening, Woodchester (Ricardo's immediate neighborhood), and Bisley, with which Minchinhampton shared the boundary settlement of Chalford; region 2 = Stonehouse, King's and Leonard Stanley, Rodbourough, Randwick, Painswick, and Pitchcombe (industrial parishes in Stroud's hinterland); region 3 = Stroud parish, including the market town and its environs. Note especially, for all three regions, the large differences between observed and expected values; these accounted for the extremely high chi-square value. It is clear, however, that the votes for Ricardo in region 1 contributed most to the overall difference.

banks, government annuities and life insurance, and "friendly" societies, each designed to give the working classes economic security while promoting a spirit of independence among them.[84] His savings bank bill required government to assume liability for deposits in order to safeguard from bank failures "these (almost sacred) savings of the poor and working classes." His annuity scheme facilitated the purchase of deferred annuities; these seemed "preferable for guarding against old age since [they are] not subject to the vagaries of sickness, accident or trade depression the way payment by instalment is." Scrope complained, too, that friendly societies had received little or no protection from the state, leaving many with defective accounts and open to fraud. He thought, nonetheless, that the fact of their existence "speaks loudly the general prevalence among these classes of the virtues of forethought, of the desire of self-support and of economy with a view to that end." Liberal paternalism aimed at promoting such habits, a fact to which Scrope indirectly attested in correspondence with Edwin Chadwick. "I think you will be quite right," Scrope wrote consolingly, "in claiming for yourself the merit that is due you in so much of all that is good in the P[oor] L[aw] Acts & administrative improvements of the last fourteen years."[85]

Despite the growth of collectivist public policy, evident in Scrope's legislative initiatives, by the 1830s a critical shift had occurred within the Whig synthesis of paternalism, deference, and individualism. Whig-Radicals began to accord free-market principles greater legitimacy than previously. In 1816 Minchinhampton's paternalists had acted freely against depression induced unemployment and generally treated the poor more generously. By the 1830s, efforts at amelioration had assumed the less direct form of preventive adjustments to market conditions, while concern for the growth of autonomy among the working classes, already evident in 1816, had fully blossomed, a change in emphasis symbolizing the emergence of a liberal-industrial society throughout Stroudwater.

Summary and Conclusion

This chapter has offered an institutional analysis of a theme that has permeated all of part I: the essential compatibility between

Nonconformity and the Establishment. It has argued that a spirit of cooperation, fostered by Chapel leaders and supported as a matter of principal by lay Anglican lords, rested on a Whiggish belief in tolerance and a social foundation of class collaboration, which the reciprocal habits of paternalism and deference reinforced.

Analysis of the operations of the surviving manor courts revealed how Nailsworth, despite its status as an outlying district, remained incorporated administratively within a wider community. This finding reaffirms conclusions regarding Nailsworth's relative autonomy, previously arrived at through studies of land-holding and Nonconformist settlement.[86] Ties of dependence, furthermore, were shown to have coexisted with a spirit of independence among members of the working class, affirming in this way earlier conclusions regarding the social consequences of tenurial arrangements. Ties of dependence partly assumed the form of surviving customary obligations owed the lord of the manor by his tenants; this chapter has focused on how successfully the lord enforced such obligations, especially the duty to pay suit-of-court.

Since refusal to fulfill this particular obligation represented alienation from customary authority, analysis of attendance patterns would indicate whether such alienation remained more pronounced among the working, middle, or upper classes, and whether religious differences among suitors affected their propensity to absent themselves. A chi-square statistic was employed to test for significant differences in both cases. If the chi-square value had been significant, we might have concluded that one or more of the classes suffered a greater degree of alienation, or that Dissenters were less prone to attend at court. However, the results revealed that no significant variation by social class or religion existed among unexcused absentees, suggesting that all classes, whether Anglican or Nonconformist, were alienated roughly to the same degree. Still, almost all unexcused suitors paid fines levied for absenteeism, behavior that acknowledged the lord's authority and thereby revealed an ambivalence between the mentalités of autonomy and deference.

Since local manorial courts had been in a state of decay, it was necessary to consider further the extent to which parochial institutions had assumed their governing powers. The parish had appropriated almost all powers of civil administration, except for the election of constables, whose appointments it continued to share with the Court Baron, and for the supervision of whatever communal agricultural practices remained. The institution of Justice of the Peace, furthermore, superseded the jurisdiction of the Court Leet in prosecuting legal infractions. Nonmanorial landowners operating within the parochial framework appropriated the paternalist tradition of customary lordship. This became manifest in the routine patterns of disbursement of poor-relief funds and in diverse schemes to relieve the poor and unemployed, particularly during periods of economic distress. Through these efforts the parish came to function in a truly corporatist way, as a sphere of local community that fully included Nonconformists.

Whig landlords were thus able to forge a social and political alliance based on religious tolerance and social solidarity. In the Stroud-wide elections to the newly reformed House of Commons, this alliance revealed the extent to which a "deference community" still persisted at Horsley, Avening, and Minchinhampton, yet showed in its aftermath how far modern interest-group politics came to predominate throughout the rest of the Stroud region. The Whig synthesis of individualism, deference, and paternalism made possible the Establishment's collaboration with Nonconformists throughout Stroud and thereby helped mediate the region's emergence as a liberal industrial society. It is the underlying structure of this transformation, in the spheres of population change, manufacturing industry, and class relations, to which we must now turn.

Part II

From Community to Society

Chapter Five

Birth, Death, Migration, and Dissent

The "demographic revolution," which gathered momentum in England between 1750 and 1850, described an intermediary pattern of population growth lying between preindustrial and modern demographic regimes. Whereas high mortality and high fertility governed preindustrial populations and low mortality and low fertility characterized modern ones, the period between them witnessed an initial decline in mortality coupled with a rise in fertility, followed again by rising mortality. The combination of declining mortality and rising fertility, however, had induced a population explosion, the underlying causes of which demographers have generally ascribed to economic conditions rather than cultural values or religious attitudes.

Studies of English population have nevertheless cited the growth of religious nonconformity during this period as a major impediment to the accurate reconstruction of demographic behavior. Demographers have relied heavily on Church of England registers of baptisms, burials, and marriages and have treated Protestant Dissenters from the Church of England mainly as a factor of underestimation in the Anglican record. Such treatment can be misleading, however, considering the mediating role social and cultural historians, from Elie Halèvy to E. P. Thompson, have assigned evangelical Nonconformity in the emergence of modern English society.

This chapter seeks to reconcile the concerns of historical demog-

raphers with those of social and cultural historians by treating
Nonconformity as an independent element in the demographic
revolution. It does so by focusing primarily on Nailsworth village
and Horsley parish, where Nonconformists seem mostly to have
settled, and by using such quantitative methods of analysis as
compound-interest growth rates of births and burials and multiple
regression.

Population Change: An Overview

During the Industrial Revolution, the "populous village" of Nailsworth had transformed itself into a small town.[1] Urbanization had
accompanied the process of regionalization as the Vale simultaneously lost its isolated character. The greater frequency and
intensity of trade depression between 1825 and 1850, however,
imposed constraints on population growth and urbanization,
aborting Nailsworth's development into a flourishing urban
manufacturing center. By 1850 a trend toward sustained gradual
decline had set in, as both economy and society reestablished a
precarious equilibrium.

   Table 24, constructed from the decennial census lists,[2] provides
an overview of population change during this crisis period. It
offers a periodic breakdown for Horsley and Avening parishes,
which together included Nailsworth, as well as for Stroud parish,
which contained the town of Stroud, the principal market center
of the region.

   Stroud parish's pattern of population growth reflected the
expansion of the town's physical environs,[3] and as the regional
center of a rural-industrial district, its economy remained equally
dependent on both agrarian and manufacturing sectors. Horsley
and Avening, on the contrary, retained a distinctly rural character
throughout the period, despite Nailsworth's partial urbanization
and Horsley's greater dependence on woolen manufacturing. Because Horsley was significantly more industrial than Avening,[4] its
pattern of population change reflected more faithfully the fluctuations of the trade cycle.

   Horsley had a much higher mean population density than Avening despite a much lower growth rate. Its growth rate fell and later
slowed in the first and third decades, when serious depressions

TABLE 24. *Population Growth in Overview: Stroud, Avening, and Horsley Parishes, 1801–1851*

Parish	$\overline{X}^a$	1801	1811	1821	1831	1841	1851
Stroud	1,255	5,422	5,321	7,097	8,607	8,680	8,798
			−1.86%	+33.3%	+21.3%	+0.85%	+1.40%
Avening	285	1,507	1,602	2,016	2,396	2,227	2,321
			+6.30%	+25.8%	+18.8%	−7.10%	+4.20%
Horsley	525	2,971	2,295	3,565	3,690	3,064	2,931
			−1.55%	+21.9%	+3.50%	−16.9%	−4.30%

[a] Average population density in square miles.
Source: Printed census; see text.

occurred, and declined much more steeply when conditions deteriorated further. The years 1836 and 1837, taken together, proved to be a critical turning point. An unusually severe depression in the cloth trade in 1837 and the introduction of the New Poor Law a year earlier caused outmigration to accelerate. Although prosperity returned by 1840 and remained throughout most of the decade, new and severe depressions occurred in 1842 and 1848/49, which contributed to the region's long-term economic decline. By 1851 Stroud and Avening had partially recovered, but Horsley's condition continued to worsen. The rising frequency of outmigration after 1836 was the main cause of Horsley's population loss, and its extent can be estimated from the decennial census figures. Nailsworth's population appears separately in the printed census lists only in 1821 but could be calculated from the census enumerators' returns for 1841 and 1851. Its population for other census years has been estimated from the decennial growth rate of Horsley and Avening combined and the percentage change in Nailsworth's population from 1841 to 1851. Population estimates for lower Nailsworth, in Avening, and for Nailsworth district, in Horsley, likewise, were needed for 1801 to 1831; the former, when added to the Horsley figures for their respective years, yield the actual decennial population levels for the locale[5] (see table 25).

It was also necessary to construct estimates of decennial population levels based solely on natural increase by adding births and

TABLE 25. *Population Estimates for Nailsworth, 1801–1851*

Year	1801	1811	1821	1831	1841	1851
Horsley and Avening	4,478	4,527	5,581	6,086	5,291	5,252
Trend value	5,021.1	5,079.8	5,138.6	5,197.4	—	—
Nailsworth	(434.0)	(454.1)	898	(1,242)	881	731
Nailsworth in Avening	(170.0)	(177.7)	(351.4)	(485.9)	364	270
Nailsworth in Horsley	(264.0)	(276.4)	(546.6)	(756.0)	517	461

Note: All bracketed numbers are estimates of Nailsworth's population when census figures were unavailable; for the method of calculating these values, see text, n. 5.
Source: Printed censuses in Parliamentary Papers and census enumerators' lists for 1841 and 1851, Home Office 107/362 and 107/1966, respectively.

TABLE 26. *Geographic Mobility at Horsley-Nailsworth, 1801–1851*

	1801	1811	1821	1831	1841	1851
a. Actual population	3,141	2,473	3,916	4,176	3,428	3,202
b. Closed-model population	3,141	3,125	3,280	3,634	4,042	4,539
c. a–b: geographic mobility	—	−652	+636	+542	−614	−1,337

Source: See text and appendix D.

subtracting burials from each year, starting with the census figure of 1801. These estimates represent a closed model of population growth based on the resident population and help to account for migration patterns; differences between actual and closed-model decennial figures represent the extent of geographic mobility (see table 26).

Between 1801 and 1811, 652 people migrated from Horsley-Nailsworth. The more rapid introduction of carding engines and shearing frames rendered some grades of woolworkers redundant, and a serious recession occurred in 1808.[6] The loss of 21 percent of the 1801 population was high, but in 1811 the woolen industry still verged on a great expansion. Apart from the recessions of 1816/17 and 1819, general prosperity prevailed until 1826 and by 1821 was reflected in a 58 percent population increase, the result of immigration. Immigration accounted for a further 6.6 percent increase by 1831, although clearly the rate of population growth began to slow.

Stagnation in the cloth trade after 1825 precipitated the slow-down. The fact that a respectable level of immigration could be recorded, however, indicates that stagnation had not yet become critical. The beginning of economic decline coincided with the more rapid growth in the number of loom factories as larger clothiers garnered a greater share of a shrinking market. In fact, the rise of loom factories induced the influx of migrants, despite the declining trade. Manufacturers began employing strangers from outside the county while many local residents remained unemployed.[7] By 1841 chronic stagnation passed into severe depression, which, combined with the New Poor Law, caused 15 percent of the population to migrate; a decade later more than a third of the population had left.

Concern had grown among the landed and employing classes regarding the social consequences of economic stagnation. When confronted with a trade crisis in 1816/17, the leading inhabitants of Minchinhampton, led by David Ricardo, the elder, employed redundant workmen to repair roads and paid them from a fund raised by voluntary subscription.[8] By 1832 these same classes were beginning to embrace paternalist solutions to unemployment tinctured by laissez-faire practices; they began adopting schemes to promote emigration rather than depend on public-works projects. In 1832, for instance, Gloucester parishes assisted emigration by granting three- to four-year advances to pensioners on their allowances and assigning them land in the colonies on condition of their resigning all future claims. Half the money would be paid in England, a free passage would be provided, and the emigrants would receive the remainder on their arrival.[9]

Between 1832 and 1836, a partial revival of the cloth trade made the issue of emigration less pressing. Between 1837 and 1842, however, two especially severe depressions occurred. In 1839 the emigration of more than fifty members of the Shortwood Baptist Church to New South Wales led the deacons of that church to establish a "holy day" devoted entirely to prayer to mark the seriousness of the occassion.[10] Schemes for promoting emigration had thus gained a new urgency. This was especially true because distress had become so acute that the more direct, traditional forms of paternalism could no longer provide an antedote. Nor could normal parochial relief, since the rates had become excessively burdensome, in the view of those required to pay them.[11] After 1836, moreover, poor law unions instead of parishes regulated relief, and the law now prohibited outdoor assistance.

Nevertheless, it was still possible for parishes to borrow funds in order to assist emigrants.[12] Such assistance was limited to the provision of clothing, the rest of the cost having been assumed by the Australian government. The colonial government created a fund from the sale of land to cover the costs of transportation and resettlement, amounting to £35 per married couple.[13] David Ricardo, the second, lord of the manor at Minchinhampton, strongly supported this scheme and calculated that his parish could borrow up to a £1,000 toward realizing it. Such a sum could be repaid within five years at an average annual sum of £224 including interest, and a small annual rate of 15d. in the Pound sufficed to discharge the debt.[14]

Other Gloucester parishes enacted similar schemes. The *Gloucester Journal* reported in 1837 that several families from Horsley had embarked for Australia: "There appears among the poor of these districts," the *Gloucester Journal* observed, "a strong prevailing disposition in favor of emigration to this promising colony, to which numerous parties have already gone."[15] In the same year, the colonial government of South Australia announced the embarkation of several emigrant ships and the provision of free passage for married couples of the working classes, ages fifteen to thirty.[16] In 1839 the Commissioners for the Colonization of South Australia organized a public meeting at Nailsworth "for the purpose of explaining the principles of emigration to...the working classes." Between 200 and 300 persons attended and departed from the meeting in a hopeful spirit.[17] In general, the efforts of local, national, and colonial governments, operating within the context of increasing distress in the manufacturing districts, had resulted in accelerated outmigration. Nationally, between 1825 and 1831, 103,218 persons had emigrated; between 1832 and 1841, 429,775 had emigrated, representing an increase of 316.4 percent.[18] The Horsley-Nailsworth experience reflected the national trend, which persisted throughout the 1840s. By 1851 the true population of the area had fallen 6.6 percent, although an estimate of the closed-model population registers a continuing increase.[19] The difference between them shows a net loss through outmigration of 1,337 persons. This level of outmigration, furthermore, represented a 118 percent increase over that of the previous decade. Indeed, the true population in 1851 was only slightly larger than it had been in 1801.

These findings show, in the first place, that industrialization promoted geographic mobility among the local population. The preindustrial era, in general, was hardly marked by immobility,[20] but the growth of a protoindustrial economy in the countryside from the late seventeenth century had tended to induce residential stability.[21] Outmigration from rural-industrial districts, which shifted toward factory production but failed to urbanize, was caused primarily by the less traditional factors of technological displacement and the vagaries of the trade cycle.[22] Because the Industrial Revolution was associated with capital-intensive reorganization and in such areas with long-term economic decline, the tempo of outmigration was bound to have increased. For the most part, migration of this sort tended to occur over long distances and was often motivated by the needs of subsistence.[23]

Outmigration, as an economic barometer, also conditioned the pattern of natural increase by making the social composition of the remaining population less industrial and, as David Levine has shown for the comparable village of Shepshed, by causing the working classes who remained to restrict their fertility.[24] Noneconomic factors, however, such as the cohesiveness of religious community life, may have induced some would-be migrants to remain behind, or delay departure, and to engage in normal reproductive practices. The period of greatest socioeconomic change had coincided with the intensification of anomie as well as its antithesis, the evangelical revival. We can study the effects of economic and religious-cultural conditions on natural increase by analyzing the time series of Anglican and Nonconformist baptisms and births and, from this vantage point, engage in a fuller discussion of the causes of population growth during this critical era.

Natural Population Change:
Horsley-Nailsworth, 1775–1851

The Industrial Revolution was accompanied by self-sustaining population growth, the causes of which historical demographers have debated extensively.[25] Attempts to explain this change have focused on the issue of whether the crucial cause was a rising birth rate or a falling burial rate. Those who have argued for the primacy of the birth rate have emphasized the impact of economic growth on fertility,[26] while those who have advocated the primacy of the burial rate have regarded economic growth as a by-product of population increase.[27] Nonconformity, as already noted, has been treated in this debate solely as a factor of underestimation in the Anglican record.[28]

This section describes local trends in baptisms, births, and burials for the period 1775–1838,[29] using aggregative analyses of Horsley's Anglican registers,[30] as well as the birth and burial registers of the Dissenters's chapels at Nailsworth.[31] With compound-interest growth rates, it is possible to assess the relative importance of births and burials to the overall pattern of population growth and, at the same time, compare the contributions of Anglicans and Dissenters to the composition of the general growth rate in births. Using multiple regression in time series between 1804 and 1838, it is also possible to determine the effects of economic and religious-cultural changes on short-term fluctuations in births. Before reporting these findings, discussion of the sources on which they are based is necessary, since the combined use of Anglican and Nonconformist registers within a local setting is comparatively unusual.[32]

The Anglican registers of Horsley were chosen because of their consistency and because Horsley itself was more representative of the industrial population than was Avening. Together with Nonconformist registration of births and burials at Shortwood and Forest Green, they represent the best set of demographic records for the industrial population, consonant with the constraints of a local study.[33] A partial exception was made with respect to marriages. Since the law required Dissenters to marry in the parish church, the Avening registration figures were added to those of

Horsley in order to compensate for the possibility of under-registration.[34]

Horsley's baptismal registers have been supplemented by baptismal registration at the Nailsworth Episcopal Chapel. Nailsworth baptisms between 1794 and 1812 represented the incidence of underregistration among Anglicans caused by the locality's relative isolation. Using a ratio of Anglican baptisms at Nailsworth to Horsley parochial baptisms, adjustments were made in the figures for the earlier period, 1775–1793.[35] After 1812, the number of Nailsworth Episcopal baptisms fell dramatically. This change coincided with the introduction of standardized forms to replace the old registration books. The cause was undoubtedly the virtual ending of Nailsworth's isolation, however, as residents had grown accustomed to regular intercourse with the surrounding hinterland. Although the Episcopal Chapel's baptisms have been added to the parochial figures for the 1813–1838 period, the latter may be regarded as substantially representative of all recorded Anglican baptism for the Horsley-Nailsworth region.[36]

Apart from the problem of deliberate underregistration, a difficulty that normally arises with the use of Anglican registers is the extent to which baptisms are truly representative of births.[37] For Horsley, baptismal dates appearing in the parochial registers closely approximate the actual date of birth. Between 1786 and 1812, indeed, the incidence of the number of children over one year of age presented for baptism became more evident. However, Horsley's vicar made note of the ages, a practice that emphasized their exceptional character. Moreover, when infants were presented for baptism beyond the normal two-week period from the date of birth, the vicar recorded their actual birth dates. Again, adjustments of yearly totals were made when the baptismal and birth years did not coincide. The intervals between births and baptisms ranged from 2.5 to 41 weeks, and the median interval was 18.5 weeks. The average number of child baptisms was four per year; they represented a very small proportion of mean Anglican baptisms for the period, which stood at fifty-eight.

Nevertheless, the practice of delayed baptism could have served as a source of underregistration in Anglican baptismal and burial records. Wrigley and Schofield have shown, for instance, that baptism delayed by one month could have seriously affected the number of infant births registered, since infant mortality was often high. They have suggested that between 1775 and 1824 the number of Anglican baptisms at the national level could be inflated by 1.074 for every recorded baptism, and between 1825 and 1875, at the ratio of 1.090; burials could be inflated correspondingly at the ratios of 1.045 and 1.070, respectively.[38] Accordingly, I have applied these inflators to the data collected in appendixes E and F.

From 1813, following the introduction of standardized registration forms, references to the age at baptism or to the birth date ceased, although there was nothing in principle to prevent the continuation of the practice. If the numbers of delayed baptism were small in the pre-1813 period, they probably dwindled to insignificance thereafter. The remoteness of Horsley's outlying districts was responsible for this practice and, as noted previously, ceased to be a factor in the later period.

Nor had a Baptist influence necessarily contributed to delayed baptism.[39] It is true that many of the Anglican laity attended the Shortwood Baptist Church as hearers, but the Baptists drew a careful distinction between the status of member and hearer. They made believers' baptism the condition for membership and prescribed a minimum age of sixteen. There were very few instances of Anglican baptism having occurred so late. Indeed, Baptists were more likely to have influenced Congregationalists, since Dissenters were especially prone to attend each other's services. However, when the Forest Green minister announced his intention to delay the baptism of members' children because of a sudden scruple regarding infant baptism, the church meeting dismissed him soon thereafter.[40] The members preferred infant baptism, despite the presence of a strong Baptist church, with whose followers they had had regular intercourse. The Anglican laity could hardly have been influenced more greatly.

The Forest Green Congregationalists and the Shortwood Baptists each maintained birth records that provide considerable additions to the Anglican totals. The Congregationalists recorded births and baptisms for the entire period from 1775 to 1836. Baptist births, drawn from a marriage register of 200 Baptist families, were recorded only for the period 1800–1836; therefore, earlier Baptist births were estimated from the church membership roll, using annual conversions and annual membership losses as independent variables in a regression model:[41]

$$\text{Baptist births} = 8.84 + (0.24 \times$$
$$\text{conversions}) + (0.31 \times \text{membership loss})$$
$$[2.187] \qquad\qquad [1.542] \; (41)$$
$$[[0.36]] \qquad\qquad [[0.24]] \; N = 37$$

Since both registers recorded actual births, the problem of "representativeness," which arose in the case of Anglican baptisms, is not an issue in quite the same way.

Congregationalist registers provided the most continuous series. Not only do they cover a longer period, but both birth and baptism dates were frequently recorded; the residence of the parents and the maiden name of the mother are sometimes included as well. A government official, responsible for collecting them, exaggerated their degree of incompleteness when he noted that "many births and baptisms have never been entered, others but partially."[42] There was undoubtedly some omission, but his remarks apparently referred only to the one register in which he inscribed them. When all Congregationalist registers are counted, they yield in combination a continuous series in which the only notable defect is the occasional omission of the date of baptism; the date of birth is usually recorded instead. Where the reverse was true, estimates of the birth date were extrapolated from the mean interval between births and baptisms during the decade of the 1820s.[43] For the entire period, 675 Congregationalist births were recorded, equaling 12.3 percent of all births: that "Dissenters viewed baptism strictly as a religious ordinance," as the government official maintained, is an argument that rather favors more complete registration, as this statistic suggests.

The problem of assessing the degree of underregistration in these sources is difficult, however, because we are dealing with a much smaller population than the Anglican, and one subject to an independent structure of growth. The distinction between member and hearer, already noted, was critical. Hearers usually fluctuated between Church and Chapel,[44] and were likely to have had their children baptized in the former. Births or baptisms recorded in Dissenters's registers were only those of members' children. Special factors, therefore, could have influenced Nonconformist birth registration: the age-sex composition of the membership and its potentially irregular growth pattern. Even with a large membership, the number of births might have remained small if the proportion of married members of childbearing age was insufficient. However, membership growth was sufficiently high among Baptists after 1800 to suggest the existence of a normal population, and as we shall see, this growth strongly affected a rapidly rising growth rate in Baptist births.

The Shortwood church roll, from which membership figures have been derived, is especially complete; it records dates of baptism and death, dates and places of emigration, and exclusions. Migration was the most troubling factor since members, prior to their departure, did not always obtain a formal letter of dismissal to a new Baptist church and would therefore remain on the register until the minister sorted out the record. Fortunately, the minister made periodic adjustments so that the document on which analysis has been based appears trustworthy.

As a group, Dissenters' registers offer a reasonably complete picture of Nonconformist demographic trends. In general, Baptist births had the greatest impact; from 1800 to 1836 alone, they numbered 746, or 42 percent of all Nonconformist births during the entire period under study. Congregationalist births, however, increased dramatically from 1820 as a result of the schism that occurred at the Forest Green Church in that year.[45] Quaker births, which numbered only forty for the period under study, were also added to the Nonconformist totals. If we include the estimates of Baptist births for the 1775–1799 period, the total number of Nonconformist births reaches 1,799, or 32.8 percent of all births recorded between 1775 and 1836. The magnitude of this figure suggests that recorded Nonconformist births, including estimates, may be treated as representative of all such births.

It is possible, then, to compare the growth rates in Nonconformist and Anglican births to determine their importance with respect to the growth rates in all births from 1775–1838. Such a comparison also requires analysis of the varying responses of Anglican, Baptist, and Congregationalist births to economic fluctuations. The dichotomy between sect and denomination is especially relevant in this respect. All religious groups, except the Quakers, became more denominational during the period under study, a change that undermined their cohesiveness as communi-

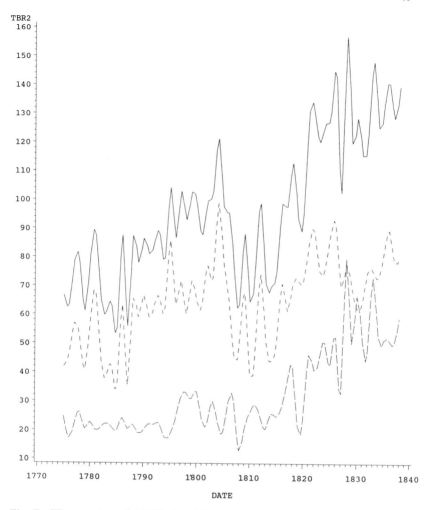

Fig. 7. Time-series of All Births, 1775–1838.

Key: Solid Line = All Births/Baptisms
Small Broken Line = Anglican Baptisms
Large Broken Line = Dissenter Births

ties and their abilities to resist exogenous shocks emanating from a changing economy. Yet there were differences in degree among them. Because of a stable competent ministry, the Baptists achieved an optimal balance between the large membership growth issuing from the evangelical revival and the persistence of sectarian practices. Their stronger sense of community immunized

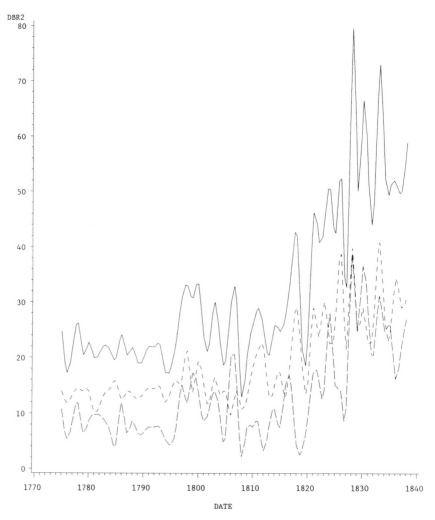

Fig. 8. Time-series of Nonconformist Births 1775–1838.

Key: Solid Line = All Dissenter Births
Small Broken Line = Baptist Births
Large Broken Line = Congregationalist Births

them more effectively (although never completely) against the
negative consequences of economic change.

If we compare the growth rates of Anglican and Nonconformist
births, we can see how their importance to the general growth rate
in births shifted during the 1775–1838 interval (see figs. 7 and 8
and table 27). Births are plotted in time series in figures 8 and 9,

TABLE 27. *Compound-Interest Growth Rates in Births, 1775–1838*

	Anglican baptism	Dissenter births	Total
1775–1799	2.01	0.92	1.7
1800–1838	0.64	3.26	1.5
1775–1838	0.74	2.20	1.2

Note: These figures measure average percent per annum changes.
Source: Parochial and Dissenters' Chapel registers; see text.

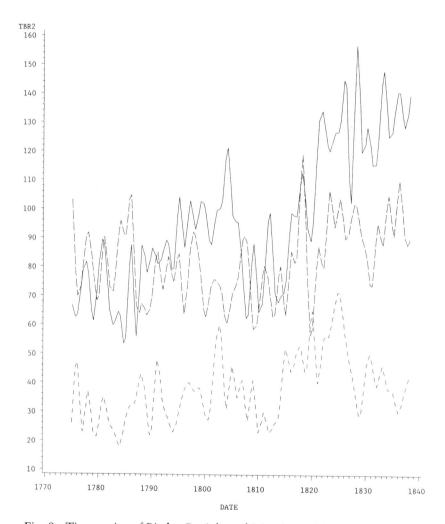

Fig. 9. Time-series of Births, Burials and Marriages 1775–1838.
Key: Solid Line = All Births/Baptisms
Small Broken Line = Marriages
Large Broken Line = Burials

and their growth rates appear in table 27. The subperiods, 1775–1799 and 1800–1838, corresponded broadly to the phases of protoindustrialization and industrial takeoff, respectively. The second phase also marked the intensification of the evangelical revival. In the first phase Anglican births grew faster than Dissenters' births but tapered off significantly in the second phase, when Dissenters' births rose rapidly. The rising general growth rate in births over the entire period was due mainly to the growth in Nonconformist births after 1800. The volume of Nonconformist births was perhaps more sensitive to religious revival than to economic flux, while the reverse seems to have been true for Anglicans.

This analysis becomes complicated, however, by the fact that the second phase was a period both of prosperity and contraction, as well as one of structural transformation of the economy. The shift to the factory system and depressions in the cloth trade induced anomie and could be expected to have had a damping effect on population.[46] Economic growth, although the product of structural transformation, could also bring intervals of prosperity that would stimulate reproduction. Membership growth in Nonconformist churches might have benefited in either case; some joined out of despair and others, from feelings of optimism. We need to examine the effects of short-term fluctuations in economic indices on Anglican and Nonconformist births to obtain a better picture of the causal relations (see table 28).

Multiple-regression analyses accomplished this task by using the residuals of average annual wheat prices[47] and the original observations of cloth manufacturing output[48] as one-year, lagged independent variables for the 1804–1838 period. The unstandardized coefficients of both independent variables, as revealed in table 28, proved strong predictors of Anglican baptisms. The negative direction of the coefficient for "Rswheat" (residuals of wheat prices) meant that a decline in price in any given year stimulated reproduction, while a corresponding rise in cloth manufacturing output had a similar effect, and vice versa. By contrast, only cloth manufacturing output significantly affected reproduction among Dissenters, suggesting that as a group they were more proletarian, since the level of output necessarily serves as a surrogate for employment in the industry; the volume of their births, in other words, remained unaffected by agricultural rhythms (see table 29).

TABLE 28. *Regression Coefficients: Wheat Prices (Residuals) and Cloth Production on All Baptisms and Births,* 1804–1838

D-var	I-var	df	b	t	Prob > t	B	Applies to the whole model				
							F	Prob > F	R^2_{adj}	DW^a	Ar
Anglican baptism	Rswheat	1	-2.65	-2.93	0.0062	-0.41	9.634	0.0006	0.3435	1.41	0.27
	Cloth	1	0.000033	3.29	0.0025	0.46					
Dissenter births	Rswheat	1	-0.99	-0.86	0.397	-0.13	5.330	0.01	0.2079	1.45	0.24
	Cloth	1	0.000041	3.16	0.003	0.49					
Total Baptist births	Rswheat	1	-3.65	-2.17	0.038	-0.30	10.040	0.0004	0.3540	1.4	0.26
	Cloth	1	0.000075	3.95	0.0004	0.55					

Key: "Rswheat" = residuals of wheat prices; "Cloth" = annual cloth output (in tables 29, 35, and 36 also); R^2_{adj} = adjusted R^2; b = parameter estimate, or slope; t = t-ratio; Prob > t = probability of obtaining a value greater than t; B = standardized b; F = F-ratio; Prob > F = probability of obtaining a value greater than F; Ar = first-order autocorrelation coefficient.

[a] The term DW refers to the Durbin-Watson statistic; values over 1.7 indicate no problem with autocorrelation; values between 0.82 and 1.7 lay within an ambiguous zone, and their degrees of significance depend on the size of the autocorrelation, reported next to DW. Values below 0.82 clearly have the problem of autocorrelation. See Wonnacott and Wonnacott, *Econometrics,* pp. 142 and 147.

TABLE 29. *Regression Coefficients: Wheat Prices (Residuals) and Cloth Production on Nonconformist Births,* 1804–1838

D-var	I-var	df	b	t	Prob>t	B	F	Prob>F	R^2_{adj}	DW[a]	Ar
								Applies to the whole model			
Baptist births											
	Rswheat	1	−0.242	−0.453	0.6534	−0.06	6.875	0.0034	0.2626	1.76	0.12
	Cloth	1	0.000022	3.68	0.0009	0.55					
Congregationalist births											
	Rswheat	1	−0.63	−0.924	0.362	−0.156	2.006	0.151	0.05	1.4	0.26
	Cloth	1	0.0000138	1.787	0.08[a]	0.302					
Dissenter births											
	Rswheat	1	−0.994	−0.939	0.355	−0.14	5.558	0.0087	0.216	1.5	0.27
	Cloth	1	0.000038	3.21	0.0031	0.49					

Note: This analysis is based on the uninflated values for Baptist, Congregationalist, and the total of Dissenters' births, appearing in appendix E. The total of Dissenters' births in previous analyses was inflated to compensate for the possible effects of delayed baptism on infant mortality, principally in order to facilitate comparisons with Anglican baptisms. This inflation factor had no effect, however, on the regressions of the original observations of Baptist and Congregationalist births and, in fact, produced only very marginal increases in their totals. For these reasons, I chose to dispense with the inflation factor in making intra-Nonconformist comparisons.

[a] Although falling slightly below the 0.05 level, I find a probability of 92.0 percent to be acceptably significant.

Nevertheless, Baptists had a more proletarian following than did Congregationalists, as table 29 illustrates. Both responded positively and significantly only to cloth-manufacturing output, but this tendency was more clearly marked among the Baptists.

In general, these findings suggest that levels of outmigration among Anglicans and Dissenters differed, with the remaining Anglican population becoming less industrial. Dissenters, because of the greater cohesiveness of their community life, retained more of an industrial working-class following, although important differences were still discernible among them. Congregationalist births, as noted earlier, increased rapidly from about 1820, and this trend coincided in that same year with the schismatic formation of a new Congregationalist church at Lower Forest Green. Those who remained at Upper Forest Green did so because of an intense attachment to that church's history and traditions; those who moved to Lower Forest Green followed the lead of wealthier members of the original congregation who sought a larger following by closer proximity to Nailsworth, which had grown into a small town.

The schism reflected the unavoidable tension between sectarian and denominational tendencies. The church at Upper Forest Green retained greater élan as a community, while the church at Lower Forest Green, although benefiting initially from its new locale, appeared more vulnerable to subsequent trade depressions, which by 1845 severely damaged its membership stability.[49] Still, when combined in time series, the births of both Congregationalist churches appear especially high after 1820. The Shortwood Baptists bridged the sect/denomination divide more successfully; despite their complaints about membership turnover,[50] they maintained greater cohesiveness throughout the entire period and retained, as we have seen, more of a working-class following.

Evangelical religion, combined with a more effective ministry, made possible this greater cohesiveness and in doing so contributed to the growth in Baptist births. A multiple regression of cloth output, annual male and female conversions, and total annual membership loss shows only the first and last variables explaining variance in Baptist births.[51] When cloth output and membership loss increased, Baptist births rose, despite the absence of a correlation between the independent variables (see table 30).

TABLE 30. *Regression Coefficients: Cloth Production, Conversions, and Members Lost on Baptist Births, 1804–1838*

D-var	I-var	df	b	t	Prob > t	B
Baptist births						
	Cloth	1	0.0000497	3.262	0.0028	0.403305
	Male con-versions	1	0.290144	1.530	0.1369	0.222142
	Female con-versions	1	−0.045533	−0.342	0.7350	−0.051169
	Total mem-bership loss	1	0.576898	4.837	0.0001	0.575423

Note: $F = 12.054$, $df = 4$, $N = 33$, Prob $> F$ 0.0001, $R^2_{adj} = 0.5726$; $DW = 1.423$, first-order autocorrelation coefficient $= 0.281$.

Baptist births, in other words, rose in response to a more productive industry, however much this higher productivity issued from a declining number of firms. A declining number of firms meant higher average unemployment and increased migration, which accounted for a meaningful proportion of Baptist membership loss. Such loss should theoretically have had a damping effect on reproduction, but instead we find an increase in the number of births.

The intensity of Baptist evangelicalism explains this apparent anomaly. The conversion rate tended to rise during periods of trade depression because of the pervasive anomie induced by such crises, although a high level of membership loss, attributable to either rising mortality or higher outmigration, accompanied and modified these gains. New converts, both male and female, contributed little to a rise in Baptist births; however, among old members who stayed behind, reproduction increased. Baptist births rose at times when members displayed an especially strong attachment to their community and thereby offset the constraining effects of industrial involution. Evangelicalism, in other words, gave hope where despair and falling births might otherwise have prevailed. This effect of religious culture on the growth in Baptist births can be further illustrated by adding another membership

TABLE 31. *Regression Coefficients: Cloth Production, Members Lost, and Total Membership on Baptist Births, 1804–1838*

D-var	I-var	df	b	t	Prob > t	B
Baptist births						
	Cloth	1	0.00000389	0.716	0.4795	0.096756
	Total membership loss	1	0.452854	4.237	0.0002	0.451696
	Total membership	1	0.035732	3.494	0.0015	0.490351

Note: $F = 24.043$, $df = 3$, $N = 33$, Prob > F 0.0001, $R^2_{adj} = 0.6769$; $DW = 1.716$, first-order autocorrelation (auto-R) = 0.101.

variable to the same regression model, the effect of which appears in table 31.

Total membership (the annual base membership after adjustments for losses and conversions) reflected the changing strength of the Baptist church as a community and appears in time series in chapter 9 (fig. 21). Total membership loss remained highly significant, but fluctuations in cloth output ceased to have any effect. Total membership proved to be highly significant as well; since total membership was also correlated with cloth output, it absorbed a great deal of the variance this last variable had once explained,[52] thereby revealing how much the cohesiveness of Baptist community life could shield members from exogenous shocks.[53]

Despite the effects of membership loss, in other words, the sharp growth in total membership until 1850 shows that the communal life of the Baptist church retained a high tensile strength. This durability enabled its members to weather the anomie of the Industrial Revolution and long-term economic decline that paradoxically accompanied it; a high growth rate in Baptist births was the result.

A combination of economic and cultural conditions, therefore, determined the growth rate in all births. Demographers have sometimes underestimated cultural considerations, but these findings show that the concept of community, informed by a religious bond, vindicates their importance to the demographic revolution. The contribution of a rising growth rate in births to overall population growth remains to be considered. To do so, we must compare the growth in all births to the movement of burials.

A combination of economic and cultural conditions also affected the growth rate in burials. Those who have argued for the primacy of its fall in explaining population advance have stressed the centrality of eighteenth-century medical progress.[54] Defenders of the primacy of a rising birth rate have treated the falling burial rate as only a by-product of a shift in the age structure of the population, itself the result of economic factors, and have dismissed the significance of medical advances. They have suggested, moreover, that the progress of industrialization in the early nineteenth century caused the burial rate to rise.[55] Before comparing births and burials at Horsley-Nailsworth in light of this controversy, we must construct the time series for burials.

The growth in burials for the Horlsey-Nailsworth area, like the growth rate in births, was calculated from a composite of values drawn from Anglican and Dissenter registers. The Shortwood Baptists maintained a burial register from 1808 that doubles the number of burials recorded in the Horsley parish register (Baptist burials for the 1775–1807 period were estimated).[56] Indeed, most of those buried at Shortwood were not members of the Baptist church. Shortwood burials, therefore, added significantly to the total number of burials for the region. Nonconformist burials also included the burial registration figures for the Quakers and Congregationalists, each of whom had maintained separate grounds. The number of Quaker burials was predictably small, but Congregationalist registration was simply incomplete. Nevertheless, their registers provided sufficient detail to make estimates for missing years.[57] If burials in Congregationalist grounds seemed few, however, this was due to the Congregationalist practice of using the Baptist burial ground: On May 31, 1827, Mary Heskins, the wife of Francis Heskins, carpenter, had been buried, and "both [were] inter'd by Mr. Edkins [*sic*]," the Congregationalist minister.[58] By combining Quaker, Congregational, Baptist, and Anglican registration figures, together with the inflators employed by Wrigley and Schofield,[59] an accurate growth rate in burials for the region can be established.

The findings are summarized in tables 32 to 34, and the

TABLE 32. *Compound-Interest Growth Rates in Burials and Total Births, Horsley-Nailsworth, 1775–1838[a]*

Period	Burials	Births
1775–1799	−0.35	1.7
1800–1838	0.99	1.5
1775–1838	0.28	1.2

[a]Expressed as percent per annum.
Source: See text.

TABLE 33. *Crude Vital Rates at Horsley-Nailsworth, 1781–1841*

	1781	1791	1801	1811	1821	1831	1841
Population	2,894	2,994	3,141	2,473	3,916	4,176	3,428
Total births	70	80	92	103	114	125	136
Total burials	76	79	81	83	86	88	90
Crude birth rate	24	27	30	42	29	30	40
Crude burial rate	26	26	26	34	22	21	26

Note: Births and burials represent the trend values for these years, plotted between 1775 and 1841. Observations between 1837 and 1841 are estimates derived from a SAS forecasting program; see appendixes D, E, and F.
Source: The population is for Horsley-Nailsworth, taken from tables 24 and 25 for the 1801–1841 period; population levels for 1781 and 1791 are backward linear estimates.

observations are plotted in time series in figure 9. The findings support the neo-Malthusian view, which defends the primacy of rising births. A rising growth rate in births of 1.7 percent per annum in the late eighteenth century clearly outstripped a falling growth rate in burials of −0.35 percent per annum. If burials had moved faster, they might have qualified as an independent variable, the decline of which resulted from advances in medical science. Since burials moved more slowly, their general decline more likely resulted from a previous fall in the age at first marriage, which neo-Malthusians have identified as the primary cause of population growth. The growth rate in burials, furthermore, had begun to rise during the early nineteenth century, although moderately.

TABLE 34. *Crude Vital Rates: England and Wales, 1781–1841*

	1781	1791	1801	1811	1821	1831	1841
Crude birth rate	35.5	38.4	33.9	39.9	41.1	35.2	35.9
Crude burial rate	29.7	25.3	28.0	26.5	23.5	22.4	21.9

Source: Calculated from Wrigley and Schofield, *The Population History of England*, pp. 208–209, table 7.8, which contains population figures, and pp. 500–501, table A2.3, which contains annual numbers of births and deaths.

When expressed as crude vital rates, we can see a similar pattern at work (see table 33). The burial rate remained low and flat between 1781 and 1801, rose noticeably between 1801 and 1811, and fell precipitously in the following two decades, only to rise moderately during the 1830s. From 1791 the birth rate remained noticeably higher than the burial rate, although fluctuating in a similar way.[60] Nationally, as table 34 reveals, the death rate fluctuated more erratically between 1781 and 1811; it fell noticeably thereafter and to levels not much higher than those at Horsley-Nailsworth. Indeed, national death rates throughout this period did not greatly differ from those at Horsley-Nailsworth, except in 1811. National birth rates, however, were significantly higher in only 1781, 1791, and 1821; this difference simply reflected local variation.[61] In 1801, 1811, 1831, and 1841, national birth rates closely approximated those of the locality and sometimes fell below them.

The rising growth rate in burials at Horsley-Nailsworth during the early Industrial Revolution implies a general deterioration of living standards. However, the fall in the crude burial rate after 1811 and its relative flatness thereafter suggests otherwise for most of the period under study. Indeed, an analysis of mortality by age-sex cohort shows industrialization to have had a less catastrophic effect than anticipated.

Mortality by Age-Sex Cohort, 1808–1838

Age data for the study of mortality at Horsley-Nailsworth were available only from the Anglican and Baptist registers, covering

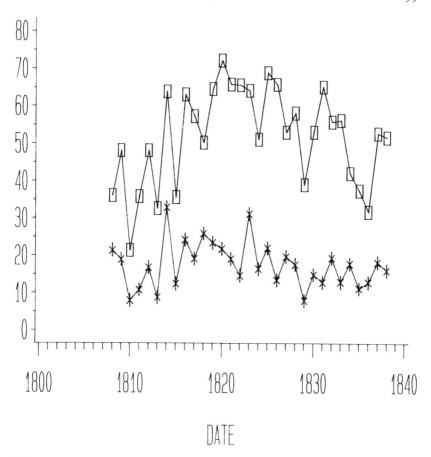

Fig. 10. Time series of infant mortality as percent of births and youth burials, 1808–1838.

Key: Star = Infant Burials as P.C. of Births
Square = Infant Burials as P.C. of Youth Burials

the 1808–1838 period (see fig. 10). Nonetheless, burials from these sources constituted the great majority of all recorded burials. Infant mortality represented an important part of all burials, but adult burials naturally predominated.

Infant burials, when expressed as a percentage of all births,[62] showed no substantial trend; nor did child and adolescent burials (ages two to twelve and thirteen to seventeen, respectively) when expressed as a percentage of infant, child, and adolescent burials combined (see fig. 11). This absence of a trend suggests that neith-

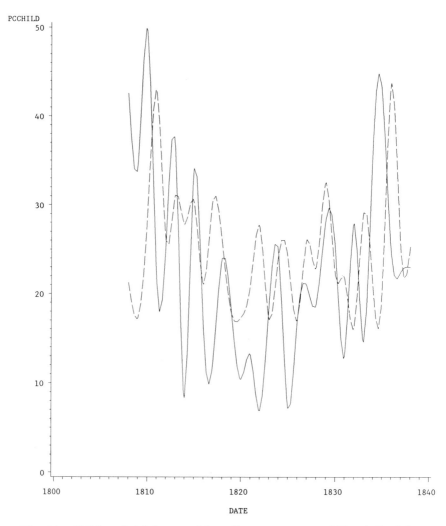

Fig. 11. Child and Adolescent Mortality as per cent of Youth Burials, 1808–1838.

Key: Solid Line = Children 2–12 Years
        Broken Line = Adolescents, 13–17 Years

er the partial urbanization of Nailsworth nor the industrialization of Horsley had significant long-term effects on the mortality of the younger cohorts.[63] Nevertheless, the agrarian sector of the economy still exercised some influence.

Regression analysis of the residuals of wheat prices and annual cloth output, as one-year lagged independent variables, on infant, child, and adolescent burials, respectively, showed only the residuals of wheat prices as having any effect. Infant burials, in absolute numbers, were revealed to be sensitive to changes in wheat prices, although inversely; a rise in wheat prices, which reflected scarcity, registered a fall in infant mortality (see table 35). In years of rising wheat prices malnutrition must have caused fewer pregnancies to be brought successfully to term,[64] while also resulting in higher mortality among women of childbearing age, as the regression analysis in table 36 clearly indicates (see also figs. 12 to 14).[65] At other times a more normal and apparently higher number of births could be registered.

The sensitivity of infant and female mortality to wheat prices echoed a preindustrial, Malthusian pattern, while the effect of the trade cycle involves more directly the controversy concerning living standards under industrialization.[66] The absence of any effect of trade-cycle fluctuations on child and adolescent mortality clearly supports the optimists in this debate; a more selective impact is apparent, however, in a similar analysis of adult mortality. Regressions of the residuals of wheat prices and cloth output, as one-year lagged independent variables, on adult mortality (table 36) reveals only the mortality of males above age sixty-five responding to trade-cycle fluctuations; in their case, mortality responded positively to rises in production. Age, combined with the intensification of work under the factory system, easily explains such vulnerability, but the immunity demonstrated by other adults overshadows this finding to favor the optimists' position.

In terms of gender, female burials accounted for 53 percent of adult burials, while male burials represented 47 percent. The difference may have been due partly to the uneven incidence of outmigration, about which contemporaries speculated, and which seems to have been reflected in the sex ratio of the population. Contemporaries certainly complained about the demoralizing impact of outmigration, which accelerated, as we have seen, during

TABLE 35. *Regression Coefficients: Wheat Prices (Residuals) and Cloth Production on Infant, Child, and Adolescent Burials, 1808–1838*

D-var	I-var	df	b	t	Prob>t	B	Applies to the whole model				
							F	Prob>F	R^2_{adj}	DW	Ar
Infant burials[a]	Rswheat	1	−1.51	−2.89	0.007	−0.48	4.271	0.02	0.18	2.4	−0.2
	Cloth	1	0.000022	0.37	0.713	0.06					
Child burials	Rswheat	1	0.02	0.06	0.948	0.01	0.163	0.85	−0.06	1.8	0.11
	Cloth	1	0.0000023	0.56	0.574	0.10					
Adolescent burials	Rswheat	1	−0.12	−0.39	0.695	−0.07	0.463	0.63	−0.03	2.0	−0.04
	Cloth	1	0.0000030	0.86	0.394	0.16					

[a]Infant burials have been inflated to adjust for the registration effects of delayed baptism; see n. 38 and accompanying text. The same regression, when performed on uninflated values, yielded virtually identical results.

TABLE 36. *Regression Coefficients: Wheat Prices (Residuals) and Cloth Production on Adult Burials by Age Cohort, 1808–1838*

D-var	I-var	df	b	t	Prob>t	B	F	Prob>F	R^2_{adj}	DW	Ar
							Applies to the whole model				
Males 18–49							2.185	0.13	0.075	2.1	−0.03
	Rswheat	1	−0.36	−1.50	0.14	−0.26					
	Cloth	1	0.0000038	1.40	0.17	0.25					
Females 18–49							2.569	0.09	0.09	2.2	−0.11
	Rswheat	1	0.37	2.03	0.05	0.35					
	Cloth	1	0.0000022	1.058	0.29	0.18					
Males 50–64							0.117	0.88	−0.06	2.1	−0.06
	Rswheat	1	−0.06	−0.39	0.69	−0.07					
	Cloth	1	−5.42461	−0.29	0.77	−0.05					
Females 50–64							0.373	0.69	−0.04	1.7	0.12
	Rwsheat	1	−0.17	−0.78	0.43	−0.14					
	Cloth	1	8.12857	0.32	0.74	0.06					
Males 65+							4.865	0.01	0.21	1.9	0.02
	Rswheat	1	−0.14	0.28	−0.50	−0.61					
	Cloth	1	0.0000098	3.06	0.004	0.50					
Females 65+							0.667	0.52	−0.02	2.3	−0.09
	Rswheat	1	0.13	0.41	0.68	0.07					
	Cloth	1	0.000004	1.09	0.28	0.20					

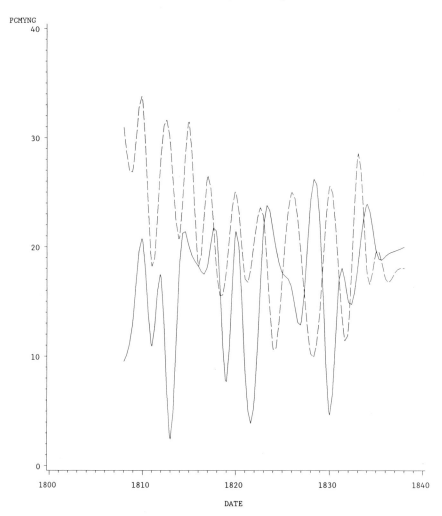

Fig. 12. Young Adult Mortality, Ages 18–49, by Gender, 1808–1838
As Percent of Adult Burials.

Key: Solid Line = Males
Broken Line = Females

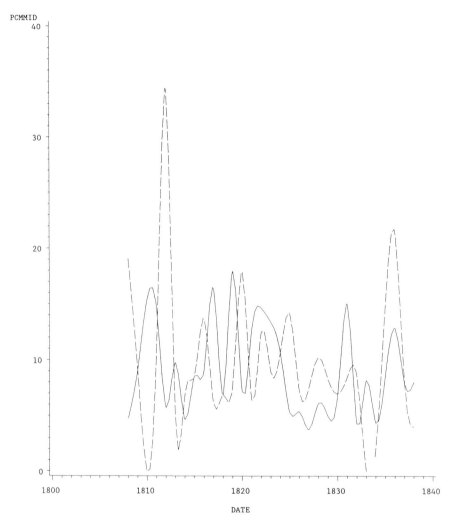

Fig. 13. Middle Ages Mortality, Ages 50–64, by Gender, 1808–1838
As Percent of Adult Burials.

Key: Solid Line = Males
      Broken Line = Females

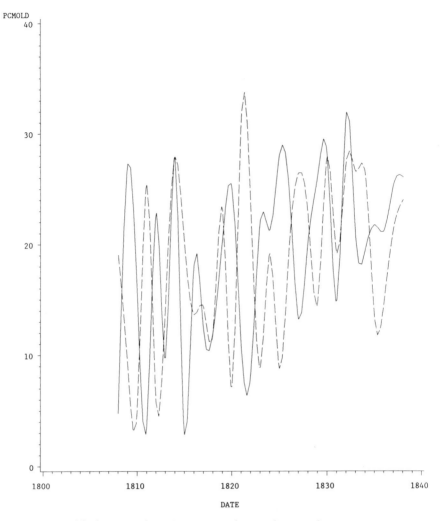

Fig. 14. Elderly Mortality, Ages 65 and over, by Gender, 1808–1838
As Percent of Adult Burials.

Key: Solid Line = Males
Broken Line = Females

the 1840s.[67] Further examination is required, however, to determine the extent of decline in the quality of life over this period; analyses of age-sex configurations can facilitate resolution of this issue.

The Age-Sex Structure in 1841 and 1851

Age pyramids have been constructed for the sample districts of Shortwood, Newmarket, Forest Green, and Winsoredge. These were the most important of the Vale hamlets, since they contained a much higher proportion of the industrial population than did Nailsworth village, however less urbanized they remained. The age pyramids appear as figures 15 and 16 with accompanying tables 37 and 38, respectively. Table 39 summarizes the pyramid structures by age groups only and presents the results of difference-of-proportions tests, designed to measure the extent of change during the decade.

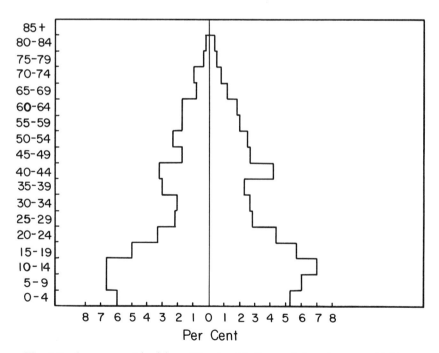

Fig. 15. Age pyramid of four Horsley-Nailsworth hamlets, ca. 1841.

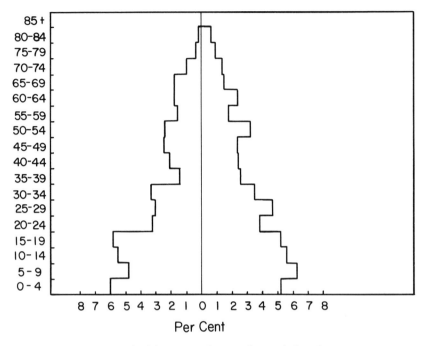

Fig. 16. Age pyramid of four Horsley-Nailsworth hamlets, ca. 1851.

The pyramids depict unevenly distributed population loss. Net loss for the entire sample was 3.2 percent, just below the 6.6 percent figure for Horsley-Nailsworth.[68] The sex ratio continued to favor women, although not as much as in 1841. Table 37 shows that very few age cohorts experienced change. Among the very young, ages zero to nineteen, only those in cohort ten to fourteen fell significantly as a proportion of the population. At the opposite end of the pyramid, among the aged, only cohort sixty-five to sixty-nine increased significantly. The middle cohorts, ages forty-five to sixty-four, hardly changed, but among young adults, ages twenty-five to thirty-four, and the early-middle-age cohorts, thirty-five to thirty-nine and forty to forty-four, the changes were startling. The proportion of young adults increased significantly, while the proportion of the early-middle-age cohorts declined correspondingly. The negative impact of outmigration therefore registered in the early-middle-age cohorts, in a fall in the proportion

TABLE 37. *Age-Pyramid Data Values, 1841 (for fig. 15)*

	Males		Females		Total	
Age group	N	%	N	%	N	%
0–4	78	5.95	70	5.34	148	11.29
5–9	86	6.56	79	6.03	165	12.59
10–14	86	6.56	93	7.09	179	13.66
15–19	65	4.96	75	5.74	140	10.68
20–24	43	3.28	57	4.35	100	7.63
25–29	29	2.21	38	2.90	67	5.11
30–34	27	2.06	36	2.74	63	4.80
35–39	39	2.97	30	2.29	69	5.26
40–44	42	3.20	55	4.19	97	7.40
45–49	22	1.68	35	2.67	57	4.35
50–54	30	2.29	33	2.51	63	4.80
55–59	22	1.68	27	2.06	49	3.74
60–64	22	1.68	23	1.75	45	3.43
65–69	11	0.83	16	1.22	27	2.06
70–74	12	0.91	10	0.75	22	1.68
75–79	4	0.30	7	0.53	11	0.83
80–84	3	0.22	5	0.38	8	0.60
Totals	621	47.34	689	52.53	1,310	99.90

Note: The hamlets analyzed include Newmarket, Shortwood, Forest Green, and Winsoredge. The overall sex ratio is 1,109 women per 1,000 males.

of the very young, and, equally, in a rise in the proportion of the aged. The apparent stability of most of the cohorts, however, together with an increase in the proportion of young adults, seems to have offset the tendency toward decline. The issue to be addressed is whether the trend toward decline was more or less important than the trend toward improvement.

This question can be answered by grouping the frequencies of the changing age cohorts into the variables "decline" and "improvement" and testing their differences in a contingency table against the years 1841 and 1851 (see table 40). Although the variable "decline" continued to show significantly higher frequencies than did the variable "improvement," the former fell in number while the latter increased. Chi-square analysis reveals the overall differences to have been significant, and the weight of each cell

TABLE 38. *Age-Pyramid Data Values, 1851 (for fig. 16)*

Age group	Males		Females		Total	
	N	%	N	%	N	%
0–4	76	5.99	66	5.20	142	11.19
5–9	61	4.81	80	6.30	141	11.11
10–14	70	5.52	71	5.59	141	11.11
15–19	74	5.83	66	5.20	140	11.04
20–24	40	3.15	48	3.78	88	6.94
25–29	38	2.99	60	4.73	98	7.72
30–34	42	3.31	45	3.54	87	6.86
35–39	18	1.41	30	2.36	48	3.78
40–44	27	2.12	32	2.52	59	4.65
45–49	31	2.44	31	2.44	31	2.44
50–54	30	2.36	40	3.15	70	5.52
55–59	20	1.57	23	1.81	43	3.39
60–64	21	1.65	19	1.49	40	3.15
65–69	21	1.65	19	1.49	40	3.15
70–74	12	0.94	18	1.41	30	2.36
75–79	4	0.31	12	0.94	16	1.26
80–84	3	0.23	8	0.63	11	0.86
Totals	588	46.28	680	53.63	1,268	99.9

Note: The overall sex ratio for the same hamlets treated in table 37 is 1,156 women per 1,000 men.

frequency shows the improvement variable in 1851 to have made the greatest contribution.

On balance, the trend toward improvement offset the trend toward decline, despite the overall net loss of population. Indeed, the residual population in 1851 may have been even more robust. The depressions of 1842 and 1848/49 forced out many of the early-middle-age cohorts with their families; however, the stabilization of the factory system during this decade, combined with the otherwise prosperous character of the period, permitted a significant rise in the number of young adults, while most other cohorts remained stable. In general, these findings affirm the impression of population loss through outmigration from the mid-1830s, but they also suggest that contemporary complaints about the consequences of such movement, while prophetic, were still

TABLE 39. *Summary of Age-Pyramid Data, 1841–1851 with Difference-of-Proportions Tests*

Age groups	1841		1851		Z-score	P[a]
	Freq.	Prop.	Freq.	Prop.		
0–4	148	0.112	142	0.111	0.00	0.5
5–9	165	0.125	141	0.111	1.10	0.14
10–14	179	0.136	141	0.111	1.93	0.03[b]
15–19	140	0.106	140	0.110	−0.32	0.37
20–24	100	0.076	88	0.069	0.01	0.49
25–29	67	0.051	98	0.077	−2.70	0.00[b]
30–34	63	0.048	87	0.068	−2.71	0.00[b]
35–39	69	0.052	48	0.037	1.85	0.03[b]
40–44	97	0.074	59	0.046	2.98	0.00[b]
45–49	57	0.043	62	0.048	−0.60	0.27
50–54	63	0.048	70	0.055	−0.80	0.21
55–59	49	0.037	43	0.033	0.55	0.29
60–64	45	0.034	52	0.041	−0.93	0.18
65–69	27	0.020	40	0.031	−1.77	0.04[b]
70–74	22	0.016	30	0.023	−1.28	0.10
75–79	11	0.008	16	0.012	−1.02	0.15
80–84	8	0.006	11	0.008	−0.06	0.27
	$N_1 = 1,310$		$N_2 = 1,268$		% change = −3.2	

[a] Significance levels of 0.05 or less were regarded as the appropriate probability levels, at which differences between frequencies could be considered significant. A 0.05 significance level means that there is a 95 percent probability that the difference is significant.

[b] The difference between proportions was significant. For a discussion of difference-of-proportions tests, see Blalock, *Social Statistics*, pp. 229–230.

TABLE 40. *Qualitative shift in Age Composition, 1841–1851*

	1841	ev[a]	w	1851	ev	w	Total
Improvement	130	(162)	(6.2)	185	(153)	(6.8)	315
Decline	372	(339)	(3.0)	288	(320)	(3.2)	660
	502			473			975

Note: $\chi^2 = 19.445$; $df = 1$, $\chi^2 \geq 3.841$ at the 0.05 significance level; ev = expected value under the null hypothesis; w = weight or contribution of each cell frequency to chi-square.

premature in 1851. Population loss was sufficiently significant, however, to have aborted the area's development into a large urban manufacturing center, despite its industrialization and passage through the demographic revolution.

Summary and Conclusion

There has been considerable debate regarding the character of the demographic revolution. This chapter supports the neo-Malthusian view, which has argued for the primacy of the rising birth rate. The compound-interest growth rate in births at Horsley-Nailsworth, the most industrial part of the Vale settlement, dramatically outstripped the falling growth rate in burials; comparative analysis of local and national crude vital rates revealed a similar pattern.

Yet the rising growth rate in births after 1800 owed much to the Evangelical Revival as manifest among Nonconformists, especially the Shortwood Baptists. The rising growth rate in Nonconformist births diverged so dramatically from that of the Anglican after 1800 as to suggest the existence of a religious-fertility differential.[69] Multiple-regression analyses revealed, furthermore, that only Baptist births remained especially sensitive to trade-cycle fluctuations and that high Baptist membership growth offset their negative consequences. The same analyses suggest that Anglicans and Congregationalists each lost a significant working-class following through outmigration. The Revival had stimulated an atmosphere of communal solidarity most successfully among Baptists, ameliorating the anomie of industrialization and finding expression in their demographic behavior. Cultural as well as economic considerations clearly contributed to population changes.

The movement of population also revealed the effects of industrialization on living standards. The growth rate in burials at Horsley-Nailsworth rose slightly after 1800, a pattern conforming to a national trend and suggesting some deterioration. When examined by age-sex cohort, however, multiple-regression analyses on balance supported the optimists' argument in this national debate.[70] Infant burials showed a negative sensitivity to wheat price fluctuations, while burials of women of childbearing age responded positively, both echoes of preindustrial experience and patterns that departed from national trends.[71] Neither child, adolescent, nor young adult mortality showed sensitivity to trade-cycle fluctuations; only burials of males sixty-five years and over did so.

Trade-cycle fluctuations had the additional effect of stimulating outmigration after 1800, with the outflow reaching crisis proportions after 1826. Although outmigration accelerated under the pressure of more frequent and intense trade depressions, a comparative analysis of age structures of a sample of Nailsworth hamlets in the 1840s revealed that the crisis had passed by 1851 and a temporary restabilization was achieved. Nailsworth eventually declined by attrition, in proportion to the gradual decay of its cloth trade after midcentury.

Chapter Six

Capital and Labor in the Industrial Revolution

"These valleys," wrote a Nailsworth local historian in 1880, "were [once] the center of the West of England cloth trade..., but trade declined, workmen and their families were driven elsewhere, mills were closed, and the masters were finding their occupations gone."[1] Gloucester possessed a thriving woolen trade from the late twelfth century until the Industrial Revolution, but between 1750 and 1850, Yorkshire usurped its long-standing premier position.[2] The lower district, containing Uley, Dursley, and Wotton-under-Edge, fell into disarray by 1835, while the Stroud district declined more gradually between 1830 and 1880.[3]

The anomaly of a declining economy in the midst of the Industrial Revolution has long vexed economic historians. Since Lipson and Clapham wrote a generation ago, scholars have ascribed the cause of decline mainly to entrepreneurial failure by Gloucester clothiers.[4] This emphasis, however, has been misleading. Lower district clothiers, Yorkshire's main competitors in coarser cloths, failed because of technical constraints on their ability to supply markets, and not because of their refusal to cultivate demand. Stroud clothiers, although plagued by the same difficulties, persisted longer because of the uniqueness of their fine cloth specialties. Despite their privileged market position, they showed themselves willing and able to exploit "a field for adventure" overseas.

The distinctive pattern of Industrial Revolution in Gloucester was instead responsible for the failure of the woolen trade. First, the business cycle contributed to the growth of large-scale production units, which proved unviable in many cases. Second, capital formation in the adoption of new machinery followed classic patterns, but the use of steam power proved more problematic. Finally, the transition from cottage industry to the factory system profoundly altered the conditions of labor, but in a manner contributing to long-term economic decline.

The Course of the Business Cycle

Between 1800 and 1850, the most important trade depressions occurred in 1803/04, 1807/08, 1811, 1816, 1819, 1825/26, 1829, 1832, 1834, 1837–1842, and 1848/49.[5] The Napoleonic blockades caused the depressions of 1807/08 and 1811;[6] the collapse of demand following the end of the French Wars, and the fall in East India Company exports, following its loss of monopoly rights in India, precipitated the depressions of 1816 and 1819, respectively.[7]

The situation grew more complex after 1825. The crisis of 1826, the major divide of the era, began in the autumn of 1825, following the weaver strikes of the spring and summer, and the nationwide financial panic of November–December.[8] Economic stagnation continued in 1827 and 1828; although 1828 is thought to have marked an upturn in the trade cycle,[9] Mann conceded that the West already began feeling stiff competition from Yorkshire.[10] The *Gloucester Journal* noted only three bankruptcies, but four clothiers retired from trade, and seven others sold their mills.[11] The effects of the 1829 depression were still felt the following year. A partial revival had begun in the autumn of 1829, but the rate of profit remained low.[12] The year 1830 witnessed a large number of sales and leasing of mill property, and this trend continued into 1831. Thus, between 1825 and 1832, a pattern of continuous stagnation characterized developments in the cloth trade (see table 41).

Scholars have usually regarded the interval 1832–1836 as a period of prosperity.[13] In Gloucester, however, economic recovery was, in fact, precarious. The loss by the East India Company of its monopoly of the China trade in 1833 very likely contributed to the closing of those mills in the lower district specializing in lighter

TABLE 41. Bankruptcy and Mill Sales by Type of Sale, 1803–1839

| Year | Bankruptcy and sales by retirees from trade | | Sales by nonbankrupts | | | | | |
	Bankrupts	Decline in trade	Machinery and stock	Machinery at mill	Machinery and mill	Mills to let	Mills for sale	Total
1803/04	5	0	2	1	0	2	0	10
1805	7	2	0	0	0	0	2	11
1806	8	1	1	0	1	1	2	14
1807	3	0	2	0	0	1	1	7
1808	3	3	3	0	0	0	0	9
1809	2	0	2	0	0	1	2	7
1810	1	2	0	0	0	0	1	4
1811	3	1	1	0	0	0	2	7
1812	2	0	1	0	1	0	5	9
1813	2	1	0	0	1	1	1	6
1814	2	0	0	0	1	1	1	5
1815	6	0	0	0	0	0	1	7
1816	4	0	1	0	0	0	1	6
1817	3	2	1	0	0	2	2	10
1818	1	0	0	1	0	0	1	3
1819	4	1	2	0	0	2	1	10
1820	2	5	0	0	0	2	3	12
1821	7	2	0	0	1	0	1	11
1822	1	1	0	0	1	2	0	5
1823	2	0	0	0	1	0	1	4
1824	2	0	0	1	0	1	4	8

1825	4	1	0	2	1	1	3	12
1826	7	0	1	0	0	0	1	9
1827	3	3	0	0	1	0	0	7
1828	3	4	1	0	1	1	6	16
1829	2	1	2	1	1	2	1	10
1830	1	3	2	2	2	5	6	21
1831	4	0	0	0	0	2	5	11
1832	3	0	0	2	0	0	0	5
1833	0	0	0	0	3	3	3	6
1834	1	2	0	1	0	1	1	5
1835	4	3	1	0	2	0	3	13
1836	0	1	1	1	1	3	5	10
1837	2	2	2	0	3	1	3	13
1838	2	1	0	1	1	0	0	5
1839	2	2	0	0	3	3	5	12

Source: Gloucester Journal; see text.

cassimeres and stripes.[14] Producers of superfines at Stroud, however, were reported doing a brisk business, despite the high price
of wool: "Black superfines may be called the staple made of this
borough," the *Gloucester Journal* reported, "and of those, well
made...goods meet a ready sale."[15] Stroud clothiers, moreover,
showed themselves sufficiently enterprising to fill the void in
coarser lines left by the East India Company, despite Yorkshire
competition. "[B]esides [the sale of Black superfines], it is surpris-
ing the quantity of cloths now making for the China market."[16]

The trend did not continue. The high price of wool soon produced "an extreme flatness" in the trade, which by March 1834
had existed "for the last four months." Yet employment was not
too badly affected, since "the fine makers are working their old
stock of wool into the market." Still, forecasts remained gloomy:
"This Summer will be one of the worst for dearth of employment
we ever had," because of the scarcity of foreign orders and satura-
tion of the home market.[17] By July 1834 the *Gloucester Journal*
could report "the still improving state of the fine cloth market."[18]
By October, however, the full force of the crisis finally materialized: "Trade is dull and most transactions are done at a loss.
Wool, though rather lower, continues...firm, but the manufacturers refuse to give the prices asked."[19] A month later, the failure
of three London houses connected with the wool trade compounded the general apprehension.[20] Yet, by the end of 1835 a
notable improvement had set in, which very likely continued into
1836.[21]

The years 1832–1836 witnessed the triumph of fine-cloth
manufacturing as the principal staple of the Gloucester trade, with
the industry now concentrated around Nailsworth and Stroud.[22]
At the same time, uneven and precarious recovery, rather than
unrelieved prosperity, characterized the period. Although the depression of 1834 may have been comparatively minor, it nevertheless produced a corrosive effect. Mere anticipation of its arrival
contributed to a general atmosphere of insecurity, which partial
economic revival in 1833 and 1835/36 failed to offset.

The depression of 1837–1842 gave the coup de grace in the
short term to any hope of continuous prosperity. The severity of
its impact demographically has already been noted for the
Horsley-Nailsworth area.[23] The depression proved especially dev-

TABLE 42. *Mill Property in Gloucestershire, 1831–1841*

District	Mills working		Mills void	Rental value (£)		Loss of rent (£)
	1831	1841		1831	1841	
Chalford, Painswick, Stroud	100	63	37	22,919	9,480	13,439
Uley	5	1	4	2,970	70	2,900
Wotton	20	11	9	3,600	1,045	2,555
Dursley	8	2	6	1,600	310	1,290
	130	77	56	31,089	10,905	20,184

Source: *Gloucester Journal*, 15 January, 1842.

asting to the lower district. At Uley, 1,000 people reportedly emigrated,[24] and the value of mill property plunged drastically. A group of mills at Kingswood, which rented for £500 in 1814, carried an annual rental value in 1839 of only £100.[25] A dramatic shrinkage in the number of firms throughout Gloucester, but especially in the lower district, had accompanied this fall in value. Samuel S. Marling, a leading Stroud clothier, analyzed the condition of the Gloucester trade at a Bath anti-Corn Law meeting in 1842. His evidence, reproduced in table 42, illustrates the Stroud region's preponderance over the decade 1831–1841; the fall in number and value of Stroud mills, although considerable, was far smaller than at the lower district, an area already in decline by 1831.

At Stroud, a general economic revival took place toward the end of 1842 that lasted to the end of the decade and was led by superfines producers, who busied themselves plying the China market.[26] The few who remained in business after 1850 concentrated on producing superfines until the last quarter of the century, when Stroud followed the lower district into decay.[27]

The business cycle often increased the incidence of bankruptcy over the 1800–1842 period and hence contributed to the decay of Gloucester's woolen trade. The trend in the turnover of firms

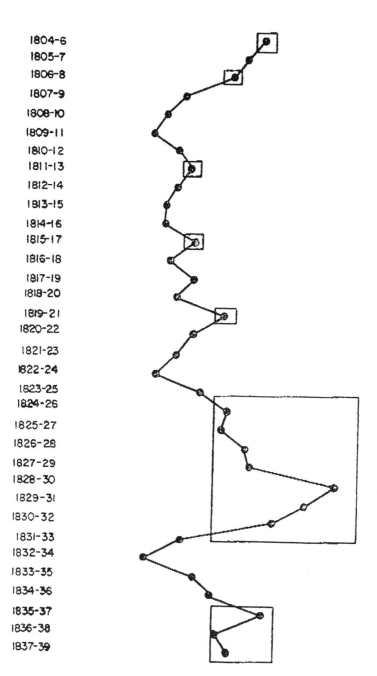

Frequencies: Bankruptcies+Sales+Lettings

Fig. 17. Three-year moving averages of business turnover, 1804–1839.

has been constructed from bankruptcy notices and sales advertisements placed in the *Gloucester Journal* and is illustrated in figure 17.[28] The squares plotted around particular averages or groups of averages indicate where a trough probably affected turnover significantly, or where an annual recession coalesced with a protracted period of stagnation.[29] The business cycle over this period helped to eclipse the small clothier and led to a concentration of ownership in larger, more heavily capitalized firms, many of which subsequently failed.

Construction of large-scale cloth mills began in the 1790s. Until 1826 the mills engaged principally in the preparatory processes of carding and scribbling, spinning, and the finishing processes of fulling, dyeing, and shearing. The early stages of the Industrial Revolution, moreover, took place in these particular branches of production.[30] Only rarely did the mills contain weaving sheds. Until 1826, weaving remained largely a traditional craft, undertaken by master artisans who employed journeymen and apprentices on a small scale.[31]

Many of these mills grew impressively large. In 1812 the five-story main building of Stonehouse Mills measured 70 feet long by 23 feet wide at its narrowest end, and it encircled an area upward of 2,000 square feet on each floor.[32] The premises contained jenny shops 170 feet long by 18 feet wide that held over eighteen spinning jennies of eighty spindles each, as well as weaving sheds and a dye house of comparable dimensions. New Mills, at Kingswood, considered "one of the largest and most powerful watermills in the West of England" in 1829, measured 150 feet long by 30 feet wide and was six stories high; five waterwheels on a high fall of 20 feet powered the mill.[33] An unnamed three-story cloth mill in the same vicinity stood 137 feet long by 31 feet wide and was powered by three waterwheels and a 20-horsepower Boulton and Watt steam engine. Its combined use of both energy sources produced a considerable sixty ends of cloth per week.[34] Uley Mills, when sold in 1837, belonged to Edward Sheppard, the largest clothier of the lower district. A combination of water and steam, with engines of 40-, 28-, and 20-horsepower, drove the entire complex and produced 100 ends of cloth per week.[35] Uley Mills contained, among a mass of ancillary items, thirty-nine scribbling and carding engines, fifteen spinning mules with 100 to 200 spindles each, and fourteen spinning jennies.[36]

Amid these large mills, many small clothiers could be found before 1825. Instead of occupying mills, they usually conducted their trade from workshops adjoining their homes. Cottagers undertook spinning and weaving for them, and fullers and dyers often performed the finishing work. In 1820 the occupier of Froome Hall Mills, for instance, advertised his services of slubbing, shearing, milling, and roughing to any clothier wishing to hire them.[37]

The inventory of the establishment of J. B. Hill, sold in 1813, typifies the style of the wealthier small clothier. His home and business included two parlors, four bedrooms, three attics, a brewhouse, and workshops, which produced ten to fourteen ends of broadcloth per week.[38] "The House," noted its sales advertisement, "has been in the country trade for some years and if [a buyer] wishes to extend the business, he can get any quantity of wool spun into yarn in the neighborhood."

Smaller, less substantial clothiers usually held more than one occupation. William Keene was a clothier and cordwainer; John Harmer, a clothier and shopkeeper; and Richard Aldridge, a clothier and victualler.[39] However, a shopkeeper operating as a clothier might still have done so on a respectable scale. William Nichols possessed a stock in trade that included some of the most up-to-date machinery of the day: five 70-, one 50-, and two 40-spindle jennies; one 40-spindle billie; and two scribbling engines of 28 and 24 inches in length, all of which were powered by a horsewheel.[40] Small clothiers often relied on horsepower, and horsewheels were notable among clothiers' effects in early *Gloucester Journal* advertisements.[41]

The emergence of large mills, however, helped to drive smaller clothiers out of business. James Hubbard, a druggist at Nailsworth, recalled in 1838 that "formerly . . . there were from 40 to 50 [small clothiers] in the neighbourhood; but the operations of the larger manufacturers, when trade became limited, has swept them away."[42] Hubbard's observation can be supported quantitatively from the sales advertisements of mills, machinery, and stock that appeared in the *Gloucester Journal*.[43]

Table 43 groups these references into four main categories and breaks them down by several time intervals.[44] The findings indi-

TABLE 43. *Sales of Mills, Machinery, and Stock, 1804–1839*

	1804–1810	1811–1817	1818–1825	1826–1832	1833–1839	Total
Machinery and stock	21	5	5	7	3	41
Machinery at mill	4	4	10	12	12	42
Mills to let	6	7	6	8	13	40
Mills and machinery, and mills for sale	8	17	31	44	31	131
Total	39	33	52	71	59	254

Note: $\chi^2 = 57.05$; $df = 12$; significance at 0.001: $\chi^2 \geq 32.909$.

cate that a dramatic change in sales patterns took place.[45] A much larger than expected number of sales of small-clothier property transpired between 1804 and 1810 and remained consistently smaller than expected throughout the later periods. Mill sales by larger clothiers followed a reverse pattern. Actual sales were much smaller than expected in the 1804–1810 interval and much larger than expected between 1826 and 1832. Small clothiers failed in significant numbers early in the period, while the reverse was true of large clothiers. By the 1830s, the preponderance of large-clothier property in sales notices shows how far their mills had come to dominate the industry.

Between 1825 and 1835, moreover, these clothiers expanded mill premises to include weaving shops, made greater use of steam power, and began to replace the spinning jenny with the mule.[46] Indeed, this pattern of modernization refutes the argument of entrepreneurial failure often used to explain Gloucester's economic decline and for this reason merits closer scrutiny.

Capital Formation

Sales advertisements for the *Gloucester Journal* have made possible the documentation of capital formation processes in Stroud, Nailsworth, and the lower district. The mills appearing in these advertisements were each sold at various intervals, so that the timing of changes in the composition of capital can be easily located. These changes, moreover, clearly typified the capital formation processes occurring throughout Gloucestershire.

In 1805, Lightpill Mill, near the town of Stroud, housed five scribbling and carding engines, four shearing machines, and a gig mill.[47] The late occupant's effects contained neither jennies nor billies, suggesting that cottagers still performed the task of spinning. By 1824, no change had occurred.[48] Five years later, however, fourteen new scribbling and carding engines, all in their first cards, were put up for sale, together with twelve 80-spindle jennies, eight 60- to 70-spindle billies, seven cloth cutters, and eighteen shearing frames. The appearance of the jennies and billies indicated that spinning had been incorporated into the mill work, and the larger number of cutters, shearing frames, and engines pointed to significant growth in productive capacity. A 12-horsepower Boulton and Watt steam engine, moreover, had been added to the inventory.[49] By 1836, the mill worked sixteen engines instead of fourteen; a cloth steaming apparatus to render wool more malleable had been added; and a new 14- to 20-horsepower steam engine had replaced the older model. The mill was now capable of producing thirty ends of cloth per week.[50]

Fixed capital formation at Lodgemore Mills, also near Stroud, occurred even more dramatically, since the occupier, N. S. Marling, had constructed many of its extensive buildings between 1824 and 1831.[51] Lodgemore, one of "the most capable and desireable clothing establishments in the West of England," relied heavily on steam power, and with the use of water power produced an optimum 100 ends of cloth per week.[52] Similar developments took place at Nailsworth. In 1813 Dyehouse Mills housed "several [carding and scribbling] engines" in a loft and "newly erected machinery mill."[53] The advertisement did not mention jennies or billies, which meant that cottage spinners were still being employed. A mill located "at a convenient distance," moreover, undertook the fulling work. By 1828, Dyehouse Mills had been transformed into a complete factory. Its machinery included broad and narrow looms, housed in its weaving shops, with a 100-spindle mule for spinning.[54] A 14-horsepower steam engine complemented the use of water in powering the mill site.

At Inchbrook Mill, in Nailsworth, only two scribbling and carding engines, two jennies, and one billy were being employed in 1820.[55] By 1832, its occupier had added a 200-spindle mule and introduced an 8-horsepower steam engine to complement the supply of water.[56] Three years later five scribbling and carding engines and two 200-spindle mules were in operation.[57] Following its sale in 1835, Inchbrook Mill passed to the ownership of Playne and Smith, clothiers from neighboring Dunkirk Mills.[58] Playne and Smith also ran Egypt and Hope Mills,[59] the previous tenants of which either succumbed to bankruptcy[60] or retired from trade.[61]

The type of large mill found at Stroud in the post-1825 period was more commonplace at Uley, Dursley, and Wotton-under-Edge in the early 1820s.[62] Stroud's fine-cloth specialties, with which Yorkshire could not compete and for which markets were relatively inelastic, brought less pressure on the region to innovate, although it did so in any case. The lower district's concentration on coarser cloths brought direct competition from Yorkshire, however, thereby forcing the region to develop more rapidly.

Hillsely Mill at Hawkesbury, near Wotton, had been used as a grist will in 1805. By 1821, however, it had become "a capital clothing mill with a steam engine of 25 horsepower, [able to drive] the whole of the machinery during a scarcity of water." At Kingswood, one mile from Wotton, "a most complete and newly erected clothing manufactory, capable of making 40 ends per week," and containing two gig mills, six rooms for machinery, and a steam engine, was put up for sale in 1819. At Uley in 1823, a clothing factory was sold that produced forty-five to fifty ends per week and was powered by a strong stream and two 8-horsepower steam engines. At Dursely in 1824, an almost identical mill was put up for sale; it, too, produced forty-five to fifty ends per week and was powered by a well-running stream and two steam engines of 8- and 10-horsepower. Finally, a cloth factory at Cam, built in 1822 and sold three years later, utilized a 20-horsepower steam engine.[63]

Gloucester had clearly adopted on a wide scale all the machinery associated with the Industrial Revolution and, with the partial exception of the steam engine,[64] broadly kept pace with Yorkshire in this enterprise. By 1815 spinning jennies were appearing regularly in *Gloucester Journal* advertisements as part of the stock-in trade of mill owners and occupiers.[65] According to Mann, the jenny and slubbing billy had been successfully introduced into the West of England after 1785, while the use of the mule first appeared in 1828 and spread rapidly after the strikes of 1829.[66] However, the sales of two mules in 1828 indicate that this type of machine must have been introduced earlier, since a lag very likely existed between the purchase and resale of each item.[67] In 1818 broad and narrow looms began to appear in the sales of ordinary mills,[68] although in small quantities and only intermittently until 1827.[69] Both the number of looms and the frequency with which they appeared in advertisements increased after 1826, and from 1830 they became permanent features of these notices.[70] According to the master weavers, "loom factories" in 1827 could house at a conservative estimate about 4,000 such devices.[71]

Although the timing of change differed between districts, the Gloucester woolen trade had clearly industrialized. The Industrial Revolution and the impact of the trade cycle permitted capital to concentrate in fewer firms, a trend that persisted at Stroud after the collapse of the lower district. Before 1826, capital concentration occurred because competition from newly capitalized mills gradually eliminated the small clothier. In this phase, the degree of concentration was really more relative, since the number of mill occupiers probably increased during the 1815–1825 period.[72] After 1826, when trade entered a critical period of stagnation, capital concentration assumed an absolute form, as successful clothiers acquired vacated mills.

The history of the Playne family firm vividly illustrates this tendency. In 1824 the prosperity that the family had experienced since 1795 led to the division of family assets between the brothers William and Peter and the subsequent creation of two firms. William remained at Longfords Mill, and Peter established his firm at Dunkirk.[73] Eventually, as we have seen, Peter's firm acquired Inchbrook, Hope, and Egypt Mills and benefited from capital-generating processes undertaken by its predecessors.[74] It was also true that successful clothiers, by virtue of capital accumulated elsewhere, frequently modernized the mills they occupied as leasehold property. N. S. Marling undertook the modernization of Lodgemore Mills during a seven-year period of his tenancy;[75] he belonged to a substantial clothier family and had previously occupied other mills in the Stroud region.[76] If the Gloucester woolen trade had therefore successfully industrialized, why did "deindustrialization" occur and virtually at the same moment? The answer hinges on the extent and nature of Gloucester's employment of steam power.

Yorkshire clothiers adopted steam power sooner than did Gloucester clothiers, and scholars have generally agreed that earlier innovation in this area gave the North a critical advantage.[77] Yorkshire clothiers benefited from significantly lower coal and transport costs, which encouraged them to innovate,[78] and in 1800 they employed nearly eighty steam engines. According to Mann, Gloucester clothiers began to adopt steam power gradually from 1819 but not on a sufficiently wide scale until 1829, when the gap between counties seems to have widened appreciably.[79]

This interpretation, however, contains several defects. When comparing Gloucester to Yorkshire, one must first distinguish between Yorkshire's principal subregions. Most of the early Yorkshire steam engines were concentrated in the East Riding, around Leeds and Bradford, where the water supply was less satisfactory, rather than at Huddersfield and Saddleworth in the West.[80] West Riding clothiers, according to Gregory, "had started to take more interest" in steam engines around 1800; but the division between East and West Riding persisted as late as 1835 and began to narrow only in the following three years.[81] West Riding seems to have occupied an intermediary position between Gloucester and the East Riding; a comparison between Gloucester and the West Riding, therefore, seems more appropriate than the county by county analyses undertaken by both Gregory and Mann.

Furthermore, comparisons between Gloucester and Yorkshire with respect to the adoption of steam power have usually based themselves erroneously on an 1838 parliamentary return.[82] In order to explain Gloucester's lack of competitiveness, Mann has shown that its mills relied more heavily on water than on steam, and Gregory has demonstrated that the aggregate capacity of Gloucester steam engines in 1838 fell considerably below Yorkshire's.[83] However, the return does not register the true extent of Gloucester's reliance on steam power over the entire course of the Industrial Revolution nor gives a clear indication of the timing of that county's economic decline.

Gloucester clothiers began adopting steam engines in more reasonable numbers and at higher capacity during the 1820s than Mann has implied,[84] and the economy of the lower district and much of Stroud's had already collapsed by 1838. Many mills that utilized steam had thus long ceased to operate.[85] The depression of 1829 was especially severe, and the number of working mills at the lower district was already low by 1831.[86] Any comparison between Gloucester and Yorkshire and 1838 must therefore adjust for the far fewer number of Gloucester mills remaining in operation and must not accept the level of its aggregate steam-power capacity at face value. The smallness of this capacity at this time was the result, not the cause, of economic decline.

Tables 44 and 45 summarize the power conditions of West Riding and Gloucester Mills in 1838. Although the West Riding clearly outstripped Gloucester in numbers of operational mills and in aggregate steam-power capacity, a per capita analysis reveals a less dichotomous relationship between the two regions. The West Riding surpassed Gloucester marginally in per capita steam power capacity, while Gloucester surpassed its rival more significantly in total per capita power because of heavier reliance on water. When improved carefully, however, water power easily matched the productivity increases effected by steam.[87] Gloucester's per capita power advantage in 1838 indicates the persistence of a competitive industry, regardless of the extent to which previous crises had reduced its size; it also suggests that the causes of industrial decline must be sought elsewhere, perhaps in the manner of innovation itself.

Gloucester clothiers used steam engines more regularly and at higher capacity than scholars have usually admitted. High coal and transport costs, combined with the cheapness of operating water, constrained Gloucester clothiers from substituting steam engines for water power. Still, the construction of mill ponds and waterwheels required more capital than that needed for investment in the equivalent amount of steam power.[88] For this reason, too, Gloucester clothiers shied away from complete substitution. When faced with the choice of upgrading existing water-power structures or supplanting them altogether with steam, clothiers often made the more rational decision to add a waterwheel or expand existing ponds and leets.[89] Otherwise, the capital costs of

TABLE 44. *Steam and Water Power in Gloucestershire and West Riding, Yorkshire Woolen Mills, ca. 1838*

Region	Number of mills		Steam engines, waterwheels, and HP intervals						
			50+	*40–49*	*30–39*	*20–29*	*10–19*	*0–10*	*Total*
West Riding	600	SE:	13	21	74	87	138	44	377
		SHP:	790	855	2003	1931	1875	296	7750
		WW:	1	2	7	27	91	109	237
		WHP:	60	80	226	370	1114	593	2443
Gloucestershire	96	SE:	1	3	6	8	22	9	49
		SHP:	50	125	157	171	287	53.5	843.5
		WW:	0	0	3	8	42	166	219
		WHP:	0	0	90	180	526	922.5	1718.5

Note: SE = number of steam engines; SHP = steam horsepower; WW = waterwheels; WHP = water horsepower.
Source: British Parliamentary Papers 1839, XLII, "Accounts and Papers," return of mills: Horner's and Saunder's districts for the West Riding, and Howell's district for Gloucestershire.

TABLE 45. *Per Capita Power in Gloucestershire and West Riding, Yorkshire Woolen Mills, ca. 1838*

Region	Number of mills	SE/M	SHP/M	SHP/E	WW/M	WHP/M	WHP/W	Total HP/M
West Riding	600	0.6	12.9	20.6	0.4	4.1	10.3	17.0
Gloucestershire	96	0.5	8.8	17.2	2.3	17.9	7.8	26.7

Note: SE = number of steam engines; SHP = steam horsepower; WW = number of waterwheels; WHP = water horsepower; total HP = total horsepower; /M = per mill; /E = per engine; /W = per waterwheel.
Source: British Parliamentary Papers, 1839, XLII, "Accounts and Papers," return of mills: Horner's and Saunder's districts for the West Riding, and Howell's district for Gloucestershire.

the original structures would burden profits,[90] while the costs of adding to them, if kept within strict limits, were probably lower than full-scale investment in steam. Nevertheless, clothiers sometimes purchased one or more steam engines instead and used them to supplement the flow of water. Steam engines clearly enhanced the productivity of water mills,[91] and by using them in this manner, Gloucester clothiers sought to extract the cost advantages offered by both energy sources while minimizing their disadvantages. The mixed use of steam and water, however, created problems of excess capacity, which rendered firms vulnerable to failure.

Although scholars have long recognized such usage, they have treated the relationship between the two energy sources dichotomously: Steam power served either as an adjunct to the water supply in emergency situations or as a complete substitute for it.[92] Gloucester clothiers actually combined both energy sources routinely on a year-round basis because of the endemic irregularity of the water supply.

Gloucester clothiers used steam power to increase output directly or indirectly. Sometimes they connected their engines directly to machinery and in this way ran entire buildings of a mill complex, while water operated others.[93] Otherwise steam engines were connected to the waterworks of a single mill and used to supplement a weak water flow or substitute for water entirely during dry seasons, or sometimes they served as pumps to facilitate the flow from lower to upper mill ponds.

By using steam engines in this manner clothiers might increase capital costs without increasing output to a compensating degree. Unit capital costs would thus remain high, and excess capacity would result. Excess capacity might occur if the amount of steam power employed was either too great or too small. A balance needed to be found, and this was something difficult to estimate.

Analysis of a sample of mixed powered mills, advertised for sale or rental in the *Gloucester Journal* by bankrupts, their assignees, or those retiring from trade, and reproduced in table 46, has shown the need to distinguish between mills using large engines and those using smaller engines.[94]

Large engine mills generated sufficient steam power to produce directly the higher levels of output noted in advertisements while

TABLE 46. *Steam- and Water-Powered Cloth Mills*

Name of mill or parish	Year	Ends per week	Steam HP	High-/ low- powered	Water HP	Total HP
At Avening	1825	35	32	H	(31.3)	63.3
Lightpill Mill	1834–1836	30	17	L	(20.7)	37.7
A cloth mill	1824	43	20	H	(22.8)	42.8
Cooke's Mill	1824	20	10	L	(15.7)	25.7
Dyehouse Mills	1828–1830	30	14	L	(18.5)	32.5
A newly built mill	1821	30	14	L	(18.5)	32.5
A mill at Cam	1825	60	20	H	(22.8)	42.8
Uley Mills	1837	100	88	H	(71.1)	159.1
A mill at Uley	1823	48	16	L	(19.9)	35.9
Avening Great Mill	1833	30	28	H	(28.5)	56.5
Lodgemore Mills	1832	100	40	H	30.0	70.0
A cloth mill	1830	40	12	L	(17.1)	29.1
Hathaway's Mill	1831	(30.4)	8	L	(14.3)	22.3
Hillsley Mill	1821	(46.6)	25	H	(26.3)	51.3
Toghill's Mill	1827	(34.2)	12	L	(17.1)	29.1
A fulling mill	1821	(34.2)	12	L	(17.1)	29.1
Slad Mill	1836	(47.5)	26	H	(27.0)	53.0
Rookhouse Mill	1832	(39.9)	18	L	(21.4)	39.4
Seville's Mill	1837	(38.0)	16	L	(19.9)	35.9
Woodchester Mill	1839/40	(51.3)	30	H	(29.9)	59.9
At Woodchester	1828	(34.2)	12	L	(17.1)	29.1
Peghouse Mill	1830	(31.4)	30	H	(29.9)	59.9
Newcombe's Mill	1839	(34.2)	12	L	(17.1)	29.1
Freame's Mill	1827	(30.4)	8	L	(14.3)	22.3
Inchbrook Mill	1832–1835	(30.4)	8	L	(14.3)	22.3
Harrison's Mill	1829	(34.2)	12	L	(17.1)	29.1
Oldland's Mill	1832	(38.0)	16	L	(19.9)	35.9
Dutton's Mill	1835	(34.2)	12	L	(17.1)	29.1
Wallington's Mill	1830	(36.1)	14	L	(18.5)	32.5
A cloth mill	1830	(70.4)	50	H	(44.1)	94.1
A cloth mill	1830	(41.8)	20	H	(22.8)	42.8
A cloth factory	1830	(36.1)	14	L	(18.5)	32.5
Blue Mills	1828	(32.9)	10	L	(16.7)	26.7
Merritt's Mill	1839	(41.8)	20	H	(22.8)	42.8

Note: The figures in parentheses were arrived at through linear estimators; see Urdank, "Economic Decline," p. 431, n. 21. A detailed catalog of *Gloucester Journal* advertisements for the sale of cloth mills has been assembled in Urdank, "Dissenting Community," appendix 5.1.

compensating simultaneously for the irregularity of the water flow. Although the water supply, when enhanced by steam, contributed to greater output, the full thrust of steam's indirect effect necessarily became attenuated,[95] and productivity advances remained moderate. Had large engine users relied solely on the direct effect of steam, productivity would have been much greater, or less steam power would have been needed to achieve the higher levels of output advertised.

Small-engine mills, in contrast, generated insufficient steam power to produce directly the levels of output advertised. Half of the capacity of steam was directed toward output, while the other half compensated for the irregularity of the water supply. Neither effect, however, was very significant. Small-engine users enjoyed comparatively better water flows and must have thought their mills required less steam power to compensate for the irregularity in the water supply. Unfortunately, they underestimated the amount of steam power needed. Productivity advances thus remained minimal, and unit capital costs undoubtedly rose, thereby contributing to failure.

In general, large-engine mills employed too much steam power, relative to output levels, while small-engine mills employed too little. For these diametrically opposite reasons, both types of mill suffered fatally from excess capacity.

Capital formation, whatever its degree of success, affected the conditions of labor. In the long term, excess capacity, by promoting bankruptcy and retirements, led to the decay of the woolen trade and consequently to the loss of employment. The rhythm of the business cycle encouraged capital concentration, but employment opportunities actually declined, although the volume of production continued its steady advance.[96]

The adoption of machinery inadvertently led to structural unemployment by replacing labor in the productive process. A. R. Fewster accurately predicted that handloom weavers would follow the paths of scribblers and shearmen,[97] and Peter Playne opined that the weavers were "racing against steam." "The slightest rise for wages," Playne maintained, "would cause [the] general adoption of power-[looms] throughout the country."[98] It was a race his own weavers lost.[99] Factory organization had created a surplus weaver population even prior to the advent of powerlooms;[100]

moreover, as the mule, with far greater number of spindles,[101] superseded the jenny, spinners began to suffer the same condition.

In the short term, however, the impact of capital formation on labor was more complex. Did factory labor represent an improvement over the conditions of cottage industry? From the manufacturer's standpoint it certainly did, since by acquiring complete control over the instruments of production, he could establish his own regime of work discipline. For labor, however, the answer was less simple. Although custom-minded weavers may have protested against factory life, changes in the sexual division of labor, labor productivity, and earnings produced mixed results.

Capital and Labor

Under the system of protoindustrialization, or cottage industry, the family often served as the primary unit of production, with all members contributing their earnings to its common budget. "In the weaver's household," Scott and Tilly have written, "children did carding and combing, older daughters and wives spun, while the father wove."[102] Yet customary practices persisted longer than this characterization suggests; master weavers often rented or purchased workshops to house the looms used by their journeymen, who necessarily worked away from their homes.

Although the size of the weaver population of the early nineteenth century is difficult to estimate, a Horsley census of householders for 1811 offers some idea of its importance.[103] The list records the tenurial status of the household head as a tenant or "landlord" and thus offers a measure of the likely proportion of extant master weavers, since the prosperous ones among them probably owed rather than rented their workshops.[104] George Ford of Elcomb, Uley, in a typical example, put up two lots for sale in 1817 that he described as "desireably situated for a weaver"; they included "a new-built messuage...with broad and narrow loom shops [and] a new-built tenement adjoining the above," which presumably served as a dwelling.[105]

Table 47 presents a breakdown of landlords and tenants by occupation, mean household size, percentage of respective occupational group, and percentage of all listed householders.[106] The findings show that weavers accounted for nearly 30 percent of all Horsley householders, a significantly higher percentage than

TABLE 47. *Craftsmen, Weavers, and Laborers, Horsley Parish, ca. 1811*

Occupation and tenurial status	N	Percent of all occupants	Percent of all household heads	Mean number of household heads	Coefficient of variation
Craftsmen all	92[a]	100	15.9	4.88	48.2
Craftsmen landlord	31	33.7	5.2	4.65	54.0
Craftsmen tenant	58	63.0	9.7	4.74	46.2
Weavers all	176[b]	100	29.6	5.06	46.6
Weavers landlord	47	26.7	7.9	5.19	51.6
Weavers tenant	114	64.8	19.2	4.96	45.6
Laborers all[c]	99	100	16.6	5.01	45.1
Laborers landlord	14	14.1	2.3	5.50	43.8
Laborers tenant	85	85.9	14.3	4.98	46.8

Note: The total number of household heads contained in the census listing equals 595; the total number in this table constitutes 62 percent of the whole. The table does not include several social groups, such as gentlemen, yeomen, widows, clothiers, or small shopkeepers, who are listed in the census but whose presence does not touch the point being analyzed.

[a] Craftsmen included masons, tailors, carpenters, cordwainers, glaziers, sawyers, pargeters, plasterers, saddlers, shearmen, wheelwrights, millwrights chairmakers and blacksmiths. Three had no discernable tenurial status.

[b] Fifteen weavers were listed as nonresidents, and while included in the total, were excluded from analysis by tenurial status. All were tenants, but since they were nonresidents, they were probably also master weavers who had rented working premises.

[c] The census listing drew no distinction between agricultural laborers and day laborers associated with the cloth trade.

craftsmen or laborers. Weavers, moreover, were as likely to have been landlords as their fellows in other crafts,[107] and as might have been expected, landlord-laborers represented a far smaller proportion of all laborers listed.[108] Clearly, large numbers of master weavers could be found in 1811, and they enjoyed a social status equal to that of other independent craftsmen.[109]

From 1800, however, the independent status of master weavers

TABLE 48. *Occupations of Household Heads in Horsley Parish,
ca. 1811 and 1841*

| | 1811 | | 1841 | | |
Occupation	N	%	N	%	% change
Weavers	176	29.6	101	15.4	−42.6
Spinners	21	3.5	14	2.1	−33.3
Shearers	21	3.5	0	—	−100.0
Clothworkers	7	1.2	47	7.2	+571.4
Subtotal	225	37.8	162	26.2	−28.0
Laborers	99	16.6	191	29.2	+92.9
Artisans	92	15.5	99	15.1	+7.6
Clothiers	20	3.4	4	0.6	−80.0
Total	595[a]		655		

[a] See the general notation in table 47.
Sources: 1811 manuscript census (see n. 103 and text); 1841 census enumerators' lists (PRO Home Office 107/363).

began to erode slowly. "Loom shops" first appeared in that year, and several years later Parliament repealed the Tudor Statutes, which had long protected the customary structure of the trade.[110] Still, between 1814 and 1825, master weavers believed strongly enough in the durability of their craft to have trained a surfeit of apprentices;[111] loom shops did not pose a serious threat to them until 1827.

The rise of capital-intensive factories by 1841 eliminated the master weaver's traditional status and reduced demand for skilled woolworkers generally. Table 48, based on comparative census data,[112] shows Horsley weavers having declined by 40 percent of all household heads between 1811 and 1814. Spinners, although initially small in number, fell by a third. Shearmen disappeared entirely, and unskilled clothworkers rose in number by more than 500 percent. Woolworkers as a group declined by 28 percent as the number of day laborers increased 93 percent, while the 80 percent fall in the number of clothiers suggests a growing concentration of capital.

Still, among journeymen outworkers, a family-centered approach

TABLE 49. *Occupations of Factory Weavers' Wives, ca. 1838*

Occupation	Number
Weavers	59
Spinners	13
Clothworkers[a]	45
Laborers	3
Seamstresses	4

[a] Quillers, burlers, reelers, pickers, and warpers.
Source: *British Parliamentary Papers*; see text.

to work predominated during the era of protoindustrialization and remained intact in the first stages of transition to the factory system. Early factory masters permitted operatives to hire their wives (see table 49) and children as assistants and therefore used the family as an agency for labor recruitment.[113] "Sir, it is the parent who makes the contract, and who sanctions the work of the child," W. H. Hyett, M.P. for Stroud, remonstrated against the first factory act; "and I apprehend that the wisdom of Mr. Sadler . . . will have some difficulty in finding a stronger safeguard for the child, than the natural affection of the parent."[114]

This traditional system gradually deteriorated, as labor recruitment began to base itself more fully on the free market. The Gloucester weavers, who in 1827 complained of the rise of "loom factories," also directed their protest against its unsavory, residual consequences. Manufacturers, they asserted, began employing "strangers in those factories, from other counties . . . [who] not infrequently . . . became the fathers of illegitimate children."[115] By individualizing labor recruitment, the factory system thus eroded the primacy of the family as an economic unit and even threatened its social stability.[116]

A repatterning of the division of labor within the household began to occur. As men moved into the factories, women became increasingly confined to the domestic sphere, although some continued to work, however irregularly. Four of the largest mills in the Stroud, Eastington, and Nailsworth areas in 1839 employed a total of 195 male weavers, only three of whom were unmarried. Of the remaining number, about one-third of the wives had no

TABLE 50. *Mean Earnings of Weavers' Wives by Occupation, ca. 1838*

Occupation	Mean (s)	Standard deviation	Percent mean household-head income	Mean household-head income
Weavers	4.6	2.18	30.0	15.27
Spinners	3.9	1.39	24.5	15.93
Clothworkers	3.25	1.72	19.7	16.43

Source: *British Parliamentary Papers*; see text.

occupation, while the others were employed in various capacities in the cloth trade.[117] Where the wife did not work, the burden of supporting the household fell on the husband and the children; where she did work, her industrial labor very likely remained subordinated to her household duties.[118] The percentage distribution of mean earnings of wives who wove cloth, depicted in table 50,[119] reflected this tendency.

Although women weavers contributed nearly one third to the total household income, the mean of 4.6s (4s.7d) was far below what they would have earned as factory weavers but roughly equal to what they could be expected to have earned as cottagers.[120] Women, of course, worked in factories, but because of the persistence of the domestic system, albeit in a weakened form, they did not necessarily precede men, as they had in the cotton industry.[121] Nor were there as many female occupations. Of nineteen total available occupations, apart from weaving and jenny spinning, men occupied eleven, children three, and women five.[122] Weaving and spinning were mixed occupations, albeit male-dominated.

In the heyday of the domestic system, weaving had been strictly confined to males. Women may have assisted their journeymen husbands by taking a turn at the loom; or if they took up the trade more regularly, they did so indirectly through service in a household, since master weavers excluded them from apprenticeship. The Napoleonic wars altered this situation. The shortage of male labor, combined with the great demand for cloth, created opportunities for women to become weavers more formally.[123]

Nevertheless, weaving remained a predominantly male occupation. At Horsley parish in 1811, while the ratio of female house-holders to all household heads was 99:526, or 18.6 percent, the ratio of women weavers, listed as householders, to all weaver householders was only 7:195, or 3.6 percent.[124] As the domestic system came into competition with the factory, more women entered the trade, but mainly as outdoor weavers. By 1841, at Horsley, their proportion had increased to about 36.0 percent of all weavers.[125] In a sample of forty Gloucester mills, however, they accounted for only 26.0 percent of all handloom weavers, representing a significantly lower proportion.[126]

The condition of female spinners altered more dramatically. Spinning had begun as a female occupation under the domestic system and remained so for some time after the introduction of the jenny. Hargreaves's original invention contained only eight spindles, but by 1810 the jenny could accommodate sixty, seventy, and eighty spindles.[127] Although contemporaries, as late as 1838, still regarded jenny spinning as a female occupation, males had begun encroaching on this preserve as early as 1811.[128] With the in-crease in spindle capacity, the operation of jennies required greater physical strength; large jennies were routinely employed in mills and those with seventy and eighty spindles, at the very least, were probably male-operated. When manufacturers adopted the mule in the late 1820s, it displaced jenny spinning by about 60.0 percent.[129] Mules, with 100 to 200 spindles, required male labor even more than did larger jennies, especially after employers began arranging them in facing pairs, so that one spinner might operate two machines.[130] If males became mule spinners, working regu-larly in factories, then women remained at the jenny, laboring ir-regularly at home amid their domestic duties.[131] The Industrial Revolution greatly transformed spinning and weaving. Unlike scribblers, carders, and shearmen, who were entirely displaced by innovation, spinners and weavers became bound more closely to the rhythm of machinery. Spinners were forced to master rising spindle capacities with speeds of up to 6,000 revolutions per minute; experienced spinners averaged three and one half draws per minute over a fifty-seven-hour week.[132] The progress of both jenny and mule spinning resulted in the production of finer yarns, which, with other changes in weaving, greatly affected weaver productivity.

The fly shuttle, widely adopted in Gloucester by 1798, enhanced weaver productivity by shortening the average labor time between a quarter and a third.[133] Where once two weavers had been required to operate a loom, one working the warp and the other the weft, the fly shuttle enabled one weaver to perform both operations.[134] In 1824 manufacturers altered a customary work rule by lengthening the warping bar from 16-hundreds to 20-hundreds while increasing the number of shoots per yard in the weft.[135] Because of the use of finer yarns, this innovation produced a denser fabric.[136] "[O]f late years," the weavers complained, "the work has been drawn so small that it requires a great deal of time and attention to do justice to the manufacturer."[137] Indeed, the combination of all these changes, compounded by the discipline of the factory, greatly intensified the weaving process.[138]

This intensification affected men and women differently, since males eventually came to dominate both spinning and weaving. Where it is possible to compare the productivity of the sexes, we find males adapting more completely to the new structure of work. Male factory weaver productivity in 1838, for instance, stood at 1,044 yards per weaver per annum, while female factory weavers produced at a significantly lower rate of 930 yards per weaver per annum.[139] For this reason, some manufacturers preferred to employ male weavers and sought to legitimate paying females at a lower rate, as master weavers had done in an earlier period. "Women are not so regular in their time as men," Peter Playne contended, "nor so able to perform the work in the same time. Thirty men will do as much work as forty women, and the outlay for looms, buildings, etc., is greater for a number of females than for male weavers."[140] The altered structure of work affected semi-skilled labor, such as warping or piecing, according to the degree of its synchronization with a skilled occupation.[141]

A comparison of factory weaver productivity with that of the outdoor weaver best illustrates the effect of the new structure of work on the labor process. Factory weavers produced 1,974 yards per weaver per annum, while outdoor weavers produced only 701.7 yards per weaver per annum.[142] Preindustrial journeymen weavers worked as long as necessary to earn their customary wage. This meant that they worked seriously only three to four days of every week.[143] Changes in the structure of work, which foreshadowed the factory system, gradually subjected them to a more rigorous regime. Under the factory system, where the clothier governed the conditions of labor, however, former journeymen worked longer and more regularly than possible under the master weaver's direction.[144]

This change produced both positive and negative consequences. On one hand, the acceleration and increased laboriousness of weaving clearly made work more stressful, although far less so than in the Lancashire cotton industry.[145] On the other hand, factory discipline imparted a new sense of order, which made weavers more self-possessed. "The factory system," one employer remarked, "decidedly tends to improve the men, to break through the sluggish habits for which weavers have been so notorious; it tends to make the men at once punctual and industrious."[146] By doing so, the factory enhanced their capacity for self-organization, expressed collectively through a trade union, or by individual initiative in pursuit of higher earnings. Evidence given by the weaver Thomas Cole illuminates this point especially well:

In the factories more work is done, as the men are evaluating each other. . . . Looms are in much better order in the shop factories than they were at the houses of weavers; people . . . had not the notion of putting them in order; a man can earn more now at a loom . . . from improvements in the tackle. . . . [T]he men do earn more money than they could out; in short they settle their minds to work . . . ; they did not used to be so active in the master's houses; they often would get out of the loom and daudle their time, and have a drop of beer, etc. Thinks the factory system has given the men more settled habits, and there is not so much time spent in the public houses as used to be. Has heard many shopweavers say that if the wages were a little higher, they would be much more content to work in a factory than out of it; has heard many of the men who work for Mr. Playne say so; Isaac Kaynton and Joseph Cole, my son, are of the same opinion.[147]

Thomas Cole's belief in the superiority of the factory system was a mark of deference, conditioned by a teetotalist, Nonconformist sensibility; it displayed an identification with his employer's view on the issue of worker control that most weavers believed contrary to their interests.[148] Once a master weaver, Cole relinquished his independence with almost casual equanimity: "was formerly a master weaver, and kept two looms, but went into the factory because his employer put out little work."[149] Apparently, no resentment lurked behind his decision to have done so. Nonetheless, this pattern of deference was paradoxical because it stemmed from the memory of his earlier, independent position. His assessment of the work habits of journeymen weavers was based on his experience as their former employer, and on this basis it displayed an unwitting empathy with the clothier.[150] Thomas Cole, in other words, accepted in principle the clothier's claim of authority over his weavers, because he had once exercised the same power as a master in his own house.[151]

Such agreeability, however, could dissipate under altered circumstances. Festering grievances could easily subvert a deferential temperament informed by individualism. Because he had been a master weaver, Thomas Cole was also sensitive to injustice at the workplace, a sensibility partially informed by a Nonconformist conscience. Under proper conditions, he might even have emerged as a strike leader, despite admonitions from his chapel's deacons.

Cole had been baptized at Shortwood in 1806 and excluded from membership in 1834.[152] Although the church roll did not state the reason for his exclusion, circumstantial evidence suggests that it may have been the strike against William Playne at Longfords Mill that same year.[153] Baptists were known for excluding members who engaged in strikes, and the Shortwood deacons, in particular, explicitly lamented their members' attraction to trade unionism.[154] Cole was not completely uncritical of the factory system: "[Its] greatest injury, witness thinks, . . . is the walking to and from the shop."[155] He was clearly dissatisfied with the wages paid by Mr. Playne; his delicate reference to that manufacturer in the context of his general approval of factory earnings must be understood as a veiled criticism. It may have been possible to earn more as a factory weaver, because of better looms and the faster pace of work, but manufacturers often used this fact to legitimate paying lower piece rates; between 1825 and 1838, wages underwent a great fall.[156] Cole admitted, moreover, that he no longer worked as a factory weaver "in consequence of some strife with the foreman."[157]

The great majority of factory weavers did not share Cole's generally favorable appreciation of the factory system, despite his assertion to the contrary. In a survey of over 190 weavers at four

TABLE 51. *Weavers' Attitudes toward the Factory: A Parliamentary Survey, ca. 1838*

	Former Status		
Condition	*Master*	*Journeyman*	*Total*
Improved	3	9	12
Not improved	90	89	179
Total	93	98	191

Source: *British Parliamentary Papers*; see text.

mills in Stroud and Nailsworth undertaken by a parliamentary commissioner, the respondents overwhelmingly rejected the proposition that their condition might have improved since entering the factory. Table 51 presents the joint distribution of their answers by their former status of master or journeyman.

These results are of special interest because factory weavers, on average, earned more than did outdoor weavers (approximate weekly earnings for factory weavers were 11s. 9d. per week; for outdoor master weavers, 8s. 1½d.; outdoor journeyman weavers earned 6s. 10¼d.).[158] Clearly, wages were not the sole criterion by which factory weavers measured their standard of living. Their distaste for working in a mill setting, rather than in intimate surroundings, and their chronic fatigue, caused by the need to walk to work, were more important considerations. Finally, most perceived factory work as less prestigious than craft labor. Master weavers forfeited their independence and could no longer entertain the ambition of becoming clothiers, while journeymen relinquished the hope of one day establishing their own shops (see data presented in table 52).[159]

Under the factory system, "training to the loom" could be undertaken without having to preserve the "mysteries of the craft." Youths, formerly trained as "colts" by master weavers,[160] could be given a fair chance to compete with their former employers, with output alone determining the level of their skill. Nevertheless, rewards were not always commensurate with effort

TABLE 52. *Earnings and Productivity of Factory Weavers by Former Status, ca. 1838*

	N	Average price paid[a]	Average weekly earnings	Average chain length (hundreds in chain)	Average weaver time[b]
Master	93	£1.15s. 4⅓d.	10s. 7d.	17.58	17.5
Journeyman	98	£1.13s. 3½d.	10s. 7d.	17.53	16.5

[a] t = 2.354, df = 193, t ≥ 2.326 at 0.02 probability.
[b] t = 1.778, df = 190, t ≥ 1.65 at 0.05 probability (one-tailed test); the two-tailed test, however, is not significant since t ≥ 1.960 at 0.05 probability.
Source: British Parliamentary Papers; see text.

under the factory regime. Among the weavers surveyed, former masters on average were still paid a higher price per piece, although they were generally less efficient than former journeymen. All weavers wove the same average length of chain, but former journeymen tended to finish the piece one day sooner, and after deductions for defects in the finished product, their average weekly earnings equaled those of their former masters.[161] The fact that former journeymen worked faster, produced fewer defects, and yet were paid at a lower gross price per piece affirmed the weavers' suspicion that once the clothier knew their speed, he would try to lower their wages. They could draw little consolation from the fact that their wages were higher and employment more regular than those for outdoor weavers. Whereas the factory system may have enhanced productivity, the existence of an outdoor surplus weaving population paid at lower rates merely served to restrain the legitimate claims of factory weavers for even higher wage rates. Threats of dismissal and black-listing were also grizzly warnings to disaffected factory weavers, who unionized in spite of them.

Wages for all categories of workers, furthermore, were declining over the course of the thirty-year period prior to the parliamentary commissioner's inquiry. The negative consequences of this fall were apparent only from 1829, and became more pronounced after 1835. Wheat prices, depicted in figure 18, were falling at an average rate of 2.9 percent per annum, as a result of the

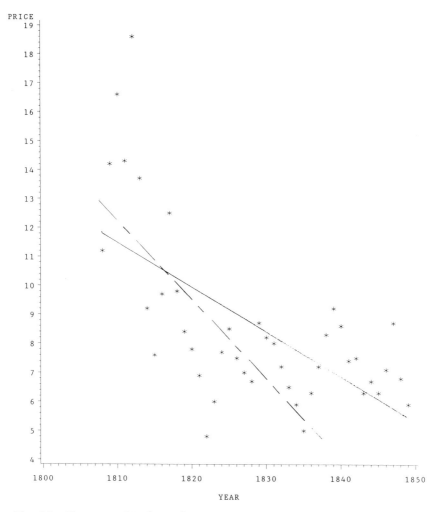

Fig. 18. Gloucester Market Wheat Prices, 1808–1849.

Key: Solid Line (1808–49) : Price = 11.7 − 0.15 (time)
  Broken Line (1808–37) : Price = 12.9 − 0.26 (time)

chronic agricultural depression of the postwar years.[162] The movement of wheat prices, of course, determined the fluctuations in the price of bread, which could account for as much as 45 percent of a weaver's budget.[163] A comparable annual wage series is not available, but one is extant for the period by yearly intervals, grouped according to when the actual fall in wages occurred. Table 53 pre-

TABLE 53. *Wages and Wheat Prices by Occupation, 1808–1838*

	1808–1816	1817/18	1819–1828	1829–1835	1836	1837	1838
Wheat	13.17	10.66	7.1	7.07	6.3	7.2	8.3
% change	—	−19.08	−33.2	−0.68	−10.8	+14.3	+15.3
Weavers	16.0	16.0	13.0	12.0	11.0	10.0	10.0
% change	—	0.0	−18.8	−7.7	− 8.3	−9.0	0.0
Spinners (males)	24.0	23.0	22.0	21.0	20.0	20.0	20.0
% change	—	−4.4	−4.3	−4.5	−4.7	0.0	0.0
Warper (female)	10.0	9.0	8.0	7.0	7.0	7.0	7.0
% change	—	−10.0	−11.1	−12.5	0.0	0.0	0.0
Cutters (males)	21.0	20.0	20.0	18.0	16.0	14.0	13.0
% change	—	−4.7	0.0	−10.0	−11.1	−12.5	− 7.2

Source: British Parliamentary Papers; see text.

sents the data for selected occupations, including the variations in wheat prices for the same intervals.

The percentage fall in wheat prices far surpassed the fall in wages through 1828, which suggests that the standard of living was improving.[164] This was valid even for weavers, who experienced the largest fall in wages of all listed woolworkers (−18.75 percent). Between 1829 and 1835, the fall in wheat prices slowed significantly, while wage rates declined at a faster pace for the first time. Between 1836 and 1838, the situation grew more critical. Wages continued to fall in 1837 and remained stationary in 1838, and for the first time, in 1837, wheat prices began to rise modestly.

The practice of paying in truck, which spread after 1825, compounded the decline of the standard of living in this latter period. Payment of wages in kind, or "truck," enabled the manufacturer to lower his workers' earnings indirectly by 15 or 20 percent.[165] He required workers to buy goods in his shop, or at one in which he held an interest. These goods sold at higher prices, were of inferior quality and were usually underweight. Although legislative measures were proposed to suppress the practice, such legislation was easily evaded; either penalties were too lenient, or proving any but the most flagrant violations became too difficult. Many of those successfully prosecuted at Horsley Petty Sessions were repeat offenders because fines were nominal. Most trucksters, however, were too delicate in their proceedings to be found in technical violation of the law. "[The] workman earned his wages," one legal commentator observed, "under the impression created by the course of dealing that he was to lay out the same at some particular shop favoured by the manufacturer."[166] Noncompliance, or complaints regarding the inferiority and exorbitant prices of goods, would result in dismissal:

[If] they did [complain], the master would make but little reply; but, in a few days, or at the next settling, some trifling fault is found, or "not being in want of so many hands," they are turned off, but not a word is said about the shop. The workman is left to draw his own inference. The workmen know this and are therefore compelled . . . to submit to silence.[167]

Dealing in truck was more widespread during periods of economic depression, since less efficient manufacturers were desperate to save their establishments by reducing labor costs; the existence of a surplus labor population facilitated their task. Because dealing in truck conferred a competitive advantage, it gave "respectable" manufacturers, who paid money wages, a reason to reduce their rates. The parliamentary commissioner estimated that one in five weavers in 1838 was paid in kind. Truck undoubtedly contributed to the general fall in wages in the post-1836 period. Public opinion, however, was against the practice, since it clearly enslaved and thoroughly demoralized the worker. Once economic conditions improved, the truckster enjoyed fewer opportunities, and because of the opprobrium of respectable society, he found plying his trade more difficult.

The parliamentary commissioner's wage series ends in 1838, but the fall in wage rates may have slowed during the prosperous years between 1843 and 1847. Improvement in the terms of trade, together with extensive outmigration in the previous period, should have enabled workers to command a better price. Wheat prices continued their linear decline, although at a slower rate; for the 1808–1849 period, the growth rate was −1.77 percent per annum. Wheat prices were slightly higher in the 1840s, but their advancement was too weak to alter the general trend significantly. Agitation for repealing the Corn Laws developed, nonetheless, in response to this slowdown. Since the clothiers found it in their interest to diffuse pressure for higher wages, the agitation revealed, indirectly, the extent of this pressure, which the Chartists had partly instigated. Scholars have generally regarded the mid-1840s as years of economic advance.[168]

In general, the trend in the standard of living of woolworkers, especially weavers, conformed to an apparent cyclical pattern. Deane and Cole were probably correct in suggesting that wages rose during the Napoleonic wars; the high wage levels, in the parliamentary commissioner's series, for the 1808–1816 period affirm their conclusion. Real wages suffered, however, since wheat prices rose proportionally higher.[169] Table 54 presents average wheat prices as a percentage of the average earnings of several categories of workers for each interval of the series.

For weavers and cutters especially, the price of wheat as a percentage of earnings moved full circle. For weavers, it was 82.3

TABLE 54. *Wheat Prices as a Percentage of Wages, 1808–1838*

	1808–1816	1817/18	1819–1828	1829–1835	1836	1837	1838
Weavers	82.3	66.6	54.6	58.9	57.3	72.0	83.0
Spinners	54.8	46.3	32.3	33.6	31.5	36.0	41.5
Cutters	62.7	53.3	35.5	39.3	39.4	51.4	63.8

Source: British Parliamentary Papers; see text.

percent in the 1808–1816 period and 83 percent in 1838; for cutters, it was 62.7 percent and 63.8 percent, respectively. This meant that the improvement in living standards occurred absolutely only between 1816 and 1828, and probably between 1843 and 1847, although the same hard evidence is lacking with respect to wages. The 1808–1816 period, moreover, was probably better than the year 1838; both intervals were marked by severe trade depressions, but the latter was compounded by the widespread payment of wages in kind. Wage rates probably never rose sufficiently to bridge the gap with rising productivity, even in the prosperous years of the mid-1840s and post-1850 period.[170] Insofar as the "quality of life" argument in the standard of living debate relates to the problem of exploitation,[171] we must conclude that the factory system produced a deleterious effect, despite the comparatively benign effect of cloth production on juvenile and adult mortality, as recorded in chapter 5.

Summary and Conclusion

The revolution in woolen manufacturing in the Stroud and lower districts of Uley, Dursley, and Wotton-under-Edge marked the transition from a protoindustrial to a factory-based system. The most distinguishing characteristic of this transition has been its comparative failure to revolutionize local society. Although improvements in communication (coupled with the growth of industry) fostered regionalism, significant urbanization did not take place, and a net loss of population occurred over the period.

Indeed, the cloth districts entered into decline virtually at the point of consolidation of the factory system, and contrary to the experience of the northern textile trade.

Excess capacity, induced by structural defects in the industry's power-supply system, rather than the alleged entrepreneurial failure of its clothiers, explained Gloucester's inability to remain competitive. Because of intensified competition and the vulnerability of smaller firms to trade depression, large capital-intensive firms came to predominate earlier at Gloucester, whereas a plethora of small firms coexisted with giant establishments at Yorkshire as late as mid-century. Gloucester's small firms did not necessarily operate inefficiently; large firms, because of greater capitalization, proved better equipped to glean greater shares of a declining market. After 1825, however, even this stratum began to experience a rising rate of bankruptcy and retirements from trade. The lower district collapsed as early as 1831 because concentration on coarse items brought it into direct competition with Yorkshire. Nailsworth declined more gradually because its unsurpassed fine cloths partially protected the locality from northern competition, but the loss of the coarse trade adversely affected it as well. Gloucester's woolen industry ultimately fell victim to market forces, and in this respect, its experience illustrates how contingency could accompany the process of modernization.[172]

Despite this failure, industrialization had an impact on labor that can be associated with a modernizing trend. The emergence of the factory system gradually undermined the protoindustrial household economy, in which each family member found a place in a delicately balanced internal division of labor. This picture of the protoindustrial household can be overdrawn, however, since it assumes the absence of traditional craft distinctions between master, journeyman, and apprentice, which, in fact persisted quite late. Still, the factory system induced "functional differentiation" in spinning and weaving, separating work from the home even when wives and children continued to labor elsewhere.

Wives and daughters who spun or wove at home, following the emergence of the factory, engaged in a less synchronized work rhythm than their predominantly male factory counterparts. Moreover, as factory workers, women generally engaged in less skilled and comparatively less demanding occupations; nor did they always work alongside other family members. A reconstitution of the family as a productive unit within the factory quite possibly occurred after midcentury; until 1850, however, this study affirms the traditional functionalist view.

Apart from its impact on the gender-based division of labor, the factory system greatly improved labor productivity, particularly among former journeymen and apprentices. More rigorous work discipline fostered habits of self-discipline and individual autonomy. Under then prevailing conditions of stagnation, however, the new regime also promoted exploitation. Falling wage rates conspired with more intensive expenditure of effort and a slowdown in the rate of falling grain prices to produce a limited decline in living standards for the critical period of transition, from 1828 to 1842. Still, how artisans and industrial workers responded to the factory system, in the forms of strikes and protests, reveals the truly subjective side of the issue behind changing living standards and remains to be examined.

Chapter Seven

Class Formation and the Growth of Social Stability

The capitalization of the woolen trade completed the proletarianization of its workforce. Although accompanied by social conflict, this process ultimately gave rise to social stability. The circuitous growth of stability can be studied through the changing forms of protest occurring between 1825 and 1848. This chapter begins with a reconstruction of the great weaver strike of 1825, which stood as a watershed in the history of popular protest throughout Gloucestershire. Because of its transitional quality, the strike recalled the customary form of protest characteristic of weaver strikes dating back to the 1720s and 1750s.[1] The last phase of the 1825 strike did, however, anticipate the more distinctive class confrontations of the post-1830 period, setting the stage for further scrutiny of them and for analysis of the subsequent growth of stability. The present chapter, therefore, pinpoints the timing of proletarianization among weavers and recreates the process by which a new social equilibrium had emerged.

The Weaver Strike of 1825

The Gloucester weaver strike of 1825 followed a national pattern of trade union revival after Parliament's repeal of the Combination Acts in 1824. However, the strike also marked a turning point in the evolution of the county's woolen trade from a protoindustrial to a factory-based system. Indeed, the strike embodied in its form the developing state of the industry by combining characteristics of preindustrial "risings" with those of modern industrial disorders.

Scholars have little appreciated the strike's transitional quality, however, treating it inevitably as a straightforward confrontation between capital and labor. They have depicted the weavers as a homogeneous social group, their strike movement as autonomous, and their conflict with the clothiers as a unitary, year-long struggle for higher wages.[2] Such treatment, moreover, reflects widely held assumptions about the nature of class and class consciousness in the English Industrial Revolution.[3]

This chapter offers a different perspective. Master weavers organized and led the strike, but their interests sometimes differed from those of their journeymen and apprentices. Nor was their movement completely autonomous, since the deference they displayed permitted elements within the employing and governing class to manipulate them. Those engaged in such manipulation pursued the interests of their own social group, however sincerely they invoked the values of paternalism. Indeed, the dominant pattern of conflict followed a traditional vertical arrangement; a hint of modern class conflict emerged only in the final phase of the strike.

The strike occurred in three phases, each corresponding to changes in both the collective attitudes of its participants and the character of their demands. These demands contained customary features that gave the weavers an initial basis for cooperation with some of the largest clothiers of the region. Only in the final phase of the strike did weaver adherence to custom "radicalize," although the change confined itself to a minority. In this way, the strike eventually assumed some of the dimensions of a modern labor dispute and thereby anticipated the genuine class confrontations of the post-1825 period.

The narrative reconstruction of the strike illustrates its transitional quality in detail. First, the economic issues that helped determine its configuration need to be outlined. Second, the terms "deference" and "paternalism" have controversial meanings and require theoretical clarification as prelude to their usage.

In 1824 manufacturers increased the size of the woven piece without increasing weaving rates correspondingly. The increase ran from 16-hundred length chain to a maximum of 20-hundreds,

TABLE 55. *Weaving Rates Negotiated in 1825*

		Colored Cloths		White Cloths	
Hundred per ell	Odd beers	Sum requested (s.d)	Sum offered (s.d)	Sum requested (s.d)	Sum offered (s.d)
1600[a]		1.9	1.9	1.6	1.4
1600[b]			1.9		1.5
1600[b]	2		1.9½		1.5½
1600[b]	4		1.10		1.4
1700[a]		1.10	1.9	1.7	1.5
1700[b]			1.10		1.6
1700[b]	2		1.10½		1.6½
1700[b]	4		1.11		1.7
1800[a]		1.11	1.9	1.8	1.6
1800[b]			1.11		1.7
1800[b]	2		1.11½		1.7½
1800[b]	4		2.0		1.8
1900[a]		2.0	1.10	1.9	1.7
1900[b]			2.0		1.8
1900[b]	2		2.0½		1.8½
1900[b]	4		2.1		1.9
2000[a]		2.1	1.11	1.10	1.8
2000[b]			2.0		1.9
2000[b]	2		2.1½		1.9½
2000[b]	4		2.2		1.10

[a] The weavers' asking prices and the clothiers' counteroffer.
[b] The final settlement at Dursley and Stroud, May–June 1825. The weavers obtained their requested rates in colored cloths and compromised on the rates for white cloths.
Source: British Parliamentary Papers, Sessional Papers, 24 (1840): 396, 454; *Gloucester Journal,* 22 November 1824.

as recorded in table 55, and rose by 900 shoots per yard in the abb from 1,600 to 2,500 shoots per yard.[4] Since manufacturers paid by the piece, the change brought them larger profits at the weaver's financial expense while further intensifying his labor. Such intensified exploitation, and the violation of custom it represented, forced the weavers to react.

In their petition of 1824, master weavers complained about the greater laboriousness of their work and also about the low wages of their journeymen, the high cost of subsistence, and their own

low profit margins.⁵ Accordingly, they proposed a pay scale standardized to apply to all manufacturers and designed to yield a
compensatory average rise in weaving rates.

However rational an approach this may have seemed, some
confusion attended their objectives. At first they defended their
prices because of the higher average wages these would bring but
later denied that they intended to secure a general pay raise. In
November 1824 they declared "with deepest humility and most
profound respect that [our] wages have not been raised for 94
years."⁶ By June 1825, however, they confessed that "an advance
is not the point for which we are contending. . . ; our only aim has
been to bring the unfeeling and unfair-dealing part of the manufacturers up to one general standard."⁷

Closer scrutiny of the weavers' petition reveals several important defects in their approach. First, their proposed pay scale only
partially compensated them for the increased labor time required
under the new work rule. The increase in the number of shoots in
the abb should have risen from 1,600 to 2,000 shoots per yard
instead of 2,500 shoots if parity were to have been maintained.
The resulting surplus of 500 shoots meant greater density of the
fabric, but since weaving rates were determined solely by the
length of the chain, the labor time required for this surplus must
have gone uncompensated.⁸ A compromise agreement was
reached that appears to have favored the weavers, but the base
rate for colored cloths contained in their list was lower than the
one already in force among several large manufacturers. These
manufacturers reduced their minimum rates accordingly and campaigned for general acceptance of the settlement.⁹ Some employers
certainly paid well below others, often by as much as 12s. to 13s.
per piece on average.¹⁰ If everyone had joined the weavers in
accepting the agreement, however, the average pay raise, "upon
the general bulk of the manufacturers," would have come to 1d.
per ell, an all too modest advance.¹¹

Had master weavers defended their demands solely on the
grounds of labor exploitation, their argument would have been
unimpeachable. They sought to justify themselves, however, as
any small employer would have done, by citing increased production costs, and in this effort they were less convincing. They
claimed, for instance, that their net pay for 1,600-chain white

TABLE 56. *The Master Weaver's Stated Expenses, ca. 1824*

Items	Costs (£.s.d.)
Glue for seizing, 3 lb	0.2.6
Harness and slay	0.2.0
Candles	0.2.6
Quilling	0.4.0
Twine, oil, shuttles, peckers, etc.	0.1.0
Rent for shop and wear-and-tear for loom	0.3.9
Journeyman's wages[a]	1.8.0

[a]Late in 1824
Source: *British Parliamentary Papers*; see text.

cloth averaged 10s.9d after deductions of 15s.9d for glue, harness, twine, and rent.[12] Yet they failed to mention that this applied only to themselves and not to their journeymen, who had to absorb these costs from their own wages.[13] Nor did they admit that several journeymen could have been at work simultaneously, thereby making the master weaver's net return very much greater (see table 56).

The combined wages of masters and journeymen ranged from 16s to a guinea or an average of 17s.6d per week, a figure that necessarily obscures the disparity in earnings between them.[14] Masters probably earned as much as spinners at 20s to 30s per week, while journeymen earned from 10s to 12s per week for a fifteen- to sixteen-hour day.[15] The journeyman supported the master weaver's call for higher wages because he felt that he would benefit from an increase, but it is doubtful that each shared this concern to the same degree.

Master weavers, for instance, justified their call for higher weaving rates partly on the basis of a rising cost of living, which, they insisted, had transpired over the course of a century.[16] This "long view" was clearly erroneous, however, since they neglected to mention the fall in wheat prices that began toward the end of the French wars. From June 1812, the highest point in table 57, to December 1824, when strike negotiations began in earnest, wheat prices declined at an average rate of 0.5 percent per month, and

TABLE 57. *Three-Month Moving Averages of Wheat Prices (in Shillings per Bushel), 1804–1826*

Months	1804/05	1805/06	1808/09	1809/10	1812/13	1813/14	1816/17	1817/18	1819/20	1820/21	1823/24	1824/25
January–March	6.5	11.4	8.4	14.0	16.5	15.3	6.0	18.0	9.2	8.0	4.6	6.4
February–April	6.4	12.0	8.7	14.0	17.6	15.6	6.3	17.0	9.1	8.2	5.0	6.9
March–May	6.4	10.8	9.2	13.6	18.6	15.3	7.6	16.0	8.8	8.3	5.6	7.5
April–June	6.4	11.5	10.2	13.2	19.8	14.8	8.6	14.5	8.4	8.2	6.2	8.0
May–July	6.5	11.6	10.9	12.7	19.9	14.5	9.2	13.0	8.1	8.2	6.7	8.1
June–August	6.7	13.6	11.4	12.9	20.6	14.3	9.3	11.3	8.1	8.1	7.0	7.9
July–September	7.3	13.8	11.6	13.7	20.8	13.6	9.7	10.0	8.1	8.0	7.1	7.8
August–October	8.0	14.0	12.4	14.9	20.2	12.9	11.3	9.3	8.1	7.7	6.8	7.6
September–November	9.7	13.4	13.4	15.5	19.1	11.9	12.8	8.3	8.1	7.4	6.5	7.5
October–December	10.6	12.9	14.1	15.7	17.2	11.3	14.3	8.5	8.0	6.7	6.2	7.4
November–January	11.4	12.3	14.2	15.5	15.9	10.3	15.8	8.5	7.9	6.3	6.3	7.2
December–February	11.4	12.0	14.0	15.5	14.9	9.9	17.0	8.5	7.8	5.8	6.3	7.4

TABLE 57. *Continued*

	1806/07	1810/11	1814/15	1818/19	1821/22	1825/26
January–March	12.1	15.6	9.7	8.5	5.8	7.8
February–April	12.0	16.0	9.2	9.6	5.8	8.5
March–May	12.6	16.8	8.7	10.4	5.8	8.8
April–June	12.6	17.5	8.1	11.1	5.8	9.0[b]
May–July	12.3	17.7	7.9	10.8	5.7	8.9
June–August	12.1	17.5	8.6	10.3	5.8	8.8
July–September	12.0	16.9	9.3	10.0	7.3	8.7
August–October	11.9	16.6	10.1	9.7	8.3	8.6
September–November	11.7	16.5	10.0	9.7	9.1	8.6
October–December	11.2	16.8	9.8	9.6	8.2	8.5
November–January	10.6	16.6	8.8	9.4	6.9	8.5
December–February	10.2	16.3	8.3	9.3	5.6	8.5

	1807/08	1811/12	1815/16	1819/20	1822/23	1826
January–March	10.2	15.4	8.1	9.2	4.8	8.3
February–April	10.3	14.5	8.6	9.1	4.8	7.8
March–May	10.4	13.7	8.4	8.8	4.7	7.4
April–June	10.3	13.3	8.3	8.4	4.7	
May–July	10.1	13.2	8.3	8.1	4.7	
June–August	9.9	13.0	8.3	8.1	5.0	
July–September	9.9	13.7	7.8	8.1	5.0	
August–October	9.9	15.0	7.1	8.1	5.1	
September–November	9.6	16.2	6.3	8.1	4.8	
October–December	9.3	16.5	6.0	8.0	4.8	
November–January	8.6	16.5	6.0	7.9	4.6	
December–February	8.6	16.5	6.0	7.8	4.5[a]	

[a] Prestrike low point.
[b] Midstrike high point.
Source: Gloucester Journal; see text.

from January 1817 to the end of the same period, the rate of decline averaged 0.8 percent per month.[17]

Bread, however, could account for as much as 45 percent of the journeyman's budget; thus, the rise in wheat prices between 1821 and 1824 was of much greater moment to him.[18] Between December 1821 and December 1824, wheat prices, although remaining comparatively low, rose gradually at an average rate of 1.5 percent per month. Between December 1822 to February 1823, the lowest point in the series, and April to June 1825, the period of strike activity, the growth rate averaged 1.8 percent per month. In this last interval, wheat prices reached their highest levels since early 1819, a factor that probably contributed to the outbreak of violence in early June.

In general, master weavers seemed less concerned about winning a serious pay raise than standardizing weaving rates. These goals were not incompatible in principle but were made so in the course of negotiations and in this way conflicted with the interests of the journeymen. "Although it may be said that . . . the weavers struck for an advance in wages," the parliamentary commissioner concluded, "it was in fact only for an equalization throughout the County."[19]

Master weavers were still more custom-minded than market-oriented. Although they proposed a pay scale based on the calculation of labor time and legitimated their claims by invoking production costs, defects in their approach show how incomplete their appreciation of the rules of the marketplace remained. Custom strongly informed their notion of a just price but led them to undervalue the proper rate of return to labor.[20] More significantly, they sought to create guildlike control over the price of labor, even if this meant accepting lower average pay raises. Control over pay rates was especially important to them because it embodied their aspirations for independence. Custom, in other words, was a notion drawn from the traditions of both the laboring and middle classes, and its persistence retarded the formation of the weavers into a mature proletariat.

The structure of the wage relationship, in particular, tended to reinforce a middle-class sensibility of independence. This structure was based on the face-to-face relations between master weavers and clothiers, which persisted despite the scattered nature of cottage industry. Master weavers delivered woven cloth directly to their clothiers and received payment in return. If the clothier were short of cash, he gave the master weaver a promissory note and thereby became indebted to him.[21] The master weaver then deducted his journeymen's wages, as indicated in table 56, and if he paid his journeymen in kind (a frequent practice), he deducted 5d. to 6d. per shilling or about 50 percent of their money earnings.[22] He also deducted a rent charge for their use of his looms and a charge for technical assistance and general assistance in loom maintenance. Besides these charges, the master weaver kept for himself the cost of his own labor, which included the time lost delivering the finished product,[23] and a small profit. The standardization of weaving prices would have secured his profits and his traditional status as an artisan-employer.

Low-paying manufacturers became the true object of weaver protest in 1825 because they created economic insecurity and violated prescriptive norms of respectability in order to remain competitive. Master weavers, consequently, sought allies among higher-paying manufacturers by appealing to both their self-interest and paternalist values. If the weavers' proposed scale were universally adopted, they humbly contended, "the low priced manufacturer, who have been impoverishing and distressing the workmen...to render their goods cheaper in the market, to the great injury of the fair trader..., will have few or none to work for them...and your petitioners will ever pray for your prosperity." This appeal grew out of deferential habits and a local tradition of paternalism, and a history of collective disturbance based on such attitudes affected the strike's entire configuration.

The terms "deference" and "paternalism" have complex and often controversial meanings. E. P. Thompson, for instance, has dismissed paternalism as nothing more than "a studied technique of rule" and deference as perfunctory gesturing.[24] However, more recent scholarship has successfully revived both concepts.[25] Patrick Joyce has shown that paternalism in later Victorian Lancashire often represented an amalgam of sentiments. Altruism and employer self-interest in social control often intermingled comfortably.[26] Joyce insists, too, on the "real inwardness" of deference, with workers "subscri[bing] to a moral order that validate[d] their own subordination."[27] Deference, by embracing a degree of self-abasement, thereby assured the stability of the social system. For Howard Newby, workers usually acceded the legitimacy of their employer's authority, but they did so believing in a structure of mutual obligations.[28] In Newby's formulation, deference and feelings of self-worth could be compatible; if employers failed to fulfill customary obligations, deference collapsed and class antagonism emerged instead.

Joyce and Newby have based their insights on the experiences of urban industrial workers.[29] Their judgments apply equally well to Gloucester's rural-industrial districts, where large-scale manufacturing developed in the absence of urbanization. The scattered nature of Gloucester's parochial settlements, located in wood-pasture regions,[30] did not impede face-to-face relations between employers and workers, nor between the Establishment generally and the lower classes, as is sometimes alleged.[31] Master weavers, as we have seen, did not transact business through intermediaries but dealt directly with their employers. By 1825, spinning, preparatory and finishing processes were carried out largely on mill premises, bringing other clothworkers into direct contact with manufacturers. Labor recruitment, moreover, was still conducted on a familial basis. This practice reinforced the traditional integration of the household economy and the world of work and served as the basis of communal solidarity that included the employer.[32]

Among Gloucester's leading clothiers, Edward Sheppard of Uley Mills was known especially for his paternalism. He opposed the factory acts, for instance, believing that "the charges of cruelty toward those persons whom it has been the practice of [the clothiers'] lives to rear up, to protect and support" were grossly unfounded.[33] In 1824 he was one of two clothiers to advance weaving rates voluntarily by an average of 1d. per ell,[34] but he was also among "the biggest manufacturers [who] had to reduce their [minimum] wages to the standard named by the weavers."[35] By lowering his base rate and agreeing simultaneously to effect a marginal average pay raise, Sheppard acted from a combination of self-interest and altruism. Concern for the stability of his neighborhood, another hallmark of paternalism,[36] also encouraged him to compromise. "I felt it my duty," Sheppard contended, "to take a very active part in proposing the terms of arrangement [between clothiers and strikers] in apprehension of what would be the result of all the factories being at a stand."[37] Sheppard, by the weight of his authority, carried virtually his entire district in accepting this agreement. Sheppard's gentry status, as much as his occupation, informed his paternalism.[38] It was not uncommon for large Gloucester clothiers to own landed estates and to be lords of manors, and as gentlemen-clothiers they frequently served their communities as magistrates.[39] The "gentlemanly ethic" of paternalism,[40] usually associated only with magistrates,[41] was, in fact, widely shared in Gloucester by a highly synthetic governing class of mill owners, Justices of the Peace, and manor lords.[42] For this reason, it is permissable to use the term "paternalism" generically rather than in a restricted typological sense, as in "J.P. paternalism."

Nonetheless, the governing class of a given community need not always have remained united in its fundamental interests. Joyce and Newby imply that such unity is the sine qua non of social stability, and they portray the maintenance of stability as the "structural function" of paternalism.[43] When division occurred among the elite, however, paternalism and deference easily conduced to collective action and even violence, as one section of the governing class sought to mobilize its resources against another. Such division manifest itself especially in the operations of preindustrial crowds.[44] A paternalism-deference mode of collective action has a historiographic lineage in John Walsh's study of anti-Methodist "tumults," Walter Shelton's work on eighteenth-century food riots and M. E. James's reconstruction of the sixteenth-century Lincolnshire rebellion.[45] James's study offers an especially apt description of this pattern that is worth quoting at length:

The methods used ranged from riots in market towns to mass popular demonstrations involving the armed occupation of the shire capital and the drafting of programmes of political demands. . . . At the same time, however, the contention is that these were constrained within a framework of form and convention which aimed at limiting the disruptive effects of the movement, and the amount of damage that might result, particularly to the landed governing class. . . . Thus while the rebellion assumed the initial form of popular commotions, which were accompanied by some . . . popular violence, the leadership of the "commons" soon gave way to that of J.P.s and gentlemen, although supposedly "coerced" into this position. Respect for established authority...was maintained throughout; and when, as the movement began to disintegrate, some of the popular leaders sought to assert themselves against their betters, the majority of the commons supported the latter.[46]

Behind the Lincolnshire rising, James has concluded, stood the covert interests and leadership of a wing of the governing class.

In 1825 conflicts of interest divided Gloucester clothiers and thereby made possible a similar pattern of collective action. Almost all clothiers from the lower district reached an early agreement with the weavers, but a majority of the Stroud clothiers opposed it. Because Sheppard and his followers produced far fewer cassimeres than did their Stroud counterparts, they lost nothing by accepting the "weavers' prices."[47] However, by settling early, Sheppard also thought they had acted for the benefit of the trade.[48] William Playne of Longfords Mills, near Stroud, believed, however, that they had fomented the strike,[49] and he adhered to this view as late as 1838. "There has not been a strike," he contended, "but what some masters were at the bottom of it."[50] As we shall see, Playne's belief was not entirely unfounded, since magistrates who shared Sheppard's paternalism were to be found inciting weavers to riot.

Social distinctions among weavers were no less a critical factor. The strike, as already noted, was organized by and reflected the interests of master weavers. Journeymen and apprentices participated, but in an auxiliary capacity, and when other members of the laboring classes demonstrated solidarity, they did so spontaneously. The weavers made no effort at this time to organize less skilled clothworkers. Master weavers saw themselves as small employers no less than as workmen, and many of the more successful among them aspired to become clothiers.[51] The demands of the strike centered initially around the issue of pay but escalated into a more comprehensive program informed by middle-class aspirations.[52] Master weavers who aspired to become clothiers empathized with their social superiors, and empathy can serve as a basis for deference.[53] When events frustrated such ambitions, however, some turned militant.

The first phase of the strike was moderate, peaceful, and deferentially conducted in the lower district but yielded to violence at Stroud, following the pattern of the Lincolnshire rebellion. The third phase shifted back to the lower district and was also accompanied by violence, but in a manner suggesting the radicalization of the remaining strikers. We can see more clearly how this pattern unfolded by reconstructing, as far as possible, the narrative of events.

Approaching the strike as a unitary phenomenon is perhaps understandable in one sense since the weavers' committee succeeded in mobilizing followers from all parishes in both the Stroud and the lower districts. A Wotton magistrate, P. B. Purnell, reported to the Home Office in January 1826 that since April 1825 five or six meetings ranging from 700 to 10,000 weavers took place not far from his residence. "To these meetings," he contended, "the different companies are marched in regular order, separated according to their different parishes, and headed and marshalled by their respective delegates [who] are chosen men, twelve to each parish."[54] Nonetheless, despite such considerable unity, the strike evolved in three stages because of the competing interests of the two districts.

First Stage

The strike began on April 29, 1825 after the weavers' petition of 1824, requesting changes in the rates of pay, met with little response from the clothiers of both districts. Three days later the weavers met in a large assembly with some manufacturers at Caincross, but without reaching agreement, whereupon several hundred shuttles were immediately collected.[55] During the next several days, meetings of 3,000 were held on Break Heart and Stinchcomb Hills, and by May 8 a settlement with the clothiers of the lower district had been reached. Sheppard was eager for an agreement, not only for the reasons already cited but also from awareness that the Tenth Hussars at Bristol had been alerted "in consequence of the state of insurrection in which the weavers of Gloucestershire were."[56] On this last point, he was quick to assure the Home Office of "the orderly conduct of the weavers, who have not shown any disposition to riot." They had agreed to return to work, but only for those clothiers who had accepted the new prices. They were to meet at Selsley Hill, "a middle spot between the districts," on May 9 "when they divide their shuttles and go to work." By May 18, Sheppard was able to report, the weavers at the lower district had returned to work for all but "three or four masters who refuse to give the prices agreed."[57]

On May 11 the weavers once again "congregated on Selsley Hill," this time "to the number of not less than six thousand, for the purpose of learning the sentiments of the manufacturers of the Stroud and Nailsworth districts."[58] Several manufacturers had agreed to the prices, but they were too few to satisfy the weavers. Another meeting was therefore held at Nympsfield, on the border of Nailsworth, at which "it was strenuously urged that they should resume their labour for those gentlemen inclined to accede to the prices." This suggestion, however, "was obstinately resisted ...until the whole of the manufacturers had expressed their compliance." The weavers remained "orderly and respectful to their superiors" nonetheless, conducting themselves throughout in a "quiet and peaceful demeanor, even when assembled in the greatest numbers."

Many Stroud clothiers were not in a position to meet the prices, so they argued, because many cloths were already under contract to the East India Company,[59] and those who produced lighter cassimeres felt these types of cloths varied too greatly with respect to the labor required to justify the weavers' desire to standardize their prices.[60] A further consideration, one "Old Manufacturer" contended, was that "they consider the principle of a manufacturer putting his name to the demands of his work-people, as establishing a destructive precedent." Given such a viewpoint, Edward Sheppard's behavior appeared truly astonishing, and his competitors suspected him of attempting to undermine them. "Some manufacturers," William Playne bitterly complained, "have gone so far as to make the workmen [who] arise not to weave these articles at a [lesser] advance than from 33s. 4d. to 45s. such when they only ask from 20 to 25s."[61] Playne's belief that clothiers fomented the strike led him to request that "the troops...not be withdrawn from Bristol unless as many...were quartered at Cheltenham, Tetbury, Sodbury or Malmsbury."[62] Clearly, he anticipated future difficulties. At a time when the weavers of the lower district had returned to work, about one-third of the clothiers at Stroud refused to accept the weavers' prices, and a few even closed their factories in protest.[63]

Second Stage

The strike at Stroud suddenly turned violent at the beginning of June. Attempts to negotiate had proved ineffective, and some weavers began to accept work "under price." A crowd descended on the Wyatts at Vatch Mill, near the town of Stroud, having seized several ends of cloth from strike-breakers with the aim of returning them to the manufacturer.[64] When they arrived, "they conducted themselves in a . . . tumultuous manner, and made such demonstrations as to call from Mr. George Wyatt a threat . . . [which] led to a scuffle, and ultimately to a complete riot." The rioters were arrested, but the next day, when brought before the magistrate, "many thousands [of malcontents] . . . making use of very violent language" disrupted the proceedings against them. The rioters demanded that the authorities free those arrested and threatened otherwise to destroy the building. When the Wyatts's foreman made his way to give evidence, "he was seized . . . and carried down to the pond of Little Mill, where they ducked him." When Peter and George Wyatt approached to give evidence, they were assaulted and severely beaten. The crowd proceded to their home and seized eight of their men, who had acted as special constables the preceeding day, and ducked them in the pond at Vatch Mill. At about the same time, rioters entered Frogmarsh, a small village near Nailsworth, and ducked fourteen weavers who refused to turn out to demonstrate. On Monday, June 6, two days later, the same pattern of rioting and ducking took place at Chalford, in Bisley, and at Minchinhampton and Woodchester, near Nailsworth.[65] As a result, the Tenth Hussars were finally called in from Bristol.[66] By the evening of June 6, when the Hussars finally arrived, the riots had ceased. However, at the town of Stroud "the mechanics thronged the streets until Tuesday,"[67] apparently with impunity and numbering eight to ten thousand,[68] "when the principal cloth manufacturers determined upon acceding to their demands for an increase of wages."[69] The presence of the militia, for obscure reasons, was not sufficient to intimidate the crowd, and the bench of magistrates remained inexplicably silent.

The simultaneous eruption of violence at Stroud and Frogmarsh, followed almost immediately by riots at Chalford, Minchinhampton, and Woodchester, suggests an element of coordination. Indeed, people widely held clothiers responsible for the violence that accompanied strikes.[70] Direct evidence for such an assertion is difficult to locate but is not entirely absent in cases of magistrates who, motivated by paternalist sentiment, desired a settlement on the "weavers'" terms. The case of Richard Aldridge, a Chalford magistrate, is significant for this reason; it is especially important because, in the role he played, his influence apparently stretched beyond the confines of his parish.

An Assize jury acquitted Aldridge in April 1826 of having directed the weavers' riot at Bisley,[71] although the judge clearly prejudiced its members in his favor. In his charge, the judge proclaimed the defense witnesses to have "given their evidence in a much more respectable manner than [those] for the prosecution," and he thought that "this was a case of very grave doubt, because it was very difficult to conceive why a respectable magistrate . . . should go two miles from his own house, to mix himself with a pack of blackguards and encourage them to acts of mutiny and sedition toward their employers."

The report of the Court's proceedings very cursorily summarized the evidence of the more "respectable" defense witnesses[72] and therefore cannot be readily assessed. However, evidence for the prosecution was reported in considerable detail and is compelling. Had the judge not swayed the jury (which deliberated for only three minutes), it seems likely that it would have rendered a different verdict. In general, the prosecution witnesses testified that Aldridge sought to get the weavers back to work for those clothiers who had agreed to their prices but adamantly refused to tolerate any weaver working "under price." On two occasions he encouraged weavers to take violent action against strike breakers. He was later observed by a shopkeeper, a weaver who had worked under price, and the millman of the clothier who employed her (all of whom witnessed these events independently), as having led a massive demonstration against that clothier's mill and openly directing the ducking of several strike-breakers.

William Pettit, a weaver and member of the thirteen-man executive committee of the Union, testified that Aldridge met with several hundred weavers on Bisley Common and had asked whether the work had been returned "to the clothiers who refuse to give the price." When they told him it had not, he appeared angry and retorted, "then I shall consider it a mark of dishonesty if you don't," after which they all agreed they would do so the next morning. At this same meeting, he encouraged them "to work for the gentlemen who would give the [full] price." When Reuben Hunt, the president of the weavers' committee, met with Aldridge on May 23, the latter advised him that a certain manufacturer "would pay full wages . . . and said it was a pity so many weavers accepted payment in truck instead of money."[73] Aldridge had clearly offered the weavers his patronage, acting from a combination of paternalism and concern for the interests of the higher-paying manufacturers.

On May 24 he reportedly met with the weavers' committee at the Duke of York House to advise them that "you must have your shuttles out and go to work," for those clothiers who would give the price and afterward bought two gallons of beer for the committee members. The weavers returned the shuttles soon thereafter, and Revd. Mansfield "preached a sermon the Friday in Witsun week, on occasion of peace being restored in the neighborhood."

One must recall that at their initial meeting with the Stroud clothiers at Selsley Hill during the second week in May, the majority of the weavers insisted on continuing the strike until they had succeeded as completely in the lower district. This goal remained their objective until Aldridge's critical intervention at the Duke of York on May 24, but when pressed, they deferred on this issue. It became apparent (as Aldridge's comment to Reuben Hunt had shown) that through his good offices, the more recalcitrant clothiers could be persuaded to agree to the prices. Yet despite Mansfield's sermon, such mediation did not finally restore peace to the neighborhood, since some clothiers persisted in paying below the weavers' scale.

The mutually supporting evidence provided by the weavers, John Ridler, Nathaniel Young, and John Workman, revealed that as early as May 12 Aldridge was willing to sanction violence against weavers who "worked under foot," as well as against the clothiers who employed them. John Ridler stated that Aldridge had ordered him "to take those who worked under foot, where there was water handy, duck them; and where they were not handy to water, to take them upon the Common and kick their—

well, and he would see them righted." Young and Workman, who had accompanied Ridler to Aldridge's, corroborated his testimony.

On the afternoon of June 6, two days after the Stroud and Frogmarsh riots, and the same day of the riots at Minchinhampton and Woodchester, several witnesses saw Aldridge at the head of a demonstration of weavers. John Eye, a Chalford shopkeeper, saw him on horseback at the corner of the shop, "and he continued riding for sixty or seventy yards, backwards and forwards," apparently waiting for the weavers who "passed by in a body" a quarter of an hour later. In a half hour, they returned, "and they had some fore-beams with cloth upon them, belonging to Mr. Davis, the clothier." According to Amos Tyler, the crowd had come to his house and taken away some work belonging to Davis, that his wife had been weaving. Handy Davis, the clothier involved, testified that on the same evening half-woven cloth was brought back to him by a crowd of unknown weavers numbering over 1,000, with Aldridge leading their way on horseback. "He rode on horseback; the weavers followed him with their work upon their shoulders, and he said 'put the work down, but don't injure it'"; to have done so would have been a capital offense. Thomas Hyde, Davis's millman, gave an even more compelling account of this incident that is worth quoting at length, for it captures the spirit of deference that lay at the heart of the weavers' relationship to Aldridge:

He saw Mr. Aldridge coming down on horseback, in front of a great number of people[,] bringing his master's work. When they came, Mr. Aldridge put his stick against the gates to try if they were fast, and finding they were so, he then rode round the corner of a wall, and said "here, I want to speak to some of you." A great number were going to him and he said "I don't want you all." He then said something in private to some of them, and after that turned his horse and rode through them. They made way for him and *reverenced* him as he passed [emphasis added].

After that Mr. Aldridge said, "Well my men, we are all standing idle in the road here, filling up the road doing nothing. Are you going to fetch any back? He then said, 'if you are going, go with me, but if not leave off.' They then dispersed from the factory, and the witnesses opened the gates and took in the work."

According to "a vast number of witnesses," Aldridge then proceeded to organize the ducking of Nathaniel Gardner and George Oldham, two weavers who had worked under price. They reported having heard him exclaim: "Duck him! It will do him no harm, and make him know better than to take the work out under foot again!" The crowd "gave three cheers after the ducking was over, in which Mr. Aldridge joined, waving his hat in the air."

Aldridge's defense admitted that his client "perhaps might have used indiscreet expressions," but pleaded extenuating circumstances. "He alone," the defense claimed, "had to stem the fury of a misguided rabble, without. . . the aid of a solitary constable." His intention, ostensibly, had been "to temporize with those by conciliatory means whom he was not able to cope with by force," until military aid arrived.

Yet the defense unwittingly had shown under cross-examination of a prosecution witness, Handy Davis, that Aldridge had not bothered to appoint special constables until the morning of June 7, well after the arrival of the Hussars at Stroud. He had not taken the same elementary precautions that P. B. Purnell followed at Wotton later in the year, namely, "keep[ing] in a body of my own labourers as special constables. . . and by swearing in and arming all the principal inhabitants of the parish as special constables."[74] The evidence suggests that Aldridge, having instigated the demonstration that culminated in ducking of the two weavers, momentarily lost control and panicked.

The entire proceeding, from the arrival at Davis's mill to the ducking episode, had occurred between 5:00 and 6:00 P.M. By 6:30 P.M., however, "a great mob" was reported amuk in Chalford proper. At the same time, Aldridge was found scurrying to the home of Daniel Cox, a clothier, to warn him of impending danger to his property. Cox bolted himself in his mill and armed his people with sticks, pitchforks, and billhooks. However, the arrival of the weavers proved anticlimactic; no attack transpired because Aldridge was able to lead them away after all. He then returned to Cox's residence later that evening and in obvious agitation composed a letter to the Duke of Beaufort, the Lord Lieutenant, requesting military aid. "What then," Cox reproached him, "you have nursed the baby so long that it is too big for you!" By this late hour, Aldridge had undoubtedly heard of the arrival of the Tenth

Hussars at Stroud and of their intention to visit Chalford.[75] His letter to the Duke, and his hasty swearing-in of constables the following morning, appear as desperate but nonetheless successful efforts to transfer responsibility for the outbreak of violence to those whom he had misled.

Nor had Aldridge confined his activities to his own locality. One of the defense witnesses noted at the strike's outset that the Chalford vestry called a meeting on Aldridge's advice, "and [invited] the neighboring clothiers. . . to attend, for the purpose of seeing whether the differences between the weavers and their employers could be adjusted." At the same time, Aldridge met regularly with the weavers' executive committee, which coordinated the strike throughout both main districts. Just as Edward Sheppard exerted his immense influence in the lower district to gain acceptance of the "weavers'" prices, so Aldridge had made the same effort in the Stroud region. Sheppard succeeded peacefully in the first months of the strike. At Stroud, however, no manufacturer of comparable stature existed to take the same stand; William Playne, who approached Sheppard in status, had different interests. Greater pressure on recalcitrants was required, and this fact explains Aldridge's provocative behavior. He succeeded, too; despite the arrival of the Hussars, as we have seen, a general strike of the "mechanics" brought many of the remaining clothiers around.

Third Stage

In late November 1825 the Wotton riots showed a significant shift in pattern. By this time, those weavers who remained on strike had become more militant and acted with greater independence, even if they represented only a minority; the complicity of the magistracy remained a possibility nonetheless, if only indirectly. The weavers acted more violently, in some respects, than they had at Stroud and Chalford in early June, and in a manner that pointed to the greater autonomy of their movement. Rioting at Wotton took the form of planned violent attacks on the property of two clothiers who paid wages below the union's price. The attacks were organized under the guidance of a pensioner, a former sergeant who was called "General Wolfe,"[76] and thereby acquired a quasi-military aspect.

The weavers directed their first attack against Thomas Neale, who specialized in cassimeres. After several meetings, in the open air and at the Swann Inn, about 100 weavers, marching in rank order, seized the cloth and loom beams from one of Neale's weavers and set them afire, thereby committing a capital offense. Later, they moved onto North Nibley and attacked the home of one of Samuel Plomer's weavers. On the next day, November 24, 300 weavers marched in two-by-two formation through the streets of Wotton to the house of another of Thomas Neale's weavers, seized the cloth and beams, and carried them to Neale's mill, where they proceeded to cut the cloth and to stamp on it. Neale armed himself and his workers, and withdrew into his mill; and when the rioters began throwing stones and daring Neale to fire, he and his men discharged several guns, injuring twelve men and one woman, all of whom were nonresidents of the town. The magistrates, who appeared on the scene shortly thereafter, conducted an inquiry, with the injured weavers testifying before them. "And after deliberate investigation," the *Gloucester Journal* noted, "Messrs. Neale and their men, who had fired upon the rioters, were admitted to bail." The authorities took no measures at this time against the rioting weavers and permitted them freely to disperse. After the magistrates withdrew, the weavers regrouped and attacked Neale's dwelling, breaking all of its windows within the space of fifteen minutes. The appearance of special constables, whom P. B. Purnell had organized, prevented them from doing further damage;[77] at the same time, Purnell made an appeal to the Home Office for military assistance.[78]

Aftermath and Discussion

The *Gloucester Journal* offered no explanation as to why the magistrates failed to arrest the rioting weavers immediately, nor why their investigation centered on Thomas Neale's efforts to protect his property, an unusual reversal of emphasis. Some rioters, of course, were finally arrested and admitted to bail for their appearance at the next Quarter Sessions. "[B]ut almost all those against whom warrants have been directed have left the country [and] a proceeding... against the leader of the weavers has... failed for want of due proof."[79] Those who appeared before Quarter Sessions were not indicted for a capital offense, "but... met with merciful prosecutors who only indicted them upon the minor charge."[80] Of the nine brought to trial, two were given prison terms of two years, one was given an eighteen-month sentence, and the others were imprisoned from three months to one year.

It was undoubtedly difficult to obtain prosecutions because of tacit sympathy for strikers, or because of the union's power to intimidate, as well as for the costs involved in attending and prosecuting at Quarter Sessions.[81] At the same time, most magistrates had little stomach for seeing prosecutions through; P. B. Purnell, a singularly militant antiunionist, proclaimed himself an exception. "I am the only magistrate," he insisted, "who has faced the weavers at one of [their] meetings..., and I was the only magistrate who remained to support the chairman [at Quarter Sessions] through the whole of the late trials." On one occassion he had helped an alleged victim of union violence with the costs of prosecution. However, he had to step down from the bench in this particular case since "it is improper that a magistrate who has to judge should be indirectly a prosecutor"; the effort, by implication, failed.

A residue of sympathy for the union prevailed among the magistracy as a whole, but this no longer meant that they were in a position to control or direct its activities, as Aldridge had done during the second phase of the strike. The attacks on Plomer's and Neale's manufacturies were desperate and gratuitous acts, for these clothiers had been among the few of the lower district who refused to give the weavers' prices from the outset.[82] If little could be gained, why then were such acts undertaken?

The answer lay in the growing militancy and independence of the union. Its demands had escalated far beyond the initial concern with wages. From an ad hoc association with limited goals, embracing the broad mass of weavers, it was gradually transformed over the course of the strike into a militant movement of a minority, who entertained more comprehensive ambitions. Purnell summarized for the Home Office the rules formulated by this minority, characterizing them as "manifestly absurd and founded on... false data." They included the following items:

1. That work should not be taken out under price. 2. No one work where there are more than three looms. 3. That no one shall weave without having served seven years apprenticeship. 4. That every weaver shall be-

long to the union. 5. That only union journeymen shall be employed.
6. [That] *a limited number of weavers [be made] clothiers* [emphasis
added]. 7. That a . . . benefit [be] promised to aged members should the
funds permit after a long period.[83]

The first, third, and fourth items, which together demanded a
closed shop, seemed to point toward modern trade unionism;
when placed within the context of the entire program, however,
they revealed a profoundly traditionalist, petit bourgeois mentality. The "union," in fact, assumed the anomalous aspect of a
medieval guild, paradoxically enchancing its "radical" image.[84]
Master weavers deemed it more important to have had fixed weaving rates than to have bargained for a serious increase; they found
it especially desirable to reaffirm the hierarchical distinctions
between master, journeyman, and apprentice and to make these
designations universally applicable. The demand to limit the number
of looms per workshop was part of the weavers' long-standing
opposition to loom shops, which accepted unapprenticed labor
and thereby threatened their status as small employers. Loom
shops first appeared between 1802 and 1806[85] but became a
serious issue only in the post-1826 period.

The union's intention to assist some weavers in becoming
clothiers holds special interest, since members' subscriptions were
used primarily as a loan fund for this purpose. "The benefit of the
Society's cause," Purnell remarked sarcastically, "is ordered to be
effected by lending 100 Pounds to a weaver on security, receiving
in return 10 Pounds a year for twenty years."[86] This item most of
all highlighted the middle-class ambitions of the master weavers.
Despite the financial sacrifices expected of all members, the provision could hardly have been aimed at improving the condition of
everyone, but more readily satisfied the aspirations of the elite
among them. After all, only the most prosperous master weavers
could possibly have qualified for such a loan. This bias against
poorer members becomes especially obvious when one recalls that
the rules made the promise of an old-age benefit conditional on
whether "the funds [should] permit after a long period."

The union's militant leadership, it must be emphasized, had
formulated this program. Purnell believed that the journeymen
and apprentices who accepted such tutelage had been either

coerced into doing so or were duped by leaders interested only in personal power. Nothwithstanding his prejudices, there may have been some truth in the allegation, considering the later history of Timothy Exell, the reputed "King of the Weavers" of the 1825 strike. During the 1830s he campaigned vigorously against Chartism, and, according to Julia de Lacey Mann, "asked for but did not obtain a reward for his exertions towards suppressing it."[87] Master weavers may have been militant in pursuing their own interests as an elite, but such efforts hardly made them full-fledged proletarians or even progressive. Although E. P. Thompson correctly emphasized the nostalgic and defensive qualities of their struggle in the Industrial Revolution period, he clearly exaggerated their opposition to capitalism and their commitment to communitarian values.[88] A more genuine proletarian radicalism developed among weavers, however briefly, with the completion of the transition to the factory system.

Strikes and Protests, 1827–1848

Ensuing labor conflicts between 1827 and 1830 found weavers resisting the reduction of wage rates established by the 1825 strike, the proliferation of payment in truck, and the building of loom factories. Where it was not possible to prevent the establishment of such factories, the union of master weavers tried to become the bargaining agent for factory weavers in order to retain a semblance of control over the craft. The strikes of the 1830s indicate the extent of their failure, since factory weavers and operative mechanics acted on their own behalf. During this decade a modern form of industrial unionism supplanted a preindustrial, craft association.

The emergence of industrial unionism, however, transpired unevenly. When strikes failed, their organizations ceased to exist or went underground and had to be resurrected at a later juncture. A certain development marked this process, since the issues over which workers called strikes broadened during the 1830s and became politicized. Disputes regarding wages combined with protests against the loss of traditional agrarian rights and the introduction of machinery into the factory. During some of these episodes, a latent tradition of militant Dissent surfaced, contradicting the deference of chapel leaders, and at the same time a Chartist influence became apparent. However, the return of prosperity between 1843 and 1847 and a diversionary anti-Corn Law agitation, led by clothiers and supported by official Nonconformity, blunted the radical edge. The anti-Corn Law agitation, in particular, reestablished cordial relations between the classes and thereby laid the groundwork of mid-Victorian stability.

The strike waves of 1825 were brought to an end by the trade depression that began that December. "[T]he very depressed state of the clothing manufacture . . . causing the failure of most of the small and several of the considerable manufacturers," P. B. Purnell wrote in April 1826, "has made [the weavers'] union more tractable."[89] With a surplus laboring population, the union lost its ability to pressure employers, although by the last phase of the strike its rank-and-file support had dwindled considerably. The clothiers lowered wages from the standards previously agreed to and began systematically to establish "loom factories" as measures of security. The strike had revealed their vulnerability to collective action by the weavers; the ease with which shuttles could be gathered and discipline enforced discomforted many, despite successful "tension management" by figures of authority.

By 1827 the growth of loom shops had caused considerable anxiety among weavers.[90] They regarded the new system not only as a usurpation of their craft but also as an innovation that threatened the fabric of traditional community life. They complained bitterly about the influx of "foreign" labor from neighboring counties at a time of high local unemployment and insisted that "these strangers [frequently became] the fathers of illegitimate children who . . . are left chargeable to the parish."[91] Increasing illegitimacy not only undermined family stability but also placed greater burdens on the poor rates at the worst possible time.

The weavers charged, moreover, that loom factories were doubly exploitative: through competition, they were "calculated to lessen the profits of [outdoor] weavers, already small," while gouging the factory weavers. Master weavers were being forced to sell their looms and other tools, the union contended, "at half their real value, and the same are then let for hire," often to the same weavers, "at the exorbitant charge of 9s. or 10s. for each piece of cloth wove[n] thereby."[92] If the weaver rented his dwelling and workshop, he therefore paid two rents, at least one of which was usurious. Loom renting was clearly a transitional practice. Since it implied a degree of possession by the user, factory weavers could retain a semblance of their artisan status, even if required to occupy space on the factory floor.

Master weavers correctly insisted that loom factories, when established under stagnating conditions, lowered wages. They cited an "opulent manufacturer near Nailsworth, and another . . . near Woodchester" as typical examples of clothiers who, in 1827, paid "lower wages to the journeymen than. . . could [be] obtain[ed] in the master weaver's house," although they were in a position to pay 1d. more out of every shilling in wages."[93] They were also able "to render shop rent cheaper than master weavers can, and by purchasing some articles in larger quantities, gain a profit thereby."[94] These were only some of the economies of scale rendered by the factory. The weavers claimed, however, that the cost of hiring a foreman, amounting to 2s. $4\frac{1}{2}$d. per piece, reduced the loom factory clothier's rate of profit to a paltry $3\frac{1}{4}$d. This seems hardly credible, considering the other advantages cited; nor does it take into account the greater productivity of labor under the new regime. In the long term, factory weavers received significantly higher rates, relative to the prevailing average wage; however, this occurred at a time when the profession of master weaver had already become degraded.[95] The clothiers countered by charging master weavers with oppressing their journeymen, and there may have been some truth in the allegation. In 1828/29, master weavers launched a new series of strikes with the dual aim of resisting the fall in wage rates and eliminating payment in kind. The weavers succeeded in attracting a wide array of support from several classes of society, including laborers and shopkeepers.[96] Not all weavers believed in the strikes, nor in the union itself, which occasioned lively debate in the pages of the *Gloucester Journal*.[97] One, called "Veritas," a disaffected union member,[98] offered pithy opposition to its activities. While "truck may be oppressive and illegal," he conceded, the true cause of "low wages and irregular modes of paying the workmen" was the imbalance between the supply and demand for labor.[99] This, he argued, was caused, in turn, by the greed of the master weavers themselves, "who are the worst trucksters, and who by urging forward so many apprentices, colts and journeymen—by pressing too many hands upon the trade, in order to fatten upon their earnings—have completely over-stocked the market."[100]

Far from remedying the evil, by striking for an advance in wages, a combination, Veritas maintained, was only "calculated to divert a portion of the trade from the neighborhood—still lessening the demand for labour, and thereby reducing the work people to greater want, if not to entire destitution." The weavers' union offered a deft reply, but failed to rebut the charge that master weavers, in fact, resorted to truck. Instead, it blamed the origin of truck on the clothier and absolved the master weavers from all moral responsibility for engaging in the practice:

> What occasioned the master weaver to pay his Journeymen in truck? Was it not in consequence of the long credit which the clothier demanded of the master weaver, and which the circumstances of the journeymen were not equal to? It has not been an unfrequent case, that the Master Weaver had been obliged to give the Clothier twelve (or more) months credit, and then to take a bill payable two months after that date; thus the straitened circumstances of the Clothier, in some instances, and his covetousness in others, introduced the Truck system into the country. The contracted capital of the Manufacturer frequently required the appropriation of the Master Weaver's wages, whilst the Master Weaver himself was necessitated to run into debt for goods to pay his journeymen.[101]

Both master weaver and clothier, in other words, resorted to truck from necessity; however, pleading necessity, as the union did for the weavers, was as morally objectionable as pleading it for the clothiers. If the clothier demanded long-term credit, was the master weaver not in a position to refuse it? Perhaps not in 1826/29, when capital was "constricted" and employment scarce. However, neither truck nor the use of long-term credit began then. Both practices were certainly well established in 1825, a year of prosperity. Richard Aldridge, the rioting Bisley magistrate, at the time remarked to the president of the strike committee: "I hope the next man that takes out work under foot again, or takes anything for it except money—any truck—will have it thrust down his throat...with a shuttle."[102] The weavers' union, however, failed to make truck an issue in 1825. As Veritas suggested, the plea of necessity was only partially correct: "for the master weaver originated truck, when the manufacturers paid in cash."[103] As the master weavers admitted, "we see nothing objectionable in the wish of any individual to 'fatten'...by his trade." With such a businesslike approach, surely they needed little encouragement to pay their journeymen in kind.

Agitation by master weavers in 1828/29, opposed to truck and low monetary wages, pointed to the metamorphosis of their organization from an artisan association to an industrial union. In 1825 they mainly sought to standardize wages, even if large clothiers could thereby lower their base rates. In 1829, however, weavers sought to forestall wage cuts, or raise rates where possible, even if they could achieve these objectives only on a firm-by-firm basis. Significantly, too, they ceased to complain about loom factories.[104] Instead, they made efforts to become the bargaining agent for "operative mechanics" and in this manner tacitly conceded recognition to the factory system.

In one notable case, they demanded the reinstatement of Joseph Daniels, a worker at Peter Playne's factory who had been dismissed for acting in liaison with them. "The truth is," the union contended, "Mr. Jones [our agent], came to your factory, sent for your work-people, and declared to them that it was not your intention to comply with...our statement; consequently, the disturbances took place with which you appear incensed."[105] Joseph Daniels, they insisted, bore no responsibility for the events in question and therefore merited reinstatement. The appearance of union agents at the factory gates marked a significant but futile effort to regain control of their craft by organizing industrial workers.

The depression of 1829, however, engulfed this union, led by master weavers.[106] Several years later a new union reconstituted itself but drew its membership entirely from factory workers. In August 1833 the new union launched itself with the publication of "The Weavers' Guide, An Address to the Gloucestershire Operative Weavers." It purported to show "the legality, justice and necessity of their uniting together by forming associations for their individual and collective security against all attempts to diminish their exceeding low wages [*sic*]."[107]

In particular, the guide described "an easy method of conducting associations...in every town, village and hamlet," which would enable the weavers to "act in concert with one another" without violating the law. Five months later a strike organized from Nailsworth against the Playne factories at Longfords and Dunkirk resulted from this new drive.[108]

The *Gloucester Journal* reported that "the operations of [Playnes'] extensive works are nearly at a stand [and about] half the looms formerly kept by these houses" were incapacitated; the average loss to the district, as a result, was £500 per week. According to the weavers, the strike was caused primarily by the Playnes "paying for fine work a full fifteen per cent less than Messrs. Maclean and other respectable manufacturers." The weavers also demanded an advance of 8s. on the price of stripes, which were coarser products, although "this would not be insisted [upon] if [the Playnes] would give the price for fine work."[109] The Playnes claimed that "we are paying, for three-fourths of our work, the highest price in the country. For the remaining fourth, we find that some manufacturers are giving more and many less."[110]

The *Gloucester Journal* supported the Playnes' assertion editorially and warned presciently of the danger of losing stripe work to Yorkshire. "A large order for stripe, which Messrs. Playne have relinquished in consequence of the strike [was] undertaken by Mr. Gott of Leeds," one of the largest manufacturers in Yorkshire.[111] The *Journal* warned further that if the weavers persisted, they ran the risk of being supplanted by power looms.[112] The strike ended with a short-term victory for the weavers.[113] They obtained a wage rise for fine work, but shortly thereafter Playne, one of Gloucester's largest stripe producers, discontinued that product line.[114]

Nonetheless, the weavers extended the strike to other stripe manufacturers, who complained that "the prices offered...in London are so low and the advices from China...so discouraging"[115] that they were unable to comply. The strike persisted in the midst of a trade depression, emboldening the clothiers, who met in council, to threaten a suspension of all operations, at least until trade conditions improved.[116] This threat probably enabled them to lower wages further. By 1838, wages for broadcloth had declined by 35 percent from the standard set in 1825; cassimere rates had declined by 38 percent and stripes, by 50 percent.[117]

Power looms also began to be introduced from this period, as the *Gloucester Journal* had predicted. In 1838 handlooms still greatly outnumbered them.[118] However, the new technology eventually gained broad acceptance; other machines, such as the spinning mule, were already widely used. Factory weaving predominated in 1838, and outdoor weaving had become a degraded craft: an industrial proletariat had been fully formed.[119]

Agrarian changes, as we have seen, further contributed to this process of class formation.[120] Common arable fields and wastes at Horsley, Avening, and Minchinhampton became fully enclosed during the late eighteenth to early nineteenth century, while the Court Baron of Minchinhampton restricted usage of its common pasture to the larger landowners of the parish. Cottagers had long engaged in agricultural by-employment and enjoyed common pasture rights, as well as forage rights on the wasteland. As they entered the factory, however, they found these traditional rights circumscribed.

By 1838 their loss of commoners' rights brought forth a Stroud-wide protest of laborers and operatives. Amid demands for the restoration of their rights, the protestors also voiced complaints against the "selfish introduction of machinery." Opposition to machinery for replacing labor in production signaled tacit acceptance of the factory regime and thereby revealed the progress of class formation.[121]

The militancy of this opposition highlighted the growth of a working-class consciousness, articulated in the language of religious dissent. The operatives formed a new "Union Association" and elected "Elders," drawn exclusively from among Dissenters, in emulation of the Chapel hierarchy: "operative mechanics avowedly unconnected with the conspiracy of the Church Ministry."[122] They called for "a complete restoration of the native rights of the people...to enjoy the free customs of their forefathers over the common...lands for the rearing of their stock." They attributed their loss to "the Bishops, Clergymen, Magisterial-Lawyers and other representatives of a factional Mother Church under 'a secret Orange Vestry Oath'." In contrast to the narrow self-interestedness of the master weavers of 1825, the protestors acted on behalf of the entire industrial population, as its "captain-centre-bit" or pivot, and articulated their solidarity with religious fervor. At the end of their meeting, "under a joyous shew of uplifted hands," they chanted: "When I'm rich I ride by chaises. Now I'm poor, I walk—By Jasus!"

The collective identification of Jesus as savior of the poor, especially under conditions of self-perceived oppression, suggests the rise of chiliastic feelings.[123] Chiliasm, however, conflicted with moderate Nonconformist evangelicalism, and for this reason Chapel deacons discouraged it. As laborers and operatives engaged increasingly in strikes, their heightened religious fervor led them to forsake Chapel life.

In 1825 divisiveness among members of the Shortwood Baptist Church had grown so acute that the church business meeting created a court to arbitrate "and . . . exercise discipline where necessary." The court consisted of the minister, deacons, and seven members.[124] Some Baptists "had taken a prominent part in the disturbances," while several others "were equally emphatic in their denunciation of the whole affair."[125] External conditions produced "a criminal indifference to the best interests of the church," instead of the "penitence, humility and great heart searching" for which the deacons had hoped.[126] Throughout that strike, no new members were baptized, and only in its aftermath did recruitment resume.[127]

Between 1829 and 1830 "[t]he Union formed by the work-people in the district grew in numbers and influence" at the expense of organized religion.[128] Weekly meetings were held in alehouses, but participants always prayed at their commencement and sang hymns at their closure. "Many of our member," the deacons lamented, "foresook our own prayer meetings for these assemblies."[129] At the height of social conflict, working people tended to abandon Chapel life; but in the trough of defeat and despair, prodigals returned seeking comfort.

In conflict were the two faces of enthusiasm. Moderate evangelicalism, espoused by Shortwood deacons, emphasized human frailty and evoked the image of a merciful God, which left the believer prostrate before his savior. Millenarians conjured an image of God as a revenging judge; since they strongly believed in their own Election, they acted in all matters with confident self-righteousness.

Weavers and operatives embraced both forms of enthusiasm.

When, in 1829, the weaver Veritas attacked the union, he drew a threat, couched in millenarian language, from "Brother Standfirm":

Where wilt though hide theyself from the vengeance of an Almighty and all-seeing God? in whose presence thou hast most solemnly declar'd, that thou never wouldst act in opposition to our Society! Remember thy declara-tion..., that thy camest of thine own free will, and with a pure intent...; and bear in mind the awful visi-tation from God upon Anna-nia and Sapphira, for deliberately telling a falsehood, whose crime will not bear the slightest comparison (for heinousness) with one who breaks his obligation.[130]

Alternatively, a weaver could write the following ditty,[131] which articulates the sentiments of Christian resignation and class collaboration the Shortwood deacons favored:

> True—Our interest and our Masters'
> Are united close in one;
> We must share, in their disasters;
> Should they fail we are undone!
> If our wages now are made less,
> tis because the trade is dull;
> Should hereafter wealth their toil bless,
> They will pay our claims in full.

> But to not will mad Dissensions
> Benefit or comfort bring;
> From unreasonable pretensions
> Nought but misery can spring.

> Are you Christians? Pray revere, then,
> What the Sacred Scriptures say:
> "Fear you God, and love your Brethern,"
> And the King with faith obey.

> Closely stick, then to your labours,
> Nor abroad tumultuous roam:
> Be in love with all your neighbours,
> Follow peace, and keep at home.

> Like a weaver's shuttle truly,
> Soon your vital thread is run;
> Who would be rewarded duly,
> Duly must his work be done.

Clearly, biblical fundamentalism could be invoked to legitimate divergent social outlooks. Millenarians voiced a militant response even if, tactically, strikes should have been avoided under depressed economic conditions. Advocates of Christian resignation correctly perceived the difficulties involved in such actions. By elevating a short-term policy of social peace into a metaphysical good, however, they defended the employers' interests. Could one reasonably have expected clothiers as a group to raise wages once prosperity returned? Many of them believed, after all, that only low wages could enhance labor productivity.[132]

These differences became politicized in 1839 with the advent of anti-Corn Law agitation and the appearance of Chartists in the region.[133] Although opposition to the Corn Laws had existed among clothiers for a considerable period,[134] not until 1839 and 1840 did they begin to hold public meetings to articulate their sentiments.[135] They held two such meetings at Stroud in 1839 and 1841, respectively, and during the second one, the Chartists intervened.

The anti-Corn Law agitators based their efforts on free-trade principles. By allowing the importation of foreign grain duty-free, the clothiers hoped to bring down the price of bread in order to lower wages. "Therefore, to that extent what you have been told [by the landed interest] is true," admitted one speaker, "it is the tendency of wages to accommodate itself to the price of food" that clothiers aimed for.[136] Convincing the workers to follow this course was a more difficult matter. The same speaker offered the following argument:

Although the tendency of the abolition of the Corn Laws, and an attendant decrease in the present high price of food, might be to create a corresponding lowering of wages, yet the condition of the labourers would very soon be improved by the increased demand for their industry.[137]

Once full employment was realized, it would be possible for the workers to request a wage increase; and their masters, the speaker suggested, would be graciously forthcoming.

Anthony Rogers Fewster, a Quaker highly respected by the workmen of the district, advanced this same line of reasoning at the second, more highly charged meeting.[138] A Chartist presence had rendered the scene considerably more turbulent. One Chartist, "shabbily dressed, forced himself upon the platform and with the cheers of the crowd made himself joint-chairman." The crowd hooted down most of the gentlemen attempting to speak, but Fewster deftly sidestepped interruptions by appealing to religious sentiment:

Perhaps they thought the clothiers were selfish people—("yes they are")—perhaps they thought farmers were selfish and that the upper classes were selfish ("yes, yes"). Why so they were, and so were they who called out "yes, yes." We were all selfish people; for he must tell them that selfishness was in the heart of man, and there it would remain and rankle in his bosom till the evil principle was subdued by a higher principle from above. . . . Suppose . . . the staple trade of this district could be increased. Suppose instead of a thousand pieces of cloth 1,500 pieces should be required, was it not plain that those who made the cloth must be benefitted?

Such would be the consequence, Fewster contended, of the repeal of the Corn Laws.

Charles Hooper appeared next and, as one of the highest-paying employers of the district, was "universally cheered as 'the king of the clothiers'." Hooper addressed the issues of wages and machinery, a heckler having raised the latter by shouting: "If they want revenue, let them tax steam—let them tax machinery." Hooper responded to the wage issue by blaming the workmen who, he contended, dishonored themselves by competing with each other in offering to accept lower rates; and he treated all opposition to machinery as reactionary: "One might well condemn the use of the plough. If there was a demand for manufactures, the more machinery they had, the better would their situation be." Hooper failed to admit that machinery quite possibly had contributed to unemployment and falling wage rates. "Machinery [could] be a blessing to the country," replied Charles Harris, the Chartist leader, but for the manner of its introduction. "[W]hen any new machinery was introduced which took away the labour of any man," he contended, "that man should have a percentage allowed to him out of the income of that machinery sufficient to maintain him." Harris derided the social consequences of capitalist innovation while maintaining that a new social basis for the utilization of machinery would be created once Parliament granted the Charter.

Harris's proposal mobilized workers by focusing on problems of immediate concern while linking their solutions to the larger political issues of the day. His approach illustrates the method of a shrewd tactician, who sought to prevent secondary issues from diverting his followers. Those so diverted, in his estimation, were "either willing slave[s] or hired fool[s]." Without an explanation of the causes of low wages and unemployment, however, merely waving the banner of the People's Charter proved insufficient. He needed to expose the anti-corn Law movement as diversionary and as representing alien class interests.

Reading from a statistical return, Harris showed exports of machinery increasing yearly and concluded "that foreign countries were going to produce for themselves and not come to the English market." The manufacturers, therefore, "wanted cheap bread only because they wanted cheap labour to compete with their new rivals." The forecast was prescient and his appreciation of the clothiers' motives accurate.[139]

The Chartists, however, were unable to sustain a wide measure of support among the working classes, despite the radicalization of laborers and operatives evident in the Stroud-wide protest of 1838. At Stroud, Chartist agitation subsided quickly and remained innocuous in other parts of Gloucestershire, largely as a result of the hostile campaign conducted by Timothy Exell, the "King of the Weavers" of the 1825 strike.[140]

Meanwhile, the clothiers, led by Lord Ducie, persisted in their campaign against the Corn Laws. As in the case of parliamentary reform agitation in 1830–1832, the anti-Corn Law movement attracted very large audiences.[141] When the clothiers refused to lend support to a political movement, however, working-class allegiance proved especially weak. The attempt to generate interest in the reform bill of 1848, which reflected the impact of the Chartists, met with overt hostility from clothiers and little popular enthusiasm.[142] When the Chartist revival occurred in 1848, "it found no support in western manufacturing districts."[143] The Anti-Corn Law League succeeded beyond its nominal objective. By diverting attention from falling wage rates and focusing on wheat prices, the clothiers defeated an independent working-class sociopolitical movement. A modern working class, like its preindustrial predecessors, deferred to the social leadership of its masters.

Summary and Conclusion

The strikes and protests occurring between 1825 and 1848 highlighted the process of class formation in the Industrial Revolution. This chapter has devoted much attention to the 1825 strike because it served as the pivot of this transition. The strike of 1825 was neither a simple confrontation between capital and labor nor a unitary phenomenon in its chronology, as often supposed. Although class confrontation emerged as an element of the conflict, a paternalist-deference mode of collective action, characteristic of preindustrial "risings," actually predominated. This pattern materialized because a community of interest existed between sections of the gentleman-clothier class and the master weavers. The former, motivated by a combination of economic interest and paternalist sensibility, had every incentive to "accept" the weavers' prices and could rely on magistrates who shared their outlook. Most master weavers sought primarily to establish a customary, fixed scale of prices. Yet as the strike progressed, the growth of weaver militancy, however much confined to a minority, induced the adoption of other, more corporatist demands. The growth of weaver militancy found its reciprocal expression in the changing attitudes of magistrates, which corresponded further to the three different phases of the strike.

The first phase, deferentially and peacefully conducted, ended with a settlement at the lower district. The second phase, located in the Stroud region and accompanied by popular violence, followed the deferential pattern of the sixteenth-century Lincolnshire rebellion. The magistrate, Richard Aldridge, in this instance assumed the leadership of the commons "though supposedly coerced into this position." The third phase, shifting back to the lower district, was likewise characterized by violence, but in a manner that illustrates the emancipation of the participants from upper-class tutelage. In this latter context the attitude of the magistracy (with one notabe exception) holds special interest: paternalist solicitude, when faced with genuine militancy, translated into a collapse of authority rather than violent repression.

This distinctive strike rhythm, moreover, substantiates Howard Newby's and Patrick Joyce's dialectical appreciation of the relationship between paternalism and deference. However, it does so by introducing a more dynamic element into their model: the sectional interests that could divide members of the governing class. Newby and Joyce are correct in suggesting that the network of paternalism and deference legitimated the existing structure of authority and thereby promoted social stability. Stability, however, was its ultimate consequence. In the short term, sectional groupings within the governing class, motivated by a combination of self-interest and paternalism, could tap a reservoir of deferential feeling in order to destabilize a situation. Edward Sheppard combined altruism with self-interest by acceding to the weavers' prices in order to bring peace to the lower district. However, Richard Aldridge, who shared Sheppard's outlook, provoked weaver violence against recalcitrant clothiers of the Stroud region in order to force a settlement. "Tension management," the mechanism by which paternalism and deference maintained stability,[144] could assume diverse forms.

Aldridge's methods, however, did not succeed completely. The example of violence he established made possible the emergence of an independent militant minority among the master weavers and therefore the partial breakdown of deference. The appearance of this minority became manifest not only in concerted acts of violence but also in the formulation of a full-fledged program transcending the weavers' initial concern with weaving rates. In some respects the program foreshadowed aspects of modern trade unionism; in others it revealed the master weavers' traditionalist yet petit bourgeois outlook.

The transitional state of the woolen industry had created this contradiction. Weavers may have become more dependent on large clothiers for employment and on production for the international market, but they had not yet emerged as a proletariat. The structural and status differences between masters, journeymen, and apprentices resisted such a development. Weaver militancy intensified in the decade following the 1825 strike, as the cloth trade entered a protracted decline, and as manufacturers made vigorous efforts to establish loom factories. A genuine proletarian radicalism among weavers emerged, however briefly, once the transition to the factory system was complete.

The structure and composition of weavers' strikes altered fundamentally between 1826 and 1834. Between 1827 and 1829, master weavers began protesting against the rise of loom factories and then shifted to a campaign against the growing tendency among clothiers to pay in truck. Toward these ends they began for the first time to organize factory weavers and other clothworkers, but the depression of 1829 completely destroyed their efforts. In 1833/34, when unionism finally reappeared, factory operatives served as the organization's new constituency and granted leadership to a now degraded class of cottage workers. A new proletarian militancy became manifest, furthermore, in wide protests against the erosion of traditional agrarian rights and the introduction of machinery in manufacturing. In this context, popular religious mentalités came to the forefront to resist modernization.

Religious mentalités, indeed, continued to inform popular perceptions of the social world. Among Dissenters, two principal strains could be found. A liberal enthusiasm, espoused by Chapel deacons, emphasized personal duty, humility, and resignation; the poor, perceived as dependent people, required "watchful superintendence" because of a presumed propensity to sin. A radical enthusiasm, informed by an autonomous reading of Scripture, and often embraced by plebeian Chapel-goers, treated the poor as the first among God's chosen and believed them capable of self-assertion. This second outlook tended toward millenarianism, which became manifest outside the confines of the Chapel during periods of acute social conflict.

During these intervals, working-class Dissenters abandoned the Chapel for the union meeting or protest assemblage. The Chapel's fortunes usually resumed when millenialist fervor subsided following the collapse of such movements. This finding affirms Eric Hobsbawm's original observation and Deborah Valenze's more recent conclusion that under conditions of anomie, millenarian enthusiasm could articulate a social militancy in defense of custom and independently of politics. Nevertheless, social militancy potentially configured with political action. The Stroud laborers' movement of 1838 thus antedated the appearance of Chartists in the region but provided a basis for their subsequent agitation.

The Chartists directed their intervention at Stroud in 1841 against the Anti-Corn Law League and the interests of the clothiers, which inspired the League's activities. Throughout the 1830s proletarian militancy had arisen spontaneously and without an explicit ideology. The debate between Chartists and Anti-Corn Law Leaguers amounted to an ideological competition for working-class loyalty and illustrated the mechanism through which Victorian social stability finally emerged. Class cooperation formed the leitmotiv of working-class consciousness by 1850 and issued directly from the Anti-Corn Law League's successful promotion of both laissez-faire doctrine and the legitimacy of middle-class social authority.

Baptist and Congregationalist diaconates, dominated by clothier families, long promoted the same liberal ethos. The Short-wood deacons' hostility to strikes revealed their liberalism with exceptional clarity and found expression in debates among weavers over the legitimacy of taking such action. Official Nonconformity ameliorated the anomie of the uprooted and disoriented in a liberal paternalist fashion, during the early phases of industrialization. By 1850, however, it had reconciled an emergent working class to a new social order centered on the factory. Still, not all Nonconformist churches registered indentical reactions to modernizing trends. Part III of this book offers two case studies of contrasting experiences, one of the Nailsworth Society of Friends and the other of the Shortwood Baptist Church.

Part III

Contrasting Communities:
Two Case Studies in Dissent

Chapter Eight

An "Introversionist Sect": Nailsworth's Society of Friends

Religious sentiment played a crucial role in the transition to modern English society. Laborers and artisans, as we have seen, used millenarian language to resist the erosion of a customary way of life; yet the Dissenters' churches that many attended directed their zeal into more conservative channels. In Gloucestershire, evangelicalism stimulated the reawakening of the older sects, with the one great exception of the Society of Friends.

Shedding an earlier pietism, the Nailsworth Society of Friends became an "introversionist sect" and remained so throughout its history.[1] Bureaucratic sectarianism in church order and discipline signified the Quakers' rejection of the world; yet a rationalist and quietist spirituality enabled them to undertake in elitist fashion the general reform of the social order. The Society of Friends embodied a hybrid form of religious organization, intermediary between Wesleyan Methodism and New Dissent. Yet because of its hostility to evangelicalism, the Quaker church order stood as a counterexample to the religious sensibility of the age and for this reason merits special attention.

Organizational Change and Decline

The Quakers arrived at Nailsworth in the 1650s and were the first Dissenters to build a meetinghouse.[2] Throughout their history the Quakers prized their autonomy to an obsessive degree and for this reason never attracted a large membership, although they permitted nonmembers to attend their prayer meetings. Between 1660 and 1834 the Society experienced a great fall in membership and a marked change in social composition, which gave it a more pronounced lower-middle-class character.

These changes can be traced from the minutes of the Society's Monthly Meeting, the Society's marriage records, and a membership listing covering the period 1812–1834.[3] The minute books document the shift in qualitative terms, and the marriage records and membership listing provide quantitative evidence. The decline in membership became manifest not only in the failure of Quakers to recruit more members than they were losing but also in the membership's extraordinary geographic mobility, which the Society's highly centralized organization facilitated.

Table 58 gives the decennial distribution of Quaker marriages of members resident at Nailsworth, Avening, Horsley, and Minchinhampton. It also provides an occupational breakdown for grooms with known occupations for the three watershed periods of decline. This decline is appropriately measured by the frequency of local marriages, since the Quakers, unlike other Dissenters, refused to marry within the parish church, as required by law until 1837. Marriages at Quaker meetinghouses, furthermore, were restricted only to members; "mixed marriages" with outsiders were strictly forbidden.[4]

The period from 1660 to 1719 witnessed the maximum number of marriages, averaging 14.5 decennially. Of the eighty-seven marriages for the period, fifty-one, or 58.6 percent, of the grooms had known occupations, and of these thirty-two, or 62.7 percent, were artisan broadweavers. The Society's occupational structure assumed a pyramidal shape, which is depicted in figure 19.

The middle class, consisting of clothiers, dyers, drapers, fullers, and mercers, occupied the top of the pyramid; petty retailers, broadweavers, and other artisans, constituting the great majority, occupied the center; and clothworkers, who represented a proletarian element, made up the least significant proportion at the bottom. Except for the absence of the gentry, Quaker social structure broadly conformed to the configuration of contemporary local society in this preindustrial period.[5]

From 1720 to 1759 a significant decline in the number of mar-

TABLE 58. *Quaker Marriages with Known Occupations of Grooms, 1660–1839*

	Total marriages	Clothiers	Other cloth manufacturers	Retailers	Artisans	Weavers	Clothworkers
1660–1669	13						
1670–1679	17						
1680–1689	17	3	3	4	7	32	2
1690–1699	14						
1700–1709	14						
1710–1719	12						
1720–1729	3						
1730–1739	5						
1740–1749	8	2	4	0	2	2	0
1750–1759	7						
1760–1769	2						
1770–1779	1						
1780–1789	0						
1790–1799	0						
1800–1809	1						
1810–1819	1						
1820–1829	2						
1830–1839	0						

Note: The difference between the first watershed period (1660–1719) and the second period (1720–1729) is obviously significant ($t = 6.25$, $df = 8$, Prob $|t| > 2.306$ at 0.01 level of significance).

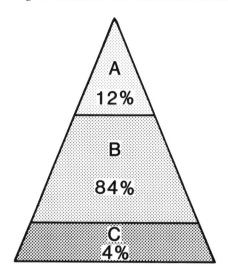

Key: **A – the Middle Classes**

       B – Artisans

       C – the Working Classes

Fig. 19. Social pyramid: status of Quaker grooms, 1660–1719.

riages took place.[6] Of the twenty-three marriages recorded, ten, or 43.5 percent, of the grooms specified their occupations. Unlike the previous period, this sample revealed severe distortions in Quaker social structure. Although the upper middle class remained the same in number and composition, a dramatic shrinkage occurred among the lower-middle-class and proletarian sectors at a time when the advance of industrialization should have led to an increase. This distortion persisted, moreover, until a Quaker presence at Nailsworth finally disappeared in the 1850s.

Quaker marriages after 1760, however, do not fully portray the degree of membership stagnation. Once again they reveal a significant fall in the number of marriages, suggesting a further decline in strength, but they do not record occupational information for any of the grooms. The membership list for the period 1812–1834

TABLE 59. *Quaker Membership, 1812–1834: Occupations and Residence*

Occupation and status	Number
Middle class	
Bankers	1
Maltsters	1
Brewers	1
Mealmen	1
Yeomen	2
Lower middle class	
Schoolteachers	5
Druggists	1
Shopkeepers	4
Bakers	1
Artisans	
Watchmakers	1
Shoemakers	1
Engineers	2
Others	
Servants	4
Widows and spinsters	4

Residence by proximity to Nailsworth	Number
Nailsworth	16
Woodchester	2
Rodborough	4
Minchinhampton	4
Stroud	3

offers a more complete picture. Table 59 gives the frequency distribution of each occupation. The upper and lower middle classes clearly predominated, but this time neither weavers nor any proletarian elements appeared. Moreover, only twenty-nine members were recorded for the entire period, during which an extraordinarily high turnover occurred (depicted in tables 60 and 61).

Table 60 describes the joint distribution of membership acquisition by type of dissolution. Twenty-one, or 72.4 percent, came from outside the locality; of these, fourteen, or 48.3 percent of the whole, were dismissed to other locations because of migration. Only three, or 10.3 percent, were born in the locality and re-

TABLE 60. *Quaker Membership Turnover by Type of Acquisition and Dissolution*

		Membership dissolved by			
Acquisition	Death	Resignation or disownment	Dismissal	Non-dismissal	Total
Certification from	3	2	14	2	21
Birth	2	0	0	1	3
Conversion	0	3	2	0	5
Total	5	5	16	3	29

Note: Total number of members equals 81; four had no occupation listed; the rest were members of families and their occupations were not included. Thus, a sample of 26 equals 35.8 percent of the whole.
Source: See text.

mained there until death or the end of the period covered by the document. Five, or 17.2 percent, were converts, but three of them were either expelled or resigned, and the two others migrated.

Table 61 shows, moreover, that most of those who migrated had lived in the locality for only one to five years; three of those expelled or who had resigned lived there between sixteen and twenty-three years. Both of these cases demonstrate, from different standpoints, the obvious fact that the Quakers could not retain a stable membership base. The membership was hardly indigenous; most tended to migrate after a short duration, and the few converts who demonstrated strong commitments by the length of their attachment to the Society were eventually expelled or forced to resign. This pattern of continuous decline emerges clearly from the minute books of the Nailsworth Monthly Meeting. This meeting serviced a wide region beyond Nailsworth, including Painswick and Cirencester. Still, the minutes made frequent references to the activities of local Friends. In 1795 the local Friends were "in too weak a state properly to hold a preparative meeting," an activity that was crucial to the maintenance of Quaker discipline.[7] By 1805 the local Nailsworth meeting "ha[d] for a few years past declined to

TABLE 61. *Years of Membership by Type of Dissolution*

	Death	Resignation or disownment	Dismissal	Non-dismissal	Total
1–5	0	1	13	0	14
6–10	1	1	3	0	5
11–15	1	0	0	0	1
16–23	1	3	0	0	4
Life	2	0	0	1	3
Missing value	0	0	0	2	2
Total	5	5	16	3	29

Note: Except for the three members born into the sect, not one joined before 1807.
Source: See text.

meet [in] the sixth month, which the [Monthly] Meeting considers improper."[8] Again, in 1808, the minutes expressed apprehension regarding "the alteration of the number of Friends belonging" to the Nailsworth Particular Meeting.[9] By 1822 complaints were regularly heard "that several of the members in the compass of the Nailsworth meeting are not diligent in their attendance of our religious meetings."[10] By 1838 "the state of the Nailsworth meeting, . . . from its peculiar circumstances" forced the Monthly Meeting to discontinue "meetings for worship on a first day afternoon."[11] This pattern of decline, furthermore, reflected a national trend: "The New York Epistle" to the Yearly Meeting in London, reported the *Gloucester Journal* in 1837, "alluded in terms of regret to the desolation of the Society in the borders of England."[12] By 1854 the Friends had formally united the Nailsworth Monthly Meeting with the Meeting at Gloucester to create a larger regional network for want of members at the local level.[13]

Quaker church order, discipline, and theology explain to a considerable degree the Society's numerical decline and changing social composition. Together these elements defined the Quakers as an undemocratic and highly repressive body that made membership in their Society both unappealing and difficult to obtain. "That [the Society] is not popular," one commentator remarked with pride, "may easily be accounted for. . . . Its discipline is not only rigid in regard to morals, but prohibits. . . many kinds of public and private amusements, many descriptions of reading and all excessive sensual indulgences." Its style of worship, moreover, was "unostentatious, meditative and tranquil with nothing to charm the imagination"[14] and stood in marked contrast to the evangelicalism that attracted hundreds to the Shortwood Baptist Church during the same period.

Church Order and Discipline

The Friends organized their Society hierarchically and directed it centrally.[15] At the base stood the local meetings for discipline and worship. The former consisted of "preparative meetings"; these were organized separately by gender and were used to monitor the moral condition of members. Meetings for worship were held jointly, and nonmembers were permitted to attend. The Friends held meetings for worship three times during the week and twice on Sunday and held meetings for discipline at least once a month on the Sunday prior to the regional monthly meeting. Members were expected to answer the "Queries," a kind of catechism formulated by higher authorities, during meetings for discipline. The national Yearly Meeting outlined the procedure in 1757 for the women's Quarterly Meeting of Gloucester:

the answers [to the queries] of such preparative meetings [should] be delivered to the respective Monthly Meetings next ensuing, & a general answer from each Monthly Meeting [should] be drawn up in writeing [*sic*] and delivered into the Quarterly Meeting.[16]

Altogether, then, meetings for discipline and worship constituted the "particular meeting" or local chapter of the Society.

The particular meeting elected representatives to the monthly regional meeting, the Society's next highest body, which also met separately according to gender. The meeting surveyed the condition of the membership at the local level by collecting answers to the queries and writing a report based on them for the Quarterly Meeting and investigating specific violations of the Society's rules. The minute books of the Monthly Meeting, in fact, provide detailed accounts of the business, and especially the discipline, of the Society.

The Quarterly Meeting encompassed an even wider region and heard appeals from members challenging the decisions of the Monthly Meeting. It collected reports forwarded from the Monthly Meetings and sent a more generalized summary of them to the Society's Yearly Meeting in London. Conversely, it communicated to the lower bodies any changes in the Society's rules effected at the Yearly Meeting. Finally, the Quarterly Meeting elected a "General Committee" to coordinate its activities with those of the lower bodies, especially "in the maintenance, education, or apprenticing [of] its poor members actually requiring such aid."[17]

The activities of the two meetings and the General Committee were administered by a hierarchy of officials who aided in the enforcement of discipline. These included ministers, elders, and overseers of particular meetings. Elders, who included women, were elected at Monthly Meetings and acted as lay leaders. In theory they were supposed to supervise the ministry, but the post "was ...more honorific, and tended to be regarded as a compensatory status symbol for affluent...Friends."[18] Each particular meeting appointed overseers who ensured "when anything appears amiss, that the rules of our discipline be put in practice."[19] Members joined the ministry voluntarily, but such commitment required an especially superior "disposition...to piety and virtue" that all Friends could acknowledge.[20]

The Quakers eschewed a professional ministry and instead adhered to the theory of spontaneous inspiration. Although all members qualified for the office in principle, only those men and women who "spoke fairly often...and proved acceptable" actually occupied it.[21] Frequent speakers were "recorded" and distinguished from the rest of the meeting by seatings in a frontal gallery. Those who spoke less often but wished to join the ministry were inhibited only by "a difficult psychological barrier."[22]

In theory, all "stations of the church" were to be assumed from a sense of humility and even self-abnegation. Ministers, especially, were to assume their duties in a spirit of self-sacrifice, in emulation of the passion of Christ,[23] and for this reason the Society did not provide them with a maintenance. Quaker humility and otherworldliness formally contrasted with the grandeur and authoritarianism of the Church of England. As attributes of "saintliness," however, Quaker attitudes contributed paradoxically to defining a distinctive hierarchy within the Society.[24] Indeed, the "stations of the church" represented a genuine structure of authority, reinforced by the system of indirect elections to the Society's higher bodies and by the manner in which directives were communicated to the lower ones. This form of church order was "presbyterian" in character[25] and stood in sharp contrast to the congregationalism of the Forest Green and Shortwood churches. Quaker church order, in other words, facilitated control by an elite; the officers of higher bodies could not be held responsible to the local membership, and it was no easy matter to appeal their decisions.

This system did not become established, however, without opposition from the local membership. The persistent weakness of the Nailsworth particular meeting, the continual indiscipline of its membership, was in part the expression of a democratic protest against creeping bureaucratization. In 1754 the Women's Meeting at Nailsworth took special note of "the repeated advice of the Yearly Meeting at London that Elders should be appointed to take the oversight of the Flock [and] Overseers to advise the Friends where they see anything amiss."[26] The minutes record further local resistance to bureaucratization in December 1790 when the Quarterly Meeting "declined the practice of receiving representatives from the particular meetings and directed in future that appointments of representatives be at several Monthly Meetings only. . . . The particular meetings are accordingly deseired [*sic*] to decline in future making such appointments."[27]

Thus, by resisting the tutelage imposed by elders and overseers and by demanding direct representation to the higher church bodies, local Friends demonstrated their democratic inclinations. Their failure to realize democracy created demoralization, however, which led to a decline in membership.[28] As a concession, however, the Yearly Meeting introduced a provision in 1806 to allow appeal of Monthly and Quarterly Meeting decisions to a special disinterested tribunal. The reform sought to diffuse discontent by providing a grievance procedure, but the tribunal retained the right to refuse a hearing,[29] and the situation at Nailsworth did not improve significantly after its implementation.

Another aspect of the movement for greater church democracy concerned the status of women. Geoffrey Nuttall has noted that in the seventeenth century Quakers were more advanced than other Dissenters in allowing women to hold office, although this leniency was confined to the ministry and only very slowly came to include participation in business meetings.[30] In 1823 Amelia Davis, who "appeared in the ministry among us," was nominated to membership in the select "meeting of ministers and elders."[31] Yet the men's meeting had to appoint a commitee of women "to consider the propriety of recommending her"; the men clearly had retained the dominant role.[32]

In numerous matters of discipline that involved women (especially cases associated with marriage), the men always directed the women's meeting to make visitations and submit reports. This pattern created tensions that probably never were fully alleviated despite attempts to settle the matter. In 1819 the Yearly Meeting, alluding to these difficulties, rendered the following judgment:

This meeting being informed that... there is a diversity of sentiment, whether any reference should be had to the women Friends in the answers to the men's queries, think it right to express its judgement that the answers from the men's meeting are intended to refer to the state and conduct of the whole body.[33]

In general, the growth of bureaucracy greatly contributed to the Society's numerical decline; although Quaker authoritarianism affected all members, it contained a significant gender bias as well.

The severity of Quaker discipline, through the regularity of expulsions, complemented the growth of bureaucracy in contributing to membership loss. At the same time, the Society judged candidates for membership according to highly rigorous standards, which made recruitment of outsiders especially difficult. The children of members, or of former members who remained within the Society's orbit, and offspring of "mixed marriages" were usually the only ones granted membership. Recruitment, therefore, remained largely kinship based, although in theory membership was open to anyone capable of showing agreement with Quaker principles and customs.

Quaker discipline meant to ensure that Friends conformed to the profession of faith that defined membership in the Society. It is paradoxical that a church, which placed such great emphasis on the independence of the Holy Spirit in its operations on the soul, should have made formal conduct so important a test of spirituality. Richard Gilkes, a Quaker minister from Nailsworth, complained "how much the principles of Friends were misrepresented by those who said we relied upon our own works for salvation."[34] Yet only by "works" could the truth, in practice, become manifest. Thus the Monthly Meeting spent most of its time enforcing proper conduct. The frequency distribution of offenses for which members were punished during 1754–1854, including induced resignations, is as follows: marriage by a priest, eighteen; bankruptcy, seven; paying tithes, two; "misconduct," eight; resignations, four; and doctrinal expulsions, 1.

Discipline I: Courtship, Marriage, and Kinship

The most common offense committed was "marriage by a priest to a person not of our Society." The disciplinarians invoked this phrase routinely. "Marriage by a priest" violated the testimony against a "hireling ministry,"[35] a view of episcopacy that expressed the most radical Protestant tendencies of the Reformation. "To a person not of our Society" referred to a violation of the rule prohibiting "mixed marriage" that the Quakers rigorously enforced. This rule contributed to the largely kinship-based character of the Society and highlighted its sectarianism. In theory the two rules were coequal in stature, but in practice a "mixed marriage" was the more serious infraction.

The Society opposed mixed marriages on both practical and spiritual grounds. On practical grounds, it was argued, those who held "contrary opinions and habits" in religion would not be able to achieve lasting domestic harmony, nor properly to rear their children. In the words of a minute from the Yearly Meeting of 1783, "Disorder in families is thereby occasioned, generally rendering a married state . . . a state of confusion and perplexity, and laying waste that united religious care . . . for the education of their off-spring in the principles of true religion."[36]

Those who followed the impulses of mutual affection without regard to religious differences deluded themselves in thinking that a purely secular attachment could bring them lasting happiness;

such an attachment the Society regarded as a form of idolatry. God blessed a marriage only when both partners made the worship of Him, according to the "Truth," their joint object.[37] Thus marriage existed for the glory of God and as such served as the foundation of church organization. Indeed, the Friends sought "the strongest sanctions our discipline could supply" to make religion a family affair;[38] they expelled violators routinely, as in every instance where members transgressed the norms of the Society.

The Society enforced its rigid insistence on group endogamy by strict control over Friends' private lives. Quaker courtship practice, for instance, required that the parents of young couples formally approve the match, and that the monthly meeting investigate whether both parties were free from other engagements. If the prospective groom belonged to another monthly meeting, the Nailsworth Society required a certificate of commendation from it, testifying to the uprightness of his character. Betty Williams and Willam Worms, in a typical example, followed the accepted procedure by announcing their intent to marry before the monthly meeting. Each obtained parental permission, and the meeting appointed Sarah Bowley, an elder among the women, "to enquire into [Betty's] conversation and clearness from all others with respect to marriage and report to the next meeting where the young couple are desired to come."[39] All issued satisfactorily, and the meeting granted the couple permission to marry.

These investigations were far from routine matters. John Bevington of Netherton, Worcestershire, and Hester Staples of Nailsworth had announced their intention to marry in the usual fashion. However, a letter was received from the Evesham Monthly Meeting "informing this meeting, that upon inquiry into John Bevington's conduct, it appeared to be such, that they could not grant him any certificate, for which reason a stop is put to his further proceeding toward marriage."[40]

The minutes provide no further details concerning Bevington's alleged "conduct." The couple, however, considered this action to be arbitrary and refused to submit: a year later the minutes reported that Hester and John were "married by a priest." A committee investigated the matter "in a spirit of Christian love and tenderness, agreeably to our known discipline," but reported that Hester "seemed not at all dissatisfied with her late proceedings, neither desirous of continuing membership of our Society."[41] In such a manner did the strictness of Quaker rules regarding marriage lead to the needless loss of members. Hester Staples's refusal to submit, moreover, is evidence of the independence of character of many of the Friends at Nailsworth, especially the women.

Although most expulsions for mixed marriage also referred to "marriage by a priest," the evidence indicates that the former was the more serious offense. In March 1807 the women's meeting notified the men that it had discharged its duty in visiting Lucy Clark: "she being likely to be connected in marriage with a person not in profession with us."[42] Although the marriage had not yet occurred, Lucy Clark persisted in her wish to carry it forward and perhaps negotiated for permission to marry at the Friends' meetinghouse, since no mention is made of her intention to marry in Church. Her prospective groom may have been a Dissenter from another denomination.[43] A committee, composed this time of male Friends, visited her four months later and expelled her for continued intransigence.[44]

Two similar cases affirm that marriage to nonmembers was the primary reason for such expulsions. In August 1810 the minutes reported that Ann Hatcher (née Gibbs) "joined in marriage by a priest to one not of our society." During the first visitation, she acknowledged the "inconsistency" of her act but pleaded as her excuse that "she was induced to form the acquaintance with her husband, in order to marry from being told, that there was little or no doubt but he would shortly be admitted into membership, which was about six months [!] previous to his case being determined upon by the monthly meeting."[45] A committee paid her a visit a second time, during which she reaffirmed her earlier statement and added that "she discovered a considerable attachment to the Society." The meeting found her answers satisfactory, and in this singular instance took no further action.[46] Clearly, her husband's prospective membership had saved her from expulsion.

Mary Pinnock (late Gardner) was not as fortunate. In June 1811, the minutes reported that she had been married by a priest to a nonmember "without Friends knowing of such a connexion being formed." When a committee visited her in July, it discovered that she had moved to Southwark, London, and the monthly meeting requested the Friends there to make an inquiry. Her secretiveness and subsequent flight were motivated by a fear of expulsion. She may have learned from Lucy Clark's case that if the spouse had no immediate prospect of membership, openness in such matters counted little. When finally visited in London, "she expressed sorrow," abjectly, "for having taken such a step, with a strong desire that friends...not disunite her." She attended meetings regularly, while in London, and declared "her intention of continuing that practice whatever decision may be come to in her case."[47] The Nailsworth meeting thus felt "called upon to testify against such disorderly conduct" and expelled her.[48]

Control over courtship was therefore central to the proper ordering of marriage; such ordering was especially important, since Quakers treated the family as the foundation of church government. In addition, Quakers felt obliged to mediate disagreements within marriages; in this respect their meddling testified to the unprecedented degree of control they sought over members' lives. The case of Samuel and Sarah Clark suggests that the Society sought to reconcile differences that could arise from sexual difficulties. "Misunderstandings" had existed between Samuel and Sarah for some time, but the "endeavours of the Friends where the parties reside have hitherto been unavailing to reconcile the difference."[49] The monthly meeting appointed two Friends to pay them a visit, and four months later the couple could report that "the resentment and shyness between us is removed."[50]

In 1796 the minutes reported a more serious case involving William and Rebecca Wilkins of Nailsworth. The case first appeared in February 1796 and was not finally disposed of until June 1797, following visits from several deputations. The minutes first reported that "the two live in a state of separation from each other," whereupon the monthly meeting dispatched two deputations, one from the men and another from the women, to visit each party. William stated that he "objected to the term separation [;] his wife's absence was on her part voluntary and permissive on his."[51] Rebecca departed, so she claimed, because her husband "retain[ed] a woman in the house that was disagreeable to her." William refused to comment on this allegation, however, "seeing it would tend to criminate another [sic]." The suggestion that William had brought his mistress into his home was a considerable scandal, "a shade on our Society," and his refusal to yield forced the Society to disown him "to clear the reputation of truth and Friends."[52]

This case is interesting for two reasons. It demonstrates that Quaker women believed themselves to have had conjugal rights and that the Society concurred. Quaker patriarchalism was therefore not a rigid norm. William did not admit to any impropriety in his actions; the minutes only hint at the possibility. He had acted instead on the assumption of male domination of the household, and this was perhaps an equally serious offense. In denying him absolute authority, by the substance of their intervention, the Friends embraced the "closed domesticated" notion of copartnership between husband and wife.[53] Moreover, by the fact of their intervention, they denied the absolute autonomy of the family. Since the Quakers viewed church government as resting on the kinship network, the Society had, in principle, the right to interfere.

The importance of kinship becomes especially apparent when one examines how the Society treated membership applications. Many of those who had no apparent familial connection with the Society were scrutinized more carefully. Normally, a candidate for full membership attended Friends' religious services as an expression of interest in the Society. Attendance during the candidacy period also enabled Friends to observe the candidate's behavior and opinions. Indeed, the length of one's candidacy could be considerable.

In March 1792 Eli Evans of Nailsworth formally applied for membership. The meeting deferred his request for two months, although to Friends he seemed especially eager. After four visits, ending in October 1793, the meeting inexplicably denied his request.[54] He reapplied in January 1804, but the minutes reported that while "he is in a great measure convinced of our religious principles, his behavior is not entirely consistent therewith." The meeting once again deferred action for two months but finally decided that "upon further enquiry he does not support our testimony against tithes."[55] This type of scrutiny was typical; however, in this case the amount of time that elapsed before anyone could raise a serious objection seems problematic. Considering his two applications for membership and the twelve years he undoubtedly attended Friends' religious meetings, the belated discovery of his "opinion" on tithes comes as a considerable surprise. The protracted nature of his candidacy and the tone of the minutes themselves suggest a deep reluctance by the Friends to entertain the membership of an outsider.[56]

The minutes communicate a different attitude when the candidacies of members' children or the offspring of "mixed marriages" were considered. Although the Society adhered to the normal practice of inquiring into a candidate's opinions, the monthly meeting remained biased in favor of those who could demonstate a familial connection. When Samuel Clark applied for membership in 1798, a deputation was appointed "to enquire of him the grounds on which he attends our religious meetings and if it appears proper to them to enquire also if he is desireous of availing himself of the privilege of his situation as the off-spring of a mixed marriage."[57] He answered that he attended "from motives of duty" and, according to the report, "does seem desireous" to avail himself of his privileged position.

Why such a privilege should have existed in the case of the progeny of mixed marriages the meeting never made explicit; it was something admitted to only informally and had to be handled with tact. The practice of "birthright" Quakerism contradicted the formal principle underlaying the issue of membership. Modeling themselves after the children of Israel,[58] the Friends viewed themselves as a distinct people, a kind of "folk," which suggested a biological affinity accompanying the receipt of grace. The children of mixed marriages, or of otherwise fallen members, could enjoy the privilege of a more lenient treatment of their membership applications because of the presumption of a partially inherited grace. This assumption did not conform to the theory of grace formally embraced by the Friends, however, which emphasized the primacy of individual experience and conformity to a strict code of conduct.

Indeed, a degree of hypocrisy seems to have attended the practice of birthright Quakerism. Was it necessary to inquire of Samuel Clark the grounds on which he attended Friends' religious meetings if, at the same time, he could invoke a special privilege? Clearly there was an inconsistency. Clarke's answer, that it was "from duty" that he attended such meetings, was, in principle, unsatisfactory. His application was therefore reconsidered three months later, at which time it was "agreed to be left for the present and the Friends of Nailsworth preparative meeting are desired in the meantime to have him under their notice."[59] Still, Clarke was soon admitted to membership, and without the rigorous scrutiny of opinions that accompanied the membership applications of such outsiders as Elie Evans.

Social custom also influenced such attitudes. Many of those expelled for mixed marriages remained within the Society's periphery; the practice of open participation enabled them to attend meetings for worship but not meetings for discipline. The expulsion of Mary Pinnock, already cited, clearly illustrates this fact.[60] Curiously, the custom of establishing a periphery mitigated the severity of Quaker discipline. Although actual fellowship was something more desirable, loss of that status did not remove one entirely from the community. Nor was readmittance to membership automatically foreclosed.[61] Attendance at Quaker schools and religious meetings by children of a disunited member, and eventually their own formal applications for membership, strengthened the entire family's attachment to the Society.

Benjamin G. Gilkes, the son of Richard Gilkes, who had been a leading Quaker minister, offered his resignation because of what appeared to be an unavoidable marriage to an outsider.[62] Dutifully, he cited the need "in every case of unequivocal delinquency from whatever cause it may have arisen that the line of discipline should be promptly and impartially drawn."[63] Yet he also expressed the not unrealistic hope "that such a disunion will neither alienate the minds of Friends from my dear children, nor in any degree interrupt that harmony and social intercourse, which has ever been to myself a source of much real pleasure."[64] He had little to fear on either ground. The Society had expelled Elizabeth Scusa because of a mixed marriage but after several years readmitted her to membership, together with her daughter, Caroline, who had "been brought up in the practice of attending meetings of Friends." Elizabeth confessed to "the disadvantages attendant on mixed marriages"; the proof of her repentance consisted in the way she reared her daughter and in the fact that, "for a considerable time past," she had "been frequent in the attendance of our religious meetings."[65]

Thus, it was possible to circumvent the "disadvantages" of

mixed marriages by remaining personally active at the fringes of the Society and by introducing one's children to its religious life. By doing so, the disunited member maintained an aura of fellowship and contributed to the Quakers' sense of themselves as a people, unified by the bonds of kinship. The special significance this bond held for the Quakers accented their hypersectarianism.

Other forms of discipline equally expressed the extremism of Quaker sectarianism. Expulsions for bankruptcy, in their severity, caricatured the "moral economy" of a capitalist order yet were of such a conservative cast that they simulated a spirit of autarchy. Quaker sectarianism also became manifest in intolerance of doctrinal differences that in one case resulted in expulsion and in four others led to resignations, even when no actual violation of the rules occurred.

Discipline II: "Moral Economy" and Religious Orthodoxy

In several bankruptcy cases the minutes of the Monthly Meeting reveal the importance the Society attached to "sober" business dealings and, once again, the extent to which it felt obliged to regulate the personal affairs of Friends. In three cases the Society expelled the members under investigation and in two others absolved them. In each instance the Society's judgment was based on the following considerations: the extent of the individual's responsibility, whether the member in question had approached Friends for advice before his situation deteriorated, and the steps actually undertaken by him to satisfy his creditors.

These cases hold a special interest partly because they illustrate the psychological disposition of members when confronted by the discipline of their community. Some resisted the encroachments of the Society in various ways and were expelled as much for displays of independence as for technical violations of the rules. Those whom the Society absolved were judged innocent of all responsibility for their condition, or else had acted correctly by reporting their plight directly to a Friend. Expressions of contrition, conveying an aura of self-abnegation, often accompanied a willingness to accept discipline in such matters.

These cases also reveal a hyperconservative attitude toward

business activity. The degree of control exercised by the Society, together with its morality toward indebtedness, strictly upheld the sanctity of contract, but in a manner that discouraged risk-taking.[66] For the Nailsworth Quakers, the "Protestant ethic" reinforced a limited and traditionalist approach to trade.[67]

The case of James Motley illustrates these patterns especially well. In September 1804, the monthly meeting "made an assignment of the whole of his property both in present possession and reversion to trustees for the equal benefit of all his creditors," who were to receive 20s. [!] in the Pound. This was a good beginning, but the monthly meeting also wanted "to be informed whether or not he appeared sensible of the impropriety of his former conduct which brought his affairs into embarrassment."[68] In October he refused to concede guilt but by March 1805 finally expressed "sorrow" for the "impropriety." Evidently, a creeping demoralization had overcome him, reaching its nadir in July 1805 when "he [was] imprisoned in the County gaol for debt and removed to Fleet prison."[69] Motley had failed to consult Friends about his business dealings and resisted their judgment of "impropriety" for a considerable period. His attempt to satisfy his creditors and a belated acknowledgment of error, no matter how contrite, could not, however, save him from expulsion, nor from debtors' prison.

In April 1809 William Hinton found himself in a similar position. "His mode of transacting business for some time has been very disreputable," and although he agreed to disclose his financial affairs fully to Friends, he failed to make good this promise. His "harassed state of mind" made him appear "to be going on in the same state of embarrassment and failure of punctuality in his engagements, as he had done for a considerable time past." Hinton's personal deportment apparently had deteriorated along with his business affairs; and sobriety in personal habits, for the Friends, symbolized coherence and "morality" in business.

This morality failed, however, to sanction unfettered capitalistic activity. Although the Society required Friends to conduct their affairs in a manner respectful of the property rights of others, an attitude consistent with "possessive individualism,"[70] the monthly meeting applied a peculiarly conservative interpretation of this doctrine, which discouraged risk-taking and evoked a spirit of customary restrictiveness. Thus, Hinton's "great impropriety" lay in the "drawing of accommodation drafts," or short-term loans for covering current expenses, which the greater world treated as a routine business practice. Still, the Society expelled him as much for displays of personal independence as for the use of entrepreneurial methods since he also resisted Friends' importunities: "he is more inclined to resent the interference of Friends," the meeting concluded, "than to benefit by their advice."[71]

The case of Joseph Davies, expelled in 1829 for "embarrassed circumstances," further highlights Quaker conservatism in this same sphere.[72] An inquiry had revealed "that after his circumstances became embarrassed, he continued to borrow money when he knew himself to be insolvent and which now appears to have been the case for some years past." Friends did not accuse Davies of concealing this insolvency from his creditors, but only of acting imprudently. Evidently, he had hoped to save a deteriorating situation through continued borrowing; nor could he have been so insolvent as to carry on this practice "for years." His strategy may well have been the most rational choice under the circumstances and a genuine act of entrepreneurship. For the Quakers, however, granting of a promissory note violated the rules of equity even where the remotest chance of failure to honor its terms existed. Although such an attitude accorded with the contemporary legal emphasis on unconditional promise-keeping, the moral assumptions underlaying it constrained legitimate risk-taking.[73]

For Sarah and George Bond, Quaker discipline had a more salutary effect. In their case Friends gave well-received practical advice, which revealed both a prudential approach to trade and an intimate involvement in the private affairs of members. The report to the monthly meeting stated that "trade was so limited as to be inadequate to their expenses of living...and to this may be added, they met with some losses."[74] The Bonds had contemplated indebtedness to salvage their business, but before proceeding further "they advised with a Friend...and determined to wind up their affairs speedily." The Friend judged, seemingly on rational grounds, that theirs was too marginal an enterprise. His advice may have been colored as much by moral considerations, however, since the Bonds hesitated to draw this conclusion independently. The monthly meeting "read [the report on their affairs] with satisfaction" because the couple had avoided compounding their "embarrassment." More importantly, however, they had consulted Friends before acting. Quaker discipline, while demanding that the Bonds be "sensible of the situation in which they involved themselves," clearly encouraged timidity and dependence rather than self-reliance.

Indeed, a Friend could go as far as formal bankruptcy if he made a "reasonable" effort, monitored by the Society, to satisfy his creditors. Thus in July 1822 the Society found James Miller in "embarrassed" circumstances because of "overtrading and having made bad debts."[75] At first he agreed "to pay [his creditors] 5s. in the Pound on condition of their granting him four years credit, during which time he would pay the remainder with interest." Although the arrangement was sufficiently normal by contemporary standards,[76] Friends found it unsatisfactory, since their rules denied Miller the right to any consideration. Instead, they forced him to liquidate the whole of his estate for the benefit of his creditors and to pay them 10s. in the Pound. Yet even this effort proved initially unsatisfactory: "from the confused state of his accounts," a committee of inquiry reported, "we have not been able to judge ourselves in this respect." Six months later Miller paid his debt at the 50 percent rate, declaring obsequiously that he did not "consider his obligations discharged...until he had paid the whole." He wanted "to pay every man his due,"[77] and for this demonstration of "good character" the meeting dismissed his case.[78]

Thus, in several bankruptcy cases the minutes of the monthly meeting reveal that the real violation occurred where the member either failed to consult the Society regarding the state of his business affairs or had steadfastly refused to follow its advice once his situation had become known. This preoccupation with control, contrary to the Weber thesis, discouraged entrepreneurship; Friends, in adopting an unusally cautious concern for the morality of business practice, regarded the pursuit of enterprise as potentially harmful to group solidarity. "It doth not appear," commented the answer to the third query sent to the Yearly Meeting in 1775, "that any [Friends] overcharge themselves with business to the hindrance of their service."[79]

Still, despite these constraints, the Society offered a system of emotional support that relieved members of the anxiety and uncertainty they confronted as actors in the marketplace. The sense of gratified relief the Bonds clearly derived by conforming to Quaker discipline stands in sharp contrast to James Motley's "sorrow" and William Hinton's "harassed state of mind," both consequences of uninhibited freedom.

Quaker sectarianism was revealed further in the Society's strict enforcement of doctrinal orthodoxy among Friends. In four cases members resigned voluntarily, recognizing that the Society could not sanction plural affiliation, and in only one case did expulsion occur. Those who resigned wished to attend Church of England services and did so without feelings of hostility toward the Society. David Bowley, Jr. resigned "on account of his preferring the established national worship"; after visiting him, Friends recounted a friendly reception but could not report a change in his attitude.[80] Mary Roberts had resigned "from a conscientious scruple on the subject of the sacrament," and not from any objection to the Society's "pure mode of worship, general opinions and excellent discipline."[81] Another David Bowley, objecting with equanimity to the Quaker conception of grace, resigned in 1840 and drew a firm but friendly defense of the Society's system of worship from the monthly meeting.[82] These departing Friends accepted reluctantly the need to relinquish membership; for them disagreements of principle, when grounded in reason, allowed for a mutually agreeable, although by no means inevitable, separation.

Amiability was absent, however, in the one expulsion for doctrinal reasons recorded by the monthly meeting. In 1807 the Society expelled Daniel Roberts for propagating "certain visionary and absurd notions of one Joanna Southcott, which are repugnant of the religious principles of Friends," namely, her ostensible assertion that "she herself [is] an instrument divinely appointed for and necessary to the redemption of mankind."[83] The Society did not adandon Roberts lightly, however; it expelled him only "after much entreaty to reform" lasting well over a year.[84] Still, his wife and children felt obliged to resign in protest against this treatment of him: "while we remain members amongst you, we conceive ourselves to be in some degree implicated in your unjust, unfeeling and cruel treatment of him."[85]

Six years later, however, his son, Oade Roberts, reapplied for membership. The minutes report that "his seceding from the Society arose from his youth and inexperience and in submission to his parents. Yet he took the blame himself for a decision that has caused him much regret."[86] In 1818 Ann Roberts, together with her children, John and Mary,[87] followed suit. They wanted to re-join, in contrast to their earlier sentiments, "a Society with which we are connected by so many important and interesting motives." In an oblique reference to Daniel Roberts, they reported themselves "gratified... that every obstacle which might have opposed [their readmission] has long since [been] extinguished."[88] Clearly, the dual loyalty felt by the Roberts family at the time of his expulsion ceased after the lapse of a decade. Once again Quaker discipline subverted patriarchal authority; if the Friends treated the family as the foundation of church government, they also believed that each member owed primary loyalty to the Society. For Roberts's wife and three children, attachment to the community proved irresistible because of the emotional and spiritual succor it offered.

Spirituality

Besides a restrictive marriage policy and a repressive church order, Quaker spirituality provided a further obstacle to membership growth since it stood outside the mainstream of the Evangelical Revival. Geoffrey Nuttall has described Quakerism of the 1650s as an "enthusiastic movement,"[89] but by 1750 the Society clearly had grown quietist.[90] Although this change conformed superficially to the mood created by the Anglican-Nonconformist consensus of the early eighteenth century, for the Quakers it signified a spiritual withdrawal from the world, and at first a political one as well.[91] Quietism complemented the formation of a church hierarchy from 1667/68[92] and manifest itself in the way the doctrine of the "Light Within" came to be applied. In the long term, however, after enthusiasm gave way to rationalism, Quaker political activism would revive.

Quakers contributed to radical Protestant belief during the seventeenth century by formulating the doctrine of the Light Within, which offered a distinctive interpretation of how the Holy Spirit transmitted grace. Although resembling Calvinism in adhering to a concept of free grace, this doctrine was more radical in at least two respects: it posited the absolute freedom of the Holy

Spirit, even from dependence on Scripture,[93] and held forth the possibility of conversion, which a strictly interpreted high Calvinism had denied. The doctrine therefore implicitly created the possibility of universal redemption. Accordingly, the Holy Spirit entered the soul of a worshiper and led him spontaneously to an instantaneous conversion. His sudden "convincement" of Truth[94] was expected to conform to Scripture abstractly, not as the result of a close reading of biblical texts. Nor was the process by which he received Truth dependent on a preacher as the instrument of its transmission.[95] God alone inspired the reception of Truth, freely and mystically.

Thus the accent of early Quaker spirituality, prior to the Restoration, had been millenarian and enthusiastic. Psychic disturbances had often accompanied the experience of illumination. "Ah! the Seizing of Souls," recalled one contemporary observer, "and the prickings at [the] heart, which attended that Season; some fell on the Ground, others crying out under the sense of opening their States."[96] Under conditions where many anticipated Christ's second coming,[97] the doctrine of the Light Within easily induced such emotional fervor. Communal interaction, moreover, sustained a highly charged atmosphere, since enthusiasm often spread contagiously among a group of worshipers.

In the post-Restoration period, when millenarian expectations no longer seemed credible, the Quakers turned inward, and the experience of "convincement" changed correspondingly. The "quickenings" of the heart transfigured themselves into a quiet rationalism, and Quaker meetings became known for their silences.[98] Silence heightened one's capacity for reflection and established the groundwork of continuous inspiration by accenting the individualism that underlay the doctrine of the Light Within.[99]

The Society's spiritual transition, therefore, embraced a dual contradiction. The early Friends were anarchistic in organizational matters; yet their enthusiasm led them to a collectivist form of spiritual unity. As enthusiasm gave way to quietism, Quaker spirituality shifted its accent to individual experience, while in organizational matters the Society grew hierarchical and centralized. Indeed, at Nailsworth, the Society's bureaucratization resulted from, and fostered reciprocally, an atomized and inward-looking membership. By the late eighteenth century, however, this very structure had induced the formation of a "pilgrim" consciousness among Quakers that facilitated their turn toward activist reform politics.[100]

Conclusion

By the second half of the eighteenth century, the Nailsworth Quakers had eschewed their earlier enthusiasm by acquiring in its place a quietist and rationalist spirituality. Simultaneously, the Society developed an exclusive kinship-based membership while becoming rigidly bureaucratic and hierarchical. Both developments discouraged recruitment and embraced a contradiction: Quakers grew spiritually individualistic as they became organizationally corporatist. Their spirituality led them to espouse liberal humanitarian political reform, while their corporatism articulated a customary yet petit bourgeois distrust of universal market relations. The Society proved unable, however, to withstand the forces of social change and the rigor of its own discipline, as high rates of membership loss, through geographic mobility and expulsion, led to its virtual disappearance from Nailsworth by 1850.

The working classes had found Quaker spirituality and authoritarianism unappealing, favoring instead enthusiastic but democratically organized religion.[101] Nationally, the early Methodists and Welsh evangelicals were the first to attract a working-class following, and by the late eighteenth century older Nonconformist congregations had followed suit. Before 1750, as we have seen, other Nailsworth Dissenters displayed nearly as much sectarianism as did the Quakers; Congregationalists moderated their rigidities first, and the Baptists later followed their example.

Chapter Nine

Secularization and the Shortwood Baptist Church

If the Society of Friends persisted in its sectarianism, the Short-wood Baptist Church adapted to the Evangelical Revival and transformed itself into a denomination. Denominationalism, however, symbolized the "secularization" of society. Elie Halèvy understood this term to mean the appropriation of religious values by the wider culture,[1] just as Max Weber believed that a "Protestant ethic" had transfigured itself into the spirit of capitalism. But "secularization" could also mean a decline in religious belief and practice. The transition from sectarianism to denominationalism often appears in the literature as the expression of such a change, and many have attributed its causes to industrialization, greater geographic mobility, and urbanization.[2]

This chapter examines patterns of Baptist membership growth, church order, and discipline and relates them to the larger structural changes caused by industrialism. Although the growth of the Shortwood church affirmed the idea of community at a time of general dissolution of traditional communal bonds, its emergence as a denomination by 1851 led soon thereafter to the dilution of religious feeling among those failing to migrate from the locality. The religious enthusiasm felt by migrants, meanwhile, persisted and even intensified under secularizing pressures, however disassociated from the church they became. The Evangelical Revival may have contributed to Shortwood's considerable expansion, yet by doing so paradoxically fostered its institutional decline in the long term.

Membership Growth and Decline, 1775–1864

The Shortwood Baptist Church roll permits reconstruction of membership growth patterns for the 1775–1864 period.[3] Three intervals have been distinguished, which broadly followed the rhythm of economic change: 1775–1806, the era of protoindustrialization; 1806–1836, the age of factory formation; and 1837–1864, the era of definitive industrial decline. The subinterval, 1852–1864, marked an especially critical turing point in the region's economic fortunes; earlier stagnation became entrenched in these years and significantly affected the condition of the Shortwood church.

Two complementary ways of studying membership growth exist; the first examines gross additions over the course of each period, and the second examines actual membership levels. Gross additions consisted of baptisms and restorations; since Shortwood followed the custom of believers' baptism, these figures represent the actual number of conversions. "Restorations" referred to those who rebaptized themselves after a period of exclusion from membership. Actual membership levels for each year have been calculated by subtracting total annual losses from total annual additions and adding the result to the previous year's membership figure. The base membership in 1758 was sixty-six; the figure for each succeeding year, therefore, represents the cumulative increase in membership, as well as the actual membership for a particular year. Annual additions and losses and annual membership appear in time series respectively as figures 20 and 21, and compound-interest growth rate coefficients accompany them in table 62.

Significant patterns emerge. During the first period, the conversion rate faltered, as annual frequencies varied too widely to reveal any trend. Nevertheless, since outmigration remained minimal, membership levels grew at a respectable rate. The pitch of intensity of the Evangelical Revival mounted between 1806 and 1838, as the pace of economic change accelerated, and the conversion rate rose correspondingly, especially among women.[4] Since outmigration had not yet become a serious problem for the church, nor for the locality as a whole, total membership grew at a much stronger pace. Between 1837 and 1864, migration of church members

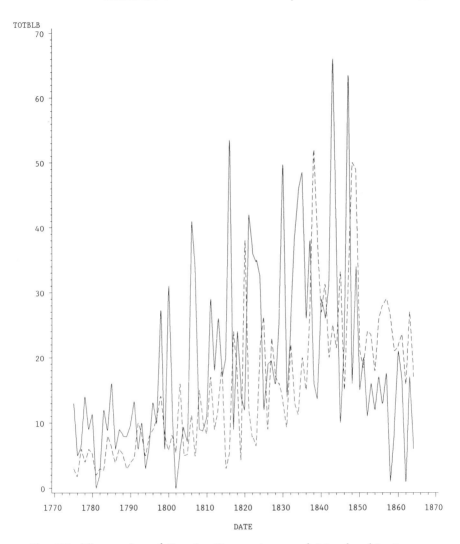

Fig. 20. Time-series of Baptist Conversions and Membership Losses 1775–1864.

Key: Solid Line = Conversions
Broken Line = Total Loses

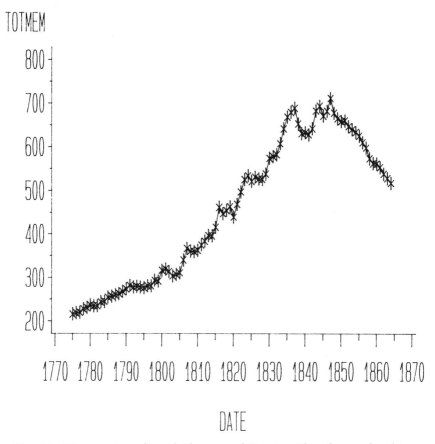

Fig. 21. Time series of total Shortwood Baptist Church membership, 1775–1864. *Source*: Shortwood Baptist Church roll (see text).

reached its highest levels, and the conversion rate fell dramatically; the growth rate for total membership also dropped for the first time in the church's history. Conversions actually reached quite high levels between 1837 and 1849, but the equally high level of outmigration negated any positive effects on membership growth these may have had. The absolute decline of conversions and total membership followed around 1850 and accelerated in 1857.

Tables 63 and 64 depict just how crucially outmigration affected membership stability. For each of the three main periods under consideration, table 63 gives a breakdown of average total mem-

TABLE 62. *Time Series of Baptist Membership Growth Rates,*
1775–1864

| | | | Mean conversions | |
	Conversions	Total membership	Male	Female
1775–1805	1.0	1.3	4.4	5.4
1806–1836	1.6	2.2	9.2	17.0
1837–1864	−5.3	−0.8	6.0	15.2

Note: Conversions and total membership are expressed as compound-interest growth rates (percent per annum); mean conversions are the average number of adult baptisms for males and females.
Source: See text.

TABLE 63. *Average Membership Losses among Shortwood Baptists,*
1775–1864
Total Losses ($\overline{X}_1$), Migrations ($\overline{X}_2$), Deaths ($\overline{X}_3$), and Exclusions ($\overline{X}_4$)

Period	$\overline{X}_1$	S_1	$\overline{X}_2$	S_2	$\overline{X}_3$	S_3	$\overline{X}_4$	S_4
1775–1805	6.29	3.2	0.7	1.5	4.09	2.3	1.54	1.6
1806–1836	14.3	7.3	2.9	5.2	8.8	3.5	2.5	2.2
1837–1864	27.2	9.5	9.6	7.7	13.1	3.8	4.4	2.8

TABLE 64. *Average Membership Losses as Percentage of Average Total*
Membership Losses

Period	$\overline{X}_1$ (%)	$\overline{X}_2$ (%)	$\overline{X}_3$ (%)	$\overline{X}_4$ (%)
1775–1805	100	11.0	65.0	24.0
1806–1836	100	20.0	62.0	18.0
1837–1864	100	35.3	48.2	16.2

bership loss by its individual components: migrations, deaths, and exclusions. Table 64 indicates the percentage of average total membership loss accounted for by each of these components in each period.

The results of these tables reveal a dramatic increase in migrations from 11.0 percent of the average total loss in 1775–1805 to 20.0 percent in 1806–1836 while increasing to 35.0 percent in 1837–1864. Deaths accounted for most of the losses in all periods, but in the last period the number of deaths declined sharply as outmigration accelerated. Not only did the great majority of migrants leave after 1837; most went to other parts of Britain or abroad. How did high geographic mobility affect their religious attitudes?

The Impact of Geographic Mobility

In 1849 Shortwood's minister, T. F. Newman, circularized members "living abroad" with the aim of discovering whether they wished their names to remain on the church roll. If for any reason they could not retain affiliation, he advised them to attend another church in the vicinity of their homes that followed "right doctrine." Nearly twenty responded to his initiative. Most wished to remain members for sentimental reasons, and those who requested formal dismissal did so reluctantly. These letters may have represented a biased sample of migrants' attitudes, since those hostile or indifferent were less likely to have responded. Still, not all potentially eager respondents found themselves in a position to write.[5] The preponderance of female correspondents reflected the sex ratio of the church membership, which suggests a degree of representativeness.[6] At minimum, these letters articulated an important body of opinion among Shortwood's migrants; correspondents gave similar reasons for attachment to the church, and several of them encountered the same obstacles in establishing a normal religious life.

M. F. Munden referred to his "unsettled state of life" and his desire to have one "spiritual home" and for this reason wished to retain full membership at Shortwood and an occasional association with the Baptist church at Hitchen, Hereford. Munden described himself as "a poor fellow entirely dependent...on my own personal and daily toils for all I have of this world's gear" and regretted that he could not offer a contribution.[7] Ann Jones, writing from Cheltenham under worse circumstances, also expressed a desire to remain on the church roll. "I should never have left Shortwood, my home," she lamented, "if I had work to have don [*sic*]." Leaving Shortwood had not improved her situation: "I was in Birmingham Union [for the poor] and now ham [*sic*] in Cheltenham Bethell Union House and I had the bad misfortune to louse [*sic*] a Sovring [*sic*], which have brought me very poor." Nostalgically, and perhaps in the hope of obtaining comfort, she added further: "I never shall forgett [*sic*] the kindness that you showd [*sic*] to me when my husband and I was living together. If any of the friends are dispose [*sic*] to come to see me I should be very glad to see them."[8]

Nostalgia, indeed, marked many of these letters. Hannah Smith recalled how, although "providential operations" had kept her from Shortwood, that church was "where I received my first spiritual good," and for this reason she wished to remain a member.[9] Sarah Green likewise responded that while circumstances had removed her from Shortwood, it was "the place where I received my earliest Christian impressions."[10] In more pathetic tones, Charlotte Boulton, writing from Cheltenham, expressed her desire to remain a member: "i still livs [*sic*] in hops [*sic*] if it is the will of got [*sic*] that somday [*sic*] i may have the privag [*sic*] of youniting [*sic*] with all my dear friends again."[11]

Nostalgia reflected the deep sense of loss felt by many migrants, especially the poor among them. The tribulations of Hannah Jones, a widow who died before receiving Newman's circular, reveal especially well the extent of this anomie; her friends, two Stockport grocers, rendered an account of them worth quoting at length:[12]

My impression is that she died for want of more nourishment. . . . During that illness when [there was] no hope of her recovery I was with her giving the little assistance I could, she requested me to go to Peter her son to ask him to come, for she wished [to see] him. . . . Peter said NO[!] I will never see her nor speak to her nor never forgive her nor never do anything for her but what the law compels me. . . . Peter would do nothing for her, then she was drove by necessity to apply to the parish. . . . I feel sorry to record the cruel conduct of Peter to his mother. He said "I

suppose she was my mother. I do not know who was my father." Peter
was informed directly of her death. His reply was "I will have nothing to
do with her."... I wrote to her son John two letters. No answer. She told
me John said [she] owed [him] £20.... As to her daughter Susan—she
was the worst. Peter's partner's wife [in the brushmaking trade] spoke
well of Hannah Jones, having lived next door for eleven years.

The kinship network had clearly failed Hannah in her time of
greatest need; her children expressed bitter hatred of her, and her
son Peter evidently nursed the grievance of his illegitimacy. Hannah's case affirms what Michael Anderson found for Lancashire's
working-class families during the Industrial Revolution: an in-
strumentalist attitude governed familial relations, however nominally close.[13]

By contrast, the Shortwood community had surrounded its
"flock" with the womblike security of Christian love. Despite the
want of opportunity for migrants to express their devotion more
formally, the intensity of their religious feeling and attachment to
Shortwood remained highly pitched. The objective difficulties
migrants faced in establishing a new spiritual home gave rise to
irregular patterns of worship that only nominally reflected the
secularizing impact of geographic mobility.

The most common mode of worship adopted by migrants was
that described by M. F. Munden, in his letter cited above, namely,
to attend other churches occasionally as a hearer. Matilde Robin,
writing from London, gave an eloquent description of the difficulties she faced in attending a Baptist church, and how she managed
to surmount them.[14] "I do not know how long or how short the
time of my residence in this locality may be," she confided, testifying at the same time to the precariousness of her situation. She was
able to "attend chapel but once in two Sundays and that is in the
evening." Yet she expressed the hope "in future to enjoy more
fully the privileges of the gospel which have borne me up for years
past." Moreover, "because I know no Baptist chapel near me, I
attend Doctor Leftchild's. He is a good plain preacher and a good
Christian...but his is an Independent chapel." She could not
bring herself to join the Independents, however, because to have
done so would have meant that "I must alter some of [my] opinions and that I cannot." Nevertheless, she went on to express the
latitudinarian view, grounded in "sound doctrine," which was

moderate Calvinist, that no sect could be excluded from heaven "that can cast away their own good works . . . rejoicing that salvation is of free grace and not of works, of free grace that none might perish."[15]

Evidently, Matilde Robin possessed decided religious views and a deep spirituality that neither the infrequency of her attendance at chapel, nor the fact that circumstances forced her to attend one of a different persuasion, mitigated. Neither was she exceptional in this regard. Servants, perhaps more than others, faced direct pressure from employers to conform to the religious discipline of their households. This problem aroused complaints in two letters sent to T. F. Newman.[16]

Hannah Neale described her movements over the course of several years and how she was eventually able to resist the pressures of her employer successfully. After leaving Shortwood, she resided at Stroud for twelve months, where she attended the Baptist chapel. She had not obtained a formal dismissal, however, "for I thought that prays [*sic*] the Lord may yet bring me back again." Then, for the next three years

I lived with people who attended the Church of England and they wished me to attend the same place of worship, but I must say it was a very great trick, so very different was that service to what I had been accustomed to here [;] and during the whole I was not . . . to meet in communion with god's people.

After returning to Stroud, she embarked on a different course:

I was determined to have the privilege of going to the chapel again. I therefore asked permission to go but was denied [*sic*] for they wish their servants to go where they go [;] but I would not give up with asken [*sic*], so I asked again and at last got safe to go to my own place.

This experience chastened her, forcing her to sacrifice the illusion that she would ever return to Shortwood. Appreciating the opportunity to attend once again the Baptist church at Stroud, she announced her intention to "enjoy the full privilege of membership there" and requested a formal letter of dismissal.

Hannah Neale's religious principles were perhaps less formed than Matilde Robin's. It was not a doctrinal issue that made her insist on choosing her own mode of worship, only the "great trick" of a foreign custom that the Anglican communion embodied. The formality of Church of England services alienated her intuitively from "god's people," as the rules of her household had done in practice. Ann Sansom, writing from Didmarton, Gloucestershire, alluded to the same difficulties, "as my master and mistress both attend Church and wish for their servants to attend there." She was more deferential toward her employers than Hannah Neale but expressed the hope "to be able to attend Mr. Michael's chapel" when her household returned to Tetbury on Lady Day. Presumably, at that time she intended to prevail upon her employers to allow her to attend chapel. How earnestly she did so would be difficult to say, although her attachment to Shortwood was genuine enough: "I must tell you dear sir that I do not feel at home anywhere but at Shortwood. . . . Dear sir I shall be very happy to give my mite at any time when help is needed."

One may conclude that geographic mobility, accelerated by a declining economy, had a contradictory effect on the religious behavior of migrants. Whereas it created barriers to their ability to worship in an accustomed fashion, anomie—created by forced mobility—increased nostalgia for the security and warmth of what for many was their first spiritual home. Indeed, many preferred an irregular mode of worship, provided they could retain their spiritual ties to Shortwood, an association that gave them fortitude. Geographic mobility, therefore, did not lead automatically to the dilution of religious feeling, however much it may have rendered religious affiliation a part-time affair. The fall in the conversion rate at Shortwood around 1850 suggests, however, that trade depression and the consolidation of the factory system may have produced a stricter secularizing effect locally.

Attendance at Shortwood, ca. 1850

The fall in the conversion rate began in the wake of the 1848 depression. In a September 1848 letter to the Western Association of Baptist Churches, the Minchinhampton Baptists described "a long dreary Winter [with] most of our people having been out of employ, and others struggling with privations from the deadness of trade."[17] Referring three years later to four recent conversions, T. F. Newman remarked sadly: "amidst [a] scene of barrenness, it is a mercy to have a little crop."[18] According to contemporaries, a fall in attendance at open communion services occurred among "hearers" at all churches and accompanied a "great fall" in conversions, especially at Shortwood. R. M. Newman, in a short history of the church, attributed this development to the advent of the factory system:

When the [people] had to walk to their work in the mills, attendances at all places began to fall considerably; the hours of work were long, and they probably rested on Sundays at home and looked after their gardens. This change brought about a great fall in membership [at Shortwood] about 1850.[19]

The fall in the rate of conversions affirms Newman's observation, although the evidence of attendance of those in full communion at Shortwood suggests that the impact of factory life had not yet come into full operation.

It is necessary to examine, as far as possible, the quality of religious experience at this time. Individuals often translated the atmosphere of a depressed economy, and the consolidation of a new form of work discipline, into feelings of personal despair. Rather than acting as a buffer against anomie, the religiosity of members living locally in 1852/53 often reinforced it. In the long term, this failure would lead to the "great fall" in attendance to which Newman had alluded; in the short term, attendance by members living locally revealed a transitional pattern.

A survey of the local membership, undertaken by T. F. Newman in 1852/53,[20] complements the earlier time-series analyses by permitting study of attendance at the moment when conversions and membership levels began to decline. Names appearing in the minister's survey were linked as closely as possible to the enumerator's lists for the 1851 census.[21] Of the 547 members listed in the survey, 177, or 32.3 percent, were sampled. Only those living locally and in the immediate vicinity of the Vale were selected because of the otherwise highly scattered membership. Besides the regularity of attendance, recorded by the survey, the census adds information regarding occupation, age, sex, and residence. "Attendance" served as a dependent variable, and the others as independent variables,[22] in a multiple classification analysis.[23]

Table 65 presents the analysis of attendance based on five variables, and table 66 contains the significance tests of the interactions

TABLE 65. *Attendance Patterns of Shortwood Baptist Church Members, 1852/53*

Variable + category	N	Unadjusted		Adjusted for independents	
		Deviation	Eta	Deviation	Eta
Class					
1 middle class	34	0.40		−1.59	
2 lower middle class	89	1.85		2.20	
3 working classes	54	−3.30		−2.62	
			0.13		0.13
Sex					
1 male	63	2.50		2.82	
2 female	114	−1.38		−1.56	
			0.10		0.12
Age (in years)	27	−0.52			
1 16–26	25	5.53		0.37	
2 27–37	31	0.70		6.56	
3 38–48	44	−1.07		1.39	
4 49–59	35	3.50		−2.57	
5 60–70	15	−14.74		3.38	
6 7–highest				−14.82	
			0.29		0.30
Region					
1 Nailsworth and hamlets	114	1.43		1.93	
2 Periphery of Vale	63	−2.58		−3.50	
			0.11		0.15
Multiple R^2					0.128
Multiple R					0.358

[a]The mean of any category is found by adding the deviation score to the grand mean of 41.07.

between them. The variable "frequency of attendance" (F_{att}) was transformed into numerical scores and broken down into the variables of class, sex, age, and region.[24] "Class" divides neatly into three groups, based on occupations listed in appendix K, and "age" is more conveniently analyzed when similarly divided into cohorts. "Region" coincides with distance intervals radiating from the center at Nailsworth village and its adjacent hamlets. The first region stands for the central Vale and the second, for the hamlets on its immediate periphery: Barton End, Horsley, Dowend, and

TABLE 66. *Significance Tests of Variable Interactions*

Source of variation			Sum of squares	df	Mean square	F	Signifi-cance of F
Main effects			7122.847	9	791.427	2.782	0.006
Class			838.330	2	419.165	1.473	0.233
Sex			752.052	1	752.052	2.643	0.107
Age			5002.190	5	1000.438	3.516	0.005
Region			1138.256	1	1138.256	4.001	0.048
Two-way interactions			8675.656	25	347.026	1.220	0.238
Class	Sex		404.778	2	202.389	0.711	0.493
Class	Age		2389.634	10	238.963	0.840	0.591
Class	Region		1454.891	2	727.445	2.557	0.082
Sex	Age		2575.259	5	515.052	1.810	0.116
Sex	Region		110.890	1	110.890	0.390	0.534
Age	Region		3112.278	5	622.456	2.188	0.060
Three-way interactions			5614.557	24	233.940	0.822	0.702
Class	Sex	Age	3044.740	9	338.304	1.189	0.309
Class	Sex	Region	491.739	2	245.869	0.864	0.424
Class	Age	Region	506.284	8	63.285	0.222	0.986
Sex	Age	Region	2025.332	5	405.066	1.424	0.221
Four-way interactions			1312.985	3	437.662	1.538	0.208
Class	Sex	Age	1312.985	3	437.662	1.538	0.208
		Region					
Explained			22726.045	61	372.558	1.309	0.108
Residual			32720.000	115	284.522		
Total			55446.045	176	315.034		

Note: The column "Significance of *F*" gives the probabilities at which the differences between categories are significant. Any value above $p > 0.05$ fails to be significant. Thus, the differences between the categories in class and sex are not significant, while those in age and region are. In the two-, three-, and four-variable interaction tests, all significant levels are greater than 0.05. Thus, between all independent variables no correlations were detected. This means that the overall equation of F_{att} = class + sex + age + region is a valid model.

Rockness districts.[25] The gender distribution of the sample reveals a preponderance of females at nearly 2:1, which corresponds to the sex ratio of conversions since 1775.[26]

In general, the findings show that attendance by class and age demonstrates the comparative health of the church, although foreshadowing future difficulties; attendance by region, however, clearly reveals a more negative pattern. No significant difference existed between the sexes, despite the much higher number of female members in the sample.

Attendance by social class shows the middle class attending nearly at the mean; small retailers, artisans, and skilled factory workers, who constituted class 2 (see table 65), attended just above the mean; laborers, unskilled clothworkers, and the miscellaneous poor, who composed class 3, attended just below it. The variation, although insignificant, suggests an incipient trend. Since evangelical Christianity provided a framework for the integration of classes,[27] the absence of significant variation implies continuity with the height of the Revival. At its height the poorest individuals very likely attended with the greatest regularity, but in our sample they attended the least frequently, a pattern suggesting incipient alienation from the Chapel community. In the long term, secularization would be associated with the alienation of the poorest strata from organized religion.[28] At the same time, class 2 showed the highest frequencies of attendance. This group included many skilled weavers who were working in factories[29] and for whom the workplace had partially supplanted the Chapel as the center of communal life. Nevertheless, the especially high attendance of weavers at 43.6 times per year indicates continuity with the height of the revival.

This purely quantitative finding, however, masks a dramatic change in their collective spirituality during the first half of the nineteenth century. Evangelicalism may have provided a framework for social integration. As Eric Hobsbawm initially observed, however, it also contained a "Ranter" potential that middle-class Chapel deacons eschewed.[30] Evidence regarding popular disorder in the Stroud region between 1827 and 1839 shows a language of protest framed by antiauthoritarian enthusiasm.[31] By 1850, however, this militancy gave way to what E. P. Thompson has accurately termed the "chiliasm of despair."[32]

Deference, sanctioned by religious feeling, had certainly coexisted with the militancy of the late 1820s and 1830s, but the latter clearly predominated. Still, despite hostility to the factory system in 1839, protestors began adapting half-consciously to its discipline. Although Chartists agitated throughout the Stroud region during the 1840s, leading clothiers successfully countered them by campaigning against the Corn Laws.[33] The depression of 1848 coincided with the final defeat of Chartism, and the combined effects of these events created an atmosphere of desperation. Many who had previously displayed a robust confidence regarding their Election came to internalize anxiety concerning their salvation. "Enthusiasm" now expressed itself more readily in deference to authority, self-abnegation, and acquiescence to an alien form of work discipline.

In 1854 the suicide of Isaac Keynton, a Minchinhampton Baptist weaver, evoked this widespread mood of psychological depression;[34] details from the inquest imply that suicide was common among the working classes of the region at this time.[35] Keynton's distress illustrates, moreover, how a Calvinist ethos, when negatively expressed, could inform deferential attitudes.

At the inquest, Keynton's wife reported that he had suffered paralysis in his limbs and had become despondent as a result. According to newspaper accounts, he had two chief concerns while in this state: fear of being unable to satisfy the manufacturer for whom he worked and depression with a general feeling of hopelessness, revealing a religious tendency.

The second witness, a fellow clothworker, corroborated Mary Keynton's testimony. He described how the deceased "often talked to him lately in a desponding way; seemed like one completely broken down. Often spoke of himself as a *reprobate*, and one for whom there was no mercy" [emphasis added]. Jeffreys, the clothworker, found the deceased drowned in Longfords Lake and had good reason for going at once to this spot: "[It] was where another man had drowned him-self some months ago, and on that occassion deceased said to him 'he could hardly bide in his loom; he could not beat it out of his head that he must go and drown him-self in the very same place.'" These two manifestations of Keynton's depression were undoubtedly related. Clearly, he viewed his paralysis as a providential act, as a sign that God had not chosen him after all, although overwork very likely caused his illness. Nor did illness permit him to satisfy his employer, a failure he treated as further proof of his own unworthiness. Nonconformity, by promoting sobriety, had long encouraged this link between virtue and utility, although sympathy for human frailty often softened normative rigor. Under the new factory system, however, a more negative emphasis finally persevered. Still, the "great fall" in attendance, much lamented by contemporaries, had not yet occurred among those in full communion, although among hearers, as we have seen, a decline in attendance accompanied a faltering conversion rate. This paradox highlights the transitional nature of the early 1850s, and attendance patterns, when examined by age cohort, affirm this observation.

Attendance, when measured by age cohort, reveals an optimistic picture for 1852/53, but darker elements present also foreshadowed a future negative trend. Referring again to table 65, "age" proved to be the most important independent variable because of its higher eta score. In general, if we count cohorts 1 and 3 together, there is a slight bias toward youth in the sample despite the high outmigration of the period; this fact suggests a comparatively healthy church membership. We have already seen that for a sample of Nailsworth's hamlets including Shortwood, the age-sex composition actually improved during the 1840s. The size of the twenty-five- to thirty-four-year cohort increased significantly, as the early middle-aged, thirty-five to forty-four years, fell correspondingly and almost all other cohorts remained stable.[36] The marginal effect of outmigration on youth shows that contemporary complaints exaggerated the problem.[37] Although Nailsworth suffered from severe trade depressions in the 1830s and 1840s, its economic decline proved to be a more protracted process, extending into the late nineteenth century.

The pattern of variation in attendance between age cohorts reinforces this impression of comparative health. The three youngest cohorts together had higher attendance than did the older ones, and the second cohort (ages twenty-seven to thirty-seven) had by far the highest, whether controlling for other independent variables or not. Young adults viewed Sunday services as an appropriate courtship setting, as much as a means for expressing religious devotion.[38] The next eldest cohort (ages sixty to seventy) attended at the second highest rate because of the proximity of death and the special concern for salvation its nearness evoked. Still, the very eldest attended least frequently because of the infirmities of age.

Those aged forty-four to fifty-nine years were the great exception to this broadly optimistic picture. Their mean attendance fell significantly below the grand mean. They were the most numerous cohort and constituted the pivotal middle-aged group; neither motives of courtship nor proximity to death could encourage higher attendance.[39] Death was neither imminent nor something, should it strike, that could rob them of the fruits of a full life. The middle-aged were more preoccupied by the cares of this world than were either their juniors or seniors and, for this reason, were the most secularized of all Shortwood's membership.

Paradoxically, the spiritual concerns of youth and the elderly could be similar. The elderly prepared for imminent death; youth did the same from fear of its unpredictability. For youth, death's suddenness amid the fullness of life was a prospect both awesome and spiritually provocative. A young woman named Harriet Dangerfield, writing to the Shortwood minister in 1849, described her own spiritual odyssey in terms that substantiate these inferences.[40] As a child, she had received instruction at the Shortwood Sunday School and "was blest with pious parents."[41] Nonetheless, her spiritual engagement evolved over a considerable period, during which she discovered the meaning of death:

About the age of sixteen I was very much concerned about my never dying soul. I had many convictions of sin but stifled them and they where [sic] has [sic] the morning cloud and the early Dew. They soon passed away and I cared nothing for them and I turned to the world a little longer, till two years and six months ago[.] Then convictions returning again and made a lasting impression upon my mind. Has [sic] I was about the busy cares of the world the thought came very powerfully [sic] to my mind where would my soul be if it should be called out of time into eternity that night. At that time I deeply felt the need of a Saviour. This led me to kneel down before god and humbly ask him to forgive me for Christ's sake. I trust and believe from that hour that he heard and answered my prayer and [made] me a new creature in Christ Jesus.

Still, Harriet did not remain entirely free from doubt about the durability of grace:

So i [sic] went on from step to step till death made its inroads in the family and removed one of my cousins Eliza Dangerfield. Has [sic] I stood by her bedside I thought if I was in her place if I should be has [sic] she was. And I prayed to god through Christ sake to prepare me for eternity. About that time I began to feel more of my own wicked heart and of my own unworthiness. I felt I could do nothing without Christ and . . . I put my whole trust in him . . . for salvation. . . . I was then brought to mourn the loss of another cousin. A few days before her death she called me to her bedside and took me by hand and said, well Harriet if you have begun to seek the Lord persevere on, he will be your guide unto death. And I felt happy at that time.

These observations illustrate a spiritual development characteristic of Baptist youth.[42] They also evoke a more universal religious sensibility, the "chiliasm of despair," already depicted in extreme form in the suicide of Isaac Keynton, and articulated in the moderate Calvinism practiced at Shortwood. By awaiting the appearance of a savior, Harriet had demonstrated a belief in free grace; yet through prayer she believed it possible to seek Election actively and in this manner demonstrated her confidence in universal redemption. Still, God's gift, not human agency, mattered most.

Harriet strictly adhered to this procedure. She composed her letter to Newman two years before baptizing herself and in the interim vacillated over whether she indeed belonged among the Elect. Not even baptism, however, could free her completely from doubts about her worthiness.[43] Although the doctrine of final perseverance should have eliminated all doubt, the Shortwood Baptists practiced only "speculative antinomianism" and expected the Saints to conform to the letter of the law. Members might lapse, but not without feelings of despair, as the case of Daniel Gill further illustrates.

Gill, a Minchinhampton Baptist, "appeared before the church and was desireous [sic] to delay his fellowship from fear of his unfitness."[44] Gill baptized himself two months later in September 1847, but during the interval, his "mind. . . [became] much exercised with a variety of convictions and temptations," and, according to the church minute book, "he has received strength by the encouraging counsel of brother Jones." Nevertheless, in March 1848 Daniel Gill was "overtaken by temptation. . . [and was] very abject by his fall from rectitude," and the church suspended him for three months.[45]

In the cases of Daniel Gill and Isaac Keynton, a morbid preoccupation with unworthiness yielded to despair. The quiet, depressive tone of Harriet Dangerfield's letter shows that she, too, bordered on despair but succeeded in establishing an emotional equilibrium, however much she may have vacillated thereafter.

She later withdrew from membership,[46] and others eventually followed her example in greater numbers.

Still, the incipient decline of the Shortwood church became manifest more fully in rates of attendance by region. Those living within the Vale attended services 42.5 times per year on average, but those residing on its immediate periphery attended only 38.5 times.[47] The difference became even more pronounced when holding other variables constant. Distances between the Vale and its immediate periphery ranged no more than two miles; by contrast, the congregation of an earlier era, as we have seen, came regularly from fifteen adjacent parishes, and some communicants traveled upward of fifteen to thirty miles.[48] This change clearly reflected a secularizing trend. With its modern discipline and requirement that workers walk to work, the factory system encouraged those living a short distance from chapel to rest on Sundays rather than attend religious services; they tended their gardens instead.[49]

Church Order and Discipline

The growth of the Shortwood Baptist Church during the first half of the nineteenth century also had stimulated the founding of other Baptist churches, first at Minchinhampton in 1765 and later at Avening in 1820. Following Benjamin Francis's example,[50] itinerant preaching soon became a prescribed duty of all ministers and lay leaders. By the 1860s, Baptist societies, operating from London, regularly gave financial support to congregations unable to finance this activity independently.[51] In 1847 the Minchinhampton Baptists established two village preaching stations to "spread the Word" to outlying settlements.[52] Archer Blackwell, one of the founding fathers of the Avening church, bequeathed money to the Shortwood deacons for the purpose of aiding this pursuit,[53] and they took a very active part in promoting it. John Heskins, the younger, elected deacon in 1807, "was called by the church [four years later] to exercise his gifts in the ministry of the Word." He fulfilled his task highly successfully in the neighboring villages and hamlets,[54] and "[h]is dwelling became . . . frequented by the pious poor who were there certain to receive both sympathy and relief."[55]

Not all churches approved of itinerant preaching. The Church of England long considered the practice incompatible with the requirements of a settled congregation.[56] In contrast, Wesleyan Methodists had founded their sect on the basis of itinerancy and invested much authority for the supervision of local societies in their preachers, whom Wesley and the "Legal Hundred" after him strictly controlled.[57] The Baptists adopted a more decentralized approach by subordinating itinerants to the authority of the local church meeting. For Baptists, members of the "gathered church" exercised absolute sovereignty over the election of deacons, the acceptance and exclusion of members, and all other business affecting the church. The Shortwood community thus developed its own special interests and loyalties, which paradoxically might sometimes conflict with village preaching.

Itinerants rarely intended to found new churches, for these could easily compete with the more established congregations. Village preachers intended only to "spread the Word" to the scattered populations of the district, who were often unable to attend a church, or to recruit a larger following for Shortwood itself. The appearance of new Baptist churches sometimes occurred as an unintended and unwelcome consequence of itinerancy. The history of the founding of the Avening church holds special interest for this reason.

Considerable divisiveness accompanied the founding of the Avening church.[58] In 1804 several members of Shortwood resident at Avening village proposed the creation of a more convenient place of worship for themselves. Although members at Shortwood, they often frequented a small house in Avening village belonging to Abraham Cox. Between 1804 and 1819 "Messrs. [S. E.] Francis, Burchell and Flint [Shortwood deacons] preached in the house when they visited Avening and sometimes in the open air." Eventually, they built a small preaching room, twenty feet by thirty feet, on a plot of ground provided by John Blackwell, an Avening landowner and a Shortwood deacon. Lewis, Flint, and Revd. Winterbotham from Shortwood presided over its opening, and with their help the congregation discharged the debt of £168 18s. ½d. in that same year. Several Shortwood deacons and one Congregationalist minister, Revd. John Pain, assumed the trusteeship; this ecumenical spirit expressed itself further in the trust deed's description of the premises' function: "a place for public worship...by Protestant Dissenters of the Baptist denomination and Calvinistic persuasion with liberty to accept the occasional assistance of ministers and preachers of other denominations of Protestant Dissenters." Until 1819, "the building was kept open by neighboring ministers and others as an evening sector only." Shortwood leaders remained content to leave the preaching room in this condition. However, the progress of the Revival caused Avening residents to consider the establishment· of a chapel:

[In 1819] the Christian friends of Avening contemplated with great pleasure the increasing attention and deep interest many of the inhabitants of the village felt...particularly among the young people, several of them enquiring their way to Zion with their faces witherward, some of them assisting at our prayer meeting in leading the devotion with acceptance.

On August 4, 1819 the Shortwood members living at Avening addressed a letter to their church, in which they reported on the situation in their village and requested the establishment of a Baptist church there. A Shortwood deacon, after an independent study, opined in his report "that [the church] ought not to sanction the measure under existing circumstances." With the exception of two votes in favor, the Shortwood meeting voted to deny the request from Avening. The meeting refused for two reasons: allegedly, the Avening people were "attempting to so dissention [*sic*] in the church and oppos[ed] the interest of Shortwood," and "it was further urged that we were so poor and illiterate that we could not support or manage such concern." The Avening people refused to accept this decision: "But we know from the Holy Scripture that the Lord despiseth not the poor nor the way of small things," and after mature deliberation, they formally erected their own chapel. They were not, of course, left entirely to their own devices, for Stephen and Cornelius Blackwell, wealthy clothiers and landowners, provided the Avening church with effective leadership.[59]

On October 31, 1819 Revd. Henry Hawkins, Baptist minister from Eastcombes, baptized eight new members, and "nearly 40 Christian friends from nine or 10 different Dissenting churches sat down with us at the 'Lord's table'."[60] Table 67 provides a break-

TABLE 67. *Attenders at Founding of the Avening Baptist Church*

Place	Number	Denomination
Shortwood	20–30	Baptist
Escombs [*sic*]	"Many"	Baptist
Tetbury	1	Baptist
Forest Green	"Many"	Independent
Stroud	1	Independent
Cirencester	1	Baptist
London	1	Independent
Littleworth (Minchinhampton)	2	Wesleyan Methodist
Chalford	1	Baptist

Source: Avening Baptist Church Book. See Mr. Frank Smith, 9 Lawrence Road, Avening, Gloucestershire.

down of this ecumenical celebration. The figures show that despite opposition from Shortwood, many of its members demonstrated goodwill by attending the convocation. By summer 1820, the two churches reestablished friendly relations. Shortwood's new enthusiasm "for our prosperity" heartened the Avening people, who in August received from the older church formal letters of dismissal for their founding members.[61]

This controversy has a broader significance for several reasons. First, it highlights the extent to which the members of independent churches prized their autonomy both as individuals and as a congregation. "As a community," the Minchinhampton Baptists wrote to the Western Association in 1848, "we are beginning to recognize the important right that every man must think and act for himself on religious subjects and nothing be allowed to arrogate worldly authority over us as a church."[62] Moreover, the arrogance displayed by Shortwood's deacons hinted at a degree of social cleavage within its own ranks and, consequently, at a growing "denominational" status. Indeed, the Shortwood leadership came to be dominated by a group of clothier families who had intermarried, as figure 22 illustrates. Others came from the lower middle class and at least one from the working class: Isaac Hillier, pig butcher and later bacon-curing manufacturer; Daniel Cook, a prosperous haymaker; Levi Chandler, a Nailsworth shopkeeper; Charles Jenkins, a baker; and Simon Dodge, a cloth spinner.[63] The

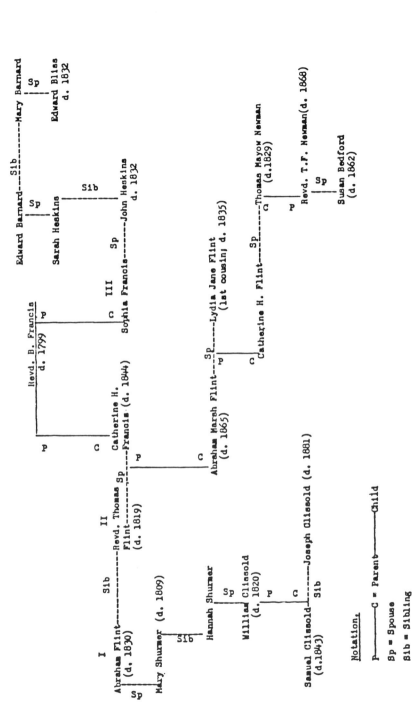

Fig. 22. Familial bonds between the clothier-deacons of Shortwood. *Source:* See text.

presence of these men gave the diaconate a more egalitarian aspect, but over the course of several generations, the network of clothier families had come to constitute the church's inner leadership.

The events at Avening, moreover, illustrate how the deacons conducted their leadership. The church membership, of course, elected them directly, as it did the minister himself. They were responsible for directing church business meetings, which sometimes required the preparation of special reports; occasionally they acted as a special tribunal, rendering judgments on controversial questions, as in 1824 when some members circulated a petition to establish a choir and to introduce instrumental music into church services.[64] In 1839 the deacons decided to visit designated districts within the neighborhood to promote contact with a "flock" that had grown impersonally large.

Finally, the Avening church incident portrays the type of communion usually practiced by Baptists of the region. Combined with an evangelical approach, "open communion" rendered the Shortwood, Avening, and Minchinhampton Baptist churches hotbeds of enthusiasm. These communities admitted all Christians to the "Lord's table" but permitted only those formally baptized, according to their ordinance, to participate in church meetings. Still, those who attended services as hearers could also attend weekday evening prayer meetings. By allowing such broad participation, these churches spread their influence throughout the region and thereby created pools from which to recruit new members. Many hearers, for instance, chose burial at the Shortwood grounds, the register of which faithfully records their status.[65]

As table 68 shows, the ratio of hearers to members buried at Shortwood remained stable at nearly 2:1 for the years 1808–1837. For the 1854–1873 period, however, the proportion of hearers to members decreased significantly. The decade 1854–1863 witnessed the maximum decline in the proportion of hearers and reflected the trend toward depopulation of the district. Although the relative proportions of hearers to members returned to previous levels in the next decade, total adult burials had nevertheless declined significantly.[66]

Despite this overall success, not every Baptist easily accepted the practice of open communion. One person writing from Chelsea in

TABLE 68. *Members and Hearers Buried at Shortwood, 1808–1873*

Decade	Mean total adult burials[a]	Mean burials of member		Mean burials of hearers[b]	
		$\overline{X}_1$	%	$\overline{X}_2$	%
1808–1817	18.6	6.7	36.0	11.9	64.0
1818–1827	22.0	7.5	34.1	14.5	65.9
1828–1837	22.6[c]	8.6	37.7	14.2	62.3
1808–1837	21.1	7.6	35.9	13.5	64.1
1854–1863	21.6	9.5	43.9	12.1	56.0
1864–1873	19.4[d]	7.2	37.0	12.2	62.8
1854–1873	20.5	8.4	40.8	12.15	59.3

[a] Adult burials include all deceased age 16 and over. The register records the age at death; Baptists regarded 16 years as the normal age at baptism.

[b] We can assume that some nonmembers interred at Shortwood were unbaptized kin of Baptist members; had they lived, some perhaps would have become baptized, especially those aged 16–24. Most hearers interred, however, fell well outside this range. The mean age of 406 hearers buried over a thirty-year period was 48.3 with a standard deviation well below this figure at 38.6. Most hearers represented in this table, therefore, were probably independent hearers.

[c] $s = 2.876$.

[d] $s = 5.188$; see n. 66 for t-test.

Source: See text.

1849 wanted to know whether Shortwood was "of strict communion principles" before requesting dismissal to it. On learning that it was "based upon the principle of open communion and not strict," he dropped all proceedings.[67] The Stroud Baptist Church adhered to open communion until 1826, when, by order of the church meeting, it decided to exclude non-Baptist hearers:

The order of this church having hitherto allowed the admission of unbaptized persons to their communion, to which the greater part of their number were consciously opposed, a meeting was called to consider the propriety thereof when the church agreed to admit only those baptized by immersion to commune with them at the Lord's table.[68]

All Baptist churches in the vicinity practiced baptism by immersion, which they connected indissolubly to believers' baptism. "The birthday of a Christian," one contemporary remarked about the Revival, "was... shifted from his [infant] baptism to his conversion, and in that change the partition line of two great systems is crossed."[69] Baptists normally required a candidate to testify about one's experiences before the church meeting and on this basis determined one's fitness for membership. Candidates needed to show, in particular, precisely how Christ had appeared to them as a savior—how, in other words, they became recipients of free grace.

If the church meeting acted as the ultimate source of authority in the matter of membership admission, it also assumed the responsibility of enforcing discipline.[70] Like the Quakers, Baptists placed much emphasis on keeping "the unity of the spirit in the bond of peace" but on crucial points displayed greater flexibility and willingness to acknowledge the reality of human frailty. They drew a clear distinction between the "slips and failings that are sinful" and those that were decidedly so. They organized class meetings so that members could watch one another's "conversation," not necessarily to condemn, but to give support and encouragement in maintaining a coherent mode of living. Ketura Smart, in a letter addressed to S. E. Francis, a senior Shortwood deacon, expressed the importance she attached to such fellowship, although she had come to reside at Horton, Gloucestershire:[71] "because during my youth you always manifested a kind and almost parental solicitude for my temporal and eternal welfare." She continued, "Nor shall I... forget the many, many happy hours I have passed beneath your roof, and in the society of friends at Shortwood." Because they often gave comfort, class meetings became the primary means through which the church cultivated a sense of community.

At the same time, these meetings provided the means for the transmission of Puritan values to a working class in formation. The Quakers, by contrast, considered a wide range of behavior as grounds for expulsion and often despite mitigating circumstances. Although exclusions accounted for a significant percentage of membership loss at Shortwood,[72] the available evidence indicates that, for the most part, they were for offenses of "gross immorality." Exclusion was the most extreme step that could be taken, and first offenders were usually suspended instead. Thus the church excluded Alice Stephenson on November 27, 1737 "for her notoriously wicked behavior and conversation... accustoming herself to get drunk and speak obscene words and railing against the church."[73] Ann Wakefield was "totally excluded" on May 18, 1755 "on a strong suspicion of fornication and an evident proof of incest with a brother."[74] Mary Webb similarly fell from favor in January 1740 for the more pathetic yet no less sinful act of "receiving wood which her children had stolen with an intention to burn it"; the church had suspended her on earlier occasions for the same offense.[75] During Benjamin Francis's ministry, exclusions were made only for "drunkenness and whoredom" or dishonesty, lying, and theft.[76] Unlike the Quakers, however, the Baptists tolerated "mixed marriages." Although article IX of the Shortwood covenant enjoined single members against "enter[ing] into conjugal bonds with any that are unbelievers," in practice Baptists defined unbelievers more literally than did Quakers, who treated them as persons "not member[s] of our society." When Benjamin Francis tested his colleague Joshua Thomas by asking, "Should a member be put by from communion for marrying one of the world, or no?" Thomas answered with Francis's tacit concurrence, "I don't think it unsuitable to marry any pious Protestant. . . . If a member be married to a pious Pedobaptist, I would not put him by, merely for that."[77] Among Baptists, therefore, some pluralism of religious affiliation at the time of marriage prevailed.

Consequently, Shortwood members generally derived a warmer sense of community than did the Quakers, particularly during the early period of the Industrial Revolution, when it was most needed. Yet it is reasonable to conclude that in the long term this sense of community failed to provide a buffer against anomie, once the factory system triumphed definitively. The eclectic nature of Calvinist doctrine provided an opening for enthusiasm at the height of the factory's emergence yet paved the way for a more thoroughgoing submission to a new order by 1850 through greater insistence on "sobriety" and appeals to the latent anxieties of its members regarding their Election.[78]

Newman's sermon from Matthew XX, on the "Parable of the Husbandman and Labourers," preached in the midst of a deep economic depression, reveals especially well the cultural values about work and poverty that evangelical Nonconformity promoted in this later period.[79] The husbandman contracted with a group of laborers in early morning to work his fields for an entire day for the equivalent of $7\frac{1}{2}$d. During the course of the day, however, the husbandman returned to the market several times (at noon, 3 P.M., and 5 P.M.) and on each occassion found new hands waiting to be employed: a surplus labor problem had clearly existed. Out of charity, the husbandman offered to employ each successive group of laborers for the same wage he paid the first group, who subsequently protested against what they perceived as unfair treatment. Those employed at later hours clearly produced much less for the same wage; Newman, therefore, depicted the husbandman's behavior as Christian generosity, while portraying the protesting laborers as mean-spirited.[80] Yet one may also argue with the protesting laborers that the husbandman had, in effect, underpaid them, and was able to do so because of an admittedly glutted labor market; the wages received by laborers hired at 5 P.M. could easily have represented the market price of their labor. In the context of a depressed economy, Newman's sermon could only have discouraged workers from challenging their employers' calls for wage reductions, supposedly effected to spread the available work around.[81]

Newman, nevertheless, conceded that poverty often resulted from circumstances beyond the control of the worker and not always from "immorality." His sermon on the "Parable of the Husbandman and the Labourers" contains this assumption implicitly, but in later sermons he articulates it explicitly:

I do not forget that sometimes the extreme of poverty is the result of vicious habits—the direct off-spring of Sin—and perhaps the existence of such cases has tended to freeze up the stream of benevolence from those whose penury has not resulted from their crimes. Now and then a case of miserable destitution may be directly traced to the habits of intemperance and profligacy. But in addition to these, and to a far greater extent, will you discover instances of individual and domestic suffering to which no taint is attached—want of employment, . . . health, the inevitable claims of a numerous family, the weakness, and decrepitude of age.[82]

By enjoining his congregation that "it is more blessed to give than to receive," Newman partially and half-apologetically reasserted the more traditional evangelical role of his church as comforter of the oppressed. Still, the Shortwood church had grown more thoroughly denominational by 1850, and the schism of 1866, which led to the formation of the Nailsworth Tabernacle, underscored this development. The Tabernacle's minutes sketch the history of the dispute, precipitated by the need to choose a new pastor, in tones that evoke the class feeling that informed it:

It would appear...that a very small minority of the richer and more influential of the members obstinately opposed the general wish of the church, threatening to withdraw their support in the event of Mr. Jackson becoming pastor. This high-handed and unwarranted conduct of the few naturally gendered bitterness and ill feeling.[83]

Sixty to eighty members withdrew to form the Tabernacle but failed to sustain themselves for any considerable length of time, and by the turn of the century the Methodists had taken over their meetinghouse.[84]

Nevertheless, the event provides an interesting counterpoint to the schism of 1707, which had led to the formation of the Shortwood church. Plebeian members had initiated each episode, but the earlier one, because of its genuine theological character, contained real possibilities for the growth of a Chapel community. The later espisode, devoid of theological meaning, simply reflected the social alienation of some and therefore contained few possibilities for the further prosperity of organized religious life. Social antagonism, however deeply felt, confined itself to a minority and thereby failed to alter the prevailing atmosphere of class collaboration; the conflict represented instead the last breath of an earlier militancy.

Summary and Conclusion

In contrast to the Society of Friends, the Shortwood Baptist Church had emerged as the premier Nonconformist community at Nailsworth and the largest of its persuasion outside London. Shortwood's history epitomized the transition from sectarianism to denominationalism, found in the sociological literature, and has thereby provided an example of "secularization."[85]

From its founding in 1707 until the advent of Benjamin Francis's ministry in 1758, the Shortwood church remained a High Calvinist, Particular Baptist sect, drawing a doctrinaire distinction between itself as an Elect and "the world." At the time the church contained a homogeneous membership consisting mainly of artisans. After 1758, although formally remaining Particular Baptist,

Shortwood adopted a moderate Calvinist and evangelical outlook, which reconciled the doctrines of universal redemption and free grace and led the Baptist community toward denominationalism. This theological shift enhanced Shortwood's capacity for spiritual tolerance and enabled it to appeal successfully to a new industrial working class while drawing its leaders increasingly from among the middle class. Its practice of open communion, especially, softened the sectarian distinction between "God's People" and "the world" and thereby stimulated overlapping attendance at different churches and even "mixed marriages" between Baptists and Anglicans.

Openness, pluralism, and spiritual universalism, however, trademarks of a denominational religious culture, led under exogenous pressures to a long-term weakening of institutional religious life, although not necessarily in the religiosity of all individuals. This weakening became evident in the impact of geographic mobility after 1840, falling conversion rates, and a shifting pattern of attendance at services in 1852/53. This last indicator, although showing positive signs, foreshadowed a future negative trend.

Evangelical communitarianism, articulated by the Shortwood Baptist Church, sought initially to recreate the integrated life of a traditional sect, but on a broad popular basis. The ideal of communal solidarity, however, obscured the consequences of exogenous pressures: the social stratification of memberships and the inherent divisiveness of their mutual relations. By the 1850s, a fully denominational Baptist community came to mirror the class structure of industrial society, and the triumph of a liberal evangelicalism over a more radical variant accompanied and facilitated this development. The "conjuncture" of demographic, social, and religious-cultural changes brought about the final transition to *gesellschaft* and a more secular way of life.

Part IV

Conclusion: The Impact of the Industrial Revolution

Chapter Ten

Synchronicity? Local Changes in the Industrial Revolution

Religious life, James Obelkevich has written of South Lindsey, "cannot be 'reduced' to its social foundations, but it is unintelligible without them. The transformation of traditional agrarian society into a society of classes transformed religion as well."[1] This conclusion applies equally well to religious life in the Vale of Nailsworth between 1700 and 1865, however much rural society there differed from South Lindsey's. South Lindsey was a vast region about the size of the County of Bedford and "a district... entirely lacking in rural industry."[2] Nailsworth, by contrast, was a textile village that grew into a small town during the nineteenth century. Its hinterland consisted of three rural-industrial parishes on the joint periphery of which the Vale rested as a boundary settlement. Those three parishes—Horsley, Avening, and Minchinhampton—were located in turn in Gloucester's Stroud district, which the Reform Act of 1832 had transformed into a parliamentary borough.

Nailsworth's pattern of Dissent also differed from South Lindsey's. Whereas Methodism dominated the religious life of that Lincolnshire region, Old Dissent, transformed into "New Dissent" by the Evangelical Revival, proliferated at Nailsworth. The importance of New Dissent to an emerging English industrial society, although generally acknowledged, has not attracted the local historian's interest in the way that Methodism has. By thus choosing to study New Dissent in a rural-industrial setting, this book has advanced our appreciation of the Halèvy thesis and enhanced our understanding of the concept of modernization.

Nailsworth's experience of modernization was in many ways classic. Initially a remote district, with an essentially hierarchical social structure, Nailsworth's progressive integration into a wider society was both reflected in and facilitated by improvements in transport and communications. Industrialization helped to bring into being a more horizontally structured, class-based society. Agrarian change, associated with the piecemeal destruction of the remnants of the traditional open-field system, paralleled the transition to the factory system. During the early nineteenth century, paternalistic attitudes among the elite came to incorporate a greater sympathy for the free operations of the market,[3] while social change and economic hardships associated with industrialization initially produced backward-looking, nostalgic forms of resistance. These subsequently gave way to more modern forms of trade-union militancy, which coexisted with widespread acceptance of—and sometimes with resignation to—basic features of industrial society.

Religious belief and practice were both affected by and helped to shape responses to modernization. Evangelical Nonconformity cushioned adherents against the psychologically destructive effects of social and economic change. Sometimes associated with and providing cultural resources for militant resistance, Evangelical Nonconformity was also frequently associated with passivity and resignation, particularly in the aftermath of failed strikes and the definitive triumph of the factory system, affirming in this way E. P. Thompson's conception of a "chiliasm of despair." Oscillation between militancy and resignation tended, however, to follow a broadly temporal course, as evangelical communities shed an early sectarianism and acquired denominational characteristics. By synthesizing denominational and sectarian characteristics, with an emphasis on the former, the Shortwood Baptists weathered most successfully the social transitions created by the Industrial Revolution, yet only forestalled their church's decline until 1850. The Society of Friends, by cleaving rigidly to sectarianism, resisted the pressures of modernization, indeed adopted a skeptical attitude toward capitalism itself, yet suffered a more rapid demise for this intransigence.

If Nailsworth's experience was in many ways classic, it was also particular. Local topography determined that the village was initially somewhat isolated and characterized by a dispersed settlement pattern. Nailsworth as a boundary settlement did not fall squarely within the jurisdiction of any one parish or manor and remained in this condition for a considerable period. This feature helped make it a center of Dissent; its Baptist community, for instance, became at one time the largest outside London. Although experiencing industrialization, the region did not urbanize appreciably, and its early history of industrialization was followed by a history of decline. The social elite of the area was generally Whig in political sympathy, and Chartism flourished only very briefly in the region, despite social conditions conducive to its growth. Besides setting forth all of these distinctive qualities, this study has developed several substantially original theses.

First, the region was dominated by large landowners and in this respect did not conform to the standard model of a district likely to foster Dissent. In fact, local Whig landowners were sympathetic to Nonconformity, partly on the grounds that it offset the weakness of the established church in the region. Local manorial courts provided further evidence that Dissenters in this neighborhood were not alienated from established authority in all its forms. The present study does not suggest, however, that Nailsworth's Dissenters were completely *subordinated* to established authority. On the contrary, it argues that the particular form tenurial relations assumed in this neighborhood served to encourage relatively independent attitudes even among the dependent, and that this circumstance was crucial for the growth of the Calvinist churches of the Vale. Just as the liberal paternalism of the elite promoted individualism among the lower classes, so among the latter could deference mingle with expressions of autonomy.

Nowhere did this combination become more manifest than in the 1825 weaver strike. The strike, because of its transitional quality, embodied elements of customary protest while foreshadowing, in its final phase, modern-style labor disputes. The nature of customary protest, however, has been the subject of controversy. Historians following E. P. Thompson have tended to argue that the crowd, in cleaving to the values of the Moral Economy, invariably acted autonomously; to the extent that they won allies from among the elite, they did so by coercing them to act as true paternalists.[4] This study argues, on the contrary, that members of the elite eagerly gave direction to popular disturbances, and were actuated in their leadership by a combination of genuine paternalism and the sectional interests of a portion of the governing class.[5] This circumstance did not deny the autonomy of strikers, as expressed in their capacity for self-organization. However, the persistence of a deferential psychology among them necessarily mitigated their autonomy, permitting the cession of the strike's leadership to figures of elite authority.

The present work points further to the denominational influences on demographic behavior. Historical demographers have routinely treated Nonconformity only as a factor of underregistration in the Anglican record, while this study finds that at Nailsworth, Dissenters—chiefly Baptists—contributed disproportionately to demographic growth in the late eighteenth to early nineteenth century. This fact reflected Nonconformist resilience in the face of social and economic change, which, in turn, reflected the emotional benefits derived from membership in a flourishing Dissenting community.

Economic historians, furthermore, usually associate a successful transition to the factory system with long-term economic advancement. "Deindustrialization," occurring in regions of cottage industry before 1850, on the contrary, they associate with the failure to effect such a transition. This study has shown that deindustrialization and social decline, at Nailsworth and its surrounding regions, coincided with the actual transition to the factory system and were caused largely by the peculiar features of this very process. This study rejects "entrepreneurial failure" as the cause of economic decline and seeks an explanation rather in a combination of market difficulties and inevitable overcapitalization.

The timing of proletarianization in regions of cottage industry has become, additionally, a controversial subject. Historians of early modern England have tended to argue that in such regions artisan occupations, in textiles especially, had already disappeared by the seventeenth century. This study has shown that in Gloucestershire they persisted through customary practice into the nineteenth century and pinpoints their demise in the decade 1825–1835.

Other topics examined have similarly occasioned debate among historians. The present work sides with those who explain population rise in terms of rising birth rates rather than falling mortality and, on balance, supports the optimists rather than the pessimists in the well-known standard of living debate. Although exploitation may have intensified during the Industrial Revolution, it did so within a limited time frame and produced insignificant effects on levels of mortality. However much artisan weavers may have resisted the factory system, their proletarianization proved ultimately a more progressive phenomenon, since trade-union organization became socially more comprehensive and egalitarian. Nailsworth's long-term social decline was caused less by the Industrial Revolution than by the failure of modern industry fully to entrench itself.

Finally, this study takes issue with E. P. Thompson's view of working-class culture in the early industrial period, arguing that working people were more receptive to capitalist values than he has suggested. Probate records revealed the extent to which an entrepreneurial spirit prevailed among a working class in formation. Master weavers, to be sure, resisted the coming of the factory, yet they did so not so much as workmen losing control of their "means of production," but as small employers lamenting their loss of status and the opportunity to advance into the clothier class. This petit bourgeois psychology registered the cultural impact of Nonconformity and in the long term facilitated adaptation to an emergent liberal industrial society.

Appendixes

Appendix A

Abstract of Particulars of Leases
Horsley Manor

Year	Occupation-lessee	Rent	Description of property
1677	Broadweaver	3s. 4d.	1 acre close of meadow, garden, and orchard
1681	Broadweaver	20s.	$\frac{1}{2}$ acre close of meadow and garden
1692	Glazier	1s.	Slaughterhouse and other houses
1692	Clothier	1s. 8d.	1 acre, dwelling, garden, and orchard
1692	Broadweaver	8s. 8d.	Messuage, garden, and orchard
1692	Carpenter	4d.	$\frac{1}{2}$ acre close of meadow, near Shortwood
1692	Broadweaver	10s.	1 acre close of pasture
1693	Broadweaver	1s.	$\frac{1}{4}$ acre, messuage, garden, and orchard
1693	Yeoman	10s.	1 acre close of meadow, 2 acres of meadow close, messuage, garden, orchard
1694	Broadweaver	5s.	Messuage, garden, and orchard; 2 acres of wood
1694	Clothworker	1s.	Messuage, garden, and orchard—$\frac{1}{4}$ acre
1694	Broadweaver	4s. 5d.	Messuage, orchard, and garden
1699	Blue dyer	1s.	3 acres close of meadow
1706	Yeoman's widow	6s. 8d.	Messuage, barn, garden, and orchard; 4 acres close meadow, 7 acres close arb.,[a] 2 acres arb., 1 acre pas.,[b] 1 acre arb. in common field, $\frac{1}{2}$ acre arb. in common field, $\frac{1}{2}$ acre arb., garden, and little paddock (10 acres arb. + 5 acres pas.)
1707	Wool sorter	4s.	Messuage, garden; 8 acres of 2 closes meadow; 2 acres arb.
1712	Broadweaver	5s.	Messuage, garden, and orchard; 1 close pas. and wood; 2 acres close pas.
1713	Yeoman	6d.	1 acre meadow; 2 acres arb.
1714	Clothier	3s.	5 acres pasture; 1 acre close meadow
1714	Yeoman	1s.	8 acres close meadow; $1\frac{1}{2}$ acres arb.
1714	Woolcomber	3s.	5 acres arb. or pas.; 3 acres in Wimbol Barrow Field (a common field)
1715	Clothier	2s.	8 acres arb.; 10 acres arb.; 1 acre arb.; $\frac{1}{2}$ acre

Year	Occupation-lessee	Rent	Description of property
1715	Clothier	10s.	10 acres arb.; 1 acre arb.; 2 acres arb.; 2 acres arb.; 1 acre arb.; 3 acres arb. (scattered strips)
1716	Clothier	5s.	5 acre close meadow; 1 acre arb.; 1 acre arb.
1716	Broadweaver	8s. 8d.	Messuage, garden, orchard
1716	Clothier	6s.	$1\frac{1}{2}$ acre arb.; $1\frac{1}{2}$ acre arb.; 1 acre arb.; $\frac{1}{2}$ acre arb.; $\frac{1}{2}$ acre arb.; 2 acres arb.
1717	Clothworker	3s. 4d.	Messuage, shop, garden, orchard, 1 acre close meadow
1721	Widow of weaver	4d.	Messuage, lately divided into two tenements
1721	Broadweaver	2s.	Two tenements with garden
1721	Broadweaver		Messuage, shop, garden, and orchard
1722	Wheelmaker	6s. 8d.	Messuage and garden
1723	Carpenter's widow	6s. 6d.	Messuage, garden, orchard; 4 acres close meadow; 7 acres; 2 acres arb. pas.; 1 acre arb.; $\frac{1}{2}$ acre arb.
1724	Broadweaver	11s.	Messuage, garden, and orchard
1724	Joyner	13s.	Messuage and water fulling mill adjoining and buildings; messuage and tenement; 1 acre arb. or pas.
1726	Clerk	1s. 6d.	$1\frac{1}{2}$ acre arb.; $\frac{1}{2}$ acre arb.; 1 acre arb.; $\frac{1}{2}$ acre arb.; $2\frac{1}{2}$ acre arb.; 3 acre arb.
1728	Mercer	6d.	"Little close of meadow ground"
1728	Broadweaver	1s.	Cottage, garden, and shop
1729	Yeoman	6d.	3 acres close of meadow
1729, 1732	Clothier	6d.	Messuage, garden, orchard; 1 acre meadow; 3 acres meadow; 2 acres grove
1730	Broadweaver	5s.	Messuage, garden, orchard—$\frac{3}{4}$ acre
1737	Widow	1s.	Cottage
1768	Yeoman	1s.	Newly erected cottage
1789	Shearman	2s.	Cottage and garden
1789	Carpenter	6d.	A piece of waste

^{a} Arable land.
^{b} Pasture.

Appendix B

Suitors and Absentees at the Court Baron, Horsley Manor, 1794–1814

Year	N suitors	N absentees	Percent absent
1794	433	389	89.8
1795	423	355	83.9
1796	381	328	86.0
1797	412	331	80.3
1798	459	373	81.2
1799	434	338	77.8
1800	419	236	56.3
1801	401	351	87.5
1802	435	393	90.3
1803	449	412	91.7
1804	432	416	96.3
1805	417	415	99.5
1806	440	399	90.6
1807	498	480	96.3
1808	475	441	92.8
1809	495	392	79.2
1810	424	364	85.8
1811	420	352	94.6
1812	380	338	88.9
1813	337	299	88.7
1814	372	352	83.8

Source: Horsley Manor Records; see text.

Appendix C

Proceedings at the Court Baron & Court of Survey for the
Manor of Horsley
(ca. 1802)
Proclamation

All manner of Persons that owe Suit & Service to this Ct Baron & Ct of Survey of Henry Stephens Esq. now to be holden in & for this Manor of Horsley draw near & give your Attendance & answer to your Names.

Jury
List of Freeholders
Leaseholders
Tenants

You that are the Lord's Tenants & are returned to be of the Homage answer to your Names.

Oath.

Your Foreman of this Homage with the rest of your Fellows shall inquire & true Presentment make of all such Things as shall be given you in Charge. The Lord's Counsel, your own, & your Fellows you shall well & truly keep; you shall present anything out of Hatred or Malice nor shall conceal any Thing out of Love From or Affection; but in all Things you shall well & truly present as the same shall come to your Knowledge————

So help you God

The rest of the Homage 4 at a time————
the like Oath that your Foreman others your Fellows have taken on their parts you & each of you shall well & truly observe and keep on your parts.
All you that are sworn draw near & Hear your Charge.

Charge.

Your Duty as being sworn of the Homage is to inquire of all such Things as relate to the Ct Baron of this Manor at which a Survey will be taken of the Lord's Estates, which I shall reduce to you under the following Heads————

You are first to enquire if Advantages have happened to the Lord by Escheats or Forfeitures————

As, if any Freehold of this Manor hath committed Felony & thereof hath been lawfully convicted, in such case Thing shall the Year Day & Month. Afterwards the land will fall to the Lord by Escheat.

Appendix D

Estimated Population Levels for Closed Model of Population Growth[a]

1802	2,995.6	1819	3,199.8	1836	3,815.6
1803	3,027.6	1820	3,236.5	1837	3,853.3[b]
1804	3,088.5	1821	3,280.2	1838	3,903.0
1805	3,115.4	1822	3,330.5	1839	3,946.2
1806	3,134.8	1823	3,344.2	1840	3,993.7
1807	3,119.9	1824	3,377.0	1841	4,041.9
1808	3,100.0	1825	3,404.5	1842	4,091.7
1809	3,129.3	1826	3,456.9	1843	4,140.9
1810	3,128.0	1827	3,463.1	1844	4,188.8
1811	3,124.8	1828	3,518.4	1845	4,231.9
1812	3,151.9	1829	3,547.4	1846	4,287.0
1813	3,159.1	1830	3,592.5	1847	4,334.0
1814	3,148.5	1831	3,634.2	1848	4,383.9
1815	3,160.2	1832	3,662.2	1849	4,434.5
1816	3,173.5	1833	3,722.7	1850	4,486.6
1817	3,187.6	1834	3,743.1	1851	4,538.6
1818	3,181.3	1835	3,785.2		

[a]The census figure for 1801, used in table 26, served as the base year for these calculations. I added to this figure the total number of births for 1802 as recorded in appendix E and subtracted the total number of burials in that same year. The result yielded a closed-model population estimate for 1803; I repeated the same procedure for each succeeding year.

[b]A Statistical Analysis System (SAS) forecasting program calculated linear estimates of Anglican and Nonconformist baptisms and births and all burials for the years 1837–1851 using the uninflated values from 1775 (see app. E). The linear equation for Anglican baptisms was: Anglican baptisms = 45.98 + 0.427 (vector of time), and for the total of Nonconformist births: Nonconformist births = 12.1141 + 0.5361 (vector of time). The estimator for burials is: Total burials = 72.1159 + 0.182 (vector of time). These estimates were then inflated, using the ratios referred to in chap. 5, n. 37 to adjust for the effect of delayed baptism on infant mortality; in this final form, they helped to estimate the closed-model population levels for these same years, following the procedure described in footnote *a* above.

Appendix E

Anglican and Nonconformist Baptisms and Births, 1775–1851

Year	a	b	c	d	e	f	g	h	i	j	k
1775	(8.9)	27	3	2.9	41.9	7	3	(13.0)	1.7	(24.7)	(66.6)
1776	(9.9)	30	3	3.2	46.2	4	1	(11.0)	1.2	(17.2)	(63.4)
1777	(12.2)	37	4	3.9	56.9	7	1	(12.4)	1.5	(21.9)	(78.8)
1778	(11.6)	35	1	3.6	51.6	11	0	(13.4)	1.8	(26.2)	(77.8)
1779	(8.9)	27	2	2.8	40.8	5	1	(13.0)	1.4	(20.4)	(61.2)
1780	(12.9)	39	2	4.0	58.0	8	0	(13.0)	1.6	(22.7)	(80.7)
1781	(14.9)	45	3	4.7	67.7	8	1	(9.5)	1.4	(19.9)	(87.6)
1782	(10.2)	31	0	3.0	44.0	9	0	(10.5)	1.4	(20.9)	(64.9)
1783	(7.9)	24	4	2.7	38.7	8	0	(12.7)	1.5	(22.2)	(60.9)
1784	(8.9)	27	3	2.9	41.9	6	0	(13.5)	1.4	(20.9)	(62.8)
1785	(7.6)	23	2	2.4	35.4	4	0	(14.6)	1.3	(19.9)	(55.3)
1786	(10.2)	31	8	4.4	63.4	11	0	(11.5)	1.7	(24.1)	(87.5)
1787	(7.6)	23	2	2.4	35.4	6	0	(13.0)	1.4	(20.4)	(55.8)
1788	(13.2)	40	8	2.4	65.5	8	0	(12.3)	1.5	(21.8)	(87.3)
1789	(12.5)	38	4	4.0	59.0	6	0	(11.7)	1.3	(19.0)	(78.0)
1790	(13.5)	41	7	4.6	66.6	6	0	(12.5)	1.4	(19.8)	(86.4)
1791	(11.9)	36	7	4.0	59.0	7	0	(13.5)	1.5	(22.0)	(81.0)
1792	(14.2)	43	2	4.4	63.4	7	0	(13.4)	1.5	(21.9)	(85.3)
1793	(13.9)	42	5	2.4	65.5	7	0	(13.7)	1.5	(22.2)	(87.7)
1794	10	44	4	4.3	62.3	5	0	(11.1)	1.2	(17.3)	(79.6)
1795	20	60	0	5.9	85.9	4	0	(13.0)	1.3	(18.2)	(104.1)
1796	11	43	5	4.4	63.4	5	2	(14.7)	1.6	(23.3)	(86.7)
1797	13	48	6	4.9	71.9	14	0	(14.9)	2.1	(31.0)	(102.9)

Year											
1798	15	38	3	4.1	60.1	10	1	(19.7)	2.3	(32.9)	(93.0)
1799	23	39	5	4.9	71.9	8	1	(12.7)	2.1	(30.8)	(102.7)
1800	9	40	4	4.4	64.2	13	0	18	2.3	33.3	97.5
1801	14	37	2	4.4	64.2	8	0	14	1.6	23.6	87.8
1802	13	51	5	5.3	77.1	9	1	11	1.5	22.5	99.6
1803	16	43	2	5.0	72.9	13	0	15	2.0	30.0	102.9
1804	18	58	6	6.8	98.8	8	1	12	1.5	22.5	121.3
1805	12	59	2	5.4	78.4	5	0	13	1.3	19.3	97.7
1806	8	51	2	4.5	65.5	18	1	9	2.0	30.0	95.5
1807	12	26	4	3.1	45.1	14	2	13	2.0	30.0	75.1
1808	10	34	3	3.5	50.5	2	0	10	0.9	12.9	63.4
1809	14	43	6	4.7	67.7	4	3	12	1.4	20.4	88.1
1810	12	19	5	2.7	38.7	5	2	17	1.8	25.8	64.5
1811	6	37	2	3.3	48.3	5	3	20	1.9	28.9	77.2
1812	29	37	3	5.1	74.1	2	1	20	1.7	24.7	98.8
1813	8	39	0	3.5	50.5	5	2	12	1.4	20.4	70.9
1814	1	40	0	3.0	44.0	9	1	14	1.8	25.8	69.8
1815	3	44	0	3.5	50.5	7	0	16	1.7	24.7	75.2
1816	5	61	0	4.9	70.9	13	1	12	1.9	27.9	98.8
1817	5	52	0	4.2	61.2	11	3	20	2.5	36.5	97.7
1818	3	63	0	4.9	70.9	11	1	27	2.9	41.9	112.8
1819	11	56	0	4.9	71.9	3	0	17	1.5	21.5	93.4
1820	5	62	0	4.9	71.9	7	1	14	1.6	23.6	95.5
1821	7	72	0	5.8	84.8	15	1	27	3.2	46.2	131.0
1822	8	75	0	6.1	89.1	15	1	22	2.8	40.8	129.9
1823	7	63	0	5.2	75.2	13	1	28	3.1	45.1	120.3
1824	6	65	0	5.3	76.3	25	1	21	3.5	50.4	126.7
1825	2	79	0	7.3	88.3	14	1	25	3.5	42.5	130.8
1826	7	76	0	7.5	90.5	13	0	36	4.3	52.3	142.8
1827	6	58	0	5.8	69.8	10	0	20	2.7	32.7	102.5
1828	4	67	0	6.4	77.4	36	0	37	6.6	79.6	157.0
1829	0	64	0	5.8	69.8	23	0	23	4.1	50.1	119.9

Year	(a)	(b)	(c)	(d)	(e)	(f)	(g)	(h)	(i)	(j)	(k)
1830	0	57	0	5.1	62.1	33	1	27	5.5	66.5	128.6
1831	1	58	0	5.3	64.3	26	0	21	4.2	51.2	115.5
1832	1	68	0	6.2	75.2	18	1	25	4.0	48.0	123.2
1833	2	67	0	6.2	75.2	29	0	38	6.0	73.0	148.2
1834	0	67	0	6.0	73.0	22	1	25	4.3	52.3	125.3
1835	4	71	0	6.8	81.8	24	0	23	4.2	51.2	133.0
1836	2	80	0	7.4	89.4	15	0	32	4.2	51.2	140.6
1837	—	(71.8)	—	6.5	(78.5)	(19)	—	(27)	4.1	(50.1)	(128.6)
1838	—	(74.2)	—	6.7	(80.7)	(25)	—	(29)	4.9	(58.9)	(139.6)
1839	—	(73.5)	—	6.7	(80.7)	(21)	—	(27)	4.3	(52.3)	(133.0)
1840	—	(75.4)	—	6.8	(81.8)	(21)	—	(30)	4.6	(55.6)	(137.4)
1841	—	(78.0)	—	7.0	(85.0)	(20)	—	(29)	4.4	(53.4)	(138.4)
1842	—	(78.7)	—	7.0	(85.7)	(23)	—	(27)	4.5	(54.5)	(142.2)
1843	—	(76.9)	—	6.9	(83.8)	(21.4)	—	(30)	4.6	(56.0)	(139.8)
1844	—	(76.8)	—	6.8	(83.6)	(22.6)	—	(28)	4.5	(55.1)	(138.7)
1845	—	(77.7)	—	6.9	(84.6)	(21.9)	—	(30)	4.7	(56.6)	(141.2)
1846	—	(76.4)	—	6.8	(83.2)	(21.3)	—	(30)	4.6	(55.9)	(139.1)
1847	—	(74.7)	—	6.6	(81.4)	(22.2)	—	(30)	4.7	(56.9)	(138.4)
1848	—	(77.2)	—	6.9	(84.1)	(22.7)	—	(30)	4.7	(57.4)	(141.5)
1849	—	(77.7)	—	7.0	(84.7)	(22.9)	—	(30)	4.8	(57.7)	(142.4)
1850	—	(78.4)	—	7.0	(85.5)	(22.7)	—	(31)	4.8	(58.5)	(144.0)
1851	—	(78.5)	—	7.0	(85.6)	(23.8)	—	(30)	4.8	(58.6)	(144.2)

Key: (a) Nailsworth Episcopal Chapel; (b) Horsley Parish Church; (c) recorded delayed Anglican baptism; (d) unrecorded Anglican baptism due to delayed baptism; (e) total Anglican baptisms; (f) Congregationalist baptisms; (g) Quaker births; (h) Baptist births; (i) unrecorded Nonconformist births due to delayed baptism; (j) total Nonconformist births; (k) grand total, baptisms and births.

Note 1: Bracketed numbers in column a are estimates based on the ratio of Nailsworth Episcopal Chapel baptisms to Horsley baptisms for 1794–1812; see chap. 5, n. 35. Those in column h, between 1775 and 1799, are estimates based on regression models using Baptist membership gains and losses in the post-1800 period; see chap. 5, n. 41 and text. Columns d and i contain additions to the original totals of Anglican Nonconformist baptisms and births, respectively, and are the estimate effects of delayed baptism on infant mortality; see chap. 5, n. 37 and text.

Note 2: See appendix D for the estimators of Anglican baptisms and the total of Nonconformist births between 1837 and 1851. A linear Statistical Analysis System (SAS) forecast was also made for Baptist births for this period: Baptist births = 8.4642 + 0.2828 (vector of time). The annual results were then subtracted from the annual totals of forecast Nonconformist births (Quaker births were assumed to have been negligible after 1836) to yield estimates of Congregationalist births. All linear estimates are bracketed. Episcopal Chapel baptisms, furthermore, were subsumed in Horsley's parochial registration after 1836.

Appendix F

Anglican and Nonconformist Burials, 1775–1838

Year	Ang.	Bap.	Quak.	Cong.	Total[a]	Year	Ang.	Bap.	Quak.[b]	Conv.	Total
1775	63	30.6	0	5.1	103.1	1814	34	36	2	6.0	80.4
1776	29	31.5	1	5.3	69.8	1815	30	23	4	3.8	63.5
1777	36	33.3	2	5.6	80.4	1816	32	42	0	7.0	85.5
1778	46	33.3	3	5.6	91.8	1817	27	46	0	7.7	83.6
1779	36	32.4	0	5.4	77.1	1818	50	53	3	8.8	119.1
1780	30	31.5	0	5.3	69.8	1819	32	34	0	5.7	74.9
1781	48	31.5	2	5.3	90.3	1820	19	32	0	5.3	58.8
1782	33	31.5	0	5.3	72.9	1821	31	45	0	7.5	87.3
1783	36	31.5	1	5.3	77.1	1822	36	33	3	5.5	79.9
1784	51	35.0	0	5.8	95.9	1823	48	45	1	7.5	106.6
1785	46	35.0	0	5.8	90.7	1824	33	45	1	7.5	93.9
1786	57	33.0	0	10	104.8	1825	39	48	2	8.0	103.8
1787	25	32.4	0	6	66.3	1826	47	32	0	5.3	89.9
1788	24	33.3	0	7	67.2	1827	36	44	2	7.3	96.3
1789	25	31.5	1	3	63.2	1828	39	45	3	7.5	101.7
1790	30	31.5	1	5	70.5	1829	41	37	1	6.2	90.9
1791	38	32.4	4	7	85.1	1830	36	36	0	6.0	83.5
1792	31	35.0	2	1	72.1	1831	36	28	0	4.7	73.8
1793	32	35.0	3	10	83.6	1832	54	30	0	5.0	95.2
1794	31	31.5	1	8	74.7	1833	38	36	2	6.0	87.7
1795	40	35.9	0	5	84.5	1834	41	47	2	7.8	104.9
1796	21	35.0	1	4	63.7	1835	48	48	0	8.0	90.9

Year						Year					
1797	36	38.7	1	6	85.4	1836	45	45	4	7.5	110.2
1798	43	36.8	1	6	90.7	1837	36	42	1	6.6	90.9
1799	33	35.0	0	6	77.3	1838	36	41	1	6.6	89.9
1800	22	32.4	0	5.4	62.5	1839					89.8
1801	33	32.4	0	5.4	73.9	1840					90.0
1802	31	35.0	0	5.8	75.0	1841					90.2
1803	24	36.8	1	6.1	70.9	1842					90.4
1804	20	31.5	1	5.3	60.4	1843					90.6
1805	31	31.5	0	5.3	70.8	1844					90.8
1806	31	34.1	2	5.7	76.1	1845					90.9
1807	48	32.4	1	5.4	90.7	1846					91.2
1808	33	39	1	6.6	82.6	1847					91.4
1809	24	26	2	4.3	58.8	1848					91.6
1810	28	29	1	4.8	65.8	1849					91.8
1811	37	32	3	5.3	80.4	1850					91.9
1812	27	35	1	5.8	71.1	1851					92.2
1813	24	30	1	5.0	63.7						

[a]These totals have been inflated to compensate for the impact of mortality on delayed baptism; see chap. 5, n. 56 for an explanation.

[b]Decimalized numbers for Baptists are estimates based on regression models; see chap. 5, n. 56 for an explanation. Decimalized numbers for the Congregationalists are based on the ratio of Congregationalist burials to Baptist burials for the 1786–1799 period. Burials for 1837 and 1838 are estimates made from a linear SAS forecast program: Anglican burials = 348 + 0.023 (vector of time); Baptist burials = 30.6 + 0.15 (vector of time); Quaker burials = 0.78 + 0.009 (vector of time); Congregationalist burials = 5.3 + 0.02 (vector of time). Thereafter, the total number of burials was forecasted on the same basis: Total burials = 72.1 + 0.18 (vector of time).

Appendix G

Gloucester Cloth Production and Mean Wheat Prices Series, 1804–1838

	Cloth production (yards)	Wheat prices (shillings per bushel)
1804	1,460,481	12.0
1805	1,464,330	11.9
1806	1,452,782	11.8
1807	1,491,276	11.6
1808	1,410,437	11.2
1809	1,448,932	14.2
1810	1,485,502	16.2
1811	1,431,609	14.3
1812	1,450,857	18.6
1813	1,445,083	13.7
1814	1,525,922	9.2
1815	1,520,148	7.6
1816	1,460,481	9.7
1817	1,512,449	12.5
1818	1,604,836	9.8
1819	1,529,771	8.4
1820	1,473,954	7.8
1821	1,531,696	6.9
1822	1,554,793	4.8
1823	1,454,981	6.0
1824	1,741,120	7.7
1825	1,790,975	8.5
1826	1,499,661	7.5
1827	1,424,175	7.0
1828	1,659,329	6.7
1829	1,507,268	8.7
1830	1,580,505	8.2
1831	1,950,350	8.0
1832	2,162,178	7.2
1833	1,420,065	6.5
1834	2,035,057	5.9
1835	1,842,188	5.0
1836	1,893,748	6.3
1837	1,721,816	7.2
1838	1,553,071	8.3

Source: See chap. 5, n. 47 and n. 48 for the wheat and cloth series, respectively.

Appendix H

Shortwood Baptists: Conversions and Total Membership, 1758–1864

Year	Conv.	Memb.	Year	Conv.	Memb.	Year	Conv.	Memb.
1758	8	66	1794	3	295	1830	49	547
1759	12	78	1795	7	294	1831	14	578
1760	3	81	1796	13	281	1832	26	582
1761	13	94	1797	11	281	1833	39	608
1762	13	104	1798	27	294	1834	46	642
1763	11	115	1799	6	292	1835	47	669
1764	11	125	1800	31	317	1836	26	680
1765	17	139	1801	11	320	1837	38	689
1766	13	145	1802	0	314	1838	16	653
1767	9	152	1803	6	304	1839	15	631
1768	7	158	1804	9	308	1840	29	633
1769	5	155	1805	9	311	1841	26	628
1770	4	154	1806	41	341	1842	34	642
1771	21	172	1807	31	367	1843	66	683
1772	12	178	1808	9	367	1844	33	694
1773	21	197	1809	9	360	1845	10	671
1774	10	206	1810	12	363	1846	26	682
1775	13	216	1811	29	375	1847	63	712
1776	5	219	1812	18	384	1848	16	678
1777	7	220	1813	26	397	1849	34	665
1778	14	228	1814	17	396	1850	15	659
1779	9	231	1815	23	416	1851	20	660
1780	11	237	1816	53	462	1852	11	647
1781	0	235	1817	9	447	1853	16	640
1782	3	235	1818	24	455	1854	12	634
1783	12	244	1819	14	463	1855	17	625
1784	9	245	1820	14	439	1856	13	610
1785	16	255	1821	42	469	1857	17	598
1786	6	257	1822	36	497	1858	1	573
1787	9	260	1823	35	525	1859	10	562
1788	8	263	1824	31	534	1860	21	561
1789	8	268	1825	12	521	1861	15	553
1790	10	274	1826	19	531	1862	1	538
1791	13	282	1827	19	527	1863	17	528
1792	6	278	1828	16	526	1864	6	517
1793	10	280	1829	28	538			

Source: Shortwood Baptist Church Roll; see text.

Appendix I

Shortwood Baptists: Total Losses (N_1), Migrations (N_2), Deaths (N_3), and Exclusions (N_4), 1758–1864

Year	N_1	N_2	N_3	N_4	Year	N_1	N_2	N_3	N_4	Year	N_1	N_2	N_3	N_4
1758	1	0	0	1	1794	5	0	2	3	1830	13	3	9	1
1759	0	0	0	0	1795	8	1	7	0	1831	10	1	7	2
1760	0	0	0	0	1796	9	2	6	1	1832	22	5	16	1
1761	0	0	0	0	1797	11	0	10	1	1833	13	1	8	4
1762	3	0	2	1	1798	14	0	8	6	1834	12	0	8	4
1763	0	0	0	0	1799	8	0	6	2	1835	20	6	12	2
1764	1	0	1	0	1800	6	2	3	1	1836	15	3	11	1
1765	3	0	2	1	1801	8	1	3	4	1837	29	9	16	4
1766	7	0	3	4	1802	6	0	6	0	1838	52	36	13	3
1767	2	0	0	2	1803	16	8	8	0	1839	37	21	13	3
1768	1	0	0	1	1804	5	0	2	3	1840	27	19	5	3
1769	8	1	6	1	1805	6	0	2	4	1841	31	11	6	14
1770	5	0	2	3	1806	11	3	5	3	1842	20	7	12	1
1771	3	0	3	0	1807	5	1	3	1	1843	25	12	9	4
1772	6	0	2	4	1808	15	0	15	0	1844	22	1	15	6
1773	2	0	0	2	1809	10	0	5	5	1845	33	9	14	10
1774	1	0	1	0	1810	9	1	6	2	1846	15	4	8	3
1775	3	1	1	1	1811	17	5	10	2	1847	33	12	14	7
1776	2	0	2	0	1812	9	1	6	1	1848	50	22	19	9
1777	6	0	4	2	1813	13	0	10	3	1849	47	18	23	6
1778	4	0	4	0	1814	18	3	12	3	1850	21	3	14	4
1779	6	2	3	1	1815	3	0	3	0	1851	19	4	11	4
1780	5	0	2	3	1816	7	1	5	1	1852	24	9	13	2
1781	2	0	2	0	1817	24	2	13	9	1853	23	7	14	2
1782	3	0	2	3	1818	16	3	8	5	1854	18	2	10	6
1783	3	1	2	0	1819	6	0	5	1	1855	26	8	16	2
1784	8	0	6	2	1820	38	28	8	2	1856	28	12	12	4
1785	6	0	6	0	1821	12	0	10	2	1857	29	8	16	5
1786	4	0	4	0	1822	8	1	6	1	1858	26	4	17	5
1787	6	0	3	3	1823	7	0	7	0	1859	21	8	10	3
1788	5	1	4	0	1824	22	11	8	3	1860	22	2	18	2
1789	3	0	2	1	1825	25	4	13	8	1861	23	5	14	4
1790	4	0	2	2	1826	9	0	5	4	1862	16	3	10	3
1791	5	1	3	1	1827	23	2	14	7	1863	27	11	12	4
1792	10	0	6	4	1828	17	3	14	0	1864	17	2	15	0
1793	8	2	6	0	1829	16	3	11	2					

Appendix J

Frequencies of Outmigration of Shortwood Baptists, 1758–1864
Local (N_1), Other Gloucester (N_2), Outcounty (N_3), Emigration (N_4)

Year	N_1	N_2	N_3	N_4	Year	N_1	N_2	N_3	N_4	Year	N_1	N_2	N_3	N_4
1758	0	0	0	0	1794	0	0	0	0	1830	0	1	2	0
1759	0	0	0	0	1795	0	0	1	0	1831	0	0	1	0
1760	0	0	0	0	1796	0	0	2	0	1832	0	3	0	2
1761	0	0	0	0	1797	0	0	0	0	1833	0	1	0	0
1762	0	0	0	0	1798	0	0	0	0	1834	0	0	0	0
1763	0	0	0	0	1799	0	0	0	0	1835	0	2	4	0
1764	0	0	0	0	1800	0	0	2	0	1836	0	1	1	1
1765	0	0	0	0	1801	0	1	0	0	1837	0	0	4	5
1766	0	0	0	0	1802	0	0	0	0	1838	0	0	8	28
1767	0	0	0	0	1803	0	8	0	0	1839	0	1	6	15
1768	0	0	0	0	1804	0	0	0	0	1840	1	2	3	15
1769	0	1	0	0	1805	0	0	0	0	1841	0	0	11	0
1770	0	0	0	0	1806	0	1	2	0	1842	1	0	6	0
1771	0	0	0	0	1807	0	1	0	0	1843	4	1	4	3
1772	0	0	0	0	1808	0	0	1	0	1844	0	0	1	0
1773	0	0	0	0	1809	0	0	0	1	1845	0	3	4	2
1774	0	0	0	0	1810	0	0	1	0	1846	1	1	2	0
1775	0	1	0	0	1811	0	0	0	5	1847	2	4	5	1
1776	0	0	0	0	1812	0	1	0	0	1848	2	1	10	9
1777	0	0	0	0	1813	0	0	0	0	1849	3	5	10	0
1778	0	0	0	0	1814	0	0	3	0	1850	0	2	2	0
1779	0	2	0	0	1815	0	0	0	0	1851	1	1	1	1
1780	0	0	0	0	1816	0	0	1	0	1852	3	3	3	0
1781	0	0	0	0	1817	0	0	2	0	1853	0	1	4	2
1782	0	0	0	0	1818	0	1	2	0	1854	1	0	1	0
1783	0	0	1	0	1819	0	0	0	0	1855	2	0	2	4
1784	0	0	0	0	1820	11	17	0	0	1856	0	1	10	1
1785	0	0	0	0	1821	0	0	0	0	1857	2	1	3	2
1786	0	0	0	0	1822	1	0	0	0	1858	1	2	1	0
1787	0	0	0	0	1823	0	0	0	0	1859	0	1	3	4
1788	0	1	0	0	1824	10	0	1	0	1860	0	0	1	1
1789	0	0	0	0	1825	0	3	1	0	1861	0	2	2	1
1790	0	0	0	0	1826	0	0	0	0	1862	0	0	3	0
1791	0	0	1	0	1827	0	0	2	0	1863	3	5	3	0
1792	0	0	0	0	1828	1	0	2	0	1864	0	0	2	0
1793	0	0	2	0	1829	2	0	0	1					

Appendix K

Occupations by Social Class Listed in Tables 65 and 66

Class 1: The middle class
Bacon-curing manufacturer
Brewer
Brush manufacturer
Farmer
Gentleman
Landed proprietor-land surveyor
Maltster
Manager of cloth factory
Umbrella crook manufacturer
Woolen cloth manufacturer

Class 2: The lower middle class
Baker
Builder (master)
Carpenter
Chairmaker
Clerk in factory
Dressmaker
Fellmonger
Gardener
Governess
Grocer
Innkeeper
Milliner
Plasterer and tiler
Printer-bookseller
Stonemason
Timber dealer
Spinner
Tailor(ess)
Cordwainer
Sleater
Journeyman-brushmaker
Weaver
Millwright
Carrier or carter
Saddler
Plumber

Class 3: Semiskilled and unskilled labor
Charwoman
Cloth cutter, burler, dresser, picker
Clothworker
Laborer

Mending daisy
Millman
Nursemaid
Pauper; formerly weaver, clothworker
Pauper-outpensioner
Quiller
Washerwoman
Unemployed, formerly weaver
Cottage industry
Servant

Appendix L

Biographical Notes of Shortwood Clothier-Deacons

Branch I: Abraham Flint (d. 1830), the son of Thomas Flint, ironmonger from Ashford and the brother of Revd. Thomas Flint, pastor at Shortwood (1800–1803). Abraham Flint moved to Horsley in 1801 and was elected a Deacon of Shortwood in 1816. He married Mary Shurmer in 1803.

Mary Shurmer's twin sister, Hannah, had married William Clissold (1779–1820) at Avening in 1802. He was the son of William Clissold, the elder, who had been elected a deacon of Shortwood about 1795. William Clissold, the younger, was a clothier who operated mills at Woodchester, the parish bordering Nailsworth, and at the hamlet of Inchbrook in the Vale itself. He had been elected a deacon of Shortwood in 1816.

William Clissold, the younger, had two sons, Samuel and Joseph, who went into partnership in operating the Nailsworth brewery, which was a sizable concern. Samuel Clissold was elected a deacon in 1839; his brother was elected one in 1845.

Branch II: Reverend Thomas Flint (d. 1819), the brother of Abraham Flint, had married Catherine Holbrow Francis, a daughter of his predecessor in the pastorate at Shortwood. Their son, Abraham Marsh Flint, joined his uncle, Samuel Enoch Francis, who was elected a deacon at Shortwood in 1816, in the cloth trade at Frogmarsh Mills circa 1823; in 1845 he purchased Nailsworth Mills and was one of the early directors of the Nailsworth-Stonehouse-Stroud Railroad. The offspring of his marriage to Lydia Jane Flint, his first cousin, was Catherine Holbrow Flint.

Catherine H. Flint had married Thomas Mayow Newman, the son of Revd. Thomas Fox Newman, the pastor at Short-wood from 1832 to 1864.

Branch III: Sophia Francis, another daughter of Revd. B. Francis, married John Heskins, the younger. He was the son of John Heskins, Sr., a clothier and a deacon at Shortwood for fifty years. John Heskins, II, was also a prominent deacon at Shortwood, having been elected in 1807, six years before his father's death.

John Heskins II's sister, Sarah, married Edward Barnard, who was elected deacon in 1816.

Edward Barnard's sister, Mary, married Edward Bliss, who was elected a deacon in 1820.

John Heskins II, Edward Barnard, and Edward Bliss were all deacons at Shortwood and were related through marriage; they were also partners in the cloth manufacturing firm at Nailsworth Mills, called Heskins, Barnard, and Bliss. Heskins and Bliss died in the 1830s. Edward Barnard went bankrupt in 1840, and although he was able to recover, Nailsworth Mills was sold to Abraham Marsh Flint (above) in 1845.

Source: GRO D2698/2/1, Pedigree of the Newman, Flint, and Clissold families; PRO PCC Prob 11/1909/229, Prob 11/1795/66: wills of John Heskins, II, and Edward Bliss, respectively; GRO D2424/2, Shortwood Baptist Church Roll.

Appendix M

THE COVENANT
ENTERED INTO BY THE CHURCH AT SHORTWOOD,
JULY 20, 1735,
And ordered to be reprinted for the use of the Members, at a Church Meeting, held January 1st, 1855.

I. That we will, to the utmost of our power, walk together in one body, and, as near as may be, with one mind, in all saint-like love to each other, as highly becomes the disciples of Christ.

II. That we will jointly strive and content together for the faith and purity of the Gospel, the truths of Jesus Christ, and the order of ordinances, honour, liberty, and privileges, of this his Church against all opposers.

III. That we will, with all diligence, conscientiously labour and study to "keep the unity of the Spirit in the bond of peace," both in the Church in general, and in particular between one another.

IV. That we will carefully avoid all cause and causes of division, as much as in us lies, and shun those that are seducers, and teachers of errors and heresy.

V. That we will sympathize and have a fellow-feeling (to our power) one with, and to another, in every condition and endeavour to "bear each other's burthens," whether we are joyful or sorrowful, tempted or otherwise; that we may be mutual helps to each other, and to answer the end of our near relation.

VI. That we will forbear and bear with one another's weaknesses and infirmities, in much pity, meekness, tenderness, and patience; not daring to rip up the weakness of any to those without the Church, nor to those within, unless it be according to Christ's rule, and gospel order, endeavouring all we can for the glory of the Gospel, and the credit of this Church, willing to cover one another's slips and failings that are not sinful.

VII. That we will, as God shall enable us cleave fast to one another; and that if perilous times should come, and a time of persecution, (which God for our non-proficiency may justly send), we will not dare to draw back from our holy profession, but will endeavour to strengthen one another's hands, and encourage one another to perseverance, let what will fall to our lot.

VIII. We do promise to keep the secrets of our Church entire, without divulging them to any that are not Members of this particular Body, though otherwise near and dear unto us; for we believe the Church ought to be as a garden enclosed, and a fountain sealed.

IX. Those of us that are, or may be, single persons, do fully design never to enter into conjugal bonds with any that are unbelievers; for we believe it a sin to be unequally yoked; that it is contrary to the rule of Christ, and the ready way to hinder our soul's peace, growth, and welfare.

X. That we will endeavour to watch over one another's conversation, and not for each other's haltings; yet as not by any means to suffer sin to rest in the bosom of our brother, but to remove it, by using all proper means to bring the person to repentance and reformation of life; and that we will endeavour to provoke one another to holiness, love, and good works.

XI. We do all purpose to attend the Meetings constantly that are appointed by the Church, both on the Lord's Day, and other days; nothing hindering, except distance, sickness, the works of necessity and mercy.

XII. That we will make conscience of praying for one another's welfare at all times, but especially in times of distress, as poverty, sickness, pain, temptation, desertion, or the like; and that we will pray for growth and peace of the whole Church in general, and for our Ministers, and the success of their ministry in an especial manner.

A. Sims, Printer, Nailsworth.

Appendix N

Mortality by Age-Sex Cohort

Year	Infant	Infant 2[a]	Child 2–12	Adolescent 13–17	M	F 18–49	M	F 49–64	M	F 65+
1808	13	13.6	16	8	4	13	2	8	2	8
1809	16	16.7	12	6	3	6	2	2	6	2
1810	5	5.2	12	7	8	13	6	0	6	2
1811	8	8.4	5	10	6	10	8	6	2	14
1812	16	16.7	9	9	6	10	2	12	8	2
1813	6	6.3	7	6	1	12	4	2	4	6
1814	22	23.0	3	10	8	9	2	3	12	12
1815	9	9.4	9	8	7	11	3	3	1	7
1816	23	24.0	6	8	8	8	4	6	8	6
1817	18	18.8	4	10	9	13	8	3	6	7
1818	28	29.3	14	15	12	10	4	4	7	7
1819	21	21.9	6	6	3	7	7	3	8	9
1820	20	20.9	3	5	6	7	2	5	7	2
1821	24	25.1	5	8	4	8	6	3	5	15
1822	19	19.1	2	8	3	10	7	6	4	11
1823	36	37.6	11	10	10	10	6	4	10	4
1824	20	20.9	10	10	10	5	5	5	10	9
1825	27	28.9	3	10	10	10	3	8	16	5
1826	18	19.3	5	5	9	14	3	4	14	11
1827	19	20.3	8	10	7	10	2	4	7	14
1828	26	27.8	9	11	12	5	3	5	10	11
1829	9	9.6	7	8	13	9	3	5	16	9
1830	18	19.3	9	8	2	11	3	3	12	12
1831	14	15.0	3	5	8	8	7	4	7	9
1832	23	24.0	12	7	7	6	2	4	15	13
1833	18	19.3	5	10	9	14	4	0	10	13
1834	21	22.5	20	11	11	8	2	1	9	12
1835	14	15.0	17	8	9	9	4	7	10	6
1836	17	18.2	14	25	9	8	6	10	10	7
1837	22	23.5	10	11	10	9	4	4	13	11
1838	21	22.5	10	11	10	9	4	2	13	12

[a]Infant burials are inflated here to account for the effect of delayed baptism; see Wrigley and Schofield, *Population History of England*, p. 97 and text.
Source: See text.

Abbreviations

Depositories and Printed Primary Sources

BM   British Museum
BPP   *British Parliamentary Papers*
Glos. Colln. The Gloucester Collection
GDR   Gloucester Diocesan Records
Glos. Jnl. *The Gloucester Journal*
GRO   Gloucester Record Office
PCC   Prerogative Court of Canterbury
PRO   Public Record Office
Stroud Jnl. *The Stroud Journal*

Book and Journals[1]

AHR   *American Historical Review*
Ag. HR   *Agricultural History Review*
Ec. HR   *Economic History Review*
EHR   *English Historical Review*
JEH   *Journal of Economic History*
JEEc. H   *Journal of European Economic History*
SAS   Statistical Analysis System
*Trans. B & G Transactions of the Bristol and Gloucester Archaeological
  Arch. Soc.   Society*
VCH Glos.   *The Victoria Country History of Gloucestershire*

---

[1] This list includes only a selected number of all journals cited.

Notes

Introduction: Background and Perspectives

1. Elie Halèvy (trans. E. I. Watkin), *A History of the English People in the Nineteenth Century: England in 1815*, I (New York, 1949); idem (trans., ed. Bernard Semmel), *The Birth of Methodism in England* (Chicago, 1971); cf. E. P. Thompson, *The Making of the English Working Class* (New York, 1963, chap. XI and Bernard Semmel, *The Methodist Revolution* (New York, 1973).

2. Halèvy has been criticized for underestimating the radical customary undercurrents within early Methodism, the persistence of popular superstition, and the Anglican origins of the Evangelical Revival; see John Walsh, "Elie Halèvy and the Birth of Methodism" *Transactions of the Royal Historical Society*, 5th ser., XXV (1975): 11–20; idem, "Origins of the Evangelical Revival," in G. V. Bennett and J. D. Walsh, eds., *Essays in Modern Church History* (London, 1966), pp. 138 ff.; James Obelkevich, *Religion and Rural Society: South Lindsey, 1825–1875* (Oxford, 1976), chap. VI; and Deborah Valenze, *Prophetic Sons and Daughters: Female Preaching and Popular Religion in Industrial England* (Princeton, 1985). Cf. J. C. D. Clark, *English Society 1688–1832* (Cambridge, 1986), pp. 235–247.

3. See, for example, Obelkevich, *Religion and Rural Society*; R. Moore, *Pit-Men, Preachers and Politics: The Effects of Methodism in a Durham Mining Community* (Cambridge, 1976); David Underdown, *Revel, Riot and Rebellion: Popular Politics and Culture in England, 1603–1660* (Oxford, 1985); and Valenze, *Prophetic Sons and Daughters*, although chaps. 8 and 12 relate more directly to economic change. However, see Keith Wrightson and David Levine, *Poverty and Piety in an English Village: Terling, 1525–1700* (New York, 1979) for a much closer integration of culture and economy, as well as Gregor Dallas, *The*

Imperfect Peasant Economy: The Loire Country, 1800–1914 (Cambridge, 1982). Cf. S. Cook, "Economic Anthropology: Problems in Theory, Method and Analysis," in J. Honigmann, ed., *Handbook of Social and Cultural Anthropology* (Chicago, 1973) and Stephen Gudeman, *Economics as Culture: Models and Methaphors of Livelihood* (London, 1986) for anthropological perspectives on economics.

4. Local studies that include discussion of Old and New Dissent deal primarily with the post-1850 period; see E. R. Wickham, *Church and People in an Industrial City* (London, 1957); Hugh McLeod, *Class and Religion in the Late Victorian City* (London, 1974); Stephen Yeo, *Religion and Voluntary Organisations in Crisis* (London, 1976); Patrick Joyce, *Work, Society and Politics: The Culture of the Factory in Later Victorian England* (New Brunswick, N.J., 1981); and Jeffrey Cox, *The English Churches in a Secular Society: Lambeth, 1870–1930* (New York, 1982). However, for two studies that deal with the classic period of Industrial Revolution, see Paul T. Phillips, *The Sectarian Spirit: Sectarianism, Society and Politics in Victorian Cotton Towns* (Toronto, 1982) and Gail Malmgreen, *Silk Town: Industry and Culture in Macclesfield* (Hull, 1985). For the inclusion of Old and New Dissent in national studies, see A. D. Gilbert, *Religion and Society in Industrial England: Church, Chapel and Social Change, 1740–1914* (London, 1976) and Thomas W. Laqueur, *Religion and Respectability: Sunday Schools and Working Class Culture, 1780–1850* (New Haven, 1976).

5. See Joanna Innes, "Review Article: Jonathan Clark, Social History and England's 'Ancien Regime'," *Past and Present*, 115 (May 1987): 182.

6. Two pioneers of this approach were, of course, W. G. Hoskins, *The Midland Peasant: The Economic and Social History of a Leicestershire Village* (New York, 1957) and, for the *Annales* tradition, Marc Bloch, [trans. Janet Sondheimer], *French Rural History: An Essay on Its Basic Characteristics* (Berkeley and Los Angeles, 1966). For recent general treatments, see J. R. Ravensdale, *Liable to Floods: Village Landscape on the Edge of the Fens, A D 450–1850* (Cambridge, 1974); Alan Everitt, *Landscape and Community in England* (London, 1985); D. R. Mills, *Lord and Peasant in Nineteenth Century Britain* (London, 1980); and Emmanuel Le Roy Ladurie (trans. Ben and Sian Reynolds) *The Territory of the Historian* (Chicago, 1979); Charles Phythian-Adams, *Rethinking Local English History* (Leicester, 1987). For more detailed local and regional studies, see Obelkevich, *Religion and Rural Society*; Margaret Spufford, *Contrasting Communities: English Villagers in the Sixteenth and Seventeenth Centuries* (Cambridge, 1974); Alan Everitt, *The Pattern of Rural Dissent: The Nineteenth Century* (Leicester, 1972); Pierre

Goubert, *Cent Mille Provinciaux Au XVIIe Siècle: Beauvais et le Beauvaisis de 1600 à 1730* (Paris, 1968); and Dallas, *The Imperfect Peasant Economy*.

7. See Dean C. Tipps, "Modernization Theory and the Comparative Study of Societies: A Critical Perspective." *Comparative Studies in Society and History*, XV (1973). Tipps focuses much attention on the ideological and political uses of the concept of modernization, both of which have contributed to discrediting it. However, as Raymond Grew has pointed out, cold-war politics are not intrinsic to the concept and can safely be discarded while retaining its essential usefulness; Peter Sterns has argued that, precisely *because* of its ethnocentric distortions, "modernization" may have "more utility in patterning the Western past than in predicting the non-Western future"; see Raymond Grew, "More on Modernization," *Journal of Social History*, XIV (1980): 180–181 and Peter Sterns, "Modernization and Social History: Some Suggestions and a Muted Cheer," *Journal of Social History*, XIV (1980): 190. For a more recent critical perspective, cf. Charles Tilly, *As Sociology Meets History* (New York, 1981). However, see E. A. Wrigley, "The Process of Modernization and the Industrial Revolution in England," *Journal of Interdisciplinary History*, III (1972), whose only real criticism is directed at the theory's contemporary practitioners for downgrading contingency and elevating historical necessity; otherwise, the fundamental elements of the concept of modernization remain intact in his treatment. For two important studies, in quite different fields, which successfully make use of the concept, see Maris Vinovskis, *Fertility in Massachusetts from the Revolution to the Civil War* (New York, 1981), and Eugen Weber, *Peasants into Frenchmen: The Modernization of Rural France. 1870–1914)* (Standford, 1976).

8. See Grew, "More on Modernization," p. 179 and Tipps, "Modernization and the Comparative Study of Societies," pp. 216–217, for the so-called revisionist position.

9. For further use of "traditional," see n. 10 (below) and the following discussion of the meaning of *gemeinschaft*; for further use of "modern," see the discussion regarding Puritanism, particularly Keith Wrightson's and David Levine's study of Terling. Their work implies that pockets of modernity can be found within a sea of tradition and foreshadow the future. Marjorie McIntosh's study of the Royal Manor of Havering between 1200 and 1500 reveals a similar finding. As a result of Royal neglect and proximity to London, the combination having made Havering an atypical manor, the inhabitants of this medieval estate developed an unusual degree of freedom by the standards of the day; the exercise of this freedom, moreover, assumed a highly commercial form.

As the author states, "Havering's individualistic medieval tenants pursued their own interests on the basis of rational considerations, taking risks in hopes of greater gain"; see Marjorie K. McIntosh, *Autonomy and Community: The Royal Manor of Havering, 1200–1500* (Cambridge, 1986), p. 2. For Marxist approaches to this transition, cf. Robert Brenner, "The Origins of Capitalist Development: A Critique of Neo-Smithian Marxism," *New Left Review*, 104 (1977). See also n. 26 (below) and text.

10. Alexander Chayanov, for instance, gave powerful expression to this definition of "traditional" in his formulation of the theory of the labor-consumer balance. Peasants, he argued, effected a balance between consumption needs and the amount of work effort needed to produce; they worked as hard as possible until their production reached the optimum necessary to satisfy these consumption needs, an optimum determined by a combination of household size and custom. They slackened their pace thereafter, even if the productivity of their labor had risen sufficiently for them to earn more than the optimum; even when the size of a peasant's farm increased in response to the growth in size of his family, a limit to further acquisition would be reached once the family itself attained a certain age. The traditionalist mentality, in other words, tended not to be accumulationist, but cleaved to familiar and secure standards. See A. V. Chayanov (Daniel Thoner, Basile Kerblay, and R. E. F. Smith, eds.), *The Theory of Peasant Economy* (Homewood, Ill.), pp. 6, 248. E. P. Thompson found this Chayanovian ethic in the mentalité of English artisans and agricultural laborers; cf. E. P. Thompson, "Time, Work-Discipline and Industrial Capitalism," *Past and Present*, 38 (1967); idem, "The Moral Economy of the English Crowd in the Eighteenth Century," *Past and Present*, 50 (1971).

11. For a summary of the attitudinal changes associated with modernization, see Wrigley, "The Process of Modernization," pp. 229–235. They include the triumph of "rationality," defined as behavior that maximizes economic returns; "merit" or "achievement" over "rank ascription" in recruitment to positions of authority; "self-interest," defined as the adoption of a personal "calculus [of] . . . pecuniary gain"; and self-control of "affect" and "much greater [personal] autonomy."

12. I am reminded of a recent advertisement appearing on Los Angeles television for the Home Savings and Loan in which a protective, comforting voice tells prospective patrons that "we guarantee the security of your investment; we take no risks." Surely, this represents the survival of traditionalism in the context of an economic order geared generally toward maximizing earnings.

13. Peter Sterns has made the point that however "teleological" the

concept of modernization appears, it does not intrinsically embrace the idea of progress; the end, in fact, might represent quite the opposite. See Sterns, "Modernization and Social History," p. 191.

14. The demographic and industrial "revolutions," for instance, are linked processes pointing toward modernity. However, religious culture and the constraints influencing the diffusion of innovation appear as contingent factors altering respectively the course and shape of each; see below, chaps. 5 and 6.

15. See Underdown, *Revel, Riot and Rebellion*; cf. John Morrill, "The Ecology of Allegiance in the English Revolution," *Journal of British Studies*, 26 (1987) and Underdown's reply in the same issue.

16. See Wrightson and Levine, *Poverty and Piety*, pp. 49–55; the authors strongly imply that this finding is an artifact of Terling's Puritan culture, but shy away from formally drawing this conclusion.

17. See Obelkevich, *Religion and Rural Society*.

18. The phrase "worldly asceticism" (ca. 1958) belongs to Max Weber; see Max Weber (trans. Talcott Partsons), *The Protestant Ethic and Spirit of Capitalism* (New York, 1976), chaps, IV, V.

19. See Paul Seaver, *Wallington's World: A Puritan Artisan in Seventeenth Century London* (Stanford, 1985) for an individual case study of such "unworldly" asceticism; cf. Deborah Valenze, *Prophetic Sons and Daughters* for emphasis on the unworldliness of Methodist sectarianism, although her study contains counterexamples of evangelicalism facilitating working-class adaptation to modern capitalist industry.

20. See Patrick Collinson, *The Religion of Protestants: The Church in English Society, 1559–1625* (Oxford, 1985), p. 249 and Halèvy, *The Birth of Methodism*, pp. 50–51.

21. Cf. Clifford Geertz, *The Interpretation of Cultures: Selected Essays* (New York, 1973); idem, *Local Knowledge: Further Essays in Interpretive Anthropology* (New York, 1983).

22. Cf. Sarah Banks, "Nineteenth Century Scandal or Twentieth Century Model? A New Look at 'Open' and 'Close' Parishes," *Ec.HR*, 2d ser., XLI (Feb. 1988), especially pp. 58–60. Banks offers a new quantitative critique of the model using correlation analysis for 106 West Norfolk parishes, although she is concerned with how well the model explains poor relief expenditure and problems of population density rather than the proliferation of Dissent.

23. See E. A. Wrigley, ed., *Introduction to English Historical Demography: From the Sixteenth to the Nineteenth Centuries* (London, 1966), chaps. 3 and 4 for the comparative utility of the two methods. Aggregative analysis is more economical in cost and allocation of time and for these reasons best fit a research strategy of total history; family

reconstitution studies must either be confined to a narrow range of demographic and economic questions or, if they wish to recreate the broader social context, as in the study of Terling, must be undertaken by a team of researchers; see Wrightson and Levine, *Poverty and Piety*, p. xii, where the authors admit as much. See also Franklin F. Mendels, "Proto-industrialization: The First Phase of the Industrialization Process." *JEH*, XXXII (1972): 241–261 for early use of the aggregative method with multivariate analysis. Sometimes, however, a single researcher is blessed by the availability of documents that accomplish the work of reconstitution in advance, because of the manner in which they were originally compiled, and in this way permit an in-depth demographic analysis over time in the context of a more broadly cast socioeconomic study. For his study of the Loire country, for instance, Gregor Dallas made use of detailed household listings, undertaken by Commune officials every five years between 1836 and 1911; see Dallas, *The Imperfect Peasant Economy*, p. 141.

24. For a lament that the "New Social History" has thus far failed to achieve this synthesis, see Roderick Floud, "Quantitative History and People's History: Two Methods in Conflict?" *Social Science History*, VIII, (Spring 1984); cf. the exchange between Fogel and Elton in Robert W. Fogel and G. R. Elton, *Which Road to the Past? Two Views of History* (New Haven, 1983).

25. Ferdinand Toennis originated the concept of gemeinschaft, which posited the existence of intimate, face-to-face communal relations based on bonds of kinship, occupation, neigborhood, and friendship; see Ferdinand Toennis (trans., ed. Charles P. Loomis), *Community and Association* (East Lansing, Mich., 1957). Sociologists of religion still characterize sects in this way; see B. R. Wilson, "An Analysis of Sect Development," in Brian Wilson, ed. *Patterns of Sectarianism: Organization and Ideology in Social and Religious Movements* (London, 1967).

26. See, for instance, J. Ambrose Raftis, *Tenure and Mobility: Studies in the Social History of the Mediaeval English Village* (Toronto, 1964); Edward Britton, *The Community of the Vill: A Study in the History of the Family and Village Life in Fourteenth-Century England* (Toronto, 1977); Zvi Razi, *Life, Marriage and Death in a Medieval Parish: Economy, Society and Demography in Halesowen* (Cambridge, 1980); Bruce M. S. Campbell, "Population Pressure, Inheritance and the Land Market in a Fourteenth-Century Peasant Community," in Richard M. Smith, ed., *Land, Kinship and Life-Cycle* (Cambridge, 1984); and Kathleen Biddick, "Medieval English Peasants and Market Involvement," *JEH*, XLV (1985). However involved in land or grain markets the medieval peasants may have been, their activities remained constrained by customary prac-

tices of risk aversion. After finding selective patterns of peasant market involvement, Biddick concludes, for instance, that "Communal efforts to ameliorate risk mediated the fuller penetration of the Medieval market"; see Biddick, "Medieval English Peasants," pp. 830–831. For a comparative perspective on the status of peasants in the transition to capitalism, cf. T. H. Aston and C. H. E. Philipin, eds., *The Brenner Debate: Agrarian Class Structure and Economic Development in Preindustrial Europe* (New York, 1985).

27. See Mills, *Lord and Peasant*; Underdown, *Revel, Riot and Rebellion*; Mack Walker, *German Home Towns: Community, State and General Estate* (Ithaca, N.Y., 1971); Joyce, *Work, Society and Politics*; and David W. Sabean, *Power in the Blood: Popular Culture and Village Discourse in Early Modern Germany* (Cambridge, 1984), especially pp. 27–30.

28. See Mills, *Lord and Peasant*, pp. 15–16, for a widely held contrary view.

29. Mendels, "Proto-industrialization," p. 246; cf. his critic, D. C. Coleman, "Proto-industrialization: A Concept Too Many," *Ec.HR*, 2d ser., 36 (1983).

30. M. E. Rose, "Social Change and the Industrial Revolution," in R. Floud and D. McClosky, eds., *The Economic History of Britain since 1700*, I: 1700–1860 (Cambridge, 1981): 225–226.

31. For theoretical considerations of the problem of "cultural hegemony," see T. J. Jackson Lears, "The Concept of Cultural Hegemony: Problems and Possibilities," *AHR*, 90 (June 1985) and Anthony Giddens, *Central Problems in Social Theory: Action Structure and Contradiction in Social Anlaysis* (Berkeley and Los Angeles, 1979), chap. 3, especially pp. 101–103.

32. See R. Currie, L. Horsley, and A. D. Gilbert, *Churches and Churchgoers: Pattern of Church Growth in the British Isles Since 1700* (Oxford, 1977), pp. 101–102; also Gilbert, *Religion and Society*, pp. 144–149.

33. Gilbert, *Religion and Society*, pp. 70, 89. The definition of "anomie" that I employ in this study, following Alan Gilbert, is a classical sociological category, derived from Durkheim. Gilbert writes: "In the unsettled era of early industrialisation, traditional authority structures began to disintegrate, social cohesion began to break down, and for individuals and families the personal security which came from integration in a stable community often gave way to anomie in the new and relatively unstructured world of the industrial shanty town or the industrial city." Again, he states: "The obverse of anomie is a heightened demand for new associational and communal foci to replace those which have been lost."

Gilbert goes on to say that the success of Nonconformist recruiting in the late eighteenth to early nineteenth century can be explained by this appeal in the industrial villages.

1: Landscape and Settlement

1. Alan Everitt, "River and Wold, Reflections on the Historical Origin of Regions and Pays," *Journal of Historical Geography*, III (1977): 2; see, as well, Craig Calhoun, "Community: Towards a Variable Conceptualization for Comparative Research," *Social History*, V (1980): 105–127.

2. "Proto-industrialization," following F. F. Mendels's now classic definition, refers here to a system of cottage industry, distinguished by production for the international market and originating in rural districts, the economies of which were based on subsistence or pastoral agriculture. See F. F. Mendels, "Proto-industrialization: The First Phase of the Industrialization Process," *JEH*, 32 (March 1972): 241–261 and P. Kriedte, H. Medick, and J. Schlumbohm (transl. B. Schempp), *Industrialization before Industrialization: Rural Industry in the Genesis of Capitalism* (Cambridge, 1981) for broad theoretical examinations of the phenomenon. For two critical appraisals, see D. C. Coleman, "Proto-Industrialization: A Concept Too Many," *Ec.HR*, 2d ser., XXXVI (Aug. 1983): 435ff. and Gay L. Gullickson, "Agriculture and Cottage Industry: Redefining the Causes of Proto-Industrialization," *JEH*, XLIII (Dec. 1983): 831ff.

3. Individually, each form of community proved conducive to the settlement of Dissenters's churches, and the Vale of Nailsworth conformed to both types; for a discussion of these community typologies, see Everitt, *Pattern of Rural Dissent*, pp. 22–26 and Mills, *Lord and Peasant*, pp. 17–19, 125; for the nature of wood-pasture regions, see Oliver Rackham, "The Forest: Woodland and Wood-Pasture in Medieval England," in Kathleen Biddick, ed., *Archaeological Approaches to Medieval Europe* (Kalamazoo, Mich., 1985), pp. 70–104 and Joan Thirsk, "The Farming Regions of England," in Joan Thirsk, ed., *Agrarian History of England and Wales*, vol. 4: 1550–1640 (Cambridge, 1967): 46–49, 67–69, 79–80.

4. For the theoretical distinction between sect and denomination, see B. R. Wilson, "An Analysis of Sect Development," in B. R. Wilson, ed., *Patterns of Sectarianism: Organization and Ideology in Social and Religious Movements* (London, 1967).

5. See Sidney and Beatrice Webb, *English Local Government from the Revolution to the Muncipal Corporation Act*, I (London, 1906): 9; see chap. 2 (below) for further discussion of the parish.

6. See Obelkevich, *Religion and Rural Society*, pp. 8–9; Everitt, *Pattern of Rural Dissent*, p. 44; Gilbert, *Religion and Society in Industrial England*, p. 98; and Mills, *Lord and Peasant*, especially chaps. 2–6.

7. *VCH Glos.*, XI: 136, 230–231; in the Stroud region, for instance, Rodborough parish had originated as a chapelry of Minchinhampton, and Stroud parish originally had been a chapelry of Bisley parish.

8. Ibid., p. 215; the Anglican chapel, established at Nailsworth in 1794, had remained unconsecrated.

9. GRO CL P/37, boundary map.

10. See fig. 3, below.

11. *BPP Population, I, Sessions 1831 and 1842–3* (Dublin, 1968; reprint). Avening parish in 1801, 1811, and 1831 included the chapelry of Nailsworth, but in 1821 Nailsworth was entered only with Minchinhampton; in 1841, it was divided appropriately among each of the parishes.

12. GRO MF447, Longtree Hundred Land Tax Returns, 1780–1794.

13. *VCH Glos.*, XI: 211.

14. Both Manor and parish were conterminous; see chap. 2 for further discussion.

15. Glos. Colln., Gloucester City Library, RF 167.2 (1–4), Horsley Manor Records, "Particulars of Leases and Rents, 1666–99."

16. Joan Thirsk, "The Farming Regions of England," in Thirsk, ed., *Agrarian History*, IV: 7–9 and passim.

17. W. I. Minchinton, "Agriculture in Gloucestershire during the Napoleonic Wars," *Trans. B & G Arch. Soc.* LXVIII (1949): 168.

18. Figure 1 is courtesy of Denis R. Mills.

19. *The Cotswoldian*, ca. 1854; A. H. Smith, *The Place Names of Gloucestershire*, XXXVIII (Cambridge, 1964): 102; *VCH Glos.*, XI: 209.

20. F. T. Smythe, *Chronicles of Shortwood*, 1705–1916 (Bristol, 1916), p. 2. Nailsworth seems to have originated as the boundary of an eighth-century Woodchester estate; see *VCH Glos.*, XI: 209.

21. *Stroud Jnl.*, 25 February 1871; see E. M. Carus-Wilson, *Medieval Merchant Venturers* (London, 1954), chap. IV for a discussion of early fulling mills.

22. See R. Perry, "The Gloucestershire Woollen Industry, 1100–1690," *Trans. B & G Arch. Soc.*, LXVI (1945): 51ff. and E. M. Carus-Wilson, "Evidences of Industrial Growth on some Fifteenth Century Manors," *Ec.HR*, 2d ser., XII (1959): 195–196.

23. See Mann, *Cloth Industry in the West of England* (Oxford, 1971): 62 for marketing, and chap. 4 (below) for the structure of the

putting-out system regionally; for the transition from the putting-out to the factory system in Gloucestershire, see chap. 6, below.

24. Beginning as by-employments, these forms of occupation persisted as such into the seventeenth century when, as the system of proto-industry advanced they began to become full-time occupations. For England generally, see Alan Everitt, "Farm Labourers," in J. Thrisk, ed., *Agrarian History*, IV: 425–429; J. Thrisk, "Industries in the Countryside," in F. J. Fischer, ed., *Essays in the Economic and Social History of Tudor-Stuart England* (Cambridge, 1961), pp. 77–88; for Gloucestershire, see ibid. and Mann, *The Cloth Industry in the West of England*, pp. 90, 92, and 102. Mann writes, for instance, that: "the village freeholder or copyholder who was also a clothier or weaver was still much in evidence in the seventeenth century," although "[m]ost weavers were people with no land or with so little that it amounted to no more than a garden."

25. Glos. Colln., RF167.1, Horsley Manor Records, Prosecutions before the manor court, ca. 1802.

26. GRO, Gloucester Dioscesan Records [hereafter GDR], Will of John Pavey, October 8, 1764.

27. See *Stroud Jnl.*, 13 May 1854, report of a meeting of the Nailsworth Literary and Mechanics Institute; cf. Dennis R. Mills, "The Nineteenth-Century Peasantry of Melbourn, Cambridgeshire," in Richard M. Smith, ed., *Land, Kinship and Life-Cycle* (Cambridge, 1984), pp. 481, 499.

28. *Glos. Jnl.*, 9 June 1806, 19 March 1810, and 29 July 1811.

29. In differences-of-proportions tests between the Vale hamlets and the inner periphery, the following Z statistics proved to be significant under the normal curve: for wool workers, $Z = 4.675$ and for agricultural laborers, $Z = 2.448$.

30. GRO P181/OV 7/1.

31. GRO GDR, Will of John Harvey, February 19, 1811.

32. For further discussion, see below, and chap 6, "Capital and Labor in the Industrial Revolution."

33. PRO Prob. 11/2113/379.

34. PRO Prob. 11/1921/14; IR26/1541; see also the example of Edward Sheppard of Uley, below, chap. 7, first section.

35. PRO Prob. 11/1560/704; IR26/601.

36. PRO Prob. 11/2149/248; GRO MF447, Minchinhampton Tithe Survey, ca. 1840.

37. PCC wills were those of testators owning property in more than one diocese; they tended to be wealthier than testators whose wills were proved in the diocesan courts, although there were exceptions.

38. Esther Moir, "The Gentlemen Clothiers: A Study of the Orga-

nization of the Gloucestershire Cloth Trade, 1750–1835," in HPR Finberg, ed., *Gloucestershire Studies* (Leicester, 1957), pp. 242–243.

39. Ibid., p. 243, the cases of George Paul and Nathaniel Wathen; see A. T. Playne, *The History of Minchinhampton and Avening* (Gloucester, 1915).

40. See *Glos. Jnl.*, 15 July 1822 for both advertisements; see also Lawrence and Jeanne C. Fawtier Stone, *An Open Elite? England, 1540–1880* (Oxford, 1984), p. 230 and Edward A. Allen, "Public School Elites in Early Victorian England: The Boys at Harrow and Merchant Taylors' Schools from 1825 to 1850," *Journal of British Studies*, XXI (Spring 1982): 88–91 and passim.

41. See R. Trumbach, *The Rise of the Egalitarian Family: Aristocratic Kinship and Domestic Relations in Eighteenth Century England* (New York, 1978), pp. 87–96; also Stone, *An Open Elite?*, pp. 221–238.

42. See G. C. Brauer, *The Education of A Gentleman: Theories of a Gentlemanly Education in England, 1660–1775* (New York, 1959); F. Musgrove, "Middle-Class Education and Employment in the Nineteenth Century," *Ec.HR*, 2d ser., XII (1959): 101–102, 109; Roy Porter, *English Society in the Eighteenth Century* (New York, 1982), p. 176; and Stone, *An Open Elite?*, pp. 243–246 for an appreciation of the comparative attitudes of businessmen and the landed elite toward classical studies and higher education, especially between 1670 and 1820. See also Allen, "Public School Elites," pp. 88–89, in which public school reform, by adapting to middle-class values, allegedly strengthened the aristocratic and landed Establishment; cf. Martin J. Weiner, *English Culture and the Decline of the Industrial Spirit, 1850–1980* (Cambridge, 1981), who argues the reverse.

43. GRO GDR, Will of Samuel Jenkins, May 22, 1838.

44. Ibid., Will of Isaac Hillier, Sepember 7, 1886.

45. Letter from E. H. Playne to "Alec," April 8, 1889, inquiring about the family genealogy. Playne Family Paper, David Playne, Bannut Tree, Avening, Stroud, Gloucestershire.

46. GRO D2424/3, Shortwood Baptist Church Roll.

47. PRO Prob. 11/1795/66, Will of Edward Bliss, the Elder, a Baptist deacon; see ibid.

48. PRO Prob. 11/1818/438; IR26/1317, Will of Nathaniel Dyer.

49. PRO Prob. 11/1851/536; IR26/1377, Will of Richard Bartlett.

50. See GRO GDR, Wills of George Ralph, March 28, 1829, George Mason, October 26, 1816; and William Stokes, the Elder, April 30, 1821.

51. GRO GDR, Will of Daniel Cook, March 8, 1838; GRO D2424/3, Shortwood Baptish Church Roll.

52. GRO GDR, Will of Cornelius Bowne, February 23, 1803; GRO

D1406, Thomas Family Papers. Bowne's trustees, James Thomas and William Biggs, were deacons of the Forest Green Congregationalist Church.

53. GRO GDR, Will of Robert Mason, January 21, 1778 and Thomas Baker, July 5, 1827.

54. PRO B3/3746-7, Court of Bankruptcy examinations. This image of an entrepreneurial laboring class conflicts with E. P. Thompson's belief in the pervasiveness of collectivist values among its members; see E. P. Thompson, *The Making of the English Working Class* (New York, 1963), p. 356; idem, "The Moral Economy of the English Crowd in the Eighteenth Century," *Past and Present*, 50 (1971).

55. GRO GDR, Will of Thomas Bird, the Elder, May 26, 1823; for other examples, see Wills of William Jennings, November 4, 1809; Thomas Young, March 15, 1834; John Arundell, Augtust 11, 1810; William Herbert, March 10, 1838; and Nathaniel Wheeler, January 15, 1800.

56. A John Webb was baptized at the Shortwood Baptish Church in 1825, two years after the testator's death; the testator's daughter, Mary Bird, may have been the same one who was baptized at Shortwood in 1795 and who died in 1844; see GRO D2424/3/517 and 1135. Thomas Bird might have attended as a hearer.

57. See H. H. Gerth and C. Wright Mills, eds., *From Max Weber: Essays in Sociology* (New York, 1958), p. 187.

58. For the survival of such an ethos in eighteenth-century Britain, see Samuel H. Beer, *British Politics in the Collectivist Age* (New York, 1965), p. 9. Beer writes: "In spite of lip service to Locke, eighteenth-century England was far from being an individualist society and, on the plane of operative ideals, the image of social reality had a strong corporatist tinge. Again, in Old Whig as in Old Tory thought, the corporatist was inseparable from the hierarchic ideal." Lawrence and Jeanne C. Fawtier Stone, by emphasizing the exclusiveness of the landed elite, strongly suggest the persistence of a customary hierarchy well past the eighteenth century; cf. Stone, *An Open Elite?*

59. See Neil Smelser, "Toward a Theory of Modernization," in George Dalton, ed., *Tribal and Peasant Economies: Readings in Economic Anthropology* (Garden City, N.Y., 1967), pp. 38–39; for a specific illustration of this tendency, see D. G. Hey, "A Dual Economy in South Yorkshire," *Ag.HR*, XVII (1969).

60. The value of personal property was recorded in diocesan wills to the nearest interval in the period after 1780; for PCC wills, values appeared in estate duty registers, PRO class IR 26. Leasehold land was included in the valuations, but freehold land was not; see letter, Capital

Taxes Office to A. M. Urdank, Inland Revenue BP 1/79, April 23, 1979. Cf. James P. P. Horn, "The Distribution of Wealth in the Vale of Berkeley, 1660–1700," *Southern History*, III (1981), especially for a correlation between personal and total wealth; and Wrightson and Levine, *Poverty and Piety*, pp. 33–34, for an analysis of wealth distribution at Terling that follows a simpler and more traditional hierarchical path.

61. Two extreme exceptions were excluded from this analysis: the estates of Daniel Cook, haymaker, and David Ricardo, the Elder, the great political economist and lord of the manor of Minchinhampton. To have included them would have seriously distorted the overall distribution. Ricardo was both banker and esquire, which affirms a pattern of mobility already cited, and his estate was valued under £500,000; see PRO Prob. 11/1676/596 and IR26/973.

62. See Anthony Giddens, *The Class Structure of Advanced Societies* (New York, 1975), p. 107. Giddens writes: "Mobility has sometimes been treated as if it were in large part separable from the determination of class structure. According to Schumpeter's famous example, classes may be conceived of as like conveyances, which may be constantly carrying different 'passengers' without in any way changing their shape. But, compelling though the analogy is at first sight, it does not stand up to closer examination. . . . In general, the greater the degree of 'closure' of mobility chances—both intergenerationally and within the career of the individual—the more this facilitates the formation of identifiable classes." Cf. Franklin F. Mendels, "Social Mobility and Phases of Industrialization," *Journal of Interdisciplinary History*, VII (1976): 193–216.

63. See "Introduction" (this volume), n. 1. Both Elie Halèvy and E. P. Thompson emphasize the role of Methodism in communicating Puritan, middle-class values to the working class, but each focuses on elements of collective subordination of one class to another, such as "work discipline." However, Puritan values also included the promotion of individual autonomy, which sometimes translated into entrepreneurial behavior, even among the working classes.

64. GRO, ROL C4, E. Witchell, *The Geology of Stroud and the Area Drained by the Frome* (Strould, 1885), pp. 1–4.

65. GRO MA 19/71, Geological Survey Map; Ordinance Survey Map, six-inch scale, Glos. XLIX (1885 ed.).

66. *VCH Glos.* XI: 207.

67. Ibid.

68. See William Cobbett, *Rural Rides* (London, 1967, reprint), p. 375.

69. GRO ROL C4, Witchell, *The Geology of Stroud*, p. 31.

70. See Jennifer Tann, "Some Problems of Waterpower—A Study of

Mill Siting in Gloucestershire," *Trans. B & G Arch. Soc.*, LXXXIV (1965): 53–77; GRO ROL C4. E. Witchell, *The Geology of Stroud*, p. 5.

71. Ibid., ROL C4. The Lias Clay is usually found at the lowest point in the Vale; it is followed in ascending order by the Supra-Liassic or Cotswold Sand, the Inferior Oolite, Fuller's Earth, the Great Oolite, and Forest Marble.

72. Ibid.

73. Data in tables 8 and 9 were derived from the acreage returns of 1801, PRO, Home Office 67/3, reprinted in W. E. Minchinton, "Agriculture in Gloucestershire"; a Minchinhampton parish valuation, ca. 1804, GRO P217a VE 1/1; the 1838–1841 tithe surveys for Avening, Horsley, and Minchinhampton, GRO MF447, the Minchinhampton Tithe Terrier, ca. 1777, GRO P217 IN 31, and the Avening tithe book, ca. 1784, GRO P29 OV1/2; for shrinkage of the wasteland at Avening and greater concentration of ownership at Horsley, see chap. 2, tables 13 and 14.

74. The estimate of arable acres sown in 1838 for each type of crop (X') is derived from the equation $X' = y/z(m)$, where y represents the acreage sown by type of crop in 1801; z, the total acreage sown in 1801; and m, the total arable acreage in 1838.

75. The Nailsworth Brewery, owned by Samuel and Joseph Clissold, deacons of the Shortwood Baptist Church [!], covered nearly two acres and was considered the most important brewery in the Stroud district. Brewing was often carried on by individuals operating on a small scale, however, as evidenced by *Gloucester Journal* advertisements; see, for instance, *Glos. Jnl.*, 27 January 1823, advertisement for the sale of "a leasehold messuage with brewhouse and workshop recently built."

76. The mean national wheat yield in 1838 was 33.1 bushels per acre; see E. L. Jones, *Agriculture and the Industrial Revolution* (New York, 1974), p. 189. For Gloucestershire, ca. 1836, the mean wheat yield was 19.6 bushels per acre, and that of barley and oats stood, respectively, at 27.1 and 27.5 bushels per acre; see R. J. P. Kain, *An Atlas and Index of the Tithe Files of Mid-Nineteenth Century England and Wales* (Cambridge, 1986), p. 234, table 38. Avening's wheat yield, at 8.2 bushels per acre, although lower than the county average, was well within the range of possible wheat yields for individual scores and akin to a medieval measure; cf. J. Z. Titow, *Winchester Yields: A Study in Medieval Agricultural productivity* (Cambridge, 1972), p. 13, table 2b.

77. GRO MF447, Horsley Tithe Survey, 1841; *Glos. Jnl.* 27 January 1823, Sale by Auction, and 7 April 1823, Sale by Auction.

78. GRO D1388/ Plan of the Estate of Edward Barnfield, ca. 1801; this theme is amply developed in E. P. Thompson, *Whigs and Hunters: The Origin of the Black Act* (New York, 1975).

79. Glos. Colln. M 10073, Revd. Messing Rudkin, *The History of Horsley* (Stroud, 1884), p. 3.

80. *VCH Glos.*, XI; 156. Unless otherwise noted, other references to specific roads have been drawn from this source.

81. E. Moir, *Local Government in Gloucestershire, 1775–1800* (Bristol, 1969), p. 1. Freestone, which was abundant in Nailsworth, "was but poorly calculated for the building of roads," according to A. R. Fewster: see the *Stroud Jnl.*, 13 May 1854, report of the proceedings of the Nailsworth Literary and Mechanics Institute.

82. *Glos. Jnl.*, 7 February 1820.

83. Ibid., 1 September 1820.

84. See chap. 5 for further treatment of the problem of geographic mobility between 1794 and 1812.

85. *Glos. Jnl.*, 15 May 1825. In a Sunday celebration, sponsored by the Waterloo Benefit Society, members were requested to assemble at Nailsworth's Clothier's Arms Inn and to march in procession to Horsley Church; they were instructed to return to the Clothier's Arms for dinner, following the minister's sermon.

86. Distances normally covered between ten and twenty miles; see T. S. Ashton, *An Economic History of England: The Eighteenth Century* (London, 1964), p. 87.

87. *Glos. Jnl.*, 19 July 1824; an advertisement records the names of the gates: Inchbrook, Sprout, Culverhouse, Woodchester, Balls Green, Nailsworth, Lightpill, Stanley, Tiltups Inn, Hazelwood, Buckholt, and Avening.

88. Ibid., 18 December 1809.

89. T. S. Ashton, *Economic History*, p. 78; wage labor was normally used to supplement unpaid statute labor from the time of the Interregnum.

90. *Glos. Jnl.*, 19 July 1824 and 22 August 1835.

91. T. S. Ashton, *Economic History*, p. 80.

92. See G. Taylor, "Types of Capitalism in Eighteenth Century France," *EHR*, LXXIX (1964), pp. 478ff. for an appreciation of Old Regime methods of financial and commerical activity.

93. T. S. Ashton, *Economic History*, p. 85, states that canal building represented a substitution of capital for labor; see A. D. Gayer, W. W. Rostow, and A. J. Schwartz, *The Growth and Fluctuation of the British Economy, 1790–1850: An Historical, Statistical, and Theoretical Study of Britain's Economic Development*, vol. I (Oxford, 1953): 38, 418 for further discussion of the eighteenth-century canal boom.

94. *VCH Glos.*, XI: 102.

95. Ibid.

96. *Glos. Jnl.*, 1 November 1824, "Stroud Canal."

97. Mann, *Cloth Industry.*, pp. 191–192 states that despite the canals it sometimes took up to four months for goods traveling to London to arrive.

98. *Glos. Jnl.*, 2 September 1805.

99. Ibid., 2 September 1804.

100. Mann, *Cloth Industry*, p. 50, cites two previously abortive schemes, one in 1730 and another in 1759, that clothiers had promoted.

101. *Glos. Jnl.*, 4 November 1805.

102. Mann, *Cloth Industry*, pp. 190–191.

103. *Glos. Jnl.*, 1 November 1824, "Stroud Canal."

104. See Peter Mathias, "Capital, Credit and Enterprise in the Industrial Revolution," *JEEc.H.*, II (Spring 1973): 124.

105. The prices of canal shares can be expected to correlate with their respective rates of profit, as reflected in dividend payments. Data on canal share prices have been drawn from Gayer et. al., *Growth and Fluctuation*, p. 370. The partial correlation was computed from the following: Given X = Stroud Canal dividends, Y = canal share prices nationally, and t = the vector of time, then $r_{xy} = 0.885$, $r_{xt} = 0.91$, $r_{yt} = 0.793$. The t-test on $r_{xy(t)}$ is: $t = 2.963$, $df = 12$; for significance at the 0.02 level, $t > 2.681$.

106. Gayer et al., *Growth and Fluctuation*, p. 418.

107. Mann, *Cloth Industry*, pp. 191–192.

108. Ibid.

109. *Glos. Jnl.*, 6 December 1834, "Great Western Railway."

110. Ibid.; see remarks of Charles Stanton and W. H. Hyett; coal was a great untapped resource of the Nailsworth valleys: Geological Survey Map, Glos. Colln. 554.231, Box 10.103 and Box 10.105.

111. *VCH Glos.*, XI: 103.

112. *Glos. Jnl.*, 6 December 1834.

113. Ibid. The Southampton-London line was to pass from Basing to Bath in order to take in the Wiltshire towns of Bradford and Trowbridge, with an extension to be built to Bristol.

114. *VCH Glos.*, XI: 209.

115. *Stroud Jnl.*, 13 May 1854, report of the proceedings of the Nailsworth Literary and Mechanics Institute.

116. Ibid.

2: Landownership and Tenure

1. This theme is examined further in chaps. 3 and 8.

2. See Obelkevich, *Religion and Rural Society*, pp. 10–13; Everitt, *The Pattern of Rural Dissent*, pp. 20–22; B. A. Holderness, "'Open' and

'Close' Parishes in England in the Eighteenth and Nineteenth Centuries,'' *Ag.HR*, XX (1972); and Mills, *Lord and Peasant*, especially chaps. 2–6; however, see Sarah Banks's critique of this model, in Banks, "Nineteenth Century Scandal."

3. See, for instance, Obelkevich, *Religion and Rural Society*, p. 12, n. 2; Obelkevich bases his analysis on the land tax return for 1831.

4. Alan MacFarlane, *The Origins of English Individualism: The Family, Property and Social Transition* (Oxford, 1978), defines individualism in terms of property right; for the correlation of property right with Dissent, see above, n. 2 as well as the two classics: Max Weber (trans. Talcott Parsons), *The Protestant Ethic and the Spirit of Capitalism* (New York, 1976) and R. H. Tawney, *Religion and the Rise of Capitalism: An Historical Study* (London, 1964).

5. For references, see above, chap. 1, n. 12 and n. 73.

6. Almost 25.0 percent of the parish's acreage remained unlisted, however; this was undoubtedly unoccupied waste, "the lord's waste," that he protected from encroachment by cottagers; see chap. 4 for a detailed treatment of the exercise of manorial authority.

7. Intermediary and small holdings among owners fell 37 and 24 percent, respectively.

8. The range was from a mean of 0.8666 to a mean of 0.4888 acres.

9. Horsley's acreage in 1784 was estimated from the land values and acreage figures in the 1784 Avening tithe survey and from Horsley's land tax assessments for that year. A regression equation, Total Acreage = $-0.2357178 + 0.3919663$ (land value) was derived from the tithe survey, and Horsley's land values, based on the assessment of 4s. per pound sterling, were substituted to yield estimates of total acreage for each landholder in the parish. Although methods of valuation for tithe and land tax could have differed, the pattern of variation between land values and acreage size are assumed to have been the same.

10. The percentage fall in acreage was respectively 34, 40, and 55.

11. John Dela Field, Esq., probably a distant relative of the late lord, Henry Stephens, occupied Chavenage manor house in 1841 but appears only to have had the "use" of the estate, the rents of which were collected by its trustee, Robert Kingscote; see the Will of Henry Stephens, Esq., February 28, 1795, PRO Prob. 11/1256/122. For the activities of the manor court under the Stephens, see chap. 4.

12. See above, chap. 1, tables 1 to 4.

13. See above, chap. 1, table 8 for the net loss of arable acreage that resulted from a sharpening of the division of labor. Adam Smith had observed that absence of specialization made preindustrial labor particularly inefficient: "A country weaver who cultivates a small farm must lose

a good deal of time in passing from his loom to his field, and from the field to his loom"; see Adam Smith (G. Stigler, ed.), *Selections from the Wealth of Nations* (New York, 1957), p. 6.

14. See this chapter (chap. 2), section on agrarian transformation.

15. See E. P. Thompson, "Patrician Society, Plebeian Culture," *Journal of Social History*, VII (1974): 387 and Roger B. Manning, *Village Revolts: Social Protest and Popular Disturbances in England, 1509–1640* (Oxford, 1988), p. 5. Manning writes that during the early modern period the survival of use-rights among the tenantry, as well as "[t]he continued exercise of seigneurial jurisdiction, the extraction of manorial dues and services, and the survival of servile tenures all modified the terms of landholding," limiting both the lords' and tenants' assertions of unqualified rights to private property. This conclusion applies equally to the late eighteenth to early nineteenth century, to the extent that remnants of seigneurialism can be found.

16. See Ivor P. Collis, "Leases for a Term of Years Determinable with Lives," *Society of Archivists Journal*, I (1955–1959) and Christopher Clay, "Lifehold Leasing in the Western Counties of England," *Ag.HR*, XXIX (1981) for close examinations of this particular form of leasehold.

17. E. Kerridge, *Agrarian Problems of the Sixteenth Century and after* (London, 1969) discusses the difference between leases as "real interests" in land and as "real chattels"; cf. A. W. B. Simpson, *A History of the Land Law*, 2d ed. (Oxford, 1986), pp. 70–73. The life tenant held "seisin" because he could transfer his holding to his heirs instead of an executor.

18. In the West of England, both copyholds for lives and lifehold leases were renewable at the expiry of each life listed in the indenture, a practice that offered additional security of tenure; see Kerridge, *Agrarian Problems*, pp. 35–36, 47.

19. The customary obligations they contained, at the very least, were payment of heriots and suit of court; the succession of lifehold leases from copyholds is depicted in Kerridge, *Agrarian Problems*; see also R. H. Hilton, *The English Peasantry in the Later Middle Ages* (Oxford, 1975), pp. 69–70, 149; F. Pollock and F. W. Maitland, *The History of the English Law before the Time of Edward I*, II (Cambridge, 1968): iii; and Manning, *Village Revolts*, p. 133.

20. See n. 17, above, on "real chattels." In eighteenth-century Norfolk, a seat of the agricultural revolution, twenty-one-year leases were regarded as long tenures; see R. A. C. Parker, *Coke of Norfolk: A Financial and Agricultural Study, 1707–1842* (Oxford, 1975), p. 54.

21. Kerridge, *Agrarian Problems*, p. 47.

22. Gloucester City Library, Glos. Colln., RF167.2 (1–4), Horsley

Manor Records, Particulars of Leases and Rents, 1562–1789; cf. *Glos. Jnl.*, 19 July 1842, the case of *Garbind vs. Jekyel*, in which the Lord Chief Justice is reported enforcing the payment of heriots to the lord of an Essex manor, although not to the amount the latter had claimed.

23. Ivor P. Collis, "Leases for a Term of Years," p. 168.

24. See chap. 4 for a detailed treatment.

25. *Glos. Jnl.*, 1 April 1816, "Manor of Horsley." We can estimate, however, that the number of leaseholders on the manor were fewer than at Minchinhampton, the estimate for which is given below. According to the series of suitors between 1794 and 1814, listed in appendix B, the trend value for the number of suitors in 1789 (the year of the last recorded lease) is 441; this means that about 10 percent of all Horsley suitors held leases from the manor.

26. GRO D1192/2; for a discussion of the evolution of tenures on the manor, especially the early commutation of labor services, see Jean Birdsall, "The English Manors of the Abbey of La Trinité at Cean," in *Anniversary Essays in Medieaval History by Students of Charles Homer Haskins* (New York, 1929), pp. 36, 38 and E. Watson, "The Minchinhampton Custumal and Its Place in the Story of the Manor," *Trans. B & G Arch. Soc.* LIV (1932): 255.

27. The results of this analysis can be expressed symbolically as $X_1 = 2.65s$, $S_1 = 3.20$; $X_2 = 3.76s$, $S_2 = 3.48$; $t = 0.62$, $df = 34$, $t > 2.03$ at the 0.05 significance level.

28. The assumption made here is that the type of property held (which might have affected the rental value) is randomly distributed among small holders and therefore should not affect the comparison.

29. Kerridge, *Agrarian Problems*, p. 48.

30. F. Pollock, *The Land Law's* (London, 1896), p. 142; cf. Simpson, *History of Land Law*, p. 252.

31. Gloucester City Library, Glos. Colln., RF167.2 (1–4), Horsley Manor Records.

32. Ibid.

33. *Glos. Jnl.*, 15 September 1823, Sale at Boot Inn.

34. PRO PCC Prob. 11/1818/66, Will of Edward Bliss; PRO, IR26/1279/81, Estate Duty Registers.

35. PRO PCC Prob. 11/1256/122, Will of Henry Stephens, Esq.

36. GRO D1812/1. Ricardo Family Papers.

37. See Ivor P. Collis, "Leases for a Term of Years," pp. 168–171.

38. Occasionally, however, wills specify the tenurial status of the property bequeathed; where freehold status is not actually specified, the property may likely have been a long-term leasehold treated as though it were a freehold, as in the case of Edward Bliss, cited above.

39. GRO GDR, Wills of W. Kemish, September 5, 1812; T. Lewis, May 25, 1825; J. Heskins, April 15, 1818; P. Howell, March 31, 1764; T. Locker, September 12, 1759; Rob Mason, January 21, 1778; Jas. Bingell, February 14, 1803; Thos. Baker, July 5, 1827; J. Sansum, June 26, 1823; H. Dee, April 22, 1797; D. Sansum, December 13, 1826; W. Dowdy, March 19, 1763; J. Harrison, October 15, 1772, J. Cull, May 12, 1779; and T. Holliday, November 8, 1774. See also chap. 6, table 47, which gives the percentage distribution by tenurial status of artisan, weaver, and laborer householders at Horsley in 1811.

40. See J. D. Chambers, "Enclosure and the Labour Supply," in D. V. Glass and D. E. C. Eversley, eds., *Population in History: Essays in Historical Demography* (London, 1965), pp. 308–310; cf. the historiographic discussion in J. A. Yelling, *Common Field and Enclosure in England, 1450–1850* (London, 1977), pp. 94–103.

41. See Joan Thirsk, "The Farming Regions of England"; Yelling, *Common Field and Enclosure*; J. R. Wordie, "The Chronology of English Enclosure, 1500–1914," *Ec.HR*, XXXVI, 2d ser. (1983) has maintained, more recently, that 70 percent of the land in England had been enclosed by 1700.

42. Chambers, "Enclosure and the Labour Supply," p. 319; see also G. E. Mingay, *Enclosure and the Small Farmer in the Age of the Industrial Revolution* (London, 1968).

43. See Yelling, *Common Field and Enclosure*, pp. 26–29, 71–93.

44. Gloucester City Library, Glos. Colln. RF167.2 (1–4), Horsley Manor Records; subsequent similar references are drawn from the same source.

45. GRO GDR, Will of Daniel Harvey, Avening, March 31, 1785.

46. GRO, D1812/1, Ricardo Family Papers, Feoffment of Premises at Avening, May 11, 1807, Hill and Dangerfield to Phillip Sheppherd.

47. Ibid. Lease Indenture, September 24, 1777, Peach to Edward Sheppherd.

48. Ibid. Deed of Exchange, February 24, 1788, Sheppherd to Walbank.

49. Ibid. Conveyance of Estates, the Shard and Samao, March 24, 1824.

50. GRO P217a/VE1/1, Survey and Valuation of the lands in the Parish of Minchinhampton, ca. 1804, for equalizing the poor rates. The parish contained altogether 390 plots of arable land, including common field lands, and 324 plots of pasture. However, mean arable acreage, at 6.4 acres per plot, outstripped mean pastoral acreage, at 3.4 acres per plot, by a ratio of 2:1. The preponderance of arable land in this wood-pasture society was undoubtedly caused by the barley requirements of

the brewing industry and the persistence of Minchinhampton Common as a communal grazing area. Nevertheless, the mean ratable value of pasture lands was significantly greater, at 14s. per acre, than the mean ratable value of the arable sector, at 6s. per acre. All pasture lands were enclosed, while a sizable proportion of arable still lay in common fields; the costs of enclosure probably accounted for the difference in ratable values; see n. 51, below.

51. Ibid.; GRO P217 IN 3/1; GRO MF 447. By 1804, the acreage held in common fields had fallen to only 589 acres; 152 plots laid in common fields, and all were devoted to arable land, while 562 plots had been enclosed, 324 of which were pasture lands. Mean enclosed acreage, at 5.6 acres per plot, outstripped mean common field acreage, at 3.99 acres per plot, by a ratio of almost 3:2; $t = 2.31$, $df = 712$, Prob > |t| 0.02. The mean ratable value of enclosed lands, at 9.66s. per acre, dramatically surpassed the mean ratable value of open field lands, at 3.25s. per acre; $t = 7.12$, $df = 712$, Prob > |t| 0.00.

52. *Glos. Jnl.*, 10 May 1813; re Minchinhampton Common.

53. Ibid., 6 March 1830, advertisement.

54. GRO D2219/1/4, Resolution of the [Minchinhampton] Court Leet, ca. 1843.

55. GRO D2219/1/5, Court Leet, Minutes of Proceedings, 1847.

56. The term "affer" comes from the Latin words *averus, avera,* which are forerunners of the word "affrus," meaning "work-horse"; see John Langdon, *Horses, Oxen and Technological Innovation: The Use of Draught Animals in English Farming from 1066–1500* (Cambridge, 1986), p. 295.

57. See chaps. 3 and 4 for the attitudes of Whig landowners and chap. 4 for evidence from manorial court records.

3: Churches and Chapels

1. For a recent study of sectarian Methodism in diverse regional contexts, see Valenze, *Prophetic Sons and Daughters.*

2. For a comparison of pre-Victorian Nonconformist and Methodist growth, see Currie et al., *Churches and Churchgoers*, and Gilbert, *Religion and Society*, p. 120.

3. On the sect-denomination dichotomy, see B. R. Wilson, "An Analysis of Sect Development," in Wilson, ed., *Patterns of Sectarianism*; Gilbert, *Religion and Society*, pp. 140–149, and Currie et al., *Churches and Churchgoers*, pp. 60, 92–93.

4. David Martin, *A General Theory of Secularization* (Oxford, 1978), p. 20; cf. Obelkevich, *Religion and Rural Society*, pp. 178–179.

5. See chap. 8 for a study of the Nailsworth Society of Friends.

6. See chap. 9 for a case study of the Shortwood Baptist Church in the nineteenth century.

7. For the model and its application to this study, see chaps. 1 and 2; for the pattern of cooperation, see chap. 4, section on Dissent and the composition of lordship.

8. Glos. Colln. M10073; Revd. M. Rudkin, *The History of Horsley* (Stroud, 1884), p. 27.

9. Ibid. The Restoration Church, from the outset, showed continuity with its latitudinarian, Cromwellian predecessor; see Patrick Collinson, *The Religion of Protestants: The Church in English Society, 1559–1625* (Oxford, 1985), p. 283.

10. BM Add. 33,589ff. 75, 77: Papers Relating to the Supression of Conventicles in the County of Gloucester, 1669–1772.

11. Ibid.

12. Ibid.

13. Ibid.

14. Rudkin, *History of Horsley*, p. 27. The "moderation" of Calvinism refers to the theological feat of reconciling the doctrine of Predestination, based on the principle of Election, with the doctrine of Universal redemption.

15. GRO D2595/1, Lower Forest Green Church Book, 1847–1854, Introductory History: Mr. George Fox, ejected from Buckle Church in 1662, had become pastor of a church at Nailsworth soon thereafter; it was this Presbyterian church, referred to by the church book as the "Nailsworth Meeting," that immediately preceded the establishment of the Forest Green Congregationalist Church.

16. Ibid.

17. See this chapter, section on origins of Dissent.

18. GRO D1460, Thomas Family Papers, Trust Deeds of the Forest Green Congregationlist Church.

19. Ibid., Indenture of Assignment, November, 15, 1688: Conveyance of Property.

20. GRO D2595/1; Thomas Small of Nailsworth, clothier, and one of the trustees was described in the church book as a "chief leader for many years." He might have become a Dissenter subsequently or remained within the Church of England while continuing to play this role, as did Samuel Sevil in his relationship with the Shortwood Baptists; for Sevil's role, see below.

21. See Charles Russell, *A Brief History of the Independent Church at Forest Green, Nailsworth* (Nailsworth, 1845, 1912), p. 12.

22. John Walsh, "Moderate Calvinism in the Church of England," unpublished paper; cf. below, n. 40.

23. An account of the riot is given in the Minchinhampton Baptist Church Book, in the possession of Revd. J. Edwards, The Manse, Windmill Road, Minchinhampton; cf. John Walsh, "Methodism and the Mob in the Eighteenth Century," in G. J. Cumming and Derek Baker, eds., *Popular Belief and Practices: Studies in Church History*, VIII (Oxford, 1972).

24. GRO D1406, Thomas Family Papers, Trust Deeds of the Forest Green Church: March 6, 1720; December 20, 1731; November 20, 1747. Throughout the late seventeenth and early eighteenth centuries, trustees were drawn from a middle- and upper-class strata. In 1720, Jeremiah Jones of Avening, gentleman, headed a list of new trustees and was followed by four clothiers and one dyer. In 1731 the trustees consisted of two gentlemen, one maltster, three clothiers, one dyer, and—significantly—one shoemaker. In 1747 the surviving trustees of 1731 conveyed their authority to one clothworker, one tallow chandler, one grocer, one maltster, and one clothier, thereby reversing the positions of the social groups involved in the leadership.

25. No accounts are sufficiently extant to allow for a detailed appraisal of the changing occupational structure of the membership of Forest Green Church or its numerical growth and decline.

26. See chap. 5.

27. Russell, *History of the Forest Green Church*, pp. 19–20.

28. Ibid., p. 21; this was the Revd. Moffat who "openly avowed that he could not baptize infants, on the usual grounds of professed Baptists."

29. Quoted in G. F. Nuttall, *Howel Harris, 1714–1773: The Last Enthusiast* (Cardiff, 1975), p. 17.

30. Russell, *History of the Forest Green Church*, p. 18.

31. GRO D1406, Thomas Family Papers, Family and Business Correspondence, 1824–1840.

32. Russell, *History of the Forest Green Church*, p. 22.

33. Ibid.

34. Ibid., p. 23.

35. Ibid., p. 25.

36. Ibid.

37. Ibid., p. 35.

38. GRO D2424/1. Shortwood Baptist Church Minute Book, 1732–1800, a brief history of the origins of the chapel as recounted by William Harding; henceforth, "Brief History." Cf. Gilbert, *Religion and Society*, p. 16 and Peter Toon, *The Emergence of Hyper-Calvinism in English Nonconformity, 1689–1765* (London, 1967).

39. GRO D2424/1, February 12, 1758. A letter to the Western Association of Baptist Churches, recorded in the church book, cites the main doctrines adhered to by the church at this time: "A confession of faith

put forward by our Brethren in the year 1689, especially the doctrine of the Blessed Trinity, Eternal Personal Election, Particular Redemption, Salvation Alone by Christ, Efficacious Grace of God and the Final Perseverance of the Saints."

40. Geoffrey Nuttall, "Calvinism in Free Church History," *The Baptist Quarterly*, XXII (October 1968): 422; for the differences between moderate and high Calvinism, see idem, "Northamptonshire and the Modern Question: A Turning Point in 18th Century Dissent," *Journal of Theological Studies*, XVI (1965) and Toon, *Emergence of Hyper-Calvinism*.

41. GRO D2424/1, Minute Book.

42. Ibid., D2424/3, Shortwood Church Roll, Copy of the Original Trust Deed of the Shortwood Meeting House in the Parish of Horsley, ca. 1768.

43. Ibid., D2424/1, Minute Book, "Brief History."

44. Ibid.

45. J. Thompson, *History of Nonconformist Congregations*, vol. I, No. 17, MS. 38.7–11, Dr. Williams's Library.

46. Ibid.

47. Ibid.

48. Ibid.

49. GRO D2424/12, J. Cave, *A History of the Shortwood Baptist Church*, ca. 1880, MSS, p. 33.

50. Ibid., pp. 48–49.

51. Ibid., D2424/1, Minute book, February 20, 1755.

52. Ibid., D2424/12, Cave, *History*, p. 61.

53. See chap. 9 (on Shortwood Baptists).

54. See Benjamin Francis, "An Elegy on the Death of the Rev. George Whitefield," unpublished MSS, ca. 1770, a poem eulogizing Whitefield. Calvinism was moderated along evangelical lines from within the Baptist community as well, principally through Andrew Fuller, who seems to have had a direct influence on Shortwood; see E. F. Clipsham, "Andrew Fuller and Fullerism," *Baptist Quarterly*, XX (1963).

55. Quoted in G. F. Nuttall, "Questions and Answers: An 18th Century English Correspondence," *Baptist Quarterly*, XXXVI (1977).

56. GRO D2424/3, Copy of the Original Deed of Trust of a Meeting House at Shortwood in the Parish of Horsley in the Country of Glos.

57. See Christopher Hill, *Century of Revolution* (New York, 1961), p. 168.

58. GRO D2424/20, "Francis and Flint Mss. Family History," app. F.

59. Ibid.

60. Thompson, *History of Nonconformist Congregations*, MS. 38.7–11, II: Gloucestershire.

61. GRO D2424/1, Shortwood Church Book, 1732–1800.

62. Thompson, *History*, MS. 38.7–11, II: Gloucestershire.

63. GRO D2424/20, "Francis and Flint," II: 14.

64. Ibid., p. 60.

65. For discussions of the correlation between universalism and enthusiasm, see Semmel, *Methodist Revolution* and Valenze, *Prophetic Sons and Daughters*.

66. GRO D2424/20, "Francis and Flint," II: 61.

67. Ibid., p. 64.

68. Ibid., p. 27.

69. See "The Trial of William Winterbotham, Asst. Preacher at Howe's Lane Meeting, Devon 25 & 26 July 1793 for Seditious Words," Dr. William's Library, PP17.7.29(6). The Government brought fourteen counts against him.

70. Smythe, *Chronicles of Shortwood*, p. 80.

71. *Glos. Jnl.*, 14 September 1839, "A New Meeting House at Shortwood."

72. GRO D2219/6/6, Nailsworth Episcopal Chapel Minute Book, Copy of Building Subscription List (1794).

73. BM Add. 34,571, f. 457: Letter from D. Ricardo, [II], to Revd. P. Bliss, May 5, 1835.

74. Ibid.

75. Ibid.

76. *Glos. Jnl.*, 1 September 1823: "New Churches." "Since the previous year ten new churches were completed and nine more were consecrated." The number already built "can afford accommodation to 7,116 persons in pews and 14,399 in free seats." Forty-four were in the progress of being built, twelve of which were due to be completed in 1824: "The whole will be capable of affording accommodation to 34,563 in pews and 39,842 in free seats." Plans for churches and chapels in nine parishes were approved, and plans for the creation of sixteen new churches "are now before the board of commissioners. Altogether, 68,442 persons in pews and 82,105 in free seats will be accommodated." Gilbert, *Religion and Society*, p. 27 has characterized these efforts as "minimal." Obelkevich, *Religion and Rural Society*, pp. 176–178, however, offers a more positive evaluation for South Lindsey, at any rate for the period after 1825.

77. Glos. Colln. JR4.3, A Charge to the Clergy of the Diocese of Gloucester, 1825.

78. Ibid., J4.57, A Charge to the Clergy of the Diocese of Gloucester, 1832.

79. GRO GDR A2/1–2, Gloucester Diocesean Book, Survey of Livings.

80. Ibid., GDR A2/2–3, Gloucester Diocesean Book, Survey of Livings.

81. Ibid., GDR A2/4–5, Gloucester Diocesean Book, Survey of Livings.

82. Ibid.

83. GRO P217 CW 2/3, Pews: Sales and Exchanges, 1789–1852.

84. *Glos. Jnl.*, 10 September 1836.

85. Ibid. Its dimensions were 45 feet by 40 feet by 13 feet high.

86. *Glos. Jnl.*, 19 July 1837, "Horsley Church."

87. Ibid.

88. Ibid.

89. Ibid., 7 April 1838; a sum of £500 was contributed by the Diocesan Church Building Society.

90. Ibid., 19 October 1833.

91. Ibid., 12 September 1835.

92. See Nuttall, *Howel Harris,* pp. 38–57; ecumenicism, too, was a chief feature of denominationalism.

93. BM Add. 40420, f. 180–185, Peel Papers, Papers Relating to the Dissenters's Marriage Bill, 1834/35.

94. Ibid.

95. Ibid.

96. *VCH Glos.*, XI: 215.

97. PRO Religious Census Returns, Home Office 129/338/7/1/2.

98. Ibid., Home Office 129/3387/1/7 and 129/338/7/1/4 and 6, for the Shortwood Baptist and Forest Green Churches, respectively.

99. See Russell, *History of the Forest Green Church*, p. 13; also Joseph Ivimey, *History of the English Baptists*, IV (London, 1811–1830): 479.

100. See chap. 9.

4: Manors, Parishes and Dissent

1. Quoted in Kerridge, *Agrarian Problems*, p. 17.

2. Ibid.; see also above, chap. 2.

3. Ibid., pp. 142–147, Coke, Document 4; for a succinct overview of the operations of the medieval manor, see Judith M. Bennett, *Women in the Medieval English Countryside: Gender and Household in Brigstock before the Plague* (New York, 1987), pp. 18–27.

4. The manor at Avening retained jurisdiction of an earlier manor

of Nailsworth, which had been united previously to the manor of Minchinhampton-Avening; see GRO D1192/2, entitled: "A Rent Role for the Mannors of Hampton, Avening, Nailsworth & Rodborough" and *VCH Glos*, XI: 212.

5. GRO D1812/1, Ricardo Family Papers.

6. See C. E. Watson, "The Minchinhampton Custumal," p. 227; see early in chap. 1, above, for the effect on the boundaries of Nailsworth tithing.

7. Kerridge, *Agrarian Prorblems*, p. 18.

8. H. M. Cam, "Manerium Cum Hundredo: The Hundred and the Hundredal Manor," *EHR*, XLVII (1932): 353–376.

9. See chap. 1, map 1 (inset) for a map of Longtree Hundred.

10. C. E. Watson, "The Minchinhampton Custumal," p. 279.

11. Gloucester City Library, Glos. Colln. RF167.1, Papers, Horsley Manor.

12. See map 1.

13. See Nathaniel J. Hone, *The Manor and Manorial Records* (London, 1912), p. 132.

14. E. M. Carus-Wilson, "Evidences of Industrial Growth," p. 193.

15. See chap. 3.

16. See Hone, *The Manor*, p. 132.

17. See Kerridge, *Agrarian History*, p. 77 for an especially evocative description of the diverse functions of the manor court; Ann Stephens, lady of the manor of Horsley, was fined 2s. 6d. in 1796 for nonattendance at court and complied with the ruling; see GRO D547a/M14, Horsley Manor Records, Annual Lists of Suitors.

18. Ibid., Horsley Manor Records; P181/OV7/1, Horsley Census Listing, 1811; D2424/3, Shortwood Church Roll.

19. Those specifically listed as refusing to comply were fined 6d, possibly for compounding their offense of nonattendance. It is not legitimate, however, to conclude from this that those appearing in lists for other years, who were also fined 6d., were likewise noncompliers, unless the document clearly designated them as such. Several of those fined 6d. in the general list for 1803 do not appear in the separate list of noncompliers compiled in that year; this sum appears simply to have been what they could afford.

20. Excused: upper middle class = 0; lower middle class = 1; working classes = 17; they have been excluded from analysis because of the low frequencies of the first two classes; $\chi^2 = 5.799$, $df = 2$, $\chi^2 > 5.991$ at the 0.05 significance level.

21. Some non-Baptists may have been Congregationalists, which may explain why their respective patterns of attendance remained similar.

22. Gloucester City Library, Glos. Colln., RF167.1, Particulars of

Presentements, Horsley Manor; GRO D2424/3. Shortwood Baptist Church Roll.

23. Gloucester City Library, Glos. Colln., RF167.1, Presentements.

24. Ibid., Summons to Appear at Court.

25. Ibid., Charge to the Jury, 1802.

26. Pollock, *Land Laws*, p. 65.

27. Ibid.

28. Gloucester City Library, Glos. Colln., RF167.1, Charge, 1802; See J. M. W. Bean, *The Decline of English Feudalism, 1215–1540* (Manchester, 1968), pp. 17–19 for the duties of the Crown's Escheator.

29. Gloucester City Library, Glos. Colln., FR167.1, Charge, 1802.

30. See chap. 2 for the erosion of commoners' rights to Minchinhampton Common.

31. *Glos. Jnl.*, 24 July 1820.

32. Ibid.

33. Webb, *English Local Government*, I: 10. Parishes, very likely, had preconquest origins; see, for instance, Charles Pythian-Adams, *Continuity, Fields and Fission: The Making of a Midland Parish* (Leicester, 1978), especially chaps. 3–6.

34. See Webb, *English Local Government*, I: 10.

35. See Norma Landau, *The Justices of the Peace, 1679–1760* (Berkeley, Los Angeles, London, 1984); J. M. Beattie, *Crime and the Courts in England, 1660–1800* (Princeton, 1986), pp. 59–67; and Keith Wrightson, "Two Concepts of Order: Justices, Constables and Jurymen in Seventeenth Century England," in John Brewer and John Styles, eds., *An Ungovernable People: The English and Their Law in the Seventeenth and Eighteenth Centuries* (New Brunswick, N.J., 1980).

36. GRO P217 OV2/2, Minchinhampton Vestry Minutes, October 31, 1805; Wrightson, "Two Concepts of Order," p. 26.

37. For a survey of cultural attitudes toward poverty, see Gertrude Himmelfarb, *The Idea of Poverty: England in the Early Industrial Age* (New York, 1985); cf. Pat Thane, "Women and the Poor Law in Victorian and Edwardian England," *History Workshop Journal*, 6, (Autumn 1978).

38. GRO P217/VE2/1, Minchinhampton Vestry Minutes, April 14, 1800.

39. Ibid.

40. Ibid., June 1818.

41. GRO P181 VE2/1-2, Horsley Vestry Minutes, 1802–1822.

42. In table 22, $\chi^2 = 39.006$, $df = 3$, $\chi^2 > 11.241$ at the 0.01 significance level.

43. GRO P212VE2/1, Minchinhampton Vestry Minutes, April 14,

1800. Experimentation among the parochial gentry in poor law reform was quite widespread at this time; see Peter Mandler, "The Making of the New Poor Law *Redivivus*," *Past and Present*, 117 (November 1987): 417; cf. Anthony Brundage, *The Making of the New Poor Law: the Politics of Inquiry, Enactment, and Implementation, 1832–1839* (New Brunswick, N.J., 1978).

44. Ibid. Minchinhampton Vestry Minutes.

45. See Thomas Malthus, *An Essay on the Principle of Population* (London, 1982; reprint), especially chap. 5; also Himmelfarb, *Idea of Poverty*.

46. GRO P217/VE2/1; the reform, however, consisted mainly in segregating children without parents from adults so as not to expose them to "immorality."

47. *Glos. Jnl.*, 23 September 1811, "Distressing Circumstances from Fire"; for the interaction between paternalism and deference in the context of the weaver strike of 1825, see below, chap. 7.

48. GRO P217/VE2/1, Minchinhampton Vestry Minutes, December 1816; see also M. W. Flinn, "The Poor Employment Act of 1817," *Ec.HR*, 2d. ser., XIV (1961) for a good discussion of gentry paternalism at this time.

49. GRO P217/VE2/1, Minchinhampton Vestry Minutes, January 4, 1817.

50. See John Locke, *Two Treatises on Government* (London, 1963; reprint), pp. 346ff., especially the section on paternal power; also C. B. MacPherson, *The Political Theory of Possessive Individualism: Hobbes to Locke* (Oxford, 1962), pp. 269–270, who finds in Locke a coexistence between "possessive individualism" and the legitimation of traditional hierarchy. For the difference between Whig and Tory approaches to paternalism, see David Roberts, *Paternalism in Early Victorian England* (New Brunswick, N.J., 1979), pp. 31, 69–73; Linda Colley, *In Defiance of Oligarchy: The Tory Party, 1714–1760* (Cambridge, 1985), p. 148; and for further theoretical discussion, see below, chap. 7.

51. See Esther Moir, "The Gentlemen Clothiers," pp. 195–290, and chap. 1, above.

52. Gloucester City Library, Glos. Colln., M. Rudkin, *A History of Horsley* (Stroud, 1884).

53. Gloucester City Library, Glos. Colln., RV1673 (1–8, abstr. B), Horsley Tithe Papers, 1797–1802.

54. GRO D1011/P2, "Plan of an Estate in the Parish of Horsley, property of the Rt. Hon. Lord Ducie," ca. 1838.

55. *Glos. Jnl.*, 18 December 1820, 1 January 1821.

56. Ibid., 22 December 1832, Countywide Elections.

57. Ibid., 16 June 1849, County Meeting.

58. See D. C. Moore, *The Politics of Deference: A Study of Mid-Nineteenth Century British Political Systems* (New York, 1976), pp. 15, 233–235.

59. GRO GDR, Will of Joseph Browning, February 27, 1770.

60. GRO D2424/3/223, Shortwood Baptist Church Roll.

61. GRO P26 OV1/2, Avening Tithe Survey, 1784.

62. Ibid., Avening Rate Book, 1801.

63. See, for instance, *Glos. Jnl.*, 28 January and 4 February 1837, "Church Rates," for reports on the large anti-church rate meetings held at Stroud; Revd. T. F. Newman, John Heskins, and Edward Barnard, the minster and clothier deacons of Shortwood, respectively, played leading roles in the protest.

64. For Fewster's appearance in the tithe surveys of Avening and Horsley, see GRO MF 447, Avening Survey, nos. 346–348, and the Horsley Survey, tithe nos. 612–620; for his role as poor law guardian, see his letter to the editor of the *Gloucester Journal*, respecting Horsley's poor rates, which appeared on February 4, 1840; see the manuscript draft of this same letter and the record of Fewster's appointment as Overseer of the Poor for Horsley, with S. E. Francis, a Shortwood Baptist deacon, in GRO D1548, Fewster Papers, miscellany. Both appointments were made on March 29, 1821, seven years before Parliament's repeal of the Penal Laws. On Nonconformist participation in parochial government, cf. Mills, "The Nineteenth-Century Peasantry," in Smith, ed., *Land Kinship and Life-Cycle*, p. 507.

65. GRO P217/VE2/1, Minchinhampton Vestry Minutes, 1 April, 1800 and December 1816.

66. For a general account of the events, see E. Halèvy, *The Liberal Awakening, 1815–1830* (New York, 1966), pp. 80–106; for the agitation in London, see I. Prothero, *Artisans and Politics in Early Nineteenth Century London: John Gast and his Times* (Folkestone, 1979), pp. 132–159.

67. *Glos. Jnl.*, 1 January 1821, "County Meeting to Address the King"; the news item reports the remarks of both Guise and Ricardo.

68. Ibid. Ceremonial and ritual were standard techniques of social control; see E. P. Thompson, "Patrician Society, Plebeian Culture," pp. 388–390, and Craig Calhoun, *The Question of Class Struggle: Social Foundations of Popular Radicalism during the Industrial Revolution* (Chicago, 1982), pp. 109–114; for their roles in the Queen Caroline Affair, see especially Thomas W. Laqueur, "The Queen Caroline Affair:

Politics as Art in the Reign of George IV," *Journal of Modern History*, LIV (1982).

69. *Glos. Jnl.*, 22 January 1821, report of Stroud meeting to petition the House of Commons; participants sought "to procure the restoration of the Queen to all her rights... and for a reform of Parliament."

70. *Glos. Jnl.*, 15 October 1831, and 19 May 1832, reports of a large Stroud-wide meeting, led by manufacturers and at which Dissenting ministers spoke; see also GRO D3393, "A Short Sketch of the Leading Characters at the Late Stroud Meeting, 1831," a polemical caricature written by a Tory sympathizer.

71. The phrase is D. C. Moore's, in *Politics of Deference*.

72. *Glos. Jnl.*, 7 January 1832.

73. See Hyett's addresses to the Stroud and Gloucester reform meetings, *Glos. Jnl.*, 25 October 1831 and 19 March 1831, respectively; also GRO D3393, "A Short Sketch," in which Hyett's appearance at the Stroud meeting is caricatured: "The breadth of the mob is incense in his nostrils which he vainly fancied will waft him to the honours of the State."

74. *Glos. Jnl.*, 7 January 1832 and 20 September 1832: One brother was Deputy Governor of the Bank of England and the other, Vice-President of the Board of Trade; and his family "occupied a distinguished place among the merchants of London for upwards of a century."

75. Ibid., 7 January 1832

76. Ibid. Edward Barnard, Baptist deacon and clothier, nominated him.

77. *Glos. Jnl.*, 31 March 1832; Scrope's campaign slogan was: "Scrope and Trade—Forever!"

78. *Glos. Jnl.*, 24 March 1832; Ricardo vehemently attacked Scrope's want of personal ties to local society.

79. *Glos. Jnl.*, 15 December 1832.

80. See *Glos. Jnl.*, 15 December 1832; and Gloucester City Library, Hyett Collection., *Gloucestershire Tracts*, ser. C, III, 1832–1882, "The Poll at the First Election of Two Members to Serve in Parliament for the Borough of Stroud."

81. *Glos. Jnl.*, 1 June 1833, Stroud Election.

82. GRO D2219/6/10, Nailsworth Loan and Sanitary Committee, Minutes of Subscriber's Meeting, May 9, 1836, chaired by David Ricardo [II]; Gloucester City Library, Glos. Colln. R205.10, David Ricardo [II], *Emigration as a Means of Relief in the Present Distressed Condition of the Poor of this Neighborhood* (Minchinhampton, 1835).

83. See Roberts, *Paternalism*, pp. 233–235. In 1835 he was joined as

M.P. for Stroud by Lord John Russell, yet another Whig paternalist; see *Glos. Jnl.*, 16 May 1835, "Stroud-Lord John Russell" and Roberts, *Paternalism*, pp. 231–232.

84. BM Add. 44566, Gladstone Papers, f. 184–191 contain Scrope's correspondence on each of these subjects.

85. Letter to Edwin Chadwick, June 12, 1847, Chadwick Papers, University College Library, University of London.

86. See chaps. 2 and 3.

5: Birth, Death, Migration and Dissent

1. See chap 1 (early).

2. *BPP, Population*. Sessions 1831, 1842/38 (Dublin, 1968; reprint).

3. *VCH Glos.*, XI: 104–111.

4. See chap. 1 (early); 29.3 percent of Horsley villagers were wool workers, but at Avening village they represented 19.3 percent; in a difference-of-proportions test, $Z = 2.13$, Prob $> Z$ is 0.02.

5. The population for Nailsworth as a whole, in years where the census gave no figures, was estimated by the ratio of the percentage change in the combined populations of Horsley and Avening between 1841 and 1851 to the percentage change in Nailsworth's population between these same years; these latter data I derived from the census enumerators' lists. The ratio was −4.0 percent to −17.0 percent, or 0.2352941. This ratio suggests that a change of 4.0 percent in the combined parochial figures meant a 17.0 percent change in the population at Nailsworth. In this analysis, I assume this general relationship to have held for earlier decades as well. Thus, for 1831, we can use the equation 9.0 percent/Y = 0.2352941, where Y is the percentage change for Nailsworth between 1821 and 1831. In this case, $Y = +38.25\%$. The formula for the percentage change can also be expressed as $Y = X_1 - 898/898$, however, where X_1 represents Nailsworth's population for 1831 and 898 is Nailsworth's population for 1821, as recorded in the printed census lists. Thus, $X_1 - 898/898 = 0.3825$; or $X_1 = 1,241.5$. For 1811, we solve for X_2; thus, $Y = 898 - X_2/X_2 = 0.9775$, or $X_2 = 454.1$. This same procedure is then repeated for 1801. Next, it is necessary to distinguish between the population of lower Nailsworth, in Avening, and Nailsworth district, in Horsley. In 1841, the latter represented 58.6 percent of Nailsworth's entire population; in 1851, it constituted 63.1 percent. The mean percentage for these two years was 60.87 percent, and I assume this to have remained broadly similar for earlier decades. Thus, the population for Nailsworth district, in Horsley, can be estimated as 60.87 percent of the entire Nailsworth population for any given decade;

once established, the population for lower Nailsworth, in Avening, can be found by subtracting the estimated population of Nailsworth district from the total population of Nailsworth. Since the population figures for Horsley parish already included those for Nailsworth district, it was necessary only to add those for lower Nailsworth to obtain the actual decennial population levels for the Horsley-Nailsworth region. The population of Forest Green, however, was not included, despite the fact that Congregationalist births and burials will be analyzed subsequently. Forest Green Congregationalists settled throughout Nailsworth; many lived at lower Nailsworth, particularly after 1820, and made extensive use of the Shortwood Baptist burial ground in Horsley. For purposes of analysis, therefore, Congregationalists are to be counted only as members of the Horsley-Nailsworth community.

6. See chap. 6 for further discussion and depiction of the trade cycle.

7. *Glos. Jnl.*, 21 July 1827, "Loom Factories."

8. See chap. 4, n. 48.

9. *Glos. Jnl.*, 21 April 1832.

10. See Smythe, *Chronicles of Shortwood*, p. 63.

11. GRO D1548, Uncatalogued, Fewster Papers; MS. letter, A. R. Fewster to the *Gloucester Journal*, ca. 1840. Fewster, then chairman of Stroud's Poor Law Union and representative to its Board of Guardians from Horsley, wrote the letter to defend his parish's failure to cut expenditure as other parishes were doing.

12. Gloucester City Library, Glos. Colln. R205.10, David Ricardo II, *Emigration as a Means of Relief*, p. 8.

13. Ibid., p. 6.

14. Ibid., p. 9.

15. *Glos. Jnl.*, 16 September 1837.

16. Ibid., 2 December 1837.

17. Ibid., 21 March 1839.

18. Ibid., 16 September 1843; for the impact of the New Poor Law nationally, see A. Redford, *Labour Migration in England, 1800–1850* (Manchester, 1964), pp. 98ff.

19. Linear estimates of births and burials for the 1837 to 1851 period were made using a SAS forecasting program to derive the closed model figures for 1841 and 1851; for the equations and estimates, see appendixes D and E.

20. See Peter McClure, "Patterns of Migration in the Late Middle Ages: The Evidence of English Place-Name Surnames," *Ec.HR*, 2d ser., XXXII (1979); R. Finlay, *Population and Metropolis: The Demography of London, 1580–1650* (Cambridge, 1981); J. H. C. Patten, "Patterns of Migration and Movement of Labour to Three Pre-Industrial East

Anglian Towns," *Journal of Historical Geography*, II (1976); and R. S. Schofield, "Age-Specific Mobility in an Eighteenth Century Rural English Parish," *Annales de Démographie Historique* (1970, 1971).

21. See Charles Tilly, "Migration in Modern European History," in J. Sundin and E. Soderlund, eds., *Time, Space and Man: Essays in Microdemography* (Atlantic Highlands, N.J., 1977), p. 189; also Chambers, "Enclosure and the Labour Supply," pp. 320–321.

22. Ibid. Tilly and Chambers assume incorrectly that industrial takeoff was a strictly urban phenomenon associated with continous economic growth. From their perspective, a rural surplus population could have arisen only from a combination of natural increase and the stagnation of traditional craft production that had failed to absorb it as a consequence.

23. See chap. 9, especially the quotations from Baptist migrants' letters. Much migration in the preindustrial era was either circular or occurred over short distances. Michael Anderson has concluded that at Preston the Industrial Revolution failed to alter this pattern since most immigrants came from that town's surrounding hinterland; see Michael Anderson, "Urban Migration in Lancashire," *Annales de Démographie Historique* (1970, 1971), pp. 24–26 for a summary of his findings. Preston was an expanding urban center, however, quite unlike Horsley and Nailsworth.

24. See David Levine, *Family Formation in the Age of Nascent Capitalism* (New York, 1977), pp. 58–71.

25. For overviews of the issue, see H. J. Habakkuk, "The Economic History of Modern Britain," in D. V. Glass and D. E. C. Eversley, eds., *Population in History: Essays in Historical Demography* (London, 1965), pp. 147–158 and E. A. Wrigley, "The Growth of Population in Eighteenth Century England: A Conundrum Resolved," *Past and Present*, 98 (1983): 121–150.

26. For the most definitive treatment, which supports this neo-Malthusian view, see E. A. Wrigley and R. S. Schofield, *The Population History of England, 1541–1871: A Reconstruction* (Cambridge, Mass., 1981), chap. 7, especially pp. 265–269 and chap. 10, especially pp. 471–430; cf. Peter H. Lindert, "English Living Standards, Population and Wrigley-Schofield," *Explorations in Economic History*, 20 (1983).

27. For the primacy of the burial rate, see T. McKeon and R. C. Brown, "Medical Evidence Related to English Population Changes in the Eighteenth Century," in D. V. Glass and D. E. C. Eversley, eds., *Population in History* (London, 1965); also, P. E. Razell, "Population Growth and Economic Change," in E. L. Jones and G. E. Mingay, eds., *Land, Labour and Population in the Industrial Revolution: Essays Presented to J. D. Chambers* (London, 1967).

28. See J. T. Krause, "The Changing Adequacy of English Registration, 1690–1837." in Glass and Eversley, *Population in History*, pp. 382–384. Wrigley and Schofield, at the national level, used the collection of Nonconformist registers deposited in the Public Record Office to effect an aggregate analysis; they showed that during 1780–1839 Nonconformist baptisms increased significantly as a percentage of Anglican baptism, from 2.8 to 6.6 percent. See Wrigley and Schofield, *Population History of England*, p. 92.

29. This analysis was extended to 1838 in order to include two peak depression years. The forecast value rather than the observed value was used for 1837 because the latter was unusually high (as pandemonium broke loose in response to the end of parochial registration) and therefore constituted a statistical outlier. On this point, see D. V. Glass, "Population and Population Movements in England and Wales, 1700–1850," in Glass and Eversley, eds., *Population in History*, pp. 231–232. Glass has speculated that this especially high registration represented in many areas "almost the whole gap between births and baptisms" resulting from underregistration, presumably including the incidence of Dissent. The forecasted value of total births is 77 percent of the observed 1837 figure and is based on an independent calculation of Anglican and Dissenter births and baptisms; see appendix F, footnote *b*.

30. GRO P181 In/1-10, 12 and 13; for the baptismal registers of the Nailsworth Episcopal Chapel, 1794–1836, see GRO MF 443.

31. Dissenters's registers included Forest Green Congregational Birth Registers, PRO RG4/2102, 1776–1785, 1782–1798; RG4/3569, 1784–1790, 1806–1815, 1820–1836; and RG4/774, 1821–1836. Forest Green Congregational Burial Register (fragment), GRO D2595/5, 1786–1799; Shortwood Baptist Church Birth and Marriage Register, GRO D2424/10; Shortwood Baptist Church Burial Register, 1808–1871, in the custody of Mrs. B. Mills, Newmarket House, Nailsworth, Stroud, Gloucestershire; Society of Friends, Birth, Marriage and Burial Registers, GRO D1340/A1/R1-R3, 1670–1836, PRO, RG6/440, 1776–1794, RG6/63, 1796–1837.

32. Denis R. Mills, however, has used Dissenters's registers in three studies; see D. R. Mills, "An Economic, Tenurial, Social and Demographic Study of An English Peasant Village, 1780–1840," Report to the [British] Social Science Research Council (1977); idem, "Aspects of Marriage: An Example of Applied Historical Studies," draft paper submitted to the Faculty of Social Sciences, Open University (1978); idem, "The Christening Custom at Melbourne, Cambridgeshire," *Local Population Studies*, XXV (1971); cf. D. E. C. Eversley, "The Demography of the Irish Quakers, 1650–1850," in J. M. Goldstrom and L. A. Clarkson,

eds., *Irish Population, Economy and Society: Essays in Honour of the Late K. H. Connell* (Oxford, 1981) and Wrigley and Schofield, *Population History of England*, pp. 89–96.

33. Minchinhampton was the most industrial of Nailsworth's surrounding parishes; yet with the exception of Watledge hamlet, Nailsworth's local life was directed mainly toward Horsley and parts of Avening. Minchinhampton was far too large and contained a sizable market town, for its demographic movements to have faithfully represented the trends at Nailsworth. The baptismal and burial registers of Avening were not included although a portion of the Vale was formally located in it. Avening was significantly less industrial than Horsley, and it was necessary to analyze birth and burial trends in the most industrial environment obtainable. With Horsley, Nailsworth Episcopal and Dissenters' registers this could be done safely while excluding Avening registers. The same option was not available for marriages. Since Dissenters, with the exception of the Quakers, married in the parish church, they probably used Horsley and Avening with equal frequency.

34. There may have been some underregistration, in any case, because of the proximity of Rodborough and Woodchester parishes which served as a kind of "Gretna Green."

35. The ratio of Nailsworth Episcopal baptisms to Horsley parochial baptisms for the period 1794–1812 was 0.33, representing the incidence of underregistration at Horsley; for the 1775–1793 period, Horsley parochial figures were therefore multiplied by 0.33 and the result added to them. Theoretically, this is an "upper-bound" estimate, since families who baptized their children at the Nailsworth chapel could have occasionally used the parish church for this purpose. In practice, however, this estimate appears realistic, since a surfeit of child and adolescent baptisms appeared in the Nailsworth register in the first year, suggesting that the parish church at Horsley had been seriously underutilized; of the 125 baptisms recorded between October 1794, and October 1795, 100, or 80.0 percent, were delayed baptisms. Six ranged from ages one to five; thirty-two from ages six to ten; forty-six from ages eleven to fifteen; ten from ages sixteen to twenty; and six from ages twenty-one to twenty-six. My estimate of baptisms for 1775–1799 accounted for all of these, except the eldest whose birth dates occurred earlier than 1775. When redistributed by year of birth, 1780 accounted for the largest number of these baptisms at eleven; my estimate for 1780 is thirteen. Between 1786 and 1799, especially, the number of delayed Episcopal baptisms, when redistributed by year of birth, fell on average well below the 1780 level, thereby reaffirming the representativeness of my estimates; for these estimates, see appendix E. I wish to thank Roger Ransom for pointing out the need for clarification about a possible upper-bound bias in the estimates.

36. After 1813, Nailsworth Episcopal baptisms decreased from a mean of 13.1 in the previous period to a mean of 3.4.

37. See B. M. Berry and R. S. Schofield, "Age at Baptism in Pre-industrial England," *Population Studies*, XXV (1971): 453–463.

38. See Wrigley and Schofield, *Population History of England*, p. 97.

39. In "The Changing Adequacy of English Registration, 1690–1837," p. 232, J. T. Krause has suggested otherwise.

40. In *A Brief History*, pp. 21–22, Russell claims that Moffat's "scruple" resulted in some underregistration but the practice of recording both birth and baptismal dates compensated for any delayed baptism that might have occurred.

41. The *t*-values appear in the single brackets and the standardized coefficients (betas), in double brackets; the first unstandardized coefficient is significant at the 0.02 level; the second, at 0.13; the adjusted $R^2 = 0.125$. Nevertheless, some bias must exist, since I am projecting backward to an earlier period a relationship between variables established in a later one. The bias, however, is certainly minimal, since the difference in growth rates of Dissenters' births between periods, as revealed in table 27, is very marked; if the bias had been significant, the growth rates should have been similar.

42. PRO RG4/3569. Dissenters submited their registers in 1840 and again in 1857; see Wrigley and Schofield, *The Population History of England*, p. 90.

43. Congregational baptismal practice was seasonal; there were two or three occassions each autumn, spring, and summer when baptism was performed. The number of baptismal dates without a corresponding birth date recorded came to sixty-three or 9.3 percent of all Congregational births. Birth dates for these cases were estimated from the mean interval between births and baptisms of 11.1 months for the completed series.

44. BM Add. 34,571, f. 457, Letter of David Ricardo, II, to Revd. P. Bliss, May 5, 1832; BM Add. 40420, f. 180–185, Peel Papers, Papers Relating to the Dissenters' Marriage Bill, 1834–35.

45. Russell, *A Brief History*, p. 24–25; the decision to establish a new church at Lower Forest Green was made arbitrarily and engendered a schism. Those who wished to remain at the old site strenuously reaffirmed their commitment to traditional ways and seem to have carried many of the membership. However, the new church undoubtedly attracted additional adherents because of its proximity to Nailsworth.

46. See Levine, *Family Formation*, p. 66 and Wrigley and Schofield, *Population History of England*, p. 478.

47. See chap. 6, fig. 18 for the wheat series; the wheat prices used are a yearly average of a one-week-per-month sample, derived from the mar-

ket chronicle of the *Gloucester Journal*. They fell at an average rate of 1.77 percent per annum and were strongly autocorrelated (DW = 0.742, first-order auto $-R$ = 0.599); for this reason, it was necessary to detrend the series and to employ instead the resulting residuals in the regression models.

48. See appendix G for the cloth production series. Cloth output estimates for Gloucester for the 1804–1822 period were obtained from a regression of national raw wool import figures on actual cloth output from Gloucester for 1823–1838. The estimator, Cloth Output = 1500469.3 + 13882.11 (raw wool imports), was based on the combined annual figures for broadcloth, narrowcloth, and cassimeres, felt and output-not-distinguished. Coarse cloth stripes were not included because of too many missing values in its series, but the other types of cloth constituted the great bulk of Gloucester's production. The estimator was then applied to raw wool import figures for the earlier period; the series did not suffer from autocorrelation (DW = 2.030, First-order auto $-R$ = −0.053). Data were derived, respectively, from B. R. Mitchell, ed., *European Historical Statistics*, abridged ed. (New York, 1978), pp. 260–261 and Mann, *Cloth Industry in the West of England*, appendix Q, p. 339.

49. See Russell, *A Brief History*, pp. 24–25.

50. See especially the correspondence between T. F. Newman and his son, cited in chap. 9.

51. All variables were lagged by one year; this assumes that the observation in any given year will produce an effect in the following year. Conversions were lagged, despite the fact that formal conversion marked the end point of a period of candidacy that could have ranged for a year or more, since baptism was a watershed in the spiritual life of a communicant; see chap. 9, the cases of Harriet Dangerfield and Daniel Gill. I also lagged the variable total membership, since it primarily represented the older members, and we need to discover how their response to membership changes in one year affected reproduction in the following year. Variation in migration, moreover, was the most important variable explaining membership losses; see chap. 9 for further study of its patterns.

52. Multicollinearity arises because cloth output clearly has an effect on annual membership levels: Totmem = −117.743 + 0.0003759866 (clothoutput); t on b-value = 5.258, Prob > 0.0001 (where "Totmem" represents total membership). In this case, however, its existence serves to illustrate the argument better. Nor does multicollinearity necessarily affect the validity of the model as a whole; on this point, see Christopher H. Achen, *Interpreting and Using Regression* (Beverly Hills, Calif., 1982), p. 82, n. 6. The steepness of total membership growth, moreover, might suggest the problem of serial autocorrelation in a regression on

baptist births. The Durbin-Watson test, however, indicated the absence of such a problem; $DW = 2.251$, first-order autocorrelation $= -0.126$.

53. Eversley, "Demography of Irish Quakers," pp. 85–88, concludes that national differences may have overriden religious affinities in determining the demographic behavior of Irish and English Quakers, although he is careful to avoid comparison between Irish Quakers and other Irish religions and has little to say about other English Dissenters. I am arguing that religious and cultural differences within a single national setting counted more heavily than usually admitted.

54. Scholars have emphasized the centrality of improved hygiene in the labor room and the spead of innoculation against smallpox from 1765; see, respectively, T. McKeown and R. G. Brown, "Medical Evidence," p. 288 and P. E. Razzell, "Population Growth and Economic Change," p. 264. Cf. Hilary Marland, *Medicine and Society in Wakefield and Huddersfield, 1780–1870* (New York, 1987).

55. See Levine, *Family Formation*, pp. 69–71 and Wrigley and Schofield, *Population History of England*, pp. 473–476.

56. Burials in the Baptist grounds for the 1775–1807 period were estimated from a two-step regression procedure. First, a regression of member deaths listed in the church roll on members buried in the burial ground yielded the estimator Members buried $= 0.931 + 0.683$ (member deaths). A second regression of members listed in the burial register on nonmembers buried there yielded the estimator Nonmembers buried $= 28.5 + 0.302$ (members buried). Using the membership listing of member's deaths for the 1775–1799 period, it was possible to use the first equation to estimate the number of members buried in the Shortwood grounds in this earlier period. These estimated values, when used in the second equation, produced estimates of nonmembers buried there as well. The estimates of members and nonmembers buried, when added together, yielded an estimate of total burials in the Shortwood burial ground for the pre-1800 period. Circumventing this two-step approach, I tried a regression of members' deaths on total burials in the post-1800 period; it yielded an estimator, Total buried $= 29.5 + 0.914$ (member deaths), which produced virtually identical results. All *b*-value proved to be significant.

57. There was a complete series only for 1786–1799; estimates were extrapolated from the ratio of Congregational to Baptist burials, which was 0.17.

58. Shortwood Baptist Burial Register, in the possession of Mrs. B. Mills, Newmarket House, Nailsworth, Stroud, Gloucestershire.

59. See above, n. 38, and accompanying text.

60. Despite outmigration, the population remained essentially normal

in composition; analysis of the age structure in the section entitled "The Age-Sex Structure in 1841 and 1851," below, shows that despite two especially severe depressions in the 1840s, the remaining population did not grow significantly older. The rise in the burial rate in decades of population loss, in other words, represented real increases.

61. The difference did not arise because of baptismal underregistration; see above, n. 34–45 and related text for problems of underregistration. The underregistration effect of one month delayed baptism, for instance, could not have caused these lower birth rates, since the appropriate inflators have been applied; see n. 38 and accompanying text. Moreover, if the burial rates at Horsley-Nailsworth were normal by national standards, and "the number of burials unrecorded because of delayed baptism depended on the number of births," as Wrigley and Schofield have shown, then it is reasonable to conclude that crude birth rates for Horsley-Nailsworth, although noticeably lower than national rates in 1781 and 1791, were "normal," too; see Wrigley and Schofield, *Population History of England*, p. 97, note in table 4.5.

62. Infant burials have been expressed as a percentage of all births. Since I have accounted for the underregistration effects of delayed baptism due to infant mortality, I assume these to have been all live births, which is the recommended procedure; see George W. Barclay, *Techniques of Population Analysis* (New York, 1958), pp. 138ff.

63. David Levine found that urbanization and industrialization at Shepshed, a village similar to Nailsworth, led to the deterioration in health and the rise in mortality of infants and children, although not of adults; see Levine, *Family Formation*, pp. 70–72.

64. See Roger Schofield, "The Impact of Scarcity and Plenty on Population Change in England, 1541–1871," in Robert I. Rotberg and Theodore K. Rabb, eds., *Hunger and History: The Impact of Changing Food Production and Consumption Patterns on Society* (Cambridge, 1986), p. 85.

65. This finding differs from Schofield's assertion, however, that in the period of the Industrial Revolution "the response of mortality to [wheat] prices weakened to the vanishing point." See ibid., p. 88.

66. A. J. Taylor, ed., *The Standard of Living In the Industrial Revolution* (London, 1975) brings together the principal articles in the orginal debate and offers some fresh theoretical pieces; see especially the editor's introduction for an excellent overview of the issues. For additional findings related to this controversy, see chap. 6, below.

67. Gloucester City Library, Glos. Colln. R205.10, David Ricardo, II, *Emigration As a Means of Relief*, p. 7; see above, table 26 and text.

68. However, the decline for Lower and Upper Nailsworth combined,

that is, Nailsworth defined in its most restrictive sense, was 17 percent; see tables 25 and 26. Still, the hamlets of Forest Green and Winsoredge were located in Avening, rather than Horsley, and the percentage decline for Horsley and Avening combined, by comparison, is 0.7; see table 24. The figure 3.2 percent can therefore be seen as reflecting an intermediary condition, characteristic of the Vale community.

69. See Joseph Chamie, *Religion and Fertility: Arab Christian-Muslim Differentials* (Cambridge, 1981); secularization occurs when the religious-fertility differential is reduced to zero or statistical insignificance. This is a suggestion, however, that requires further exploration. I am arguing here only that the superior strength of Nonconformist community life positively affected the crude birth rate.

70. See n. 4, above.

71. See Schofield, "The Impact of Scarcity and Plenty," p. 88.

6: Capital and Labor

1. GRO D2424/12, J. Cave, *A History of the Shortwood Baptist Church*, ca. 1880, MS., p. 4.

2. See Perry, "The Gloucestershire Woollen Industry, 1100–1690."

3. Mann, *Cloth Industry*, pp. 175–176, 212.

4. Albion M. Urdank, "Economic Decline in the English Industrial Revolution: The Gloucester Wool Trade, 1800–1840," *JEH*, XLV (June 1985): 427–428.

5. See Mann, *Cloth Industry*; Mann's treatment of the business cycle for West of England broadly corresponds to the national trend; cf. Gayer et al. *The Growth and Fluctuation of the British Economy, 1790–1850*, pp. 58, 110.

6. See Derek Gregory, *Regional Transformation and Industrial Revolution: A Geography of the Yorkshire Textile Industry* (Minneapolis, 1983), pp. 36–37, 104.

7. Mann, *Cloth Industry*, p. 157.

8. For a treatment of the 1825/26 crisis, see Boyd Hilton, *Corn, Cash and Commerce: The Economic Policies of the Tory Governments, 1815–1830* (Oxford, 1977), pp. 202–231; *Glos. Jnl.*, 19 December 1825 noted the failure of two local banks: that of Messrs. Turner & Morris of Cheltenham and that of Sir Peter Pole & Co. of Stroudwater.

9. Gayer et al., *Growth and Fluctuation*, p. 173; not that the modest recovery of 1827/28 could not be sustained.

10. See Mann, *Cloth Industry*, p. 170.

11. Urdank, "Dissenting Community," appendixes 5.1 and 5.2, catalogs of bankruptcy and mill sale references.

12. *Glos. Jnl.*, 17 October 1829.

13. See Gayer, et al., *Growth*, p. 244; Mann, *Cloth Industry*, pp. 175–177; and R. C. O. Matthews, *A Study in Trade-Cycle History: Economic Fluctuations in Great Britain, 1833–1842* (Cambridge, 1954), pp. 202–209.

14. See Mann, *Cloth Industry*, p. 180.

15. *Glos. Jnl.*, 9 November 1833.

16. Ibid.

17. Ibid., 22 March, 1834.

18. Ibid., 12 July 1834.

19. Ibid., 4 October 1834.

20. Ibid., 1 November 1834.

21. Ibid., 26 December 1835. The recesssion of 1834 had lasted into the early months of 1835; see *Glos. Jnl.*, 7 February 1835, report on the state of trade.

22. Mann, *Cloth Industry*, p. 170.

23. See chap. 5.

24. *Glos, Jnl.*, 15 January 1842, letter of Samuel Smith of Uley, cited at a Bath anti-Corn Law meeting.

25. Ibid., 2 November 1839.

26. Urdank, "Economic Decline," p. 428.

27. See Anon., "History of the [Playne] Family Firm," ca. 1923, MS., for a discussion of the bankruptcy of Playne & Smith at Dunkirk Mills, Nailsworth, ca. 1875, a critical failure that marked the decline of the region. William Playne's neighboring firm at Longfords Mill was one of the few to persist into the twentieth century. By the 1920s, because of its reliance on Stroud's traditional indigo dye, the firm found itself unable to compete with German woolens, made with newer chemical dyes.

28. See Urdank, "Dissenting Community," appendixes 5.1 and 5.2, catalogs of bankruptcy and mill sale references.

29. The frequencies measuring turnover, more specifically, consist of notices of Commissions of Bankruptcy awarded, which have been calculated annually from April to March (those awarded between January and March of a calendar year probably reflected a bankruptcy occurring in the previous year); sales of mills and/or machinery belonging to a bankrupt, where no reference to a Commission was found; sales or lettings in which the advertisement specifically mentioned that the owner or occupier was declining trade, although was not a bankrupt; and the sale or letting of all other mills or related property, where the reasons have not been indicated.

30. Mann, *Cloth Industry*, pp. 132–133.

31. *BPP*, 24 (1840): 448: "The master weaver," noted a contemporary observer, "rented large premises on which were buildings to hold the looms of his journeymen."

32. *Glos. Jnl.*, 20 January 1812, Sale of Stonehouse Mills; the premises, however, were occupied by several "undertenants" and not by one firm, which accounts for the especially large capacity of the mill in this early period.

33. Ibid., 21 November 1829.

34. Ibid., 26 December 1829.

35. Ibid., 29 April 1837.

36. Ibid., 1 April 1837. Sale of Machinery.

37. Ibid., 20 March 1820.

38. Ibid., 26 April 1813.

39. Ibid., 5 January 1805, 27 October 1804, 17 March 1806.

40. Ibid., 18 January 1808.

41. See Richard L. Hills, *Power in the Industrial Revolution* (New York, 1970), p. 92; Mann, *Cloth Industry*, p. 131; *Glos, Jnl.*, 19 January 1805, 27 October 1804, 17 March 1806.

42. *BPP. Sessional Papers*, 24 (1840): 426.

43. References from which these data have been drawn appear in Urdank, "Dissenting Community," appendixes 5.1 and 5.2.

44. The sales and lettings of workshops, because of their small frequencies, have been added to the category of machinery and stock without reference to a mill, which here represents the small clothier and to whom they were clearly related. Similarly, all mill sales—with and without machinery—have been grouped into one category. Sales of machinery at a mill (without the corresponding sale of the mill) and lettings of mills have been left to stand separately. The former indicated the turnover of lessees, who tended to be intermediary clothiers. Mill sales often indicated the turnover of owner and occupiers, but sometimes a mill was sold by its owner after the expiration of a tenant's lease or retirement from trade.

45. Although the text refers to the differences between observed and expected values, table 43 presents only the observed values gathered from the *Gloucester Journal*; see Roderick Floud, *An Introduction to Quantitative Methods for Historians* (Princeton, 1973) pp. 131–133 for the method of calculating expected values.

46. Mules had a minimum of 100 spindles, and jennies were found to have had a maximum of 80 spindles, although 40- to 60-spindle jennies were most common in sales advertisements.

47. *Glos. Jnl.*, 9 September 1805; Mann, *Cloth Industry*, pp. 129,

138, 141, 150, gives the following dates for the introduction of these types of machines in the West of England: scribbling and carding engines (1792); the gig mill for finishing (1793); and shearing frames, circa 1800.

48. *Glos. Jnl.*, 20 March 1824.

49. Ibid., 20 June 1829.

50. Ibid., 2 July 1836.

51. Ibid., 14 July 1832.

52. See Urdank, "Economic Decline," p. 429.

53. *Glos. Jnl.*, 21 July 1813.

54. Ibid., 4 October 1828.

55. Ibid., 6 March 1820.

56. Ibid., 16 June 1832.

57. Ibid., 17 January 1835.

58. Anon., "History of the [Playne] Family Firm."

59. Ibid.

60. PRO B3/629, Bankruptcy Examination of Edward J. Blackwell, Woolen Manfacturer, Nailsworth; Commission awarded July 14, 1829. Blackwell had occupied Egypt Mill.

61. *Glos. Jnl.*, 14 March 1829, sale by Nathaniel Wathen of his machinery at Hope Mills.

62. A possible exception was Stonehouse Mills, near Stroud, which in 1812 contained weaving shops, and was capable of employing between £20,000 and £60,000 of capital (*Glos. Jnl.*, 14 March 1812). When the machinery was sold in 1814, it included twenty-six 80-spindle jennies, ten 80-spindle reels, thirteen new shearing frames, and several narrow-looms and broadlooms (*Glos. Jnl.*, 3 January 1814). These instruments clearly belonged to the principal lessee and his undertenants; a mill of such capacity could not be run at this early date, except with the re-sources of several intermediary firms. Such a pattern of mill occupation approximated the one prevailing in the Manchester cotton industry; see R. Lloyd-Jones and A. A. LeRoux, "The Size of Firms in the Cotton Industry: Manchester, 1815–1841," *Ec.HR.*, 2d ser., XXXIII (February 1980): 73.

63. Urdank, "Economic Decline," p. 429.

64. Gloucester had actually kept pace with Yorkshire in powerlooms by 1838; thereafter, Gloucester clothiers who remained in businesss adopted them even more widely. In aggregate, however, Gloucester continued to lag behind Yorkshire, although not always on a per capita basis; in 1861 Gloucester regained a per capita parity but was rapidly outpaced by Yorkshire from 1867; see Mann, *Cloth Industry*, p. 188 and the tables on p. 220.

65. *Glos. Jnl.*, 22 September 1815.

66. See Mann, *Cloth Industry*, pp. 127, 188.

67. *Glos. Jnl.*, 4 October 1828, at Dyehouse Mills; ibid., 20 September 1828, Nathaniel Driver's stock at Peghouse near Stroud.

68. Stonehouse Mills, cited above, n. 55, was an exception.

69. *Glos. Jnl.*, 27 April 1818 and 6 March 1820, respectively.

70. Ibid., 9 June 1827, 2 August 1828, and 6 March 1830, respectively.

71. Ibid., 21 July 1827, "Loom Factories," a notice placed by the executive committee of the weavers' union.

72. Mann, *Cloth Industry*, p. 163, notes that the building of new factories and the extension of old ones "went on vigorously."

73. Anon., "History of the [Playne] Family Firm." Between 1811 and 1814, capital increased from £3,000 to £14,000, following the transfer of management from Martha Playne to her two sons, William and Peter. The firm was said to have prospered at the same rate of growth until 1824.

74. PRO B3/629, Bankruptcy Examination of Edward J. Blackwell, Woolen Manufacturer. At his bankruptcy examination, Blackwell, Egypt Mill's previous tenant, indicated that two pair of stocks, one gig mill, and four waterwheels had been constructed by the owner, Samuel Webb, while "the other part has since been erected at the joint expense of Mr. Webb and myself."

75. *Glos. Jnl.*, 14 July 1829.

76. See Esther Moir, "Marling and Evans, King's Stanley and Ebley Mills," *Textile History*, I (1971).

77. Urdank, "Economic Decline," p. 428, n. 9.

78. Gregory, *Regional Transformation*, pp. 72–74.

79. Mann, *Cloth Industry*, p. 190; ibid., p. 74.

80. Gregory, *Regional Transformation*, pp. 200–201; in the East Riding, he notes, the stream only "trickled." Steam engines began to substitute for water power in the West Riding much later: by the 1820s and then largely in response to conditions of overcrowding on rural streams; see D. T. Jenkins, *The West Riding Wool Textile Industry, 1770–1835: A Study of Fixed Capital Formation* (Edington, 1975), p. 47.

81. Ibid., Gregory, p. 203; ibid., Jenkins, pp. 76–77.

82. *BPP*, XLII (1839): 1–799, "Accounts and Papers."

83. See Mann, *Cloth Industry*, p. 186 and Gregory, *Regional Transformation*, p. 72.

84. Ibid.; Mann, p. 190. The earliest reference to a steam mill in Gloucester, in fact, occurred in 1818 in the sale of J. C. Hamblin's property. An earlier reference for the West Country occurred in 1815 in the sale of a 30-horsepower Boulton & Watt at Radstock, Somerset, but

perhaps the earliest took place at Chippenham, Wiltshire, where a factory, four stories high with rooms fifty feet by thirty-two feet, and housing six to ten machines, was said to "be driven by either steam or water." See *Glos. Jnl.*, 2 April 1804, 22 May 1815, and 12 November 1818; see also Albion M. Urdank, "Custom, Conflict and Traditional Authority in the Gloucester Weaver Strike of 1825," *Journal of British Studies* 25, (April 1986): 195, n. 7.

85. For further discussion, see below.

86. See table 42.

87. See Robert B. Gordon, "Cost and Use of Water Power during Industrialization in New England and Great Britain: A Geological Interpretation," *Ec.HR*, 2d ser., XXXVI (May 1983).

88. See Stanley Chapman, "The Cost of Power in the Industrial Revolution in Britain: The Case of the Textile Industry," *Midland History*, I (Spring 1971): 6–8, 12–13.

89. See Tann, "Employment of Power" and Gordon, "The Cost and Use of Water Power."

90. See Chapman, "The Cost of Power," pp. 8–11, especially the examples of Thackery and Arkwright.

91. Urdank, "Economic Decline," p. 429, n. 14.

92. Ibid., n. 13; Chapman, "The Cost of Power."

93. Anon., "History of the [Playne] Family Firm": "The new north mill [at Dunkirk Mills]," complained a younger member of the Playne family "has never been fully used. It is absolutely necessary that the heavy, fast-running looms should. . . be placed on the ground floor, and driven by steam at a perfectly regular speed and not by the irregular and varying water power."

94. See Urdank, "Economic Decline," pp. 430–433. Path analysis, a form of regression modeling, was used to distinguish direct and indirect causal flows and to compare the relative efficiency of large- and small-engine mills. Steam powered mills were selected from the catalog of 260 *Gloucester Journal* references in Urdank, "Dissenting Community," appendix 5.2. Table 46 (this chapter) contains all mills for which sales notices specifically indicated the amount of steam horsepower employed, and these numbered thirty-four. Twelve other sales notices referred to steam engines but gave no horsepower data and thus could not be included. The appearance of these data, moreover, occurs randomly throughout these notices. If we exclude the first 147 notices, which appeared prior to the advent of the earliest known steam engine in Gloucester (e.g., November 1818), the sample of thirty-four then represents 30.08 percent of the remaining sales notices, while the upper-bound

sample of forty-six represents 40.7 percent. A sample of thirty-four, in any case, is not unduly small, despite the fact that the true universe of steam-powered mills remains unknown. Adopting a confidence interval of 90 percent, with an error range of plus or minus 3.5 horsepower, and using the standard deviation of 15.245 of the thirty-four steam engines in our sample, we obtain an expected sample size of 34.066. See Blalock, *Social Statistics*, pp. 213–215 for the method of estimating sample sizes when the standard error of the population is unknown. Blalock indicates that the real difficulty in making such estimations comes when estimating the standard error of the population; according to him, we have to rely on a "best guess" or a pilot study if practicable. In our case, the standard deviation of the thirty-four mills is better than a "best guess" and at least as good as a pilot study.

95. A 10-horsepower engine, used to pump water for waterwheels, would not produce 10 horsepower in the machinery, according to a contemporary expert; to produce 10 horsepower of energy would require instead 16 to 20 horsepower. See R. L. Hills and A. J. Pacey, "The Measurement of Power in Early Steam-driven Textile Mills," *Technology and Culture*, XIII, (January 1972): 31.

96. *BPP*, XXIV (1840): 362; W. A. Miles, the Assistant Commissioner for Gloucester, sent to investigate the condition of handloom weavers, pointed to the concentration of capital and the growth in productive capacity of the remaining mills.

97. Ibid., p. 435.

98. Ibid., p. 434.

99. See above, n. 93; by 1870, the date of the quotation cited, the "fast-running [power]looms," referred to by the younger Playne, had clearly replaced the handloom weavers.

100. *BPP*, XXIV (1840): 386–387: W. A. Miles calculated that of the 3,000 weavers remaining in Gloucester in 1839, only 2,666 were needed to meet current production levels, leaving a surplus of 334, or 16 percent of an outdoor weaver population of 2,089.

101. See n. 127, 130, 132 and text, for a comparison of the number of spindles, and below for the mule's impact on labor.

102. J. W. Scott and L. A. Tilly, "Women's Work and the Family in nineteenth Century Europe," *Comparative Studies in Society and History*, XVII (1975): 46.

103. GRO, P181/OV7/1. Horsley Parish Census Enumerator's List, ca. 1811.

104. "There were many master weavers who were rather respectable men and who kept four to six looms in their houses if they had room,"

Mann quotes one contemporary source. "They kept journeymen and women and gave the journeyfolk about two-thirds the price of the work." Quoted in Mann, *Cloth Industry*, pp. 229–230.

105. *Glos. Jnl.*, 24 February 1817; see also *Glos. Jnl.*, 20 August 1836, sale of two tenements at Wotton with a four-loom weaving shed attached to one of them.

106. Craftsmen, such as carpenters, masons, and blacksmiths, have been grouped separately from weavers; and both categories have been distinguished from laborers. The enumerator's list did not distinguish between agricultural laborers and day laborers employed in the cloth trade.

107. Testing the difference in proportions between craftsmen-landlords and weaver-landlords, $Z = 1.200$, Prob $Z > 1.200 = 0.12$; the probability, in other words, of obtaining a Z value greater than or equal to 1.2 is 88.0 percent, which falls below the usual 0.05 level, suggesting no difference, but is an acceptably high level of significance to suggest the beginning of erosion of the status of master weaver.

108. Nor was there a significant difference in mean household size between any occupational group. By this date, journeymen and apprentices were unlikely to have lived in the master's house, especially if the master rented his work premises.

109. This point is worth emphasizing because we have become accustomed erroneously to regard country weavers as mere cottagers. See, for instance, Hans Medick, "The Proto-industrial Family Economy: The Structural Function of Household and Family During the Transition From Peasant Society to Industrial Capitalism," *Social History*, I (1976): 291–315; Buchanan Sharp, *In Contempt of All Authority: Rural Artisans and Riot in the West of England, 1588–1660* (Berkeley, Los Angeles, London, 1980) and Charles Tilly, *As Sociology Meets History* (New York, 1981).

110. See Mann, *Cloth Industry*, pp. 143–149 for an account of early weaver resistance to repeal of the apprenticeship statutes.

111. See the debates among the weavers in the *Glos. Jnl.*, 21 March, 4 and 11 April 1829.

112. GRO, P181/OV7/1, Horsley Census List, ca. 1811; PRO Home Office 107/362, 1841 census enumerators' lists.

113. See Scott and Tilly, "Women's Work," p. 52, quoting Neil Smelser, *Social Change in the Industrial Revolution: An Application of Theory to the British Cotton Industry* (Chicago, 1959), p. 188.

114. Gloucester City Library, The Hyett Collection, *Gloucestershire Tracts*, ser. C, III, 1832–1882, Speech on the Factories Regulation Bill, 1833.

115. *Glos. Jnl.*, 21 July 1827, "Loom Factories."

116. Functional differentiation of occupations accompanied the new pattern of labor recruitment; see Neil Smelser, *Social Change in the Industrial Revolution*; for a different finding, cf. Patrick Joyce, *Work, Society and Politics: The Culture of the Factory in Later Victorian England* (New Brunswick, N.J., 1981), pp. 53ff., who argues for the persistence of work and family ties in the factory after 1840. For a summary of research on this issue, see E. H. Pleck, "Two Worlds in One: Work and Family," *Journal of Social History*, X (1976).

117. *BPP*, XXIV (1840): 445–449.

118. See Scott and Tilly, "Women's Work," pp. 60–61, the case of Francesca F.

119. Clothworkers included quillers, burlers, reelers, pickers, and warpers.

120. *BPP*, XXIV (1840): 400–401, evidence given by Peter Playne. Male factory weavers earned 11s. per week, and male outdoor weavers earned $8\frac{1}{2}$s.

121. This was especially true in the case of spinning; see Joyce, *Work, Society and Politics*, p. 55 for the Lancashire cotton trade.

122. *BPP.*, XXIV (1840): 374.

123. See Ivy Pinchbeck, *Women Workers and the Industrial Revolution, 1750–1850* (New York, 1969), pp. 121, 126, 162–166.

124. In a difference-of-proportions test, $Z = 6.33$, significant at 0.00 probability.

125. The 1841 census for Horsley parish listed thirty-eight women and sixty-seven men as weavers.

126. *BPP*, XXIV (1840): 377; the proportion was 184 in 694, or 26.5 percent; $Z = 2.068$, significant at the 0.02 level.

127. H. Catling, "The Evolution of Spinning," in J. G. Jenkins, ed., *The Wool Textile Industry in Great Britain* (London, 1972), p. 110.

128. GRO, P181/OV7/1, MS. Census List, Horsley Parish.

129. *BPP*, XXIV (1840): 337.

130. Catling, "The Evolution of Spinning," p. 110.

131. The 1841 census for Horsley listed six males and fourteen females as spinners.

132. Catling, "The Evolution of Spinning," p. 110.

133. Mann, *Cloth Industry*, pp. 140, 229. Although the fly shuttle shortened the average weaving time, some weavers still took longer than on the double loom.

134. Ibid., see P. Ellis, "The Techniques of Weaving," in Jenkins, ed., *Wool Textile Industry*, pp. 125–127 for a careful description of hand-looms.

135. See below, chap. 7, the 1825 weaver strike.

136. Ibid.

137. *Glos. Jnl.*, 20 June 1825.

138. Synchronization was the crucial variable. See E. P. Thompson, "Time, Work-Discipline and Industrial Capitalism," *Past and Present*, 38 (1967): 76–86; cf. David Landes, *Revolution in Time: Clocks and the Making of the Modern World* (Cambridge, Mass., 1983).

139. *BPP*, XXIV (1840): 389; the combined productivity of males and females was 1,974 yards per weaver per annum. The male rate was 52.8 percent of the total, while the female rate was 47.1 percent. Male weavers numbered 655, and female weavers numbered 167. In a difference-of-proportions test, $Z = 2.533$, significant at the 0.005 probability level.

140. Quoted by Miles, in *BPP*, XXIV (1840): 389.

141. Warping, for instance, required "care and art," and warpers had to keep pace with the weaver; piecers, similarly, followed the pace set by the spinner. Since warping and piecing were essentially female occupations, women workers tended to imbibe factory discipline indirectly, through structural dependence on male work rhythms.

142. *BPP*, XXIV (1840): 389.

143. Mann, *Cloth Industry*, pp. 106–107.

144. Master weavers tried less sucessfully to expedite the journeyman's work; see ibid., pp. 229–230 and below, Thomas Cole's comments on journeymen weavers.

145. John Foster, *Class Struggles and the Industrial Revolution: Early Industrial Capitalism in Three English Towns* (London, 1977), pp. 91–93, cites the impact of disease, which was, however, more the consequence of urbanization. The same factory inspectors, Horner and Woolrich, who condemned northern cotton manufacturers, gave Gloucester factories a favorable report; see Mann, *Cloth Industry*, p. 247.

146. *BPP*, XXIV (1840): 389.

147. Ibid., p. 415.

148. See table 51 for a survey of weavers' attitudes toward the factory.

149. *BPP*, XXIV (1840): 415.

150. On the symbiosis between deference and empathy, see chap. 7, section on the 1825 weaver strike.

151. Other master weavers reacted competitively. Their wish to retain control over their craft produced considerable militancy among them, as we shall see. However, many also wished to become clothiers and regarded the factory system as a threat to this ambition.

152. GRO D2424/3/658, Shortwood Baptist Church Roll, baptized September 28, 1806 and excluded October 9, 1834. His brother and father, both named Jonathan Cole, were weavers and Baptists: D2424/3/ 385 and 763.

153. See Mann, *Cloth Industry*, p. 241, on the strike at Playne's in 1834.

154. See Chap. 7.

155. *BPP*, XXIV (1840): 415.

156. See tables 52 to 54.

157. *BPP*, XXIV (1840): 442: Cole returned to outdoor work, this time as a journeyman weaver, but still could not find enough employment and had to resort to potato digging, for which he was paid 4d. per bag; his wages were paid in potatoes instead of money, that is, in truck.

158. Ibid., pp. 417–419. The master weaver deducted from the journeyman's gross earnings 3d. for materials and 2d. for fetching and carrying back the work. Miles, the parliamentary commissioner, also reduced the gross earnings of the master weaver by 16 percent, in order to adjust for the effect of surplus labor.

159. See chap. 7, the 1825 weaver strike.

160. "Colts" were youths who were only partially initiated into the trade and served master weavers as assistants. The surplus of colts made it easier for clothiers to establish loom factories, since colts usually welcomed the chance to learn all of the "mysteries" of the trade. See *Glos. Jnl.*, 21 March 1829, a weaver's rebuttal against the claims made by the Association of [Master] Weavers.

161. See *BPP*, XXIV (1840): 442–446, 439 for a summary of Miles's other findings.

162. Figure 18 is based on a sample of weekly prices drawn from the *Gloucester Journal*; one week per month was selected, and a yearly average based on twelve months was computed and plotted in two time series, the regressions of which are also given. For treatments of the agricultural depression, see Hilton, *Corn, Cash and Commerce*, chaps. III–V, and Pamela Horns, *The Rural World: Social Change in the English Countryside, 1780–1850* (London, 1980), pp. 71–83.

163. *BPP*, XXIV (1840): 421, budget of James Risby; rent, at 9 percent of the total budget, was the next largest item. Wheat prices tended to correlate with the movement of prices of other consumables; see R. D. Lee, "Short-Term Variations: Vital Rates, Prices and Weather," in Wrigley and Schofield, *Population History of England*, p. 353.

164. This finding partly affirms the view advanced by Deane and Cole that the trend in living standards rose at least until 1825, although their optimism regarding the period of the Napoleonic wars seems question-

able; see P. Deane and W. A. Cole, *British Economic Growth, 1688–1959: Trends and Structure* (Cambridge, 1962), p. 27, and below, n. 169. The most recent restatement of the optimists' case dates the ostensible rise in living standards only from 1820; see Peter Lindert and Jeffrey G. Williamson, "English Workers' Living Standards: a New Look," *Ec.HR*, 2d ser., XXXVI (1983); however, see a careful critique and downward revision of their estimates in N. F. R. Crafts, *British Economic Growth during the Industrial Revolution* (Oxford, 1985), p. 101.

165. *BPP*, XXIV (1840): 459, 458ff. for all other comments related to truck unless otherwise indicated. Littleton, an M.P. from Straffordshire, reported that the difference was between 20 and 25 percent; see *Glos. Jnl.*, 24 April 1830.

166. Ibid.; *Glos. Jnl.*, 5 May 1832: Prosecutions were made under the Act of first and second William IV, clause 37; for weavers debating the origin of truck, see *Glos. Jnl.*, 21 March and 4 and 11 April 1829.

167. *BPP*, XXIV (1840): 459; evidence of Mr. Ross, a Woodchester shopkeeper.

168. See Taylor, ed., *Standard of Living*, p. xlv.

169. The point of controversy is whether wage levels could have risen at all during the war. Deane and Cole have implied that both nominal and real wages had increased between 1795 and 1816; see ibid., p. xliii. Crafts has shown that their real wage estimates for 1780–1820 were very nearly correct, while those of Phelps-Brown and Hopkins and Lindert and Williamson were far too low; see Crafts, *British Economic Growth*, p. 103, table 5.5.

170. Mann, *Cloth Industry*, pp. 250–251.

171. See Thompson, *Making of the English Working Class*, p. 203 and R. M. Hartwell and S. Engerman, "Models of Immiseration: The Theoretical Basis of Pessimism," in Taylor, ed., *The Standard of Living*, pp. 190–191.

172. See Wrigley, "The Process of Modernization."

7: Class Formation and Social Stability

1. Detailed examination of the 1825 strike serves partly for this reason as a surrogate for analysis of the type of conflict represented by these earlier struggles. We find in them the same deferential appeal to authority, the same call for standardizing pay rates, the same paternalism of the Justices of the Peace, and even the same connivance in the weavers' activities by figures of authority, following the outbreak of genuine conflict; for a glimpse of such connivance, which lay at the heart of the argument presented below, see J. L. and B. Hammond, *The Skilled*

Labourer, 1760–1832 (London, 1927), p. 158. However, see also Adrian J. Randall, "Labour and the Industrial Revolution in the West of England Woollen Industry" (Univ. Birmingham, Ph.D. dissertation, 1979), for a recent study of these earlier strikes, *albeit* from a Thompsonian perspective; cf. n. 44, below, and the accompanying text.

2. See Hammond, *Skilled Labourer*, pp. 156ff.; Mann, *Cloth Industry*, pp. 167–168, 235–236; and Randall, "Labour and the Industrial Revolution," chap. 3.

3. E. P. Thompson has offered a nominalist definition of class, based largely on the mentalité of the subject and the broader category of culture to which it gave rise. For his now classic study, see Thompson, *Making of the English Working Class*; idem, "Eighteenth Century English Society: Class Struggle without Class," *Social History*, III (1978); and idem, "Patrician Society, Plebeian Culture," *Journal of Social History*, VII (1974). See, also Harold Perkin, *The Origins of Modern English Society, 1780–1880* (London, 1969), especially chap. VI, and Trygve Tholfsen, *Working Class Radicalism in Mid-Victorian England* (New York, 1977), especially chaps. 2–4. But cf. Robert Glen, *Urban Workers in the Early Industrial Revolution* (London, 1984).

4. *BPP, Sessional Papers*, 24 (1840): 371, 451. The "chain" and "abb" are Gloucester terms for warp and weft, respectively; see Mann, *Cloth Industry*, p. 292. The length of the chain was measured by the number of threads, which were counted by the "hundred"; the hundred was a customary measure consisting of 190 threads. Two smaller customary measures were also used: One "beer" equaled thirty-eight threads, five beers equaled a hundred, and eighty beers equaled a 16-hundred chain; one "ell" equaled 84.4 threads, and thirty-six ells equaled a 16-hundred chain.

5. *Glos. Jnl.*, 22 November 1824.

6. Ibid.

7. Ibid., 20 June 1825.

8. While the absolute length of the chain increased, the number of threads per inch remained constant at 27.4. The number of shoots in the abb increased with the progressive rise in the length of the chain. If parity had been maintained, two shoots of abb per thread of chain would have been required at the 20-hundred chain level; instead we find an estimated 2.5 shoots of abb per thread.

9. *BPP, Sessional Papers*, 24 (1840): 451, 454.

10. Ibid., Samuel Marling of Ham Mills, for example, paid about of 27.5 percent below the weavers' reduced scale.

11. Based on an averaged of 40.5 ells per piece, covering the new range of 16- to 20-hundred length chains, an increase of 1d. per ell based

on the weavers' scale amounted to only 3s. 4½d. per piece or 1s. ¼d. per week when divided over a three-week period, the average time for completion of a piece. This was not sufficient to give master weavers the parity they claimed they needed with other skilled clothworkers.

12. *BPP, Sessional Papers*, 24 (1840): 452; *Glos. Jnl.*, 22 November 1824; the weavers' petition stated that the master weaver's profit per piece came to 4s. 3d., or 8.8 percent of the total price paid by the clothier, in what appears to have been a considerable underestimation.

13. *BPP, Sessional Papers*, 24 (1840): 386.

14. Ibid., Wage Series, 1808–1838, p. 374; PRO Home Office 40/18/169–170, Letter to Hobhouse, 4 May 1825.

15. *BPP, Sessional Papers*, 24 (1840): 452; *Glos. Jnl.*, 20 June 1825, letter from a journeyman weaver. Master weavers probably earned about 24s. per week, if 17s. 6d. was the average for all weavers and 11s. the average for journeymen.

16. *Glos. Jnl.*, 22 November 1824.

17. See table 57; the observations are three-month moving averages of one-week-per-month samples, drawn from the market chronicle of the *Gloucester Journal*. Growth rates were calculated from the first and last trend values of the regression lines effected on the basis of the sample of weekly prices. Wheat prices, furthermore, correlated with the movement of prices of other consumables; see R. D. Lee, "Short-Term Variation: Vital Rates, Prices and Weather," in Wrigley and Schofield, *Population History of England*, p. 357. John Bohstedt has shown that the correlation between prices and popular disturbances, while statistically significant, was weak; see John Bohstedt, *Riots and Community Politics in England and Wales, 1790–1810* (Cambridge, Mass., 1983), pp. 18–21. Master weavers, unlike their journeymen, would appear to have had different reasons for striking.

18. See *BPP, Sessional Papers*, 24 (1840): 421, budget of James Risby; also *Glos. Jnl.*, 20 June 1825, letter from a journeyman weaver, which suggests that journeymen were peculiarly sensitive to short-term variations in prices. In complaining about his low wages (10s. to 12s. per week), the writer gives their amount as a three-year average. By comparison, the nominal weekly wages of ordinary Gloucester laborers amounted to 9s. 3d. in 1824; see Gregory, *Regional Transformation*, p. 76.

19. *BPP, Sessional Papers*, 24 (1840): 451–452.

20. This finding affirms Eric Hobsbawm's original observation regarding the influence of custom on wages; see E. J. Hobsbawm, "Custom, Wages and Work-Load in Ninetenth Century Industry," in Asa

Briggs and John Saville, eds., *Essays in Labour History in Memory of G. D. H. Cole*, (London, 1960), pp. 114–115.

21. See PRO B3, Court of Bankruptcy Registers, in which examples of employees receiving promissory notes from employers for services rendered abound; see also *Glos. Jnl.*, 21 March, 4 April, and 11 April 1829, in which master weavers complained about the practice.

22. *BPP, Sessional Papers*, 24 (1840): 386. "The journeyman is always in so depressed a state," noted one contemporary, "that the moment the master weaver employs him he is obliged to give him his daily food; and hence, in a great degree, the origin of truck."

23. Ibid.

24. E. P. Thompson, "Patrician Society," p. 397.

25. See Joyce, *Work, Society and Politics*; also Howard Newby, "The Deferential Dialectic," *Comparative Studies in Society and History*, XV (1975); Moore, *The Politics of Deference*; and Roberts, *Paternalism in Early Victorian England*.

26. See Joyce, *Work, Society and Politics*, pp. 144, 148–149, 151–152, and passim.

27. Ibid., p. 95.

28. Newby, "Deferential Dialectic," p. 149; for studies of the limits of deference, see J. R. Fisher, "The Limits of Deference: Agricultural Communities in a Mid-Nineteenth Century Election Campaign," *Journal of British Studies*, XXI (1981) and Frank O'Gorman, "Electoral Deference in Unreformed England," *Journal of Modern History* 56 (1984).

29. In doing so, they have emphasized the persistence of face-to-face relations and have thereby undermined the Durkheimian notion that urban-industrial life was necessarily governed by a pervasive anomie. See Joyce, *Work, Society and Politics*, pp. 93–94 and Newby, "Deferential Dialectic," pp. 156–157.

30. Wood-pasture regions usually gave rise to scattered rather than nucleated settlements because of their hilly terrain and woodlands; see chap. 1, n. 2.

31. Some have argued that wood-pasture settlements weakened social control from the manor house and parish church and induced an antagonistic relationship between the Establishment and the lower classes; see above, chap. 2, n. 2.

32. See the remarks by W. H. Hyett, M.P. for Stroud, quoted above, chap. 6, n. 114; also Joyce, *Work, Society and Politics*, pp. 111–116.

33. Quoted in Mann, *Cloth Industry*, p. 247; Horner and Woolrich, the factory inspectors who rendered such harsh judgments of the Yorkshire clothiers, evidently concurred.

34. *BPP, Sessional Papers*, 24 (1840): 451. He did so, ostensibly, to compensate for the increase in the size of the chain; see above.

35. Ibid., p. 454.

36. See Joyce, *Work, Society and Politics*, pp. 93–94; also Newby, "Deferential Dialectic," pp. 150–151.

37. PRO Home Office 40/18/185–186, May 8, 1825.

38. Uley Mills was sold as part of Sheppard's landed estate, described in the sales advertisement as "all that manor or lordship of Woodman-scote, or otherwise Woodmanscote with Nibley, within the parish of Dursley"; *Glos. Jnl.*, 29 April 1837.

39. See Moir, "Gentlemen Clothiers"; for other gentlemen-clothier families, see above, chap. 1.

40. This phrase belongs to Howard Newby; see Newby, "Deferential Dialectic," pp. 152–155.

41. See Landau, *Justices of the Peace*, chap. 6, especially pp. 175 and 193; for instances of J.P. paternalism, see Eric Hobsbawm, "Machine Breakers," in *Labouring Men* (London, 1964), p. 16; Gregory, *Regional Transformation*, pp. 166–184; and Frank Munger, "Contentious Gatherings in Lancashire, England, 1750–1830," in Louise A. and Charles Tilly, eds., *Class Conflict and Collective Action* (Beverly Hills, Calif., 1981), pp. 75–76.

42. See chaps. 2 and 4 for the social integration of the governing class.

43. See Joyce, *Work, Society and Politics*, pp. 93–94 and Newby, "Deferential Dialectic," pp. 150–151.

44. For a different view, see Thompson, "Moral Economy of the English Crowd" and George Rudé, "The Pre-industrial Crowd," in G. Rude, *Paris and London in the Eighteenth Century* (New York, 1973). Thompson emphasizes the autonomy of the crowd even where he glimpses obliquely the license accorded it by figures of authority; Rudé takes the same view even in cases where such figures assume the leadership of the crowd directly. For a recent defense of Thompson, see Andrew Charlesworth and Adrian J. Randall, "Comment: Morals, Markets and the English Crowd in 1766," *Past and Present*, 114 (February 1987). John Bohstedt has more convincingly modified Thompson's approach, however, by describing crowd action as only partly auton-omous and by according the "vertical, reciprocal relationships between the plebs and the powerful" a central place in its dynamics; see Bohstedt, *Riots and Community Politics*, p. 203. See also David Rollison, "Prop-erty, Ideology and Popular Culture in a Gloucestershire Village, 1660–1740," *Past and Present*, 93 (1981), a compelling reconstruction of a *charivari*. Rollison depicts the conflict of interests between a capitalist farmer and his rentier landlord, with the local community mobilized in

support of the former. Rollison's anthropological characterization of the farmer as a "Big Man" is another way of describing a structure of paternalism and deference.

45. See John Walsh, "Methodism and the Mob in the Eighteenth Century," in G. J. Cumming and Derek Baker, eds., *Popular Belief and Practices: Studies in Church History,* III (Oxford, 1972); Walter Shelton, *English Hunger and Industrial Disorders: A Study of Social Conflict during the First Decade of George III's Reign* (Toronto, 1973); and M. E. James, "Obedience and Dissent in Henrician England: The Lincolnshire Rebellion, 1536," *Past and Present,* 48 (1970). These studies place the initiative for crowd action more directly in the hands of the governing class than do Bohstedt and Rollison (cited above) and thereby deprive the crowd of an even greater measure of autonomy.

46. James, "Obedience and Dissent," p. 7.

47. See this chapter, subsections entitled "First stage" (of the 1825 strike), especially comments by William Playne, cited in n. 61, and "Third Stage," n. 82.

48. *Glos. Jnl.* 13 June 1825.

49. PRO Home Office 40/18/190–191, May, 10, 1825.

50. Quoted in Mann, *Cloth Industry,* p. 237; see also Eric Hobsbawm, "Machine Breakers," in *Labouring Men,* pp. 14–15 for a similar assessment of the role of clothiers in the genesis of Luddism.

51. See subsection below on third phase of the 1825 strike and Mann, *Cloth Industry,* p. 111, for weavers desiring to become clothiers. Also see Mann, *Cloth Industry,* pp. 229–230 for examples of prosperous weavers. This self-perception was especially obvious in the debates between master weavers regarding the issue of the origin of truck; see *Glos. Jnl.,* 21 March, 4 April, and 11 April, 1829. R. S. Neale has also classified artisans of this period as "petit bourgeois"; see R. S. Neale, *Class in English History, 1680–1850* (Oxford, 1981), p. 133.

52. See below, Wooton riots, ca. 1825.

53. In "Deferential Dialectic," pp. 149–150, Newby points out that empathy must occur within a framework of suitable social distance to act as a psychological basis of deference.

54. PRO Home Office 40/19/1, January 31, 1826.

55. *Glos. Jnl.,* 16 May 1825.

56. PRO Home Office 40/18/185–186, May 8, 1825.

57. PRO Home Office 40/18/202–203, May 18, 1825, Letter from Edward Sheppard to the Home Office.

58. *Glos. Jnl.,* 15 May 1825.

59. PRO Home Office 40/18/190–191, May 10, 1825.

60. *Glos. Jnl.,* 30 May 1825, Letter from An Old Manufacturer."

61. PRO Home Office 40/18/190–191, May 10, 1825.

62. Ibid. Claiming the need for speed, he apologized for not addressing himself first to Edward Sheppard, who normally served as the clothiers' intermediary with the government. Distrust, very likely, was the real reason for Playne's contacting the government directly.

63. PRO Home Office 40/18/202–203, May 18, 1825.

64. *Glos, Jnl.*, 13 June 1825.

65. GRO Q/SG2 TRN 1825, Quarter Sessions Proceedings.

66. PRO Home Office 40/18/216–217, June 4, 1825.

67. *Glos. Jnl.*, 13 June 1825.

68. PRO Home Office 40/18/227–228, June 7, 1825.

69. *Glos. Jnl.*, 13 June 1825.

70. Mann, *Cloth Industry*, p. 237.

71. *Glos. Jnl.*, 10 April 1826; the following account is drawn from the trial report, appearing in this issue. Cf. Julia de Lacey Mann, "Clothiers and Weavers in Wiltshire during the Eighteenth Century," in L. S. Pressnell, ed., *Studies in the Industrial Revolution Presented to T. S. Ashton* (London, 1960), pp. 72–73 for a Wiltshire counterpart to Aldridge in 1739. The activities of the paternalist gentleman cited by Mann seem to have been confined, however, to pamphleteering on behalf of rioting weavers.

72. This was done perhaps deliberately, and in complicity with the judge's own bias, in order to prevent the reader of the *Gloucester Journal* from arriving at an independent judgment of this delicate matter.

73. Master weavers, in 1825, did not complain about truck because many paid their own journeymen and apprentices in this way; only in 1829, under the pressure of the growth of loom factories, would they take up the issue as a vehicle of protest: see this chapter, section on strikes and protests, 1827–1848.

74. PRO Home Office 40/19/1, January 31, 1826.

75. PRO Home Office 40/18/231, June 8, 1825.

76. PRO Home Office 40/19/1, January 31, 1826.

77. *Glos. Jnl.*, 23 January 1826.

78. PRO Home Office 40/18/392, November 25, 1825.

79. PRO Home Office 40/18/393, December 11, 1825.

80. *Glos Jnl.*, 23 January 1826. This pattern of leniency was common practice; "mercy," writes Douglas Hay of the eighteenth-century legal system, "was part of the currency of patronage." See Douglas Hay, "Property, Authority and the Criminal Law," in Douglas Hay et al., *Albion's Fatal Tree: Crime and Society in Eighteenth Century England* (New York, 1975), p. 45.

81. PRO Home Office 40/19/1ff., January 31, 1826.

82. Both were producers of cassimeres, and Plomer seems to have been the "Old Manufacturer" who had written to the *Gloucester Journal* in May 1825, for he reiterated the same position almost verbatim after the attack had been made on his mill; see *Glos. Jnl.*, 12 December 1825.

83. PRO Home Office 40/19/1ff., January 31, 1826.

84. See Craig Calhoun, *Class Struggle*, chaps. 3 and 6 for a characterization of artisan radicalism as "reactionary."

85. See Mann, *Cloth Industry*, pp. 144–148.

86. PRO Home Office 40/19/1ff., January 31, 1826.

87. See Mann, *Cloth Industry*, p. 249.

88. Lawrence Stone has rightly criticized Thompson on this point, although he is wrong to think that the struggle of the "poor" against industrialism was any less defensive; see L. Stone, "The New Eighteenth Century," *New York Review of Books*, 29 March 1984, p. 45.

89. PRO Home Office 40/19/119–120.

90. Mann, *Cloth Industry*, p. 234 dates the rise of loom factories belatedly from 1829.

91. *Glos. Jnl.*, 21 July 1827.

92. Ibid.

93. Ibid., 29 December 1827.

94. Ibid.

95. See chap. 6, section on capital and labor for a comparison between factory and outdoor weavers' wages.

96. See Mann, *Cloth Industry*, pp. 237–238.

97. *Glos. Jnl.*, 28 June 1828, 5 July 1828, 12 July 1828, contains three communications, one from a manufacturer and two from weavers, all of whom opposed the position of the union, which had claimed that, as a result of the lowering of wages, weavers could earn only 9s. to 12s. per week on average. The manufacturers claimed that for weavers in full employ the average was between 16s. and 20s., and the weaver who wrote in support of this view suggested that it was closer to 20s.

98. *Glos. Jnl.*, 4 April 1829, Veritas received a letter from "Brother Standfirm" warning him to "Remember they declaration [to support the union] in the presence of a numerous assembly," which he then passed on to the *Gloucester Journal*.

99. Ibid., 21 March 1829.

100. Ibid.

101. Ibid., 4 April 1929.

102. Ibid., 10 April 1826.

103. Ibid., 11 April 1829.

104. Mann, *Cloth Industry*, p. 239, indicates that the union was willing to drop this proposal when it joined with representatives of the mid-

dle classes in an antitruck association; the weaver, Veritas, argued that it dropped the demand for tactical reasons in order to assure a wide measure of support. See *Glos. Jnl.*, 11 April 1829.

105. *Glos Jnl.*, 21 March 1829.

106. Mann, *Cloth Industry*, p. 241.

107. *Glos. Jnl.*, 10 August 1833.

108. Mann, *Cloth Industry*, pp. 241–242, seems to regard this strike as an isolated occurrence, whereas the weavers claimed to be supported "by all other weavers in the country." Nor does she distinguish its distinctively proletarian character, in contrast to the 1825 or 1828/29 strikes. According to Playne, moreover, the strike began in December 1833, and the weavers' committee established its headquarters at the Kings Head Inn, Nailsworth; see *Glos. Jnl.*, 1, 15, and 22 February and 8 March 1834 for coverage of the strike.

109. *Glos. Jnl.*, 22 February 1834.

110. Ibid., 15 February 1834.

111. Ibid., 22 February 1834.

112. Ibid.

113. Ibid.

114. Mann, *Cloth Industry*, pp. 174–175.

115. *Glos. Jnl.*, 22 February 1834.

116. Ibid.

117. Mann, *Cloth Industry*, p. 241.

118. *BPP, Sessional Papers*, 24 (1840): 376–377.

119. See chap. 6 for broader treatment of capital formation processes and their impact on labor.

120. See chap. 2.

121. See Hobsbawm, "Machine Breakers," in which he suggests that worker opposition to machinery was neither blind nor always consistent, and Gareth Stedman Jones, *Languages of Class: Studies in English Working Class History, 1832–1982* (Cambridge, 1982) on the social implications of language.

122. *Glos. Jnl.*, 23 June 1838, "Labourers' Meeting." The Stroud protest was coordinated with the one occurring at the Forest of Dean, near Gloucester. The Dean Foresters had had a long history of resistance to enclosure; for accounts, see Sharp, *In Contempt of All Authority*.

123. J. F. C. Harrison, *The Second Coming: Popular Millenarianism, 1780–1850* (London, 1979), p. 25: "A situation of misery, oppression and seemingly hopeless struggle against powerful tyrants [are] the classic conditions for the emergence of chiliasm."

124. Smythe, *Chronicles of Shortwood*, pp. 44–45.

125. Ibid., p. 45.

126. Ibid.

127. Ibid.

128. Ibid., p. 47.

129. Ibid.

130. *Glos. Jnl.*, 4 April 1829.

131. *Glos. Jnl.*, 12 July 1828.

132. Mann, *Cloth Industry*, p. 251; in the 1870s one Gloucester manufacturer announced that he would change his wage policy if other clothiers followed suit; they chose not to.

133. Ibid., p. 249, 298.

134. *Glos. Jnl.*, 30 November, 7 December 1833, "Trade and the Corn Laws," two letters from Nailsworth.

135. Ibid., 29 January 1839, Anti-Corn Law Meeting, 29 February, 7 March 1840, at Tewkesbury and Gloucester.

136. Ibid., 29 January 1839.

137. Ibid.

138. Ibid., 22 May 1841; one Chartist spokesman, who apologized to Fewster for not getting a better hearing, had heard him "speak much on behalf of the poor many times." All other references to this meeting are drawn from this issue of the *Gloucester Journal*.

139. The trend in grain prices had declined markedly since the war, although a slight upturn was noticeable between 1836 and 1840. The "high price" of bread had certainly been overplayed; it became a problem only relatively, in relation to falling wage rates. See chap. 6 for a fuller treatment of the relationship between wheat price fluctuations and wage rates.

140. Mann, *Cloth Industry*, p. 250.

141. The Stroud Anti-Corn Law meeting of 1839 attracted between 1,700 and 2,000; and the one in 1841 had been attended by a "vast multitude."

142. *Glos. Jnl.*, 17 June 1848, "Extension of the Franchise Meeting—Stroud." The meeting started slowly and attracted only 250 to 300 people.

143. See Mann, *Cloth Industry*, p. 250.

144. "Tension management" is Howard Newby's phrase; see Newby, "Deferential Dialectic," pp. 150–151.

8: Nailsworth's Society of Friends

1. For a theoretical discussion of the concept of an "introversionist sect," see Wilson, "An Analysis of Sect Development," pp. 22–45.

2. Smythe, *Chronicles of Shortwood*, p. 5.

3. GRO D1340/A1/Z5, Quaker Membership Listing, Nailsworth Monthly Meeting; D1340/B1/M3–4, Nailsworth Monthly Meeting

Minutes, 1786–1854; D1340/A1/R3, Quaker Marriage Records, 1684–1838.

4. For the importance of group endogamy in defining the Society as a sect, see Elizabeth Isichei, "Organization and Power in the Society of Friends, 1852–1859," in Wilson, ed., *Patterns of Sectarianism*, pp. 170, 173.

5. Richard T. Vann, *The Social Development of Early Quakerism, 1655–1755* (Cambridge, Mass., 1969), p. 77, points to the extremely rapid disappearance of the gentry among Quakers after 1662; see also Barry Reay, "The Social Origins of Early Quakerism," *Journal of Interdisciplinary History*, XI (1980): 55–72 for a discussion of early Quaker social structure.

6. $t = 6.25$, $df = 8$, Prob t at 0.01 > 2.306.

7. GRO D1340/B1/M3, September 10, 1795.

8. Ibid., June 13, 1805.

9. Ibid., March 10, 1808.

10. Ibid., February 14, 1822.

11. Ibid., September 13, 1838.

12. *Glos. Jnl.*, 19 June 1837; Elizabeth Isichei, *Victorian Quakers* (Oxford, 1970), p. 111, fig. 3, shows a sharp decline in membership nationally, circa 1800–1860.

13. GRO D1340/B1/M3, January 19, 1854.

14. BM PP5.85, *Friends Monthly Meeting Magazine*, I (Bristol, 1830): 55.

15. See Isichei, *Victorian Quakers*, chap. III, for an overview of the structure of meetings and the functions of offices. She appears reluctant, however, to acknowledge the Society's undemocratic character; cf. Elizabeth Isichei, "Organization and Power," p. 190.

16. GRO D1340/B1/M5, February 22, 1757.

17. Ibid. See the eighth-minute, [Men's] Gloucester Quarterly Meeting. September 20, 1842.

18. Isichei, "Organization and Power," p. 188.

19. GRO D1340/B1/M5, Queries to Women's Meeting.

20. Ibid., D1340/A3/M2, testimony concerning Henry Wilkins.

21. Isichei, "Organization and Power," p. 186.

22. Ibid.

23. BM PP5.85, "First Principles," in *Friends Monthly Magazine*, I: 61.

24. The relationship between "humility" and the exercise of power, as manifest in the workings of the Society, recalls Friedrich Nietzsche's concept of "resentment"; see Friedrich Nietzsche (trans., ed., Walter Kaufmann), *On the Geneology of Morals* (New York, 1969).

25. See Patrick Collinson, *The Elizabethan Puritan Movement* (Berkeley, Los Angeles, London, 1976) on early Presbyterian church organization.

26. GRO D1340/B1/M5, Quaker Women's Meeting Minutes.

27. Ibid., D1340/B1/M3, December 9, 1790.

28. Ibid., September 10, 1795 and July 14, 1796. In 1795 and 1796, the Women's Particular Meeting ceased forwarding the Queries for want of members, while the men's meeting nearly united with that of Painswick, for much the same reason, and had ceased to hold more than one Sunday service.

29. Ibid., "A Selection of Rules established since the printing of the Book of Extracts in 1782," Yearly Meeting, 1806; hereafter, "Selections."

30. G. F. Nutall, *The Holy Spirit in Puritan Faith and Experience* (Oxford, 1946), p. 89; cf. Isichei, *Victorian Quakers*, pp. 94–96, 107–110.

31. GRO D1340/B1/M4, August 14, 1823.

32. Ibid.; Isichei, *Victorian Quakers*, p. 108. Indeed, the Minutes of the Nailsworth Monthly Meeting, our principal source, are really the minutes of the men's meeting.

33. GRO D1340/B1/M3, Selections, 1819.

34. Ibid., D1340/B1/M4, testimony concerning Richard Gilkes, March 13, 1823.

35. BM PP5.85, *Friends Monthly Magazine*, II: 624.

36. Ibid.

37. Ibid., I: 20.

38. Ibid., II: 623; Isichei, "Organization and Power," p. 170, 173; idem, *Victorian Quakers*, pp. 115, 136, 146–147, 158–159. The Ban on "mixed marriages" lasted nationally until 1860.

39. GRO D1340/B1/M5, Quaker Women's Meeting Minutes, December 12, 1754.

40. Ibid., December 1755.

41. Ibid., November 1756.

42. Ibid., M4, March 12, 1807.

43. Ibid.; Anthony Fewster, for example, was expelled for marrying "a person not of our religious faith in the Baptist Meeting House." See ibid., 9 November 1837.

44. Ibid., August 13, 1807.

45. Ibid., M3, September 10, 1810.

46. Ibid., March 14, 1811.

47. Ibid., November 14, 1811.

48. Ibid.

49. Ibid., M3, December 14, 1809.

50. Ibid., March 4, 1810.

51. Ibid., March 10, 1796.

52. Ibid., June 8, 1797.

53. See Lawrence Stone, *Marriage, Sex and the Family in England, 1500–1800* (New York, 1979), chap. 6.

54. GRO D1340/M3, March 8, 1792; October 10, 1793.

55. Ibid., March 7, 1804.

56. Familial connections were always reported in candidacies. Eli Evans, moreover, had been baptized at Shortwood on May 3, 1788. The Baptist church roll notes that he had joined the Quakers but was readmitted in 1814; yet soon thereafter, he discontinued his attendance and died in 1831; see GRO D2424/3/349.

57. GRO D1340/B1/M3, March 12, 1799.

58. BM PP5.85, *Friends Monthly Magazine*, I: 21, "Thoughts on Marriage."

59. GRO D1340/B1/M3, March 12, 1799.

60. See above, n. 47 and n. 48.

61. Anthony Fewster, three years after his expulsion for "mixed marriage," was readmitted to membership; see GRO D1340/B1/M4, October 8, 1840.

62. Ibid. 14 August 1828.

63. Ibid.

64. Ibid.

65. Ibid., M3, January 13, 1814.

66. See below, n. 70–79.

67. Max Weber suggested that Protestant restraint might have served as a "rational temporing of th[e] irrational impulse" to acquire wealth; see Weber, *Protestant Ethic*, p. 17. Rather than refining capitalism, as Weber concluded, the Protestant ethic can be treated as a defensive reaction against the uncontrollable growth of market transactions and as potentially anticapitalistic, or at least customary. See Thomas Haskell, "Capitalism and the Origins of the Humanitarian Sensibility," *AHR*, 90 (1985); this, I believe, is the real implication of his argument.

68. GRO D1340/B1/M3, September 20, 1804.

69. Ibid., October 11, 1804; March 1805; July 11, 1805.

70. BM PP5.85, *Friends Monthly Magazine*, I: 200. The Quakers, quite early in their history, required of their members that "none launch into trading and worldly business beyond what they can manage honourably, and with reputation; so that they may keep their words with all men."

71. GRO D1340/B1/M3, April 9, 1809; April 13, 1809; July 12, 1810.

72. Ibid., M4, January 8, 1829.

73. Nineteenth-century legal practice gradually abandoned the "doctrine of consideration" (which considered circumstances in determining contract liability) in favor of unrestricted promise keeping; see P. S. Atiyah, *Promises, Morals and Law* (Oxford, 1981), P. 4 and passim. Quakers may have acted more flexibly when both borrower and lender were coreligionists or kin; see L. S. Pressnell, *Country Banking in the Indsutrial Revolution* (Oxford, 1956), p. 114, the example of the Gurneys, and Haskell, "Capitalism."

74. GRO D1340/B1/M3, November 13, 1806.

75. Ibid., M4, July 11, 1822.

76. See the bankruptcy notices for Gloucester clothiers in the *Gloucester Journal* (references in Urdank, "Dissenting Community," appendix 5.1, pp. 531–552), and PRO Court of Bankruptcy Registers, Class B/3.

77. GRO D1340/B1/M3 June 9, 1823.

78. Ibid., June 12, 1828; the minutes noted at this time that "though repentent, his behavior has not been good subsequently and he needs to be watched."

79. Ibid., A3/M2, Elders' Meeting Minutes.

80. GRO D1340/B1/M3, November 14, 1816; December 11, 1816.

81. Ibid., M4, March 13, 1826.

82. Ibid., March 12, 1840.

83. Ibid., M3, February 12, 1807; his case is also cited in Harrison, *The Second Coming*, pp. 133, 252, n. 57.

84. Ibid., April 14, 1809.

85. Ibid., April 11, 1808.

86. Ibid., December 8, 1814.

87. Very probably, this was the same Mary who had resigned in 1826 (see above).

88. GRO D1340/B1/M3, March 12, 1818.

89. Nuttall, *The Holy Spirit*, p. 45.

90. Nuttall, *Howel Harris*, p. 54.

91. The formation of Nonconformity was based on the failure of millenarian expectations; see Christopher Hill, "Occasional Conformity," in R. Buick Knox, ed., *Reformation, Conformity and Dissent: Essays in Honour of Geoffrey Nuttall* (London, 1977), p. 220.

92. See Vann, *Early Quakerism*, pp. 91, 102.

93. Nuttall, *Holy Spirit*, pp. 29–30; see also J. Van Den Berg, "Quaker

and Chiliast: the 'contrary thoughts' of William Ames and Petrus Serrarius," in Knox, ed., *Reformation, Conformity and Dissent*, p. 193.

94. Vann, *Early Quakerism*, pp. 39–40. George Fox did not draw
any distinction between "convincement" and "conversion," but later
Quakers did; convincement became the first step in the process of conversion.

95. It was quite the reverse, at least in practice; although the Friends
adhered rigorously to the principle of the priesthood of all believers, it
was felt that god preferred certain "customary vessels" to transmit his
message. Preachers were therefore important among the early Friends;
see ibid., p. 96 and above.

96. Quoted in ibid., p. 37.

97. Hill, *Century of Revolution*, pp. 168–169.

98. See Isichei, *Victorian Quakers*, pp. 16–19 and 90 on quietism and
silent meetings and pp. 3–16 and 45–53 for the evangelical reaction
among Friends that led to the Beaconite schism. Isichei notes that
nationally, from about 1830, the Friends were divided between evangelicals and quietists and claims that the former were in the ascendant. At
Nailsworth, the quietists remained dominant; see above, n. 83, the case
of Daniel Roberts, for evidence of the Nailsworth Society's hostility to
enthusiasm.

99. Nuttall, *Holy Spirit*, p. 29. The indwelling of the Holy Spirit was
accepted in principle by the radical puritans, but the Quakers added the
proviso that its inspiration was continuous and was therefore reflected in
daily practice.

100. See Isichei, *Victorian Quakers*, pp. 188–211. As the most prominent Quaker at Nailsworth, Anthony R. Fewster had involved himself in
a variety of political activities, from peace activisim to protests against
capital punishment and slavery. See, respectively, GRO D1548, Uncatalogued, the Fewster Papers, letters from Henry Richards (Nov. 22, 1854)
and the Peace Congress (Dec. 10, 1852); letter from W. H. Hyett (March
16, 1848), on the effects of the abolition of capital punishment for
forgery; and a Draft Anti-Slavery Resolution (May 28, 1832), composed
for a meeting held that day by Minchinhampton residents.

101. For the association between enthusiasm and democracy in this
context, see Semmel, *Methodist Revolution* and Valenze, *Prophetic Sons
and Daughters*, especially chaps. 9 and 10.

9: The Shortwood Baptist Church

1. See Halèvy, (trans., ed. Semmel), *Birth of Methodism*, pp. 75–77;
idem, *England in 1815*, part III, chap. I for the classic formulation of the

"Halèvy thesis." See also Peter G. Foster, "Secularisation in the English Context: Some Conceptual and Empirical Problems," *The Sociological Review*, new ser., XX (1972), especially pp. 157–163; L. Shiner, "The Concept of Secularization in Empirical Research," *Journal for the Scientific Study of Religion*, VI (1967): 205–220; and Martin, *General Theory*.

2. See chap. 3, n. 2 and n. 3; also Gilbert, *Religion and Society*; Currie, et al., *Churches and Churchgoers; BPP*, Religious Census Report, 1852/53, vol. 1 xxxix, pp. cxxviii, cclxxxiii; and K. S. Inglis, "Patterns of Religious Worship in 1851," *Journal of Ecclesiastical History*, XI (1960): 82–85.

3. GRO. D2424/3, "Shortwood Baptist Church Roll, 1732–1865."

4. Women consistently outnumbered men in most evangelical movements in both Britain and America; see Gail Malmgreen, "Domestic Discords: Women and the Family in East Chesire Methodism, 1750–1830," in James Obelkevich, Lyndal Roper and Raphael Samuel, eds., *Disciplines of Faith: Studies in Religion, Politics and Partriarchy* (London, 1987), p. 56.

5. Evidence cited from these letters shows that migrants died or moved around a great deal and would not necessarily have received the minister's communication. A low response rate, in other words, is not automatic evidence of lack of interest among nonrespondents, assuming that the letters that survive in the archive were all that the minister had received in the first place, and this, of course, is unlikely, since some were probably lost.

6. For the sex ratio of sample members around 1850 and conversions since 1775, see tables 62 and 65.

7. GRO D2424 Uncatalogued, M. F. Munden to T. F. Newman, May 3, 1849.

8. Ibid., Ann Jones to T. F. Newman, May 3, 1849.

9. Ibid., Hannah Smith to T. F. Newman, March 24, 1849.

10. Ibid., Sarah Green to T. F. Newman.

11. Ibid., Charlotte Boulton to T. F. Newman, March 28, 1849.

12. Ibid., Ann and Thomas Wheeler to T. F. Newman, February 14, 1849.

13. Michael Anderson, *Family Structure in Nineteenth-Century Lanacashire* (Cambridge, 1971), chap. 6.

14. GRO D2424, Uncatalogued, Matilda Robin to T. F. Newman, March 1849.

15. These remarks are quintessentially moderate-Calvinist; on one hand they demonstrate a belief in free grace independently of good works, which is Calvinistic, and on the other hand embrace the doctrine

of universal redemption, which represents a moderation of predestinarian doctrine.

16. GRO D2424, Uncatalogued, Hannah Neale to T. F. Newman, March 2, 1849; Ann Sansom to T. F. Newman, February 25, 1849; cf. Valenze, *Prophetic Sons and Daughters*, pp. 125–127.

17. Minchinhampton [Baptist] Church Book, in the possession of Revd. J. Edwards, Minchinhampton Baptist Church.

18. GRO D2698, Uncatalogued, Newman Family Papers, T. F. Newman to Mayow Newman, December 16, 1851.

19. Dr. William's Library, 5106 GL 25: R. M. Newman, "A History of the Shortwood Baptist Church, 1715–1965."

20. GRO D2424/6, "Abstract of Members from the Church Roll, with a note on their attendance."

21. PRO, Home Office 107/1966; linkages were effected by comparing the names in the enumerator's lists to the names in the church roll, and ages were compared to dates of baptism. The name of any person who appeared too young to have been baptized or who died or migrated before the census was taken was discarded. Identification of more than one person in a family as a member facilitated identification of others.

22. In order to serve as independent variables, they were slightly modified; see appendix K for the list of occupations grouped into social classes and table 65 for age cohorts.

23. See Nie et al., *The Statistical Package of the Social Sciences* (*SPSS*), 2d ed., pp. 416–417 for a discussion of multiple classification analysis as a form of analysis of variance.

24. A regular attendant was someone who appeared at services at least once a week or fifty times a year; those who attended only "sometimes" were assigned a score of fifteen per year, and those who "never" attended were given a score of zero.

25. See the boundary map of the Vale in map 1 and fig. 2 (above); those residing in region II, within a two-mile radius, depicted in fig. 2, were most likely to have attended Shortwood and not the surrounding churches in Avening or Minchinhampton.

26. See table 62.

27. See Halèvy, *Birth of Methodism*; Thompson, *Making of the English Working Class*, chap. XI; Semmel, *Methodist Revolution*; and Valenze, *Prophetic Sons and Daughters*.

28. BPP, Religious Census Report, 1852/53, pp. cxxviii, cclxxxiii; see also Inglis, "Patterns of Religious Worship in 1851," pp. 82–85 and Gilbert, *Religion and Society*, pp. 146–147.

29. By 1851 outdoor handloom weavers had become virtually extinct. In the sample there were twenty-one weavers out of eighty-nine in

class 2. The weavers were grouped together with artisans because they were a skilled class of factory worker, who regarded themselves as artisans, even if traditional designations of master, journeyman, and apprentice had ceased to apply.

30. See E. J. Hobsbawm, "Methodism and the Threat of Revolution in Britain," in Hobsbawm, *Labouring Men*, pp. 23–32; cf. Valenze, *Prophetic Sons and Daughters*.

31. See chap. 7.

32. See E. P. Thompson, *Making of the English Working Class*, chap. XI.

33. See chap. 7.

34. Minchinhampton [Baptist] Church Book, List of Members, no. 315. Keynton's membership lapsed in 1848 but was restored in 1850; the record also notes that he committed suicide in 1854. Keynton's wife, Mary, was also a member (no. 316) but joined the Church of England, evidently following his death.

35. *Stroud Journal*, 27 May 1854. For comparison, see Olive Anderson, "Did Suicide Increase with Industrialization in Victorian England?" *Past and Present*, 86 (Feb. 1980), in which the author demonstrates that although no correlation existed between high suicide rates (calculated on the basis of government statistics) and industrialization, contemporaries believed that suicide occurred most frequently in industrial urban areas. For the definitive study of nineteenth-century English suicide to date, see Olive Anderson, *Suicide in Victorian and Edwardian England* (Oxford, 1987).

36. See chap. 5 section on age-sex structure in 1841 and 1851.

37. Cf. Thomas E. Jordan, "'Stay and Starve, or Go and Prosper!' Juvenile Emigration from Great Britain in the Nineteenth Century," *Social Science History*, IX (Spring 1985): 146–166, especially comparisons in tables 1 and 2.

38. Eleven of the twenty-five in the second (middle) cohort, or 44.0 percent, were unmarried.

39. The mean age of the cohort is 53.9, with a small standard deviation of 3.2, which means that most were still in early middle age. Thirty-six of the forty-four members, or 81.0 percent of the cohort, moreover, were married.

40. GRO D2424, Uncatalogued, Harriet Dangerfield to T. F. Newman, ca. 1849. According to the church roll she was baptized two years later at age twenty-four: D2424/3/1865; cf. Valenze, *Prophetic Sons and Daughters*, p. 46, the example of Hannah Yeomans.

41. GRO D2424, Uncatalogued, Harriet Dangerfield to T. F. Newman, ca. 1849.

42. Her cousin, Elizabeth Dangerfield, was probably not much older, having been baptized in 1841; ibid., 3/1559.

43. Ibid., 6/1865. T. F. Newman's survey of 1852/53 records her attending services only sometimes; note Newman's own spiritual vacillations in his daily journal, D2698/2/5, 1834/35.

44. Minchinhampton [Baptist] Church Book, Minutes, July 1847.

45. Ibid., Minutes, March 1848.

46. GRO D2424/3, Shortwood Church Roll, April 1856.

47. See table 65.

48. See chap. 3, n. 59 and text.

49. See n. 19, above; this is also reflected in the marginally significant interaction effect between class and region depicted in table 66 (92.0 percent probability).

50. See chap. 3.

51. The Baptist Union Library, London. "Records of the Baptist Home Missionary Society," Minutes, 1861–1865, Gloucester Auxiliary, p. 22: in 1861, for example, Uley Baptist Church was granted £30 and Painswick, £10.

52. Minchinchampton Baptist Church Book, Minutes, 1847.

53. GDR Will, Archer Blackwell, blacksmith, 1824.

54. GRO D2424/20. About 1,000 people attended his funeral.

55. Ibid.

56. Nuttall, *Howel Harris*, p. 13; see also Semmel, *Methodist Revolution*, chap. 5.

57. Semmel, ibid., pp. 115–116; cf. Valenze, *Prophetic Sons and Daughters*, chap. 4.

58. Avening Baptist Church Book, "Brief Account of the Building and Formation of the Small Baptist Church in the Village of Avening," in the possession of Mr. Frank Smith, Avening, Gloucestershire. The following account has been drawn from this source.

59. Stephen and Cornelius Blackwell were the descendants of John Blackwell, a prominent eighteenth-century Shortwood deacon. Both were listed as trustees of the preaching room established at Avening in 1805; in 1819, when the initial request to establish a Baptist church was made, Cornelius Blackwell added a note requesting his formal dismissal to Avening.

60. Avening Baptist Church Book, "Brief Account."

61. Ibid.

62. Minchinhampton (Baptist) Church Book, Minutes, 1848.

63. GDR Wills: Issac Hillier, September 7, 1886; Daniel Cook, March 8, 1838; Levi Chandler, June 17, 1869; PRO Home Office 107/ 1966, 1851 Census Enumerators' lists: Charles Jenkins, baker, Market

Street, Nailsworth Village, Horsley HH14, District 2; Simon Dodge, cloth spinner, Watledge, Amberley District, Minchinhampton, HH35; Simon Dodge's entire family were members and regular attenders of Shortwood; GRO D2424/3 and 6/1075, 1085, 1730, 1759 and 1608.

64. Smythe, *Chronicles of Shortwood*, p. 43.

65. Shortwood Burial Register, 1808 to the present, in the possession of Mrs. B. Mills, Newmarket House, Nailsworth, Gloucestershire. Between 1838 and 1853, no members appear to be recorded in the register, which explains the chronological gap in table 68.

66. In table 68 $t = 1.85$, $df = 41$; $t \geqslant 1.680$ to be significant at the 0.05 level.

67. GRO D2424, Uncatalogued, Letters from Leonard Smith to T. F. Newman, September 20 and 28, ca. 1850.

68. Stroud Baptist Church Book, 1824–1868; in the possesstion of Revd. J. A. Baker, The Manse, Folly Lane, Stroud, Gloucestershire.

69. Quoted in G. F. Nuttall, *Howell Harris*, p. 17; cf. L. P. Curtis, *Anglican Moods in the Eighteenth Century* (Hamden, Conn., 1966).

70. See appendix M, convenant of 1735 for general guidelines.

71. GRO D2424, Uncatalogued, March 26, 1849.

72. See table 64.

73. GRO D2424/1, Shortwood Minute Book, 1732–1800.

74. Ibid.

75. Ibid.

76. Ibid.; March 17, 1765; October 6, 1765; October 3, 1782; July 14, 1782; December 20, 1792; September 24, 1780; June 26, 1794; August 12, 1798; August 26, 1792; August 12, 1798; September 28, 1790; April 17, 1791. Only forty-two exclusions over the entire course of Francis's ministry took place.

77. Quoted in Nuttall, "Questions and Answers," p. 85.

78. GRO D2698/2/15, Sermons of T. F. Newman, 1849–1852. A number of sermons in the early part of 1849 deal with the theme of the uncertainty of life and the imminence of death and the consequent need for preparation; a sermon in 1850 stressed the need to maintain diligence, virtue, temperance, and patience (August 11, 1850).

79. Ibid., D2698/2/13, July 10, 1842.

80. Ibid. Metaphorically, according to Newman, the laborers hired later in the day symbolized the Christians and those hired in the morning, the Jews; alternatively, they could symbolize individuals who received grace later in life, when more mature and implicitly more worthy. In this manner, Newman gave new meaning to the biblical dictum that the "last shall come first."

81. See chap. 6, the example of Thomas Cole, and chap. 7, the post-

1826 strike period.

82. GRO D2698/2/13, sermon on Acts XX: 35 (Collection for the Poor), December 15, 1844.

83. GRO MF 461/1, Shortwood Baptist Church Records, Misc. D2424, acc. 3546. Minutes of the Nailsworth Tabernacle, 1866/67.

84. Smythe, *Chronicles of Shortwood*, pp. 81–82.

85. See above, n. 2.

10: Local Changes in the Industrial Revolution

1. Obelkevich, *Religion and Rural Society*, p. 313.

2. Ibid., pp. 1–2.

3. See Mandler, "Making of the New Poor Law," in which the author argues an old case with a new twist, namely, that paternalist values among the gentry had succumbed to the new ethos of classical liberalism in the early decades of the nineteenth century; his new twist is that the gentry did not require middle-class tutelage to arrive at this position. The argument advanced in this study, to the contrary, emphasizes the existence of a liberal paternalism among the gentry, which reconciled patriarchalism with individualism and could be traced back to John Locke. During the early nineteenth century, we see a shift within this synthesis to accommodate greater scope for the market, not the wholesale abandonment of paternalism.

4. For a cogent restatement of this thesis, see Charlesworth and Randall, "Comment: Morals, Markets and the English Crowd," p. 212.

5. The most recent study of village riots in England during the early modern period suggests the possibility of "aristocratic manipulation or gentry factionalism complicat[ing] the picture" of village revolts; see Manning, *Village Revolts*, p. 2.

Bibliography

Principal Manuscript Sources

LONDON

Baptist Union Library

Records of the Home Missionary Society. Minutes, 1861–1865.

British Library

Additional 40420, f. 180–185. Peel Papers. Papers Relating to the Dissenters's Marriage Bill, 1834/35.

Additional 34571, f. 457. Letter from D. Ricardo to Revd. P. Bliss, May 5, 1835.

Additional 33589, f. 75, 77. Smythe Papers. Papers Relating to the Suppression of Conventicles in the County of Gloucester, 1669–1672.

Additional 44566, Gladstone Papers, f. 184–191. Three Letters, Poulet Scrope to the *Economist*.

Dr. Williams's Library

Thompson, J. *History of Nonconformist Congregations*, vol. II, no. 17, MS. 38.7–11, ca. 1780.

Public Records Office

Court of Bankruptcy Registers and Examination Papers, Classes B/3 and B/4.

Birth Registers of the Forest Green Congregationalist Church. Class RG/4.

1841 Census Enumerators' Lists. Home Office 107/363.

1851 Census Enumerators' Lists. Home Office 107/1966.

1851 Religious Census Returns. Home Office 129/338/7/1.

Peel Papers, Home Office Correspondence. Home Office 40/18 and 40/19.

Prerogative Court of Canterbury Wills, Class Prob. 11 and Estate Duty Registers and Ledgers, Classes IR 25 and 26.

University College Library
The Chadwick Papers.

CAMBRIDGE
Cambridge Group for the History of Population and Social Structure. Aggregate Data to Avening Parish Marriage Registers.

GLOUCESTER
Gloucester Records Office
Records of Nonconformist Chapels
D2595 Forest Green Congregationalist Church Collection.
D1340 Society of Friends Collection.
D2424 and MF 461/1 Shortwood Baptist Church Collection.
MF 974 Sermons of T. F. Newman, Minister of the Shortwood Baptist Church.
Gloucester Diocesan Records
Probate Collection: Wills, Administrations, and Inventories. GDR A2/1–5 Gloucester Diocesan Book.
Family Papers
D2698 Newman Family Papers.
D1812 Ricardo Family Papers.
D1460 Thomas Family Papers.
D1548 Fewster Papers.
Manor Records
D1192/2 A Rent Role [*sic*] for the Mannors [*sic*] of Hampton, Avening, Nailsworth, and Rodborough, 1744–1745.
D2219/1/4–5 Minutes of Proceedings of the Minchinhampton Court Leet, 1843 and 1847.
D547a/M14 Horsley Manor Records, Lists of Suitors at Court.
Parish Records
D2219/6/6 Nailsworth Episcopal Chapel Minute Book, Copy of Building Subscription List (1794).
MF/443 Nailsworth Episcopal Chapel Baptismal Registers, 1794–1836.
P181 IN 1/1–10, 12, 13 Horsley Parish Registers of Baptisms, Marriages, and Burials.
P181 VE, Horsley Vestry Records.
P181 OV, Horsley Overseers' Records.
P217 CW, Minchinhampton Churchwardens' Accounts.
P217 VE, Minchinhampton Vestry Records.
P217 OV, Minchinhampton Overseers' Records.
P217 IN 3/1, Minchinhampton Tithe Terrier, ca. 1777.

P29 OV, Avening Overseers' Records: OV 1/2, Avening Tithe Book, ca. 1784 and Rate Book, ca. 1801.

MF 447, Avening, Horsley, and Minchinhampton Tithe Surveys, 1838–1841.

Hundred Records.

MF 447, Longtree Hundred Land Tax Returns, 1780–1830.

Quarter Session Records.

Q/SG 2 TRN. 1825, Proceedings.

Miscellaneous Records

D3393, A Short Sketch of the Leading Characters at the Late Stroud Meeting, 1831.

Gloucester City Library

The Gloucester Collection

RF 167.2 (1–4). Particulars of Leases and Rents, 1562–1789, Horsley Manor Records.

RF 167.1 Papers Relating to Horsley Manor.

RV 167.3 (1–8, abstr. B), Horsley Tithe Papers, 1797–1802.

Private Collections

An Elegy on the Death of the Revd. George Whitefield. By Revd. Benjamin Francis. MSS. Poem, n.d. (ca. 1770). In the possession of Mrs. B. Mills, Newmarket House, Nailsworth, Stroud.

Avening Baptist Church Book. In the possession of Mr. F. Smith, 9 Lawrence Road, Avening, Tetbury.

Minchinhampton Baptist Church Book. In the possession of Revd. J. Edwards, The Manse, Windmill Rd., Minchinhampton, Stroud.

Stroud Baptist Church Book, 1824–1868. In the possession of Revd. J. A. Baker, the Manse, Folly Lane, Stroud.

Shortwood Baptist Burial Register, 1808 to present. In the possession of Mrs. B. Mills, Newmarket House, Nailsworth, Stroud.

Letters and papers of A. W. Playne, together with a manuscript account of the history of the Playne family firms, n.d. (ca. 1890). In the possession of Mr. David Playne, Bannut Tree, Avening, Tetbury.

Printed Primary Sources

CHAPEL AND PARISH HISTORIES

A Brief History of the Independent Church at Forest Green, Nailsworth. By Charles Russel. Nailsworth: 1845, 1912. Gloucester Records Office Pamphlet Collection.

A History of the Shortwood Baptist Church, 1715–1965. By R. M. Newman. London: 1965. Dr. Williams's Library.

Chronicles of Shortwood. By F. T. Smythe. Gloucester Records Office. Shortwood Baptist Church Collection, D2424, Uncatalogued.

The History of Horsley. By Revd. Messing Rudkin. Stroud: 1884. Gloucester City Library Collection, M10073.

The History of Minchinhampton and Avening. By A. T. Playne. Gloucester: 1915. Gloucester City Library.

MAPS AND PLANS

Geological Survey Map, one-inch scale. Stroud and the Lower District. Gloucester Records Office. MA 19/71.

Geological Survey Map, one-inch scale. Horsley, Avening, and Minchinhampton, with Nailsworth. Gloucester City Library. The Gloucester Collection. 554.231, Boxes 10.103 and 10.105.

Ordinance Survey Map, six-inch scale. Nailsworth. Gloucester, XLIX: 1885 ed.

Ordinance Survey Map, six-inch scale. Nailsworth. Gloucester, XLIX: 1885 ed., with elevations. Playne Papers. In the possession of David Playne, Bannut Tree, Avening, Stroud.

Plan of an Estate of Edward Barnard in 1801. Gloucester Records Office. D1388.

Plan of an Estate in the Parish of Horsley, the Property of the Rt. Hon. Lord Ducie, 1838. Gloucester Records Office. D1011/P2.

NEWSPAPERS AND CONTEMPORARY PERIODICALS

The Gloucester Journal. The Gloucester Collection. Gloucester City Library.

The Stroud Journal. Public Record Office, London. Newspaper Collection.

The Cotswoldian. British Library main reading room index.

Friends Monthly Meeting Magazine, vol. I. Bristol: 1830. British Library. PP5.85. Main reading room.

MISCELLANEOUS

A Charge to the Clergy of the Diocese of Gloucester, 1825. By the Bishop of Gloucester. Gloucester City Library. The Gloucester Collection. JR 4.3.

A Charge to the Clergy of the Diocese of Gloucester, 1832. By the Bishop of Gloucester. Gloucester City Library. The Gloucester Collection. J 4.57.

Gloucestershire Tracts. Series C. III, 1832–1882. Gloucester City Library. The Hyett Collection.

Narrative Relating to the Present State and Former History of the Baptist Church at Shortwood, Gloucestershire (ca. 1857). By J. Cave. Gloucester Records Office. D2424/12, MS.

Reports and Selected Papers of the Statistical Committee. Papers of the Royal Commission. Royal Commission on Population. Vol. II. London: Her Majesty's Stationery Office, 1950.

Emigration as a Means of Relief in the Present Distressed Condition of the Poor of This Neighborhood. By David Ricardo. Minchinhampton: 1835. Gloucester City Library. Gloucester Collection. R205.10.

The Geology of Stroud and the Area Drained by the Frome. By E. Witchell. Stroud: 1885. Gloucester Records Office. ROL C4.

The Fall of the Great Man Contemplated: A Sermon Occassioned by the Death of the Revd. William Winterbotham. Gloucester Records Office. D2424/13.

The Trial of William Winterbotham, Asst. Preacher at Howe's Lane Meeting, Devon, 25 and 26 July 1793 for Seditious Words. Transcript of Proceedings. In Dr. Williams's Library. PP17.7.29(6).

BRITISH PARLIAMENTARY PAPERS

British Parliamentary Papers. Population. "Census Reports." Vol. I. Session 1831. Dublin: Irish University Press reprint, 1968.

British Parliamentary Papers. Religion. "The 1851 Census Reports and Tables on Religious Worship in England and Wales." By H. Mann. Vol. 10. Dublin: Irish University Press reprint, 1968.

British Parliamentary Papers. "Report on the Condition of the Handloom Weavers: The West of England." By W. A. Miles. Vol. XXIV, 1840.

Secondary Sources

Achen, Christopher H. *Interpreting and Using Regression.* Beverly Hills, Calif.: Sage Publications, 1982.

Allen, Edward A. "Public School Elites in Early Victorian England: The Boys at Harrow and Merchant Taylors' Schools from 1825 to 1850." *Journal of British Studies,* XXI (1982): 87–117.

Anderson, Michael. *Family Structure in Nineteenth Century Lancashire.* Cambridge: Cambridge Unversity Press, 1971.

———. "Urban Migration in Lancashire," *Annales de Démographie Historique* (1970, 1971): 17–26.

———. "Sociological History and the Working Class Family: Smelser Revisited." *Social History,* I (1976): 317–334.

Anderson, Olive. "Did Suicide Increase with Industrialization in Victorian England?" *Past and Present,* 86 (1980): 149–173.

———. *Suicide in Victorian and Edwardian England.* Oxford: Clarendon Press, 1987.

Armstrong, Alan. *Stability and Change in an English County Town: A*

Social Study of York, 1801–1851. Cambridge: Cambridge University Press, 1974.

Ashton, T. S. *An Economic History of England: The Eighteenth Century.* London: Methuen, 1964.

Aston, T. H. and C. H. E. Philpin, eds. *The Brenner Debate: Agrarian Class Structure and Economic Development in Pre-Industrial Europe.* New York: Cambridge University Press, 1985.

Atiyah, P. S. *Promises, Morals and Law.* Oxford: Clarendon Press, 1981.

Banks, Sarah. "Nineteenth Century Scandal or Twentieth Century Model? A New Look at 'Open' and 'Close' Parishes." *Economic History Review,* 2d ser., XLI (1988): 51–73.

Barclay, George W. *Techniques of Population Analysis.* New York: John Wiley & Sons, 1958.

Bean, J. M. W. *The Decline of English Feudalism, 1215–1540.* Manchester: Manchester University Press, 1968.

Beattie, J. M. *Crime and the Courts in England, 1660–1800.* Princeton: Princeton University Press, 1986.

Beer, Samuel H. *British Politics in the Collectivist Age.* New York: Alfred A. Knopf, 1965.

Bennett, Judith M. *Women in the Medieval English Countryside: Gender and Household in Brigstock before the Plague.* New York: Oxford University Press, 1987.

Berry, B. M., and R. S. Schofield. "Age at Baptism in Pre-industrial England." *Population Studies,* XXV (1971): 453–463.

Biddick, Kathleen. "Medieval English Peasants and Market Involvement." *Journal of Economic History,* XLV (1985): 823–831.

Birdsall, Jean. "The English Manors of the Abbey of La Trinité at Cean." In Charles H. Taylor, ed. *Anniversary Essays in Medieaval History by Students of Charles Homer Haskins.* New York: Houghton Mifflin, 1929.

Blalock, Hubert M. *Social Statistics.* New York: McGraw-Hill, 1972.

Bloch, Marc (trans. Janet Sondheimer). *French Rural History: An Essay on Its Basic Characteristics.* Berkeley and Los Angeles: University of California Press. 1966.

Bohstedt, John. *Riots and Community Politics in England and Wales, 1790–1810.* Cambridge, Mass.: Harvard University Press, 1983.

Brauer, G. C. *The Education of a Gentleman; Theories of Gentlemanly Education in England 1660–1775.* New York: Bookman Associates, 1959.

Brenner, Robert. "The Origins of Capitalist Development: A Critique of Neo-Smithian Marxism." *New Left Review* (July, Aug 1977): 25–92.

Briggs, Asa. "The Language of 'Class' in Early Nineteenth Century England." In Asa Briggs, ed., *Essays in Labour History in Memory of G. D. H. Cole*. London: Macmillan, 1959.

Britton, Edward. *The Community of the Vill: A Study in the History of the Family and Village Life in Fourteenth-Century England*. Toronto: Macmillan, 1977.

Brundage, Anthony. *The Making of the New Poor Law: The Politics of Inquiry, Enactment, and Implementation, 1832–1839*. New Brunswick, N.J.: Rutgers University Press, 1978.

Calhoun, Craig. "Community: Towards a Variable Conceptualization for Comparative Research," *Social History*, V (1980): 105–129.

———. *The Question of Class Struggle: Social Foundations of Popular Radicalism during the Industrial Revolution*. Chicago: University of Chicago Press, 1982.

Cam, H. M. "Manerium Cum Hundredo: The Hundred and Hundredal Manor." *English Historical Review*, XLVII (1932): 353–376.

Campbell, Bruce M. S. "Population Pressure, Inheritance and the Land Market in a Fourteenth-Century Peasant Community." In Richard M. Smith, ed., *Land, Kinship and Life-Cycle*. Cambridge: Cambridge University Press, 1984.

Carus-Wilson, E. M. *Medieval Merchant Venturers*. London: Methuen, 1954.

———. "Evidences of Industrial Growth on Some Fifteenth Century Manors." *Economic History Review*, 2d ser., XII (1959): 190–205.

Catling, H. "The Evolution of Spinning." In J. G. Jenkins, ed., *The Wool Textile Industry in Great Britain*. London: Routledge & Kegan Paul, 1972.

Chambers, J. D. "Enclosure and the Labour Supply." In D. V. Glass and D. E. C. Eversley, eds., *Population in History: Essays in Historical Demography*. London: Edward Arnold, 1965.

Chamie, Joseph. *Religion and Fertility: Arab Christian-Muslim Differentials*. Cambridge: Cambridge University Press, 1981.

Chapman, Stanley. "The Cost of Power in the Industrial Revolution in Britain: The Case of the Textile Industry." *Midland History*, I (1971): 1–23.

Charlesworth, Andrew, and Adrian J. Randall. "Comment: Morals, Markets and the English Crowd in 1766." *Past and Present*, 114 (1987): 200–213.

Chayanov, A. V. (Eds. Daniel Thoner, Basile Kerblay, and R. E. F. Smith), *The Theory of Peasant Economy*. Homewood, Ill.: R. D. Irwin, 1966.

Clark, J. C. D. *English Society, 1688–1832*. Cambridge: Cambridge University Press, 1986.

Clark, Peter. "Migration in England during the Late Seventeenth and Early Eighteenth Centuries." *Past and Present*, 83 (1979): 57–90.

Clay, Christopher. "Lifehold Leasing in the Western Counties of England," *Agricultural History Review*, XXIX (1981): 83–96.

Clipsham, E. F. "Andrew Fuller and Fullerism." *Baptist Quarterly*, XX (1963): 99–114.

Cobbett, William. *Rural Rides*. London: Penguin Books, 1967; reprint.

Coleman, D. C. "Proto-Industrialization: A Concept Too Many." *Economic History Review*, 2d ser., XXXVI (1983): 435–448.

Colley, Linda. *In Defiance of Oligarchy: The Tory Party, 1714–1760*. Cambridge: Cambridge University Press, 1985.

Collinson, Patrick. *The Elizabethan Puritan Movement*. Berkeley, Los Angeles, London: University of California Press, 1967.

———. *The Religion of Protestants: The Church in English Society, 1559–1625*. Oxford: Clarendon Press, 1985.

Collis, Ivor P. "Leases for a Term of Years Determinable with Lives," *Society of Archivists Journal*, I (1955–1959): 168–171.

Cook, S. "Economic Anthropology: Problems in Theory, Method and Analysis." In John J. Honigmann, ed., *Handbook of Social and Cultural Anthropology*. Chicago: Rand McNally, 1973.

Cox, Jeffirey. *The English Churches in a Secular Society: Lambeth, 1870–1930*. New York: Oxford University Press, 1982.

Crafts, N. F. R. *British Economic Growth during the Industrial Revolution*. Oxford: Clarendon Press, 1985.

Currie, Robert. "A Micro-Theory of Methodist Growth." *Proceedings of the Wesley Historical Society*, XXXVI (1967): 65–73.

Currie, Robert, Alan Gilbert, and Lee Horsley. *Churches and Churchgoers: Patterns of Church Growth in the British Isles since 1700*. Oxford: Clarendon Press, 1977.

Curtis, L. P. *Anglican Moods in the Eighteenth Century*. Hamden, Conn.: Archon Books, 1966.

Dallas, Gregor. *The Imperfect Peasant Economy: The Loire Country, 1800–1914*. New York: Cambridge University Press, 1982.

Deane, P. "Contemporary Estimates of National Income in the First Half of the Nineteenth Century." *Economic History Review*, 2d ser., VIII (1956): 339–354.

Deane, P., and W. A. Cole. *British Economic Growth, 1688–1959: Trends and Structure*. Cambridge: Cambridge University Press, 1962.

Duncan, Otis D. *Introduction to Structural Equation Models*. New York: Academic Press, 1975.

Easterlin, R. A. "The Economics and Sociology of Fertility: A Synthesis." In Charles Tilly, ed., *Historical Studies of Changing Fertility*. Princeton: Princeton University Press, 1978.

Everitt, Alan. "Farm Labourers." In Joan Thirsk, ed., *Agrarian History of England and Wales*, vol. 4: 1500–1640. Cambridge: Cambridge University Press, 1967.

———. *The Pattern of Rural Dissent: The Nineteenth Century*. Leicester: Leicester University Press, 1972.

———. "River and Wold, Reflections on the Historical Origin of Regions and Pays," *Journal of Historical Geography*, III (1977): 1–19.

———. *Landscape and Community in England*. London: The Hambledon Press, 1985.

Eversley, D. E. C. "The Demography of the Irish Quakers, 1650–1850." In J. M. Goldstrom and L. A. Clarkson, eds., *Irish Population, Economy and Society: Essays in Honour of the Late K. H. Connell*. Oxford: Clarendon Press, 1981.

Finlay, R. *Population and Metropolis: The Demography of London, 1580–1650*. Cambridge: Cambridge University Press, 1981.

Fisher, J. R. "The Limits of Deference: Agricultural Communities in a Mid-Nineteenth Century Election Campaign." *Journal of British Studies*, XXI (1981): 90–105.

Flinn, M. W. "The Poor Employment Act of 1817." *Economic History Review*, 2d ser., XIV (1961): 82–92.

Floud, Roderick. *An Introduction to Quantitative Methods for Historians*. Princeton: Princeton University Press, 1973.

———. "Quantitative History and People's History: Two Methods in Conflict?" *Social Science History*, VIII (1984): 151–168.

Floud, Roderick, and P. Thane. "Debates: The Incidence of Civil Marriage in Victorian England and Wales." *Past and Present*, 84 (1979): 146–154.

Fogel, Robert W., and G. R. Elton. *Which Road to the Past? Two Views of History*. New Haven: Yale University Press, 1983.

Foster, John. *Class Struggles and the Industrial Revolution: Early Industrial Capitalism in Three English Towns*. London: Methuen, 1977.

Foster, Peter G. "Secularisation in the English Context: Some Conceptual and Empirical Problems." *The Sociological Review*, new ser., XX (1972): 153–168.

Gayer, Arthur D., Walter W. Rostow, and Anna J. Schwartz. *The Growth and Fluctuation of the British Economy, 1790–1850: An Historical, Statistical, and Theoretical Study of Britain's Economic Development*, vol. I. Oxford: Clarendon Press, 1953.

Geertz, Clifford. *The Interpretation of Cultures: Selected Essays*. New York: Basic Books, 1973.

———. *Local Knowledge: Further Essays in Interpretive Anthropol-*

ogy. New York: Basic Books, 1983.

Gerth, H. H., and C. Wright Mills, (trans. and eds.). *From Max Weber: Essays in Sociology*. New York: Oxford University Press, 1958.

Giddens, Anthony. *The Class Structure of Advanced Societies*. New York: Harper & Row, 1975.

——. *Central Problems in Social Theory: Action, Structure and Contradiction in Social Analysis*. Berkeley, Los Angeles, London: University of California Press, 1979.

Gilbert, Alan D. *Religion and Society in Industrial England: Church, Chapel and Social Change, 1700–1914*. London: Longmans, 1977.

Glass, D. V. "Population and Population Movements in England and Wales, 1700–1850." In D. V. Glass and D. E. C. Eversley, eds., *Population in History: Essays in Historical Demography*. London: Edward Arnold, 1965.

Glen, Robert. *Urban Workers in the Early Industrial Revolution*. London: Croom Helm, 1984.

Gordon, Robert B. "Cost and Use of Water Power during Industrialization in New England and Great Britain: A Geological Interpretation." *Economic History Review*, 2d ser., XXXVI (1983): 240–259.

Goubert, Pierre. *Cent Mille Provinciaux au XVIIe Siècle: Beauvais et le Beauvaisis de 1600 à 1730*. Paris: Flammarion, 1968.

Gregory, Derek. *Regional Transformation and Industrial Revolution: A Geography of the Yorkshire Textile Industry*. Minneapolis: University of Minnesota Press, 1983.

Grew, Raymond. "More on Modernization." *Journal of Social History*, XIV (1980): 179–188.

Gudeman, Stephen. *Economics as Culture: Models and Metaphors of Livelihood*. London: Routledge & Kegan Paul, 1986.

Gullickson, Gay L. "Agriculture and Cottage Industry: Redefining the Causes of Proto-Industrialization." *Journal of Economic History*, XLIII (1983): 831–850.

Habakkuk, H. J. "Population Problems and European Economic Development in the Late Eighteenth and Early Nineteenth Centuries." *American Economic Review*, Papers and Proceedings, LIII (1963): 607–618.

——. "The Economic History of Modern Britain." In D. V. Glass and D. E. C. Eversley, eds., *Population in History: Essays in Historical Demography*. London: Edward Arnold, 1965.

——. "English Population in the Eighteenth Century." In D. V. Glass and D. E. C. Eversley, eds., *Population in History: Essays in Historical Demography*. London: Edward Arnold, 1965.

Halévy, Elie (trans. E. I. Watkin). *A History of the English People in the*

Nineteenth Century: England in 1815, vol. I. New York: Harcourt Brace, 1949.

———. (trans. Bernard Semmel). *The Birth of Methodism in England.* Chicago: University of Chicago Press, 1971.

Hammond, John L., and Barbara Hammond. *The Skilled Labourer, 1760–1832.* London: Longmans, 1927.

Harrison, J. F. C. *The Second Coming: Popular Millenarianism, 1780–1850.* London: Routledge & Kegan Paul, 1979.

Hartwell, R. M., and S. Engerman. "Models of Immiseration: The Theoretical Basis of Pessimism." In A. J. Taylor, ed., *The Standard of Living in the Industrial Revolution.* London: Methuen, 1975.

Haskell, Thomas. "Capitalism and the Origins of the Humanitarian Sensibility." *American Historical Review*, 90 (1985): 339–361.

Hay, Douglas. "Property, Authority and the Criminal Law." In Douglas Hay, Peter Linebaugh, John G. Rule, E. P. Thompson, and C. Winslow, eds., *Albion's Fatal Tree: Crime and Society in Eighteenth Century England.* New York: Pantheon, 1975.

Heaton, H. *The Yorkshire Woollen and Worsted Industries, From the Earliest Times up to the Industrial Revolution.* Oxford: Clarendon Press, 1965.

Herbert, N. M., ed. *Victoria County History of Gloucester*, vol. XI. Oxford: Oxford University Press, 1976.

Hey, D. G. "A Dual Economy in South Yorkshire." *Agricultural History Review*, XVII (1969): 108–119.

Hill, Christopher. *Century of Revolution.* New York: W. W. Norton, 1961.

———. "Occasional Conformity." In R. Buick Knox, ed., *Reformation, Conformity and Dissent: Essays in Honour of Geoffrey Nuttall.* London: Epworth Press, 1977.

Hills, Richard L. *Power in the Industrial Revolution.* New York: A. M. Kelly, 1970.

Hills, Richard L., and A. J. Pacey. "The Measurement of Power in Early Steam-driven Textile Mills." *Technology and Culture*, XIII (1972): 25–43.

Hilton, Boyd. *Corn, Cash and Commerce: The Economic Policies of the Tory Governments, 1815–1830.* New York: Oxford University Press, 1977.

———. *The Age of Atonement: The Influence of Evangelicalism on Social and Economic Thought, 1795–1865.* Oxford: Clarendon Press, 1988.

Hilton, Rodney H. *The English Peasantry in the Later Middle Ages.* Oxford: Clarendon Press, 1975.

Himmelfarb, Gertrude. *The Idea of Poverty: England in the Early Industrial Age*. New York: Random House, 1985.

Hobsbawm, Eric J. "Custom, Wages and Work-Load in Nineteenth Century Industry." In Asa Briggs and John Saville, eds., *Essays in Labour History in Memory of G. D. H. Cole*. London: Methuen, 1960.

———. "Machine Breakers." In Eric. J. Hobsbawm, *Labouring Men*. New York: Basic Books, 1964.

———. "Methodism and the Threat of Revolution in Britain." In Eric J. Hobsbawm, *Labouring Men*. New York: Basic Books, 1964.

Holderness, B. A. "'Open' and 'Close' Parishes in England in the Eighteenth and Nineteenth Centuries." *Agricultural History Review*, XX (1972): 126–139.

Hone, Nathaniel J. *The Manor and Manorial Records*. London: Methuen, 1912.

Horn, James P. P. "The Distribution of Wealth in the Vale of Berkeley, 1660–1700." *Southern History*, III (1981): 81–109.

Horn, Pamela. *The Rural World: Social Change in the English Countryside, 1780–1850*. London: Hutchinson, 1980.

Hoskins, W. G. *The Midland Peasant: The Economic and Social History of a Leicestershire Village*. New York: St. Martin's Press, 1957.

Hudson, Pat. "Proto-industrialization: The Case of the West Riding Wool Textile Industry in the Eighteenth and Early Nineteenth Centuries." *History Workshop Journal*, 12 (1981): 34–61.

———. *The Genesis of Industrial Capital: A Study of the West Riding Wool Textile Industry ca. 1750–1850*. Cambridge: Cambridge University Press, 1986.

Inglis, K. S. "Patterns of Religious Worship in 1851." *Journal of Ecclesiastical History*, XI (1960): 74–86.

Innes, Joanna. "Review Article: Jonathan Clark, Social History and England's 'Ancien Regime'." *Past and Present*, 115 (1987): 165–200.

Isichei, Elizabeth. "Organization and Power in the Society of Friends, 1852–1859." In Bryan R. Wilson, ed., *Patterns of Sectarianism: Organization and Ideology in Social and Religious Movements*. London: Heinemann, 1967.

———. *Victorian Quakers*. Oxford: Clarendon Press, 1970.

Ivimey, Joseph. *History of the English Baptists*, Vols. I–IV. London: Burditt, Button & Hamilton, 1811–1830.

James, M. E. "Obedience and Dissent in Henrician England: the Lincolnshire Rebellion, 1536." *Past and Present*, 48 (1970): 3–78.

Jenkins, D. T. *The West Riding Wool Textile Industry, 1770–1835: A Study of Fixed Capital Formation*. Edington: The Pasold Fund, 1975.

Jenkins, J. G., ed. *The Wool Textile Industry in Great Britain*. London:

Routledge & Kegan Paul, 1972.

Jensen, Richard. "Crunching Numbers by Hand: Statistical Programs for the Texas Instrument 55 Pocket Calculator." *Newberry Papers in Family and Community History*. Paper 80–3 (1981): 1–25.3.

Jones, Eric L. *Agriculture and the Industrial Revolution*. New York: John Wiley & Sons, 1974.

Jones, Gareth Stedman. *Languages of Class: Studies in English Working Class History, 1832–1982*. Cambridge: Cambridge University Press, 1982.

Jordan, Thomas E. "'Stay and Starve, or Go and Prosper!' Juvenile Emigration from Great Britain in the Nineteenth Century." *Social Science History*, IX (1985): 145–166.

Joyce, Patrick. *Work, Society and Politics: The Culture of the Factory in Later Victorian England*. New Brunswick, N.J.: Rutgers University Press, 1981.

Kain, R. J. P. *An Atlas and Index of the Tithe Files of Mid-Nineteenth Century England and Wales*. Cambridge: Cambridge University Press, 1986.

Kerridge, Eric. *Agrarian Problems of the Sixteenth Century and After*. London: George Allen & Unwin, 1969.

Krause, J. T. "Changes in English Fertility and Mortality, 1780 to 1850." *Economic History Review*, 2d ser., XI (1958): 52–70.

———. "The Changing Adequacy of English Registration, 1690–1837." In D. V. Glass and D. E. C. Eversley, eds., *Population in History: Essays in Historical Demography*. London: Edward Arnold, 1965.

Kriedte, Peter, Hans Medick, and Jurgen Schlumbohm, eds. (trans. B. Schempp). *Industrialization before Industrialization: Rural Industry in the Genesis of Capitalism*. Cambridge: Cambridge University Press, 1981.

Landau, Norma. *The Justices of the Peace, 1679–1760*. Berkeley, Los Angeles, London: University of California Press, 1984.

Landes, David. *The Unbound Prometheus: Technological Change and Industrial Development in Western Europe from 1750 to the Present*. Cambridge: Cambridge University Press, 1969.

———. *Revolution in Time: Clocks and the Making of the Modern World*. Cambridge, Mass.: The Belknap Press, 1984.

Langdon, John. *Horses, Oxen and Technological Innovation: The Use of Draught Animals in English Farming from 1066–1500*. Cambridge: Cambridge University Press, 1986.

Laqueur, Thomas W. *Religion and Respectability: Sunday Schools and Working Class Culture, 1780–1850*. New Haven, Conn.: Yale University Press, 1976.

————. "The Queen Caroline Affair: Politics as Art in the Reign of George IV." *Journal of Modern History*, LIV (1982): 417–466.

Laslett, Peter. *The World We Have Lost: England before the Industrial Age*. New York: Charles Scribner & Sons, 1971.

Lears, Jackson T. "The Concept of Cultural Hegemony: Problems and Possibilities." *American Historical Review*, 90 (1985): 567–593.

Lee, R. D. "Short-term Variation in Vital Rates, Prices and Weather." In E. A. Wrigley and R. S. Schofield, *The Population History of England and Wales, 1541–1871: A Reconstruction*. Cambridge: Harvard University Press, 1981.

Le Roy Ladurie, Emmanuel (trans. Ben and Sian Reynolds). *The Territory of the Historian*. Chicago: University of Chicago Press, 1979.

Levine, David. "The Reliability of Parochial Registration and the Representativeness of Family Reconstitution." *Population Studies*, XXX (1976): 107–122.

————. *Family Formation in the Age of Nascent Capitalism*. New York: Academic Press, 1977.

Lindert, Peter. "English Living Standards, Population and Wrigley-Schofield." *Explorations in Economic History*, 20 (1983): 131–155.

Lindert, Peter, and Jeffrey G. Williamson. "English Workers' Living Standards: A New Look." *Economic History Review*, 2d ser., XXXVI (1983): 1–25.

Lipson, Ephriam. *The History of the Woollen and Worsted Industries*. London: A & L Black, 1921.

Lloyd-Jones, R., and A. A. LeRoux. "The Size of Firms in the Cotton Industry: Manchester, 1815–1841." *Economic History Review*, 2d ser., 33 (February 1980): 72–82.

Locke, John. *Two Treatises on Government*. London: Mentor Books, 1963; reprint.

McClure, Peter. "Patterns of Migration in the Late Middle Ages: The Evidence of English Place-Name Surnames." *Economic History Review*, 2d ser., XXXII (1979): 167–182.

MacFarlane, Alan. *The Origins of English Individualism: The Family, Property and Social Transition*. Oxford: Basil Blackwell, 1978.

McIntosh, Marjorie K. *Autonomy and Community: The Royal Manor of Havering, 1200–1500*. Cambridge: Cambridge University Press, 1986.

McKeon, T., and R. G. Brown. "Medical Evidence Related to English Population Changes in the Eighteenth Century." In D. V. Glass and D. E. C. Eversley, eds., *Population in History: Essays in Historical Demography*. London: Edward Arnold, 1965.

McLeod, Hugh. *Class and Religion in the Late Victorian City*. London: Croom Helm, 1974.

MacPherson, C. B. *The Political Theory of Possessive Individualism: Hobbes to Locke.* Oxford: Clarendon Press, 1962.

Malmgreen, Gail. *Silk Town: Industry and Culture in Macclesfield.* Hull: Hull University Press, 1985.

―――. "Domestic Discords: Women and the Family in East Chesire Methodism, 1750–1830." In James Obelkevich, Lyndal Roper, and Raphael Samuel, eds., *Disciplines of Faith: Studies in Religion, Politics and Patriarchy.* London: Routledge & Kegan Paul, 1987.

Malthus, Thomas. *An Essay on the Principle of Population.* London: Penguin Books, 1982; reprint.

Mandler, Peter. "The Making of the New Poor Law *Redivivus*," *Past and Present,* 117 (1987): 131–157.

Mann, Julia de Lacey. "Clothiers and Weavers in Wiltshire during the Eighteenth Century." In L. S. Pressnell, ed., *Studies in the Industrial Revolution Presented to T. S. Ashton.* London: The Athlone Press, 1960.

―――. *The Cloth Industry in the West of England from 1640 to 1880.* Oxford: Clarendon Press, 1971.

Manning, Roger B. *Village Revolts: Social Protest and Popular Disturbances in England, 1509–1640.* Oxford: Clarendon Press, 1988.

Marland, Hilary. *Medicine and Society in Wakefield and Huddersfield, 1780–1870.* New York: Cambridge University Press, 1987.

Marrimer, Sheila. "English Bankruptcy Records and Statistics before 1850." *Economic History Review,* XXXIII (1980): 351–365.

Marshall, T. H. "The Population Problem during the Industrial Revolution." In D. V. Glass and D. E. C. Eversley, eds., *Population in History: Essays in Historical Demography.* London: Edward Arnold, 1965.

Martin, David. *A General Theory of Secularization.* Oxford: Basil Blackwell, 1978.

Martins, Susanna Wade. *A Great Estate at Work: The Holkham Estate and Its Inhabitants in the Nineteenth Century.* Cambridge: Cambridge University Press, 1980.

Mathias, Peter. "Capital, Credit and Entrepreneurship in the Industrial Revolution." *Journal of European Economic History,* II (1973): 121–143.

Matthews, R. C. O. *A Study in Trade-Cycle History: Economic Fluctuations in Great Britain, 1833–1842.* Cambridge: Cambridge University Press, 1954.

Medick, Hans. "The Proto-industrial Family Economy: The Structural Function of Household and Family during the Transition from Peasant Society to Industrial Capitalism." *Social History,* I (1976): 291–315.

Mendels, Franklin F. "Proto-industrialization: The First Phase of the Industrialization Process." *Journal of Economic History*, XXXII (1972): 241–261.

———. "Social Mobility and Phases of Industrialization." *Journal of Interdisciplinary History*, VII (1976): 193–216.

Mills, Dennis R. "The Christening Custom at Melbourne, Cambridgeshire." *Local Population Studies*, XII (1973): 11–22.

———. "An Economic, Tenurial, Social and Demographic Study of an English Peasant Village, 1780–1840." Report to the (British) Social Science Research Council (1977).

———. "Aspects of Marriage: An Example of Applied Historical Studies." Draft paper submitted to the Faculty of Social Sciences, Open University, U.K. (1978).

———. *Lord and Peasant in Nineteenth Century Britain*. London: Croom Helm, 1980.

———. "The Nineteenth-Century Peasantry of Melbourne, Cambridgeshire." In Richard M. Smith, ed., *Land, Kinship and Life-Cycle*. Cambridge: Cambridge University Press, 1984.

Minchinton, W. I. "Agriculture in Gloucestershire during the Napoleonic Wars." *Transactions of the Bristol and Gloucester Archaeological Society*, LXVIII (1949): 165–183.

Mingay, G. E. *Enclosure and the Small Farmer in the Age of the Industrial Revolution*. London: Macmillan, 1968.

———. *The Gentry: The Rise and Fall of a Ruling Class*. London: Longmans, 1976.

Mitchell, B. R., ed. *European Historical Statistics*, abridged ed. New York: Columbia University Press, 1978.

Moir, Esther. "The Gentlemen Clothiers: A Study of the Organization of the Gloucestershire Cloth Trade, 1750–1835." In H. P. R. Finberg, ed., *Gloucestershire Studies*. Leicester: Leicester University Press, 1957.

———. *Local Government in Gloucestershire, 1775–1800*. Bristol and Gloucester Archaeological Society Publication No. 8. Bristol: Gloucester Archaeological Society, 1969.

———. "Marling and Evans, King's Stanley and Ebley Mills." *Textile History*, I (1971): 28–56.

Moore, D. C. *The Politics of Deference: A Study of Mid-Nineteenth Century British Political Systems*. New York: Barnes & Noble, 1976.

Moore, R. *Pit-Men, Preachers and Politics: The Effects of Methodism in a Durham Mining Community*. Cambridge: Cambridge University Press, 1976.

Morrill, John. "The Ecology of Allegiance in the English Revolution." *Journal of British Studies*, 26 (1987): 451–467.

Munger, Frank. "Contentious Gatherings in Lancashire, England, 1750–1830." In Louise A. and Charles Tilly, eds., *Class Conflict and Collective Action*. Beverly Hills, Calif.: Sage Publications, 1981.

Musgrove, F. "Middle-Class Education and Employment in the Nineteenth Century." *Economic History Review*, 2d ser., XII (1959): 99–111.

Neale, R. S. *Class in English History, 1680–1850*. Oxford: Basil Blackwell, 1981.

Newby, Howard. "The Deferential Dialectic." *Comparative Studies in Society and History*, XV (1975): 139–164.

Nie, N. H., C. H. Hull, K. Steinbrenner, and D. H. Bent. *The Statistical Package of the Social Sciences (SPSS)*, 2d ed. New York: McGraw-Hill, 1975.

Nietzsche, Friedrich (Walter Kaufmann, trans., ed.). *On the Geneology of Morals*. New York: Random House, 1969.

Nuttall, Geoffrey F. *The Holy Spirit in Puritan Faith and Experience*. Oxford: Oxford University Press, 1946.

———. "Northamptonshire and the Modern Question: A Turning Point in Eighteenth Century Dissent." *Journal of Theological Studies*, XVI (1965): 101–123.

———. "Calvinism in Free Church History." *The Baptist Quarterly*, XXII (1968): 418–428.

———. *Howel Harris, 1714–1773: The Last Enthusiast*. Cardiff: Cardiff University Press, 1975.

———. "Questions and Answers: An 18th Century English Correspondence." *Baptist Quarterly*, XXXVI (1977): 139–140.

Obelkevich, James. *Religion and Rural Society: South Lindsey, 1825–1875*. Oxford: Clarendon Press, 1976.

O'Gorman, Frank. "Electoral Deference in Unreformed England." *Journal of Modern History*, 56 (1984): 391–429.

Olney, R. J. *Lincolnshire Politics, 1832–1885*. New York: Oxford University Press, 1973.

Parker, R. A. C. *Coke of Norfolk: A Financial and Agricultural Study, 1707–1842*. Oxford: Clarendon Press, 1975.

Patten, J. H. C. "Patterns of Migration and Movement of Labour to Three Pre-Industrial East Anglican Towns." *Journal of Historical Geography*, II (1976): 111–129.

Payne, P. L. *British Entrepreneurship in the Nineteenth Century*. London: MacMillan, 1974.

Perkin, Harold. *The Origins of Modern English Society, 1780–1880.* London: Routledge & Kegan Paul, 1969.

Perry, R. "The Gloucestershire Woollen Industry, 1100–1690." *Transactions of the Bristol and Gloucester Archaeological Society,* LXVI (1945): 49–137.

Phillips, Paul T. *The Sectarian Spirit: Sectarianism, Society and Politics in Victorian Cotton Towns.* Toronto: University of Toronto Press, 1982.

Pinchbeck, Ivy. *Women Workers and the Industrial Revolution, 1750–1850.* New York: A. M. Kelly, 1969.

Pleck, Elizabeth H. "Two Worlds in One: Work and Family." *Journal of Social History,* X (1976): 178–195.

Pocock, J. G. A. *The Ancient Constitution and the Feudal Law.* Cambridge: Cambridge University Press, 1957.

Pollard, Sydney. "Factory Discipline in the Industrial Revolution." *Economic History Review,* 2d ser., XVI (1963): 254–271.

———. *The Genesis of Modern Management.* Cambridge: Harvard University Press, 1965.

Pollock, Frederick. *The Land Laws.* London: Macmillan, 1896.

Pollock, Frederick, and F. E. Maitland. *The History of the English Law before the Time of Edward I,* vols. I and II. Cambridge: Cambridge University Press, 1968.

Ponting, K. G. *The Woollen Industry of South-West England: An Industrial, Economic and Technical Survey.* Bath: Adams and Dart, 1971.

Porter, Roy. *English Society in the Eighteenth Century.* New York: Penguin Books, 1982.

Postan, Michael. "The Chronology of Labour Services." *Transaction of the Royal Historical Soceity,* 4th ser., XX (1937): 169–193.

Pressnell, L. S. *Country Banking in the Industrial Revolution.* Oxford: Clarendon Press, 1956.

Prothero, I. *Artisans and Politics in Early Nineteenth Century London: John Gast and his Times.* Folkestone: Dawson and Sons, 1979.

Phythian-Adams, Charles. *Continuity, Fields and Fission: The Making of a Midland Parish.* Leicester: Leicester University Press, 1978.

———. *Rethinking English Local History.* Leicester: Leicester University Press, 1987.

Rackham, Oliver. "The Forest: Woodland and Wood-Pasture in Medieval England." In Kathleen Biddick, ed., *Archaeological Approaches to Medieval Europe. Studies in Medieval Culture,* vol. XVIII. Medieval Institute Publications. Kalamazoo, Mich.: Western Michigan University, 1985.

Raftis, J. Ambrose. *Tenure and Mobility: Studies in the Social History of the Mediaeval English Village.* Pontifical Institute of Medieval Studies, Studies and Texts, No. 8. Toronto: Pontifical Institute of Medieval Studies Press, 1964.

Randall, Adrian J. "Labour and the Industrial Revolution in the West of England Woollen Industry." University of Birmingham, Ph.D. dissertation, 1979.

Ravensdale, J. R. *Liable to Floods: Village Landscape on the Edge of the Fens, A D 450–1850.* Cambridge: Cambridge University Press, 1974.

Razi, Zvi. *Life, Marriage and Death in a Medieval Parish: Economy, Society and Demography in Halesowen.* Cambridge: Cambridge University Press, 1980.

Razzell, P. E. "Population Growth and Economic Change." In E. L. Jones and G. E. Mingay, eds., *Land, Labour and Population in the Industrial Revolution: Essays Presented to J. D. Chambers.* London: Edward Arnold, 1967.

Reay, Barry. "The Social Origins of Early Quakerism." *Journal of Interdisciplinary History*, XI (1980): 55–72.

Redford, Arthur. *Labour Migration in England, 1800–1850.* Manchester: Manchester University Press, 1964.

Rice, J. G. "Studying the Modernization Process at the Scale of the Locality." In J. Sundin and E. Soderlund, eds., *Time, Space and Man: Essays in Microdemography.* Atlantic Highlands, N.J.: Humanities Press, 1979.

Roberts, David. *Paternalism in Early Victorian England.* New Brunswick, N.J.: Rutgers University Press, 1979.

Rollison, David. "Property, Ideology and Popular Culture in a Gloucestershire Village, 1660–1740." *Past and Present*, 93 (1981): 70–97.

Rose, M. E. "Social Change and the Industrial Revolution." In R. Floud and D. McClosky, eds., *The Economic History of Britain since 1700. I: 1700–1860.* Cambridge: Cambridge University Press, 1981.

Rudé, George, "The Pre-Industrial Crowd." In George Rudé, *Paris and London in the Eighteenth Century.* New York: Viking Press, 1973.

Sabean, David W. *Power in the Blood: Popular Culture and Village Discourse in Early Modern Germany.* Cambridge: Cambridge University Press, 1984.

SAS Institute. *SAS/ETS User's Guide*, Version 5 ed. Cary, N.C.: SAS Institute, 1984.

Schofield, R. S. "Age-Specific Mobility in an Eighteenth Century Rural English Parish." *Annales de Démographie Historique* (1970, 1971): 261–296.

———. "The Impact of Scarcity and Plenty on Population Change in

England, 1541–1871." In Robert I. Rotberg and Theodore K. Rabb, eds., *Hunger and History: The Impact of Changing Food Production and Consumption Patterns on Society.* Cambridge: Cambridge University Press, 1986.

Scott, Joan W., and Louise A. Tilly. "Women's Work and the Family in Nineteenth Century Europe." *Comparative Studies in Society and History*, XVII (1975): 447–476.

Seaver, Paul. *Wallington's World: A Puritan Artisan in Seventeenth Century London.* Stanford: Stanford University Press, 1985.

Semmel, Bernard. *The Methodist Revolution.* New York: Basic Books, 1973.

Sharp, Buchanan. *In Contempt of All Authority: Rural Artisans and Riot in the West of England, 1588–1660.* Berkeley, Los Angeles, London: University of California Press, 1980.

Shelton, Walter. *English Hunger and Industrial Disorders: A Study of Social Conflict during the First Decade of George III's Reign.* Toronto: University of Toronto Press, 1973.

Shiner, L. "The Concept of Secularisation in Empirical Research." *Journal for the Scientific Study of Religion*, VI (1967): 202–220.

Simpson, Alan W. B. *A History of the Land Law*, 2d ed. Oxford: Clarendon Press, 1986.

Smelser, Neil. *Social Change in the Industrial Revolution: An Application of Theory to the British Cotton Industry.* Chicago: University of Chicago Press, 1959.

———. "Sociological History: The Industrial Revolution and the British Working Class Family." *Journal of Social History*, I (1967): 18–35.

———. "Toward a Theory of Modernization." In George Dalton, ed., *Tribal and Peasant Economies: Readings in Economic Anthropology.* Garden City, N.Y.: The Natural History Press, 1967.

Smith, Adam (George Stigler, ed.). *Selections from the Wealth of Nations.* Arlington Heights, Ill.: AHM Crofts, 1957.

Smith, A. H. *The Place Names of Gloucestershire*, vol. XXXVIII. Cambridge: Cambridge University Press, 1964.

Spufford, Margaret. *Contrasting Communities: English Villagers in the Sixteenth and Seventeenth Centuries.* Cambridge: Cambridge University Press, 1974.

Sterns, Peter. "Modernization and Social History: Some Suggestions and a Muted Cheer." *Journal of Social History*, XIV (1980): 189–209.

Stone, Lawrence. *Marriage, Sex and the Family in England, 1500–1880.* New York: Harper & Row, 1979.

———. "The New Eighteenth Century." *The New York Review of Books*, 29 March 1984, pp. 42–48.

Stone, Lawrence, and Jeanne C. Fawtier Stone. *An Open Elite? England, 1540–1880*. Oxford: Clarendon Press, 1984.

Tann, Jennifer. "Some Probelms of Waterpower—a Study of Mill Siting in Gloucestershire." *Transactions of the Bristol and Gloucester Archaeological Society*, LXXXIV (1965): 53–77.

———. *Gloucesterhire Woollen Mills*. Newton Abbott, Devonshire: David & Charles, 1967.

———. *The Development of the Factory*. London: Cornmarket Press, 1970.

———. "The Employment of Power in the West-of-England Wool Industry, 1790–1840." In N. B. Harte and K. G. Ponting, eds., *Textile History and Economic History: Essays in Honour of Julia de Lacey Mann*. Manchester: Manchester University Press, 1973.

Tawney, R. H. *Religion and the Rise of Capitalism: An Historical Study*. London: Longmans, Green & Co., 1964.

Taylor, A. J., ed. *The Standard of Living in the Industrial Revolution*. London: Methuen, 1975.

Taylor, George. "Types of Capitalism in Eighteenth Century France." *English Historical Review*, LXXIX (1964): 478–497.

Temin, P. "Steam and Waterpower in the Early Nineteenth Century." *Journal of Economic History*, XXVI (1966): 187–205.

Thane, Pat. "Women and the Poor Law in Victorian and Edwardian England." *History Workshop Journal*, 6 (1978): 29–51.

Thirsk, Joan, "Industries in the Countryside." In F. J. Fischer, ed., *Essays in the Economic and Social History of Tudor-Stuart England*. Cambridge: Cambridge University Press, 1961.

———. "The Farming Regions of England." In Joan Thirsk, ed., *Agrarian History of England and Wales*, vol. 4: *1500–1640*. Cambridge: Cambridge University Press, 1967.

Tholfsen, Trygve, *Working Class Radicalism in Mid-Victorian England*. New York: Columbia University Press, 1977.

Thomas, Keith. *Religion and the Decline of Magic*. New York: Charles Scribner & Sons, 1971.

Thompson, Dorothy. *The Chartists: Popular Politics in the Industrial Revolution*. New York: Pantheon, 1984.

Thompson, Edward P. *The Making of the English Working Class*. New York: Random House, 1963.

———. "Time, Work-Discipline and Industrial Capitalism." *Past and Present*, 38 (1967): 56–97.

———. "The Moral Economy of the English Crowd in the Eighteenth Century." *Past and Present*, 50 (1971): 76–136.

———. "Patrician Society, Plebeian Culture." *Journal of Social History*,

VII (1974): 382–405.

———. *Whigs and Hunters: The Origin of the Black Act.* New York: Random House, 1975.

———. "Eighteenth Century English Society: Class Struggle without Class." *Social History*, III (1978): 133–165.

Thompson, F. M. L. *English Landed Society in the Nineteenth Century.* London: Routledge & Kegan Paul, 1963.

Tilly, Charles. "Migration in Modern European History." In J. Sundin and E. Soderlund, eds., *Time, Space and Man: Essays in Microdemograpy.* Atlantic Highlands, N.J.: Humanities Press, 1977.

———. *As Sociology Meets History.* New York: Academic Press, 1981.

Tipps, Dean C. "Modernization Theory and the Comparative Study of Societies: A Critical Perspective." *Comparative Studies in Society and History*, XV (1973): 199–226.

Titow, J. Z. *Winchester Yields: A Study in Medieval Agricultural Productivity.* Cambridge: Cambridge University Press, 1972.

Toennis, Ferdinand (trans., ed. Charles P. Loomis). *Community and Association.* East Lansing: Michigan State University Press, 1957.

Toon, Peter. *The Emergence of Hyper-Calvinism in English Nonconformity, 1689–1765.* London: The Olive Tree, 1968.

Trumbach, Randolph. *The Rise of the Egalitarian Family: Aristocratic Kinship and Domestic Relations in Eighteenth Century England.* New York: Academic Press, 1978.

Underdown, David. *Revel, Riot and Rebellion: Popular Politics and Culture in England, 1603–1660.* Oxford: Clarendon Press, 1985.

———. "A Reply to John Morrill." *Journal of British Studies*, 26 (1987): 468–488.

Urdank, Albion M. "Economic Decline in the English Industrial Revolution: The Gloucester Wool Trade, 1800–1840." *Journal of Economic History*, XLV (1985): 427–433.

———. "Custom, Conflict and Traditional Authority in the Gloucester Weaver Strike of 1825." *Journal of British Studies*, 25 (1986): 193–226.

———. "Dissenting Community: Religion, Economy and Society in the Vale of Nailsworth, Gloucestershire, 1780–1850: An Economic, Tenurial, Social and Demographic Study." Unpublished Ph.D. dissertation, Columbia University, 1983.

Valenze, Deborah M. *Prophetic Sons and Daughters: Female Preaching and Popular Religion in Industrial England.* Princeton: Princeton University Press, 1985.

Van Den Berg, J. "Quaker and Chiliast: The 'Contrary Thoughts' of William Ames and Petrus Serrarius." In R. Buick Knox, ed., *Reformation,*

Conformity and Dissent: Essays in Honour of Geoffrey Nuttall. London: Epworth Press, 1977.

Vann, Richard T. *The Social Development of Early Quakerism, 1655–1755*. Cambridge: Harvard University Press, 1969.

Vinovskis, Maris. *Fertility in Massachusetts from the Revolution to the Civil War*. New York: Academic Press, 1981.

Walker, Mack. *German Home Towns: Community, State and General Estate, 1648–1871*. Ithaca: Cornell University Press, 1971.

Walsh, John. "Origins of the Evangelical Revival." In G. V. Bennett and J. D. Walsh, eds., *Essays in Modern Church History in Memory of Norman Sykes*. London: Adam & Charles Black, 1966.

———. "Methodism and the Mob in the Eighteenth Century." In G. J. Cumming and Derek Baker, eds., *Popular Belief and Practice: Studies in Church History*, vol. VIII. Oxford: Basil Blackwell, 1972.

———. "Elie Halèvy and the Birth of Methodism." *Transactions of the Royal Historical Society*, 5th ser., XXV (1975): 1–20.

Ward, J. T. *Chartism*. London: Croom Helm, 1973.

Watson, C. E. "The Minchinhampton Custumal and Its Place in the Story of the Manor." *Transactions of the Bristol and Gloucester Archaeological Society*, LIV (1932): 205–384.

Webb, Sidney, and Beatrice Webb. *English Local Government from the Revolution to the Municipal Corporation Act*, vol. I. London: Longmans, Green & Co., 1906.

Weber, Eugen. *Peasants into Frenchmen: The Modernization of Rural France, 1870–1914*. Stanford: Stanford University Press, 1976.

Weber, Max (trans. Talcott Parsons). *The Protestant Ethic and the Spirit of Capitalism*. New York: Charles Scribner & Sons, 1976.

Weiner, Martin J. *English Culture and the Decline of the Industrial Spirit, 1850–1980*. Cambridge: Cambridge University Press, 1981.

Wickham, E. R. *Church and People in an Industrial City*. London: Lutterworth Press, 1957.

Williams, Frederick. *Reasoning with Statistics*. New York: Holt, Rinehart and Winston, 1979.

Wilson, Bryan R. *Religion in a Secular Society: A Sociological Comment*. London: Watts, 1966.

———. "An Analysis of Sect Development." In Bryan R. Wilson, ed., *Patterns of Sectarianism: Organization and Ideology in Social and Religious Movements*. London: Heinemann, 1967.

Wonnacott, Ronald J., and Thomas H. Wonnacott. *Econometrics*. New York: John Wiley & Sons, 1970.

Wordie, J. R. "The Chronology of English Enclosure, 1500–1914." *Economic History Review*, 2d ser., XXXVI (1983): 483–505.

Wrightson, Keith. "Two Concepts of Order: Justices, Constables and Jurymen in Seventeenth Century England." In John Brewer and John Styles, eds., *An Ungovernable People: The English and Their Law in the Seventeenth and Eighteenth Centuries.* New Brunswick, N.J.: Rutgers University Press, 1980.

Wrightson, Keith, and David Levine. *Poverty and Piety in an English Village: Terling, 1525–1700.* New York: Academic Press, 1979.

Wrigley, E. A., ed. *Introduction to English Historical Demography: From the Sixteenth to the Nineteenth Centuries.* London: Weidenfeld and Nicolson, 1966.

Wrigley, E. A. "The Process of Modernization and the Industrial Revolution in England." *Journal of Interdisciplinary History*, III (1972): 225–259.

———. "The Growth of Population in Eighteenth Century England: A Conundrum Resolved." *Past and Present*, 98 (1983): 121–150.

Wrigley, E. A., and R. S. Schofield. *The Population History of England, 1541–1871: A Reconstruction.* Cambridge: Harvard University Press, 1981.

Wuthnow, Robert, ed. *The Religious Dimension: New Directions in Quantitative Research.* New York: Academic Press, 1979.

Wuthnow. Robert. *Meaning and Moral Order: Explorations in Cultural Analysis.* Berkeley, Los Angeles, London: University of California Press, 1987.

Yelling, J. A. *Common Field and Enclosure in England, 1450–1850.* London: Macmillan, 1977.

Yeo, Stephen. *Religion and Voluntary Organizations in Crisis.* London: Croom Helm, 1976.

Yinger, J. M. "Pluralism, Religion and Secularism." *Journal for the Scientific Study of Religion*, VI (1967): 17–30.

Index

Abb (term for weft), 210–211, 389 nn. 4, 8

Adolescent mortality, 155–157

Adult mortality, 152, 157, 205, tables 159–162

Affers (draught animals), 80–82

Age structure, 163–168; of attendance patterns at Shortwood Church, 286–288, 289–290; and mortality data, 154–163, 168

Aggregative analysis, 7, 341–342 n. 23

Agrarian rights, protests against loss of, 231, 237, 245

Agriculture, 25–26, 40–41, 55; and by-employment, 21, 237, 346 n. 24; changes in, 74–82; communal practices controlled by manor courts, 104, 110; relationship of changes in to class formation, 74–75, 237, 307–308

Aldridge, Richard (magistrate), 234; role in 1825 riots, 223–227, 229, 243–244

Altruism, mixed with self-interest among employers, 216, 217–218, 244

Amberly Church (Anglican church), 98–99, 362 n. 85

Anderson, Michael, 282, 370 n. 23

Anderson, Olive, 405 n. 35

Anglican (Church of England) records/ registers, use in demographic studies, 131, 137, 138–152, 372 n. 35, 373 n. 36, table 145

Anglicans, 87, 96–97, 110, 149; collaboration with Nonconformists, 86, 88, 101. See also Church of England

Anomie, 12, 245, 285, 301, 343–344 n. 33

Anti-Corn Law League, 242, 245–246, 379 n. 141. See also Corn Laws, movement against

Apprenticeship (Tudor) statutes, 192, 384 n. 10

Apprenticeships, parish expenditures for as poor relief, 114, 116

Apprentice weavers, 229–230, 233–234, 394 n. 73; colts, 199, 234, 387 n. 160; role in 1825 strike, 209, 219

Arable land: abandonment by clothworkers, 59, 353–354 n. 13; enclosures of, 74–79, 82

Artisans, 34, 250–253, 310; factory workers classed as, 404–405 n. 29

Australian government, assumption of emigration costs, 136

Authority, structures of, 4, 53, 309; in local Baptist church meetings, 294, 295, 298–301; in Society of Friends, 258–259, 274; transfer of from manor to parish and Justices of the Peace, 102, 106, 110

Autonomy, 296, 309–310; of crowd, 392–393 n. 44, 393 n. 45; of family for Quakers, 264

Avening (village), 23–26, 37, map 38

Avening Baptist Church, 293, 294–298

Avening manor, 17, 103, 119, 362–363 n. 4; enclosure of common fields and wastes, 77, 237. See also Minchinhampton-Avening manor

Avening parish, 17, 98, 307, map inset 18; landownership patterns, 57–59, 64, 353 nn. 6, 7, 8; population patterns, 132–135, 368–369 n. 5; registration figures, 138–139, 372 n. 33

Bankruptcy, 31; in Gloucester's woolen
  trade, 171, 175–177, 181, 378 nn. 27,
  29, 381 n. 74, table 172–173; Quaker
  moral attitudes toward, 267–270
Banks, Sarah, 341 n. 22
Baptism, 292, 298; delaying of, 139–140;
  believers', 90, 95, 276, 299–300 (*see
  also* Conversion); by immersion, 299–
  300; infant, 86, 88, 90, 95, 140
Baptisms, 137, 138–147, 276–280, 371
  n. 28; as representative of births, 139–
  142, 371 n. 29, 373 nn. 40, 43, 376 n.
  61
Baptists, 12, 198, 275, 309, 359–360 n.
  39; church order and discipline, 293–
  303; membership growth and
  economic changes, 143–144, 149–151,
  374 n. 51, 374–375 n. 52; registers as
  data source for study of mortality,
  154–155; registration of births, 140–
  141, tables 147–148; support for
  itinerant preachers, 293, 406 n. 51. *See
  also* Shortwood Baptist Church
Barley, 41
Barnard, Edward (clothier-deacon), 331
Barton End, 23, 25–26
Bath-Gloucester road, 43–44
Baxter, Richard (minister), 86, 91–92
Baxterianism, 90, 91–92, 93. *See also*
  Calvinism, moderate
Beer, Samuel H., 348 n. 58
Believers' baptism, 90, 95, 276, 299–300.
  See also Conversion
Bequests. *See* Wills
Biddick, Kathleen, 342–343 n. 26
Biggs, William, conversion experience, 88
Birthday of a Christian, shifted from
  infant baptism to conversion, 88–89,
  299–300
Birthright Quakerism, 265–266
Births, 131, 133–134, 138–154, 168,
  368–369 n. 5, 371 n. 29; baptisms as
  representative of, 139–142, 373 nn. 40,
  43, 376 n. 61; comparison of Anglican
  to Nonconformist, 142, 144–152;
  influence of cloth production on, 146–
  151, 374 n. 48; influence of wheat
  prices on, 146–148, 373–374 n. 47
Bisley, rioting and ducking in 1825, 222–
  227
Blackwell, Cornelius (clothier and lay
  leader), 295, 406 n. 59
Blackwell, John (landowner and deacon),
  120, 121, 294
Blackwell, Stephen (clothier and lay
  leader), 295, 406 n. 59

Bliss, Edward (clothier-deacon), 71, 331,
  355 n. 38
Boarding schools, curricula of, 28
Bohstedt, John, 392–393 n. 44, 393 n. 45
Bond, Sarah and George (business
  people), 269–270, 271
Boulton and Watt steam engine, use of,
  177, 180
Bowen, Samuel (minister), 93
Bowne, Cornelius (laborer), 30–31
Box (village), occupational structure, 23,
  table 24
Bread prices, 201, 215, 240, 242, 397 n.
  139
Brewing industry, 26, 41, 350 n. 75
Bristol, use of troops from in 1825 strike,
  220, 221, 222
Bristol-London railway line, 49
Bullocks, grazing on Minchinhampton
  Common, 80–82
Burder, John (minister), 90
Bureaucratization of Society of Friends,
  249, 258–259, 273–274
Burial of hearers and members at
  Shortwood Church grounds, 298, table
  299
Burials, 138, 152–157, 168, 368–369 n.
  5, 376 n. 61. *See also* Mortality
Burleigh (village), occupational structure,
  23, table 24
Business activity, Quaker discipline
  concerning morality of, 267–271, 400
  n. 70
By-employment, agriculture and industry
  as, 21, 237, 346 n. 24

Calvinism, 52, 289, 301
Calvinism, high, 94, 95–96, 272–273;
  practiced at Shortwood Baptist Church,
  93, 303
Calvinism, moderate: practiced at
  Shortwood Baptist Church, 292, 304;
  theology, 86, 87, 91–92, 93–94, 95,
  283, 358 n. 14, 360 n. 54, 403–404 n.
  15
Calvinistic Methodism, 87
Cam, cloth factory at, 181
Canal construction, 16, 42, 45–48
Capital and labor, 190–205; 1825 strike
  seen as confrontation between, 209,
  243
Capitalism, 241, 275, 311; Quaker
  attitude toward, 268–269, 308
Capitalization, 179–190, 208
Capital offense, damaging property as,
  225, 227, 228–229

Capital punishment, protests against, 402 n. 100

Carding, 177, 195; engines, 134, 180–181, 379–380 n. 47

Caroline, Queen, 119, 121–122, 123

Cash grants, as parish expenditures for poor relief, 114, 116

Cassimeres, 174, 219, 221, 236, 395 n. 82

Cattle, grazing on Minchinhampton Common, 80–82

Census of 1851, use in study of church attendance, 285, 404 n. 21

Chain (term of warp), 389 n. 4; 1824 increase in numbers per piece, 209–211, 389 n. 8, 389–390 n. 11, 392 n. 34

Chalford, violence in 1825 strike, 222–227

Chambers, Cornelius (woolcomber), 66, 76

Chambers, J. D., 75, 370 n. 22

Champion regions, 19, fig. 20

Chapel, 35, 232, 237, 288; abandonment for Union or protest meetings, 238, 245; attendance by Shortwood Baptist migrant members, 282–284

Chapel (chapelry), Anglican, 17, 96–97, 345 nn. 7, 8

Chartism, 204, 231, 232, 240–242, 245–246, 288–289

Chattel, real, 65, 69, 354 n. 17

Chayanov, Alexander, 340 n. 10

Children, 114, 190, 193; burials of, 155–157

Children of Israel, Quakers modeled after, 265

Chiliasm. *See* Millenarianism

Chiliasm of despair, 7, 288, 292, 308

Chi-square statistic, 80–82 table 16, 108–109 tables 18–20, 124 table 23, 167 table 40, 179 table 43, 379 n. 45

Church building program, Anglican, 97–100, 361 n. 76

Church meetings, local Baptist, 294, 295, 298–301

Church of England, 29, 98, 271, 309; attitude toward itinerant preaching, 294; Baptist servants pressured to attend, 283–284; erection of chapel at Nailsworth, 87, 96–97; latitudinarianism, 358 n. 9; Quaker qualities contrasted with, 258; reaction to Evangelical Revival, 96–100; relationship with Dissenting churches, 54, 84–85, 101; use of registers in demographic studies, 131, 137, 138–152, 372 n. 35, 373 n. 36, table 145. *See also* Anglicans

Church order, 258; of Baptists, 258, 275, 293–300; of Quakers, 249, 255–272

Church rates, payment by Dissenters, 120

Civil infractions, Court Baron jurisdiction over, 104

Clarendon Code, 86

Class, social, 209, 239, 288, 349 n. 62; attendance patterns at Shortwood Church by, 286–288; of Court Baron suitors, 107–109; nominalist definition of, 389 n. 3; occupations by, 329–330

Class consciousness, 209, 237–238

Class formation, 74, 237, 243, 307–308; social mobility within context of, 27–35, 51–52

Class meetings (in Baptist churches), 300–301

Clays, 39

Clissold, William (the younger) (clothier-deacon), 330

Closed (squires') parishes, 7, 56, 59, 341 n. 22

Closed shop, among weavers' demands, 230

Closes (Tynings), 76, 79

Cloth cutters, 180, 204–205

Clothiers, 20–21, 26, 178, 198, 234–235, 236; and canal financing, 46; face-to-face dealings with master weavers, 215–216, 217; as lords of manors, 118–119; master weavers' aspirations to become, 219, 230; as Quakers, 250, table 251; on relationship between wages and labor productivity, 240, 397 n. 132; as Shortwood Baptsit Church leaders, 296–298; and strike of 1825, 209–211, 215–228; and strikes and protests 1827–1848, 233–243; support for anti-Corn Laws movements, 119, 232, 240–242, 245–246, 288; wills, 27–28

Clothing: parish expenditure on for poor relief, 114; supplied by parishes to emigrants, 136

Cloth mills, 38–39, 177–190, 217; sales of, 171, 175–177, 178–179, 378 n. 29, 379 n. 44, table 172–173

Cloth (woolen) trade, 19–21, 208, 244; demographic effects of economic factors in, 133, 135, 146–151, 157, 374 n. 48, 374–375 n. 52, tables 158–159; industrialization of, 170–207; and weaver strike of 1825, 208–231

Clothworkers (Woolworkers), 23–27, 34, 192, 217; exploitation of, 211; migration of, 134–135; as Quakers,

Clothworkers (*continued*)
250, table 58, 251; role of less-skilled in 1825 weavers' strike, 219; use of arable land, 59, 353–354 n. 13. *See also* Spinners; Weavers; Weavers, factory; Weavers, master

Clutterbuck, Edmund (clothier), 27, 71–72

Coal, 46, 48–49, 183, 184

Cobbet, William, 38

Cole, Thomas (weaver), 197–198, 387 n. 157

Cole, W. A., 204, 388 n. 169

Collective (crowd) action, 219–220, 232; paternalism-deference mode of, 218–219, 243, 392–393 n. 44

Colored cloth, weaving rates negotiated for, 211, table 210

Colts (youthful apprentices), 199, 234, 387 n. 160

Combination Acts, repeal of,208

Commissioners for the Colonization of South Australia, 136

Commoners' rights, 80, 237

Common fields, enclosing of, 77–79, 237

Communications, growth of, and regionalization of local society, 42–51, 205

Communion, 298–299; open, 87, 285, 298–299, 304

Community: definitions of, 15; Shortwood Baptist Church as, 275, 282, 300–302, 303, 304

Conduct, importance to Quakers, 260, 265, 268–271

Congregationalists: birth and burial figures, 138, 140–142, 149, 152, 373 n. 43; role in Avening preaching room, 294–295. *See also* Forest Green Congregationalists

Conjugal rights of women, recognized by Society of Friends, 264

Conservatism of Quaker attitude toward business activity, 267–271

Consideration, legal doctrine of, 401 n. 73

Constables (Tithingmen), 104–105, 112, 113, 127; appointment of to deal with violence in 1825, 226–227, 228

Contracts, 268, 401 n. 73

Conversion, 88–89, 254, 299–300, 374 n. 51; Quaker doctrine on, 273, 402 n. 94; role in membership changes of Shortwood Baptist Church, 276–280, 284–285, 287

Conveyances, 67–69

Convincement, 273, 402 n. 94

Copyholds, 64, 65, 66–67, 69, 354 n. 18

Corn Law, movement against, 204, 288, 397 n. 141; support for, 119, 232, 240–242, 245–246

Cotswold Hills, 35; Sand (Supra-Liassic), 37, 39

Cottage industry, 20–21, 180, 190–193, 215–216, 310; transition to factory system, 171, 190–195, 205–207. *See also* Protoindustrialization

Cotton industry, compared to woolen industry, 197, 386 n. 145

Court Baron, 102, 104–105, 110–112; for Horsley Manor, 76–77, tables 317, 318

Court Leet, 102, 104, 105, 127; at Horsley manor, 76–77

Court of Assizes, and case involving Aldrich's actions, 223, 394 n. 72

Court of Recognition, 104

Court of Survey, 104, 110–112; for Horsley manor, table 318

Courts, customary, 104

Courts, manor, 75, 102–113, 309, 363 n. 17; attendance at, 106–113, 126, 363 nn. 17, 19, 20, 21. *See also* courts by name

Courtship, 260–263, 290

Craftsmen, 191, 199, 384 nn. 106, 107

Criminal offenses, Court Leet jurisdiction over, 104

Crowd action. *See* Collective action

Custom, 75, 102, 109–110, 210, 245, 266; weaver adherence to in 1825 strike, 209, 215

Customary obligations, 65–69, 72, 102, 126

Cutters, 180, 204–205

Dangerfield, Harriet, spiritual odyssey, 219–293, 374 n. 61, 405 n. 40

Davis, Amelia (Quaker minister), 259

Deacons, 238, 245, 288, 293–298

Dean, Forest of, protests over loss of agrarian rights, 396 n. 122

Deane, P., 204, 388 n. 169

Death, anticipation of, 290–292, 407 n. 28

Deaths. *See* Burials; Mortality

Deference, 55, 197–198, 225, 243, 309–310; co-existence with militancy, 232, 288; and collective action, 218–219, 243–244, 392–393 n. 44; empathy as basis for, 219, 393 n. 53; enthusiasm expressed in, 289; meanings, 209, 216–

217; shown by master weavers in 1825 strike, 209, 216; synthesis with paternalism and individualism, 118, 121, 125–126, 127

Denominationalism, 275, 362 n. 92; transformation of sects into, 2, 9, 12, 15, 84, 149, 308; transformation of Shortwood Baptists into, 275, 296, 302–304

Depression, psychological, as prevalent in 1850s, 288–289, 292

Depressions, economic (Trade depressions) (1825–1850), 132, 171–175, 232, 236, 290; effect on weavers' union, 235, 245; 1848, 288–289; T. F. Newman's sermons during, 301–302

Despair, and religious experience in 1850s, 7, 285, 288–289, 292, 308

Difference-of-Proportions (Z) test, 26, table 4, 384 n. 107

Difference-of-means (t) test, 33 table 6, 200, table 52, 251, table 58

Discipline (Baptists), 275, 300–303

Discipline (Quakers), 249, 255–272; concerning courtship, marriage, and kinship, 259, 260–267; concerning doctrinal orthodoxy, 271–272; concerning moral economy, 267–271

Dissent. *See* Nonconformity

Dissenters. *See* Nonconformists

Dissenters' Marriage Bill of 1835, 100

Divided parishes, 56

Doctrinal orthodoxy, Quaker enforcement of, 267, 271–272

Ducie, Lord (Henry Moreton), 119–120, 242

Ducking, used by weavers in 1825 strike, 222, 223, 224, 226

Dunkirk Mills, 181, 182, 378 n. 27

Durbin-Watson statistic, 147, 148, 150, 151, tables 28–31, 158, 159, tables 35–36

Durkheim, Emile, 391 n. 29

Dursley, 42, 181, 205

Dyehouse Mills, 180

Earnings. *See* Truck, payment in; Wages

East India Company, 171, 174, 221

East Riding, clothiers' use of steam power, 183, 381 n. 80

Economic conditions, 171–179, 189, 284, 310; effect on births and burials, 138, 146–154; effect on religious experience, 285, 288–290, 293

Ecumenicism, 100, 294–296, 362 n. 92

Edkins, Thomas (minister), 89–90

Egypt Mills, 181, 182, 381 n. 74

Elderly: attendance patterns at Shortwood Church, 290–291, table 286; mortality, table 162

Elders, in the Society of Friends, 257–258, 261

Election, 90, 93–94, 238, 292, 358 n. 14; anxiety concerning, 289, 301, 407 n. 78

Elite, 231, 249, 258, 309; division among as conducive to collective action and violence, 218–219; paternalism among, 308, 309–310

Ell (number of threads), 389 n. 4; weaving rates per, 389–390 n. 11, table 210

Emigration, colonial, 135–137

Empathy as basis for deference, 219, 393 n. 53

Employers, pressure on servants to conform to household's religious discipline, 283–284

Employment of labor through subscription schemes, 117–118, 127

Enclosure movement, 74–82, 237, 356 n. 41

Encroachment, 110–111

Enthusiasm, 87, 245, 274, 288, 301; Baptist churches as hotbeds of, 298; changes in first half of 19th century, 288–289; of early Quakerism, 272–273, 402 n. 98; among Forest Green Congregationalists, 87–88; moderate evangelicalism and millenarianism in, 238–239. *See also* Evangelicalism

Entrepreneurship, Quakers' attitude toward, 269–270

Entry fines (in manor leases), 66, 69, 82, 102

Escheats, 111–112

Esquire (title), 27, 30

Establishment: relationship to Dissent, 54, 55–56, 64, 83, 96, 102, 118, 125–127, 309; relationship with lower classes in wood-pasture region, 217, 391 n. 31

Evangelicalism, 150, 249, 274, 298, 308; and changes in collective spirituality, 288; chiliasm's conflict with moderate, 238; Halèvy thesis on, 1, 131, 337 n. 2; influence on emerging proletariat, 1–12; promotion of cultural values about work and poverty, 301–302; and Quakerism, 249, 256, 272, 402 n. 98; Shortwood Baptist Church's adaptation to, 275, 304

Evangelical Revival, 84–101, 276, 288, 295; and Dissenters' births, 146, 149,

Evangelical Revival (*continued*)
168; Old Dissent transformed into New
Dissent by, 307
Evans, Eli, consideration for membership
in Society of Friends, 264–265, 266,
400 n. 56
Exell, Timothy (weaver), 231, 242

Face-to-face relations between employers
and workers, 215–216, 217, 391 n. 29
Factory acts, opposition to, 217
Factory inspectors, judgments of
Yorkshire clothiers, 391 n. 33
Factory system, 135, 180–181, 192–200,
204–207; adaptation to discipline of,
197, 285, 288–289; effect on
secularization, 284, 293; effects on
Shortwood Baptist Church, 276–280,
285, 301–302; as eroding family work
unit, 193–194; transition to from
protoindustrial system, 11–12, 171,
205–207, 208–209, 310; transition to
paralleled by agrarian change, 237,
308. *See also* Loom factories/shops
Family, 232, 272, 281–282; Quaker discipline concerning, 260–264, 266, 400
n. 56; as unit of production, 190, 193
Family reconstitution studies, 7, 341–342
n. 23
Farmers, as middle-class occupation, 26
See also Agriculture
Fertility. *See* Births
Feudal obligations, remnants of in land
tenure, 64, 354 n. 15
Fewster, Anthony Rogers, 120, 189, 366
n. 64, 369 n. 11, 402 n. 100; expulsion
from and readmittance to Friends, 399
n. 43, 400 n. 61; on repeal of Corn
Laws, 240–241, 397 n. 138
Fields, names of, 41–42
Final perseverance of the Saints, doctrine
of, 292
Fine cloth market, 170, 174, 181, 206
Fines: as de facto rent charges, 110; for
nonattendance at manor courts, 106,
109, 126, 363 nn. 17, 19
Flint, Abraham (clothier-deacon), 330
Flint, Benjamin F. (deacon), 95–96
Flint, Thomas (minister), 95–96, 330
Fly shuttle, 196, 385 n. 133
Food: given to journeymen by master
weavers, 391 n. 22; relationship of
prices to wage rates, 240, 242. *See also*
Bread prices
"Foreign" labor. *See* Strangers

Forest Green (hamlet), age-sex structure,
163–168, 376–377 n. 68
Forest Green Congregationalists, 83, 84,
86, 101, 140, 258; birth and burial
records, 138, 140–142, 149, 152, 368–
369 n. 5; historic background, 86–90,
358 nn. 15, 20, 359 n. 24, table 91;
Shortwood Church as result of schism
among, 90–92; transformation into
denomination, 2, 9, 15
Forests, 41
Forfeitures, 111
Francis, Benjamin (minister), 93–95, 96,
293, 301, 303
Freehold, 57, 64, 69, 73–74
Freeholders: as jurors in Court Baron,
105; as parochial officials, 113
Freehold parishes. *See* Open parishes
Free seats/sittings, 98, 99, 361 n. 76
Friends, Society of (Quakers), 9, 120,
249, 255, 398 n. 12; birth and burial
figures, 142, 152; church order and
discipline, 249, 255–272, 300–301.
See also Nailsworth Society of Friends
Frogmarsh, rioting in 1825 strike, 222
Fuller, Andrew (minister), 360 n. 54
Fuller's Earth, 39–40
Fulling mills, 20, 177

Gemeinschaft, concept of, 8–9, 342 n. 25
Gender (Sex): attendance patterns at
Shortwood Church by, 286–288;
mortality by, 157–163, 168; Quaker's
preparative and monthly meetings
organized by, 256, 258, 259, 399 n. 28;
structure for Vale hamlets, 163–168.
See also Women
Gender bias in Quaker authoritarianism,
259
General Committee of the Society of
Friends, 257
General Turnpike Act of 1780, 44–45
Gentlemen, 26–27, 30; and wealth
distribution, 32–33, 52
"Gentleness," 18th-century view of, 32
Gentlewoman, 27
Gentry, 27–29, 34; disappearance among
Quakers, 250, 398 n. 5; paternalism,
116–118, 218, 408 n. 3
Geographic mobility, 11, 135–137, 275,
280–284. *See also* Immigration;
Outmigration
Giddens, Anthony, 349 n. 62
Gig mills, 180, 379–380 n. 47
Gilbert, Alan, 343–344 n. 33

Giles, Revd., 90–91
Gill, Daniel, 292, 374 n. 51
Glass, D. V., 371 n. 29
Gloucester-Swindon trunk line, 49
Governing class: manipulation of weavers in 1825 strike, 209; and paternalism-deference mode of collective action, 218–219, 243, 393 n. 45
Grace, free, 283, 291–292, 300, 304, 403–404 n. 15
Grace, Quaker theory of, 265, 271, 272–273
Grain, 41, 48, 397 n. 139. *See also* Wheat prices
Grazing lands, restricted access to, 75, 79–82
Great Reform Act, 122
Great Western Railway, 48–49
Gregory, Derek, 183
Grew, Raymond, 339 n. 7
Guise, B. W. (baronet and M.P.), 121

Halèvy, Elie, 275, 308; on transition to modern society, 1, 35, 52, 131, 337, n. 2, 349 n. 63
Harding, William (broadweaver), 90–91, 92
Harris, Charles (Chartist leader), 241–242
Havering, Royal Manor of, 339–340 n. 9
Hearers, 140, 141, 282–283, 285, 290, 298–299
Heriots, 66, 69, 72, 82, 102, 354–355 n. 22
Heskins, John, II (clothier-deacon), 121, 293, 331
Hierarchy: of officials of Society of Friends, 257–259, 274; traditional, 31–32, 35, 51
Hill, Christopher, 94
Hill, J. B. (clothier), 178
Hillier, Isaac (deacon), 29, 30, 31
Hillsely Mill, 181
Hinton, William (businessman), expulsion from Society of Friends, 268–269, 271
Hobsbawm, Eric, 245, 288, 390–391 n. 20, 393 n. 50, 396 n. 121
Holy Spirit, Quaker doctrine on, 260, 272–273, 402 n. 99
Hooper, Charles (clothier), 241
Hope Mills, 181, 182
Horsepower, use of, 178
Horses, grazing on Minchinhampton Common, 82, table 81

Horsley (village), map 38; elevation, 35
Horsley manor, 17, 76, 104, 119; courts, 104–105, 112, 318, table 317; leases, 65–67, 69, 70–71, 354–355 n. 22, 355 n. 25, table 315–316
Horsley-Nailsworth region: effect on of 1837–1842 depression, 174–175; population change, 137, 138–163
Horsley parish, 19, 85–86, 98, 237, 307; boundaries, 17, map inset 18; Anglican church reconstruction at, 99, 101, 362 n. 89; landownership structure, 59, 64, 353 nn. 9, 10, 11, table 60–61; occupational structure, 23–27, 190–192, 195, 384 nn. 106, 107, 108; outdoor relief, 114–116; population changes, 132–154, 368–369 n. 5; records of birth and burials, 138–139, 140, 152–154, 372 n. 35
Horsley Petty Sessions, 203
Humility and exercise of power, 257–258, 398 n. 24
Hundred Court, 104
Hunt, Reuben (president of weavers' committee) 224
Hyde, Thomas (millman), on Aldridge, 225
Hyett, W. H. (M.P.), 49, 122, 193, 367 n. 73, table 174

Illegitimacy, 232
Immigration, 135, 193, 232
Inchbrook Mill, 180–181, 182
Indebtedness, Quaker morality on, 268–271
Independence: and gentry paternalism, 116, 117, 121, 126; master weavers' aspiration for, 215
Individualism, 55–56, 268–269, 309, 408 n. 3; and customary practices, 102, 109–110; leaseholds as evidence of, 72, 82–83; synthesis with paternalism and deference, 118, 121, 125, 127
Industrial decline (1837–1864), Shortwood Baptist membership during era of, 276–280
Industrialization, 137, 209, 252, 275, 307–311; effect on mortality, 157, 376 nn. 63, 65; effect on secularization, 275, 284, 293; importance of New Dissent to emerging society, 307–308; and suicide, 405 n. 35. *See also* Factory system
Industrial Revolution, 138, 170–207, 243, 301–302, 376 n. 65

Industrial unionism. *See* Trade unionism; Union of weavers

Infant mortality, 140, 155, 157, 168, 376 n. 62

Inspiration, Quaker doctrine on, 257, 272–273, 402 n. 99

Investments, 3, 340 n. 12

Isichei, Elizabeth, 402 n. 98

Itinerant preaching, 293–294

James, M. E., 218–219, 393 n. 45

Jarvis, Revd., 89

Jennies, spinning. *See* Spinning jennies

Jenny shops, 177

Journeymen weavers, 190, 192–193, 196–200, 207, 383–384 n. 104, 384 n. 108, 387 n. 158; and 1825 strike, 209, 215, 219, 230; payment in truck, 233–235, 391 n. 22, 394 n. 73; treatment by master weavers, 230, 233–234; wages as issue in master weavers' 1824 demands, 210–212, 215–216, 390 nn. 15, 18, 391 n. 22

Joyce, Patrick, 216–217, 218, 244, 391 n. 29

Jury, 105, 111, 223

Justices of the Peace, 10, 102, 106, 110, 113, 127

Kerridge, Eric, 70

Keynton, Isaac, suicide, 289, 293, 405 n. 34

Kingswood, mills at, 175, 181

Kinship: failure of network for Shortwood Baptist migrant member, 281–282; Quaker discipline concerning, 260–267, 274, 400 n. 56

Labor, 171, 210; 1825 strike seen as confrontation between capital and, 209, 243; and Industrial Revolution, 189–205

Labor, gender division of, repatterning under factory system, 193–194, 206–207

Laborers (Laboring classes), 34, 215, 237–238; in 1811 Horsley Parish census, 191–192, 384 n. 106; support for weavers' strikes, 21, 233. *See also* Working classes

Labor time, 1824 proposed pay scale based on, 211–212, 215

Lancashire, 282; cotton industry, 197, 386 n. 145

Landlords, 10, 57, 191, 384 n. 107

Landowners, 27–28, 54–83; clothiers as, 218, 392 n. 38; resistance to railway route, 49; sympathy with Nonconformity, 309

Land tenure, 54–83

Latitudinarianism, 282–283, 358 n. 9

Lay leaders: as itinerant preachers, 293–294; Quaker elders as, 257

Leaseholds, 10, 55, 57, 64–73, 76, 82–83

Leases, 64–73, 82–83; at Horsley Manor, 65–72, 76, table 315–316

Legal practice on promise-keeping, in 19th century, 269, 401 n. 73

Leniency: as common practice in 18th-century legal system, 394 n. 80; shown to weavers accused of destroying property, 228–229

Levine, David, 4–5, 137, 339–340 n. 9, 376 n. 63

Lias Clay, 37, 39

Liberalism, classical, relationship to paternalist values, 408 n. 3

Lifehold leases, 65, 69, 82, 354 nn. 17, 18, 19

Lightpill Mill, 180

Light Within, Quaker doctrine of, 272–273

Lincolnshire rebellion (16th century), 218–219, 243

Littleworth (village), occupational structure, 23, fig. 25, table 24

Living, cost of, as justification for call for higher weaving rate, 212, 215

Living standards, and wheat prices, 203, 204, 207, 387–388 n. 164

Loans, 31, 230

Lodgemore Mills, 180, 182

London, canal traffic to, 46, 48

Longfords Mill, 182, 198

Longtree Hundred, 104, map inset 18

Loom factories/shops, 135, 192, 193, 230, 394 n. 73; proliferation following 1825 strike, 231–233, 235–237, 244–245, 395 n. 90. *See also* Factory system

Looms, 299–230, 237; power looms, 189, 236–237, 380 n. 64; renting, 216, 232–233; sales, 182, 380 n. 62

Lords of the manor, 10, 104–105, 118–125; clothiers as, 118–119, 218, 392 n. 38; and survival of customary obligations, 65–69

Lord's waste, 353 n. 6

Lower classes: horizontal social mobility, 31–32; relationship with Establishment in wood-pasture regions, 217, 391 n. 31

Lower district (of Gloucester): agreement between weavers and clothiers in 1825, 219, 220–221, 224, 227, 229, 243
Lower Forest Green Congregational Church, 89, 149
Lower middle class, 329; Quakers as, 250–253; at Shortwood Baptist Church, 288, 296, 298, 406–407 n. 63, table 286

Machinery, 171, 189, 236–237; opposition to, 231, 237–238, 241, 245, 396 n. 121; sales of, 178–179, 187, 379 n. 44
McIntosh, Marjorie, 339–340 n. 9
Magistrates, 218, 243; role in weavers' 1825 riots, 219, 222–227, 228–229, 243
Malting industry, 26, 41
Mandler, Peter, 408 n. 3
Mann, Julia de Lacey, 182, 231, 346 n. 24, 394 n. 71, 396 n. 108, 397 n. 132; on loom factories, 395 n. 90, 395–396 n. 104; on steam power, 183–184; on Yorkshire competition, 171, 183
Manning, Roger B., 354 n. 15
Manor courts. *See* Courts, manor
Market, 215, 308, 342–343 n. 26, 408 n. 3
Marling, N. S. (clothier), 180, 182–183
Marling, Samuel S. (clothier), 175, 389 n. 10
Marriage: legal requirement for, 100, 250; Quaker discipline concerning, 250, 259, 260–267, 399 nn. 38, 43; registration records, 138–139, 250–252, 372 nn. 33, 34
Marx, Karl, 74–75
Medical advances, and burial rate, 152
Meetings for discipline (Preparative meetings) (Quaker), 256, 266
Meetings for worship (Quaker), 255–256, 266
Mendels, F. F., 344 n. 2
Methodism, 5, 294, 307, 394 n. 63; and Evangelical Revival, 84, 87, 274; Halévy's thesis on, 1, 337 n. 2
Middle-aged people, 164–166; attendance patterns at Shortwood Church, 290–291, table 286; mortality, fig. 161
Middle class, 215, 219, 230, 329; Nailsworth Society of Friends members as, 250–253; at Shortwood Church, 288, 296, 298, 304, 406–407 n. 63,

table 286; social mobility of, 27–31, 32–35, 52
Migration, 11, 135–137. *See also* Immigration; Outmigration
Militancy, 288, 308
Millenarianism (Chiliasm), 88, 245, 249, 273, 396 n. 123; and social protests of weavers and social operatives, 238–240
Miller, James (Quaker businessman), 270
Mill ponds, 184
Mills. *See* Cloth mills
Minchinhampton (town), 37, maps, 36, 38
Minchinhampton-Avening manor, 103, 104–105, 119, 362–363 n. 4; leases, 66–67, 68–69, 70, 72
Minchinhampton Baptist Church, 284, 292, 296, 298; founding of, 293
Minchinhampton Common, 37, 113, maps, 36, 38; restricted use of grazing lands, 75, 79–82, 112, 237
Minchinhampton Manor, 103, 112–113, 119
Minchinhampton parish, 85, 98, 307, 372 n. 33; boundaries, 17, map inset 18; enclosure records, 76, 77–79, 356–357 n. 50, 357 n. 51; landowning characteristics, 59, 64, 75, table 62–63; occupational structure, 23–26; reconstruction of Anglican church, 98, 101; vestry plan for regulation of poor, 116; violence in 1825 strike, 222, 225
Minchinhampton Park School curriculum, 28
Minchinhampton-Tetbury road, 42
Mingay, G. E., 74–75
Ministers: continuity in Forest Green Congregational Church, 89–90, table 91; as itinerant preachers, 293–294; in Society of Friends, 257–258, 259. *See also* churches and ministers by name
Mixed marriages: banned by Quakers, 250, 260–263, 266, 399 nn. 38, 43; Baptist tolerance for, 301, 304; offspring of considered for Quaker membership, 265–267
Mobilization for Court Baron attendance, 105, 112
Modern, relationship to traditional, 3–5, 399–340 n. 9
Modernization, 3–5, 307–311, 340 n. 11, 340–341 n. 13, 341 n. 14
Monk, Bishop, 98

Monthly meetings (Quaker), 256–257, 258, 267–271; at Nailsworth, 254–255, 260, 261, 263–264, 268–271

Morality, Quaker concern with, 256, 260, 267–271

Moreton, Henry (Lord Ducie), 119–120, 242

Mortality, 131, 152–163, 205; role in membership losses for Shortwood Baptist Church, 280, table 279. *See also* Burials

Motley, James (businessman), expulsion from Society of Friends, 268, 271

Mules, spinning, *See* Spinning mules

Multiple classification analysis, 7

Multiple regression analysis, 7, 141 n. 41, 146–151 tables 28–31, 158–159, tables 35, 36. *See also* Time-Series forecasting

Munden, T. F. (migrant Shortwood Baptist member), 280–281, 282

"Mysteries of the craft," 199, 387 n. 160

"Nael" (Anglo-Saxon wool weight), 19–20

Nailsworth: boundary confusion, 17, 19, 51, 345 n. 11, map 18; etymology of name, 19–20; historic background, 19–21; occupational structure, 21–23, 25

Nailsworth Brewery, 350 n. 75

Nailsworth Episcopal Chapel, 96–98, 101; baptisms at, 139, 372 n. 35

Nailsworth Loan Society, 123

Nailsworth Society of Friends, 86, 101, 249–274, 308; and Evangelical Revival, 84, 93; size and social composition of membership, 250–256, 258, 274, 399 n. 28

Nailsworth Tabernacle, formation of, 302–303

Napoleonic Wars, effects on economic conditions, 171, 194, 204–205, 388 n. 169

Neale, Hannah (migrant Shortwood Baptist member), 283–284

Neale, Thomas (the elder and the younger) (clothiers), 31, 228, 229

Negelsleag Minor, early reference to Nailsworth as, 20

Newby, Howard, on deference and paternalism, 217, 218, 244, 391 n. 29, 393 n. 53

New Dissent, 1, 307. *See also* Nonconformity

Newman, Thomas Fox (minister), 96, 284–285, 292, 406 n. 43; correspondence with migrant members of Shortwod Church, 280–284, 403 n. 5; sermons, 301–302, 407 nn. 78, 80

Newmarket (hamlet): age-sex structure of, 163–168

New Mills, 177

Nietzsche, Friedrich, concept of resentment, 398 n. 24

Nonattendance at manor courts, fines for, 106–113, 126, 363 nn. 17, 19

Nonconformists (Dissenters), 1–2, 15, 17, 245, 274; baptism registrations, 140, 141–142, 371 n. 28, 372 n. 35; demographic studies' treatment of, 131–132, 137, 138, 141–152; ecumenical spirit, 296; as manor court suitors, 103, 110; relationship with Establishment, 54, 85, 86, 105, 118; role in parochial affairs, 120–121

Nonconformity (Dissent), 4, 11, 19, 35, 101; associated with individualism, 55–56; based on failure of millenarianism, 401 n. 91; chiliasm as conflicting with, 283; and composition of lordship, 10, 118–125; differing reactions to modernization, 246; and Evangelical Revival, 83, 84–101; militant tradition of surfacing in 1830s protests, 231–232; Nailsworth as a center for, 51, 52, 307–311; promotion of link between virtue and utility, 289; relationship to land ownership and tenure, 54–74, 83; relations with Church of England, 54, 84–101; role in growth of working-class consciousness, 237–240; role in Thomas Cole's attitudes toward factory system, 197–198; structural compatibility with Establishment, 102, 118, 125–127; support for anti-Corn Law agitation, 232

North Nibley, 1825 violence in, 228

Nuttall, Geoffrey, 259, 272

Oats, 41

Obelkevich, James, 5, 307

Occupations: available to mill factory women, 194, 195, 206; of Court Baron suitors, 107–109; of encroachers, 110–111; of Horsley parish householders, 190–192, 384 nn. 106, 107, 108; of Nailsworth Society of Friends members, 250–253; by social class, 329–330

Old Dissent, 307
Oligarchic parishes, 56; Avening as, 57–59
Open communion, 87, 285, 298–299, 304
Open (freehold) parishes, 7, 56, 341 n. 22
Operative mechanics, 231, 234, 237–239
Orange Vestry Oath, 237
Orthodoxy, doctrinal, Quaker enforcement of, 267, 271–272
Outdoor relief, 114–116, 136. *See also* Poor relief
Outmigration, 133–137, 168–169, 204, 370 nn. 22, 23, 375–376 n. 60; differences in Anglican and Dissenter levels of, 149; effect on age structure, 164–165; effect on Nailsworth Congregationalists, 89; effect on Nailsworth Society of Friends membership, 253–254; effects on membership of Shortwood Baptist Church, 142, 276, 277–284, 290, 374 n. 51; during 1837–1842 depression, 175; and gender differences in mortality rates, 157, 163
Overseers (Quaker), 257–258

Paine, John (minister), 89, 294–295
Painswick Baptist Church, 406 n. 51
"Parable of the Husbandman and Labourers," Newman's sermon on, 301–302, 407 n. 80
Parish churches: marriage within as required by law, 250; movement to refurbish, 96–100
Parishes, 9–10, 16–17, 104; administration of poor relief, 113, 114–116, 127, 136; authority of, 102, 106, 110, 113–118, 126–127; as model for relationship between Establishment and Dissent, 55–64. *See also* Closed parishes; Oligarchic parishes; Open parishes
Parish vestry, 106, 110, 113–118, 126–127
Parliament: reform, 119, 122; repeal of Combination Acts, 208
Particular Baptist churches, 92, 303–304
Paternalism, 135–136, 223, 224, 394 n. 71, 408 n. 3; and collective action, 218–219, 243, 392–393 n. 44; among elite, 308, 309–310, 408 n. 3; meanings, 209, 216–217; and Nonconformity, 101, 246; as promotion of working-class

independence, 116–118; synthesis with deference and individualism, 118, 121, 125–126, 127; and weavers' strike of 1825, 216, 217–218, 219, 243
Patriarchalism, 264, 272, 408 n. 3
Payment in kind (truck). *See* Truck, payment in
Pay scale, proposed by master weavers in 1824, 211–212, 215–216. *See also* Wages
Peasants, involvement in markets, 342–343 n. 26
Peel, Sir Robert, 100
Petit bourgeoisie, 34; mentality, 230, 274, 311
Pettit, William (weaver), 223–224
Pew rents, 98, 361 n. 76
Piece rates, 198, 209–210
Piecing, 196, 386 n. 141
Pinmarkers, as middle-class occupation, 26
Playne, Peter, 28, 196, 235, 381 n. 73; as mill owner, 181, 182, 189, 378 n. 27, 382 n. 93, 383 n. 99
Playne, William, 27–28, 29, 227, 381 n. 73; and 1833 strike, 235–236, 396 n. 108; on 1825 strike, 219, 221, 394 n. 62; lordship of Avening manor, 103, 119; as mill owner, 182, 198, 378 n. 27
Plomer, Samuel (clothier), 228, 229, 395 n. 82
Political activism of Quakers, 272, 274, 402 n. 100
Pollock, Frederick, 70, 112
Poor (people), 83, 94, 114–118, 120–121, 288
Poor Law, New, 114, 117, 125, 133, 135
Poor Law Unions, 10, 114, 136, 369 n. 11
Poor rates, 113, 232
Poor relief, 113, 114–116, 127, 136, 232
Population, 131–154, 174–175, 209, 311
Power and humility, 258–259, 398 n. 24
Power looms, 189, 236–237, 380 n. 64
Preachers: itinerant, 293–294; Quaker attitude toward, 273, 402 n. 95. *See also* Ministers
Preaching room, as predecessor to Avening Baptist Church, 294–295, 406 n. 59
Preaching stations, 293
Predestination, doctrine of, 91–92, 358 n. 14. *See also* Election
Preparative meetings (Meetings for discipline) (Quaker), 256, 266

Prerogative Court of Canterbury, clothiers' wills proved at, 28, 346 n. 37

Presbyterianism, 86, 90, 258

Priest, marriage by, forbidden by Quakers, 250, 260, 261–262

Priesthood of all believers, Quakers' adherence to principle of, 402 n. 95

Probate records, as evidence of individualism, 72–74, 83, 355 n. 38

Productivity, labor, 196, 233, 240, 386 n. 139

Profits: for manufacturers following piece size increase, 210; of master weavers as issue in 1824 demands, 211–212, 216, 389–390 n. 11, 390 n. 12

Proletarianization, 1, 34, 208, 237, 310–311; of small farmers, 74–75, 82; of weavers, 215, 231, 244, 396 n. 108. *See also* Class formation; Working classes

Promise-keeping, 19th-century legal emphasis on, 269, 401 n. 73

Promissory notes: Quaker moral attitude toward, 269; use by clothiers to pay master weavers, 216, 391 n. 21

Protest, 12, 208, 237–238, 288; and religious fervor, 238–240, role of paternalist elite in, 309–310, 408 n. 5; of weavers from 1827 to 1848, 231–243, 245. *See also* Strikes; Strikes, weavers'

Protestant ethic, 52, 268, 275, 400 n. 67

Protoindustrialization, 15, 16, 21, 190–195; definition, 344 n. 2; Shortwood Baptist membership during era of, 276–280; transition to factory system, 11–12, 205–207, 208. *See also* Cottage industry

Puritanism, 4–5, 85, 402 n. 63; transmission of values of, 300–301, 349 n. 63

Purnell, P. B. (magistrate), 220, 226, 228, 229–231, 232

Quakers. *See* Friends, Society of

Quarries, 39

Quarterly Meetings (Quaker), 256–257, 258

Quarter Sessions, indictments against rioting weavers, 228–229

Queen Caroline affair, 119, 121–122, 123

Queries (Quaker catechism), 256

Quietism of Quakerism, 249, 272, 273, 402 n. 98

Railway construction, 16, 42, 48–49

Rationalism of Quakerism, 249, 272, 273

Real chattel, 65, 69, 354 n. 17

Redemption, universal, 273; as doctrine of moderate Calvinism, 92, 93–94, 95, 292, 304, 358 n. 14, 403–404 n. 15

Reform Act of 1832, 307

Reform bill of 1848, 242

Religious experience, of Shortwood Baptist Church attenders, 285, 288–289, 290–293. *See also* Spirituality

Resentment, concept of, 398 n. 24

Resignation, Christian, 239–240, 245, 308

Revival, Evangelical. *See* Evangelical Revival

Ricardo, David (the elder), 121–122, 135, 349 n. 161; as lord of Minchinhampton manor, 72, 77, 103, 119

Ricardo, David (the younger), 97, 122–125, 136

Ridler, John (weaver), 224–225

Riots, 219, 220, 408 n. 5; during 1825 strike, 222–223, 224–229

Risk-taking in business, Quaker discouragement of, 268–269

Road construction, 16, 42–45

Robert, Daniel, expulsion from Society of Friends, 271–272, 402 n. 98

Robin, Matilde (migrant, Shortwood Baptist member), 282–283

Rockness, occupational structure, 23, 26, fig. 25

Rodborough Commons, grazing rights at, 80

Rollison, David, 392–393 n. 44

Rudé, George, 392–393 n. 44

Rupel, F. (minister), 97

St. Chloe School curriculum, 28

Salvation, concern for, 289, 290–292

Sands, 39

Saving banks, legislation on, 123, 125

Schofield, Roger S., 139–140, 152, 376 n. 65

Scott, Joan W., 190

Scribbling, 177, 195; engines, 180–181, 379–380 n. 47

Scrope, Poulet, as candidate for parliament, 122–125, 367 n. 74

Sectarianism, 84–85; of Quakers, 84, 249, 260–274; transition to denominationalism, 12, 149, 275, 303–304, 308

Secularization, 275, 288, 377 n. 69; and Shortwood Baptist Church, 12, 275–304

Seignory, manor as a, 104

Self-abasement, 217

Self-abnegation, 257, 267, 289

Self-interest, 216–218, 244

Selsley Hill, meeting of clothiers and weavers, 220–221, 224

Semiskilled labor, occupations, 329–330. *See also* Laborers; Working classes

Servants, employers' pressure on to conform to household's religious discipline, 283–284

Sevil, Samuel, 92–93, 358 n. 20

Sex. *See* Gender

Shearing, 177, 192, 195; frames/machines, 134, 180, 379–380 n. 47, 380 n. 62

Shelton, Walter, 218, 393 n. 45

Sheppard, Edward (clothier), 177, 217–218; acceptance of weavers' prices, 217–218, 219, 220–221, 244; and first phase of 1825 strike, 220–221, 227, 394 n. 62

Sheppard, Phillip (lord of Minchinhampton manor), 86–87

Shepphord family, 118–119; Edward (lord of Minchinhampton-Avening manor), 77, 103, 120

Shoots, 1824 increase in number per abb, 210–211, 389 n. 8

Shopkeepers, support for weavers' strike, 233

Shortwood (hamlet): age-sex structure of, 163–168

Shortwood Baptist Church, 12, 83, 84, 256, 275–304; attendance patterns around 1850, 284–293, 404 n. 24; attitude toward founding of Avening Church, 295–296; birth and burial records, 138, 140–142, 152, 375 n. 56; church order and discipline, 258, 295–303; covenant entered into, 331–332; divisiveness over degrees of enthusiasm, 238, 239; historic background, 90–96; members as manor court suitors, 109–110; membership growth and decline, 44, 94–95, 101, 135–136, 149–151, 168, 276–280, 285, 300–301; migrant members' association with other churches, 280, 282; tranformation from sect into denomination, 2, 9, 12, 15, 308

"Shrift-shire," parish defined as a, 16

Shuttles, 196, 232, 385 n. 133; collection of as beginning of strike of 1825, 220–221

Silence, role in Quaker meetings, 273

Smith, Adam, 353–354 n. 13

Social mobility, 27–35, 51–52, 349 n. 62

Social stability, 4, 208, 391 n. 31; paternalism as effort to maintain, 216–218, 244

Southampton-London railway line, 49

Southcott, Joanna, 271

South Lindsey, 307

Spindle billies, 180–181

Spinners, 190, 192, 195, 217

Spinning, incorporation into mill work, 177, 180

Spinning (spindle) jennies, 177, 179, 180–182, 190, 195, 379 n. 46, 380 n. 62

Spinning (spindle) mules, 177, 180–181, 182, 195, 237, 379 n. 46; as replacement for jenny, 179, 190, 195

Spirituality, 285, 288–293; for Society of Friends, 249, 260, 272–274

Squatters, 110

Squires' parishes. *See* Closed parishes

Statute labor, use on road construction, 44–45

Steam power, use in mills, 171, 177, 179, 180–181, 183–189, 381 n. 80, 381–382 n. 84, 382 n. 93, 382–383 n. 94, 383 n. 95

Stephens, Henry (lord of Horsley manor), 71, 119

Stephens family, lordship of Horsley manor, 119

Sterns, Peter, 339 n. 7, 340–341 n. 13

Stock, clothiers', sales of, 178–179, 379 n. 44

Stone, Jeanne C. Fawtier, 348 n. 58

Stone, Lawrence, 348 n. 58, 395 n. 88

Stonehouse Mills, 177, 379 n. 32, 380 n. 62

Stonehouse-Nailsworth Branch Railway line, 49–51

Strangers ("Foreign" labor), use in loom factories, 135, 193, 232

Streams, influence on settlement of the Vale, 38–39

Strike-breakers (1825), 222, 223–224, 226

Strikes, 12, 198; and religious fervor, 238, 240

Strikes, weavers', 208–243; 1720s and 1750s, 208, 388–389 n. 1; 1825, 208–232, 243, 309, 396 n. 108; 1828

Strikes, weavers' (*continued*)
  1829, 233–234, 243, 245, 396 n. 108;
  1833–1834, 235–236, 243, 245, 396
  n. 108
Stripes (cloth), 174, 236
Stroud (town), 15, 21, map 38
Stroud Baptist Church, communion
  practices, 299
Stroud canal company, 48, 352 n. 105
Stroud district (parliamentary borough
  after 1832), 307; 1838 protests, 237,
  396 n. 122; 1825 strike, 219–227, 243;
  parliamentary borough elections, 122–
  125, 127; woolen trade, 170, 174–175,
  205. *See also* Avening parish; Horsley
  parish; Minchinhampton parish
Stroud parish, 99–100, 132–135
Stubbs, Henry (Puritan preacher), 85–86
Subtenancies, 67–68
Suicide, as indicative of mood of 1850s,
  289, 292, 405 nn. 34, 35
Suits-of-court, 102, 109, 126; at Horsley
  manor, 66, 77, 105–110, 355 n. 25
Superfines (cloth), 174, 175
Supra-Liassic (Cotswold) Sand, 37, 39

Tax farming, 45
Tenancy-at-will, 64, 66–67
Tenth Hussars, use to deal with 1825
  strike, 220, 221, 226–227
Terling (village), 5
Term leases, 64–65, 69, 70–72, 82–83
Testifying as part of believers' baptism,
  300
Tetbury, 42
Theescombe, occupational structure, 23,
  26
Thirsk, Joan, 74
Thomas, Joshua (minister), 93, 301
Thompson, E. P., 131, 216, 311, 389 n. 3;
  on chiliasm of despair, 7, 288, 308; on
  crowd action, 309, 392–393 n. 44; on
  master weavers' militancy, 231, 395 n.
  88; on Methodist middle-class values,
  52, 349 n. 63
Tillage, acreage under in early 1800s, 40
Tilly, Charles, 370 n. 22
Tilly, Louise A., 190
Time-Series forecasting, 319 Appendix D,
  322 Appendix E, 324 Appendix F
Tipps, Dean C., 2–3, 339 n. 7
Tithes, 119, 120, 264–265
Tithingmen. *See* Constables
Tithings, 104–105
Toennis, Ferdinand, 8, 342 n. 25

Toll gates, 44, 45
Tracks, narrowness of, 42–43
Trade depressions. *See* Depressions,
  economic
Trade (industrial) unionism, 208, 230,
  231. *See also* Union of weavers
Traditional, 340 n. 10; relationship to
  modern, 3, 339–340 n. 9
"Training to the loom," 199
Transportation, 42–51, 183, 184
Truck, payment in, 203–204, 224, 231,
  233–235, 245, 394 n. 73; to journey-
  men and apprentices by master weavers,
  216, 233–235, 391 n. 22, 394 n. 74
Trusteeship, of Avening preaching room,
  294–295; of Forest Green
  Congregational Church, 87, 358 n. 20,
  359 n. 24
Tudor (apprenticeship) Statutes, 192, 384
  n. 110
Turnpike construction, 16, 42–45
Tynings (closes), 76, 79
Typologies, parochial, 55–64

Uley, 175, 205
Uley Baptist Church, 406 n. 51
Uley Mills, 177, 181, 217–218, 392 n. 38
Underdown, David, 4–5
Union Association, formed by operatives
  in 1838, 237
Union of weavers, 223, 229–235, 395–
  396 n. 104; opposition to, 233–234,
  395 nn. 97, 98; reconstitution in 1833,
  235–236
Universal redemption. *See* Redemption,
  universal
Unskilled labor, occupations, 329–330.
  See also Laborers; Working classes
Upper middle class, Quakers as, 250–253
Urban industrial workers, studies of
  deference and paternalism based on,
  217, 391 n. 29
Urbanization, 132, 157, 275, 376 n. 63

Valenze, Deborah, 245, 341 n. 19
Vatch Mill, 222
"Veritas" (weaver), opposition to union,
  233–234, 239, 395 n. 98, 395–396 n.
  104
View of Frankpledge, 104
Violence: in paternalism-deference mode
  of collective action, 218–219; in
  second and third phases of 1825 strike,
  219–220, 222–223, 224–229, 243–
  244

Wages, 194, 196, 198–200, 204, 233, 240–242, 397 n. 132; for journeymen weavers, 200, 210–212, 215–216, 217, 387 n. 158, 390 nn. 15, 18, 391 n. 22; for master weavers, 211–212, 215–216, 217, 390 n. 15; during Napoleonic Wars, 204–205, 388 n. 169; role in labor conflicts 1827–1848, 231–236, 240–242, 395 n. 97; role in 1825 strike, 209, 222, 223–224, 226, 227; and wheat prices, 201–203, 204–205, 207. *See also* Weaving rates

Wages in kind. *See* Truck, payment in

Walsh, John, 218, 393 n. 45

Warp, chain as Gloucester term for, 389 n. 4

Warping, 196, 386 n. 141

Wasteland, shrinking of, 57, 75, 82

Water power: use in mills, 180, 183–189, 381 n. 80, 382 n. 93, 383 n. 95

Wealth: as mark of status, 30, 32, 52; mean personal distribution, 32–34

Weavers, 20–21, 34, 197–202, 238–239; Horsley census of, 190–192; household as family work unit, 190, 206; outdoor handloom, 189–190, 195, 196, 199–200, 383 nn. 96, 99, 100, 404–405 n. 29; as Quakers, 250, table 251; social position, 33–34, 51–52; women as, 194–195, 196, 206, 386 n. 139. *See also* Journeymen weavers; Strikes, weavers'; Truck, payment in; Wages

Weavers, factory, 12, 195, 199, 231–233, 245; attendance at Shortwood Baptist Church, 288, 404–405 n. 29

Weavers, master, 197–199, 215–216, 217, 232–233, 386 n. 151; aspirations to become clothiers, 219, 230; as leaders of 1825 strike, 209, 219; petition of 1824, 210–212, 215–216; use of workshops and journeymen, 190–192, 379 n. 31, 383–384 n. 104

"Weavers' Guide, The, An Address to the Gloucestershire Operative Weavers," 235–236

Weaving rates, 217, 219; as issue in master weavers' 1824 demands, 209–211, 215–216, 220–221; role in 1825 strikes, 222, 223–224, 226, 229–230

Webb, Beatrice and Sydney, 16, 113

Weber, Max, 32; on Protestant ethic, 270, 275, 400 n. 67

Weft, abb as Gloucester term for, 389 n. 4

"Weorth" (Anglo-Saxon for market), 20

West Riding Mills, use of steam power, 183–184, 381 n. 80, tables 185–186

Wheat, 41

Wheat prices, 200–203, 204–205, 212–215, 387 nn. 162, 163; fluctuations in and demographic data, 146, 157, 168, 373–374 n. 47, tables 147, 148, 158, 159

Whigs, 83, 118, 125, 309; and New Poor Law, 114, 117; social and political alliance of, 119–125, 127

White cloth, weaving rates negotiated for, 211–212, table 210

Whitefield, George (minister), 87, 93

Wills: bequests of leasehold and freehold estates, 71, 72–74, 355 n. 38; as indications of social mobility, 27–31, 33–34, 52

Winsoredge (hamlet), 17, 19, map 18; age-sex structure of, 163–168, 376–377 n. 68

Winterbotham, William (minister), 96

"Wolfe, General," 227

Women, 164, 190, 195, 276, 403 n. 4; under factory system, 193–194, 206; as migrant members of Shortwood church, 280, 281–284; mortality rates, 157, 168; status within Society of Friends, 256–257, 259, 262, 264; as weavers, 194–195, 196, 206, 386 n. 139

Women's meetings (Quaker), 258, 259, 262, 399 n. 28

Woodchester, violence in 1825 strike, 222, 225

Wood-pasture society, 19, 41–42, 51, 217, 391 nn. 30, 32, fig. 20

Woolen trade. *See* Cloth trade

Woolworkers. *See* Clothworkers

Work, cultural values concerning, 301–302

Work discipline under factory system, 285, 288–289

Workhouse, maintenance of, 114, 116

Working-class consciousness, 237–238

Working classes, 242–243, 274, 282, 289, 300; attendance patterns at Shortwood Church, 288, table 286; and gentry paternalism, 116, 117–118, 126; occupations, 329–330; receptivity to capitalist values, 311; Shortwood Baptist leaders from, 296, 298, 406–407 n. 63. *See also* Laborers; Proletarianization

Workman, John (weaver), 224–225

Works: grace independent of, 283, 303–304 n. 15; relationship to salvation for Quakers, 260

Workshops, 178; journeymen weavers employed by, 190, 383–384 n. 104; sales of, 178–179, 379 n. 44

Work under price, acceptance of, 222, 223–224, 226, 227, 229–230

"Worldly asceticism," 5, 341 n. 18

Worship: patterns of among Shortwood Baptist migrant members, 282–284; Quakers' style of, 255–256, 271

Wotton, riots in 1825 strike, 227–228

Wotton-under-Edge, 205

Wrightson, Keith, 4–5, 339–340 n. 9

Wrigley, E. A., 139–140, 152, 339 n. 7

Wyatt, George (clothier), 222

Wyatt, Peter (clothier), 222

Yearlings, grazed at Minchinhampton Common, 82, table 81

Yearly Meeting, national (Quaker), 256–257, 258, 259, 260

Yelling, J. A., 74

Yorkshire, 181, 183–184, 391 n. 33; as competition for Gloucester woolen trade, 170, 174, 181, 206, 236, 380 n. 64

Young, Nathaniel (weaver), 224–225

Young adults, 164–166; attendance at Shortwood Church, 290–291, table 286; mortality rates, table 160

Designer:	U.C. Press Staff
Compositor:	ASCO Trade Typesetting, Ltd.
Text:	11/13 Sabon
Display:	Sabon
Printer:	Braun-Brumfield
Binder:	Braun-Brumfield